Unfinished Business

THE HAYMARKET SERIES

Editors: Mike Davis and Michael Sprinker

The Haymarket Series offers original studies in politics, history and culture, with a focus on North America. Representing views from across the American left on a wide range of subjects, the series will be of interest to socialists both in the USA and throughout the world. A century after the first May Day, the American left remains in the shadow of those martyrs whom this Haymarket Series honours and commemorates. These studies testify to the living legacy of political activism and commitment for which they gave their lives.

Unfinished Business
Twenty Years of *Socialist Review*

———————◆———————

Edited by the
SOCIALIST REVIEW
COLLECTIVES

VERSO

London · New York

First published by Verso 1991
© 1991 The Center for Social Research and Education

Verso
UK: 6 Meard Street, London W1V 3HR
USA: 29 West 35th Street, New York, NY 10001-2291

Verso is the imprint of New Left Books

Library of Congress Cataloging-in-Publication Data

Unfinished business : twenty years of Socialist review / Socialist
  review
    p. cm.
    ISBN 0-86091-307-4. -- ISBN 0-86091-524-7 (pbk.)
    1. Socialism. 2. Communism. 3. World politics. 4. Economic policy.
    I. Socialist review.
    HX73.U55   1992
    335--dc20

British Library Cataloguing in Publication Data

Unfinished business : twenty years of Socialist Review.
    I. Socialist Review collectives
    320.531

    ISBN   0-86091-307-4
    ISBN   0-86091-524-7   pbk.

Typeset in Monotype Bembo by
NorthStar, San Francisco, California
Printed in USA by The Courier Group

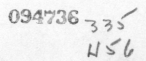

Contents

In memory of Carol Hatch:
Conscience, mentor, friend

Preface

In 1970, a new journal with roots in the New Left appeared in the United States. Its first issues were brash and wide-ranging, with articles predicting the fiscal crisis of the state, exploring the intersection of Marx and Freud, and analyzing the relation of feminism to consumer culture. Ever since those early days, *Socialist Revolution* (as the publication was then called) has been the iconoclastic conscience of the US left. Becoming *Socialist Review* in 1977, *SR*'s major role has been to bridge the gap between activists and academicians. From labor struggles to socialist feminism, from the fate of Communism to the impact of new technologies, *Socialist Review* has become a voice for a pluralistic, democratic socialism that refuses to rely on received truths or orthodoxies. Drawn from over 14,000 pages, the twenty essays gathered here represent some of the most original, insightful, and provocative writings that have appeared in *Socialist Review*. How are racial categories constructed and contested? In what ways does feminist theory force a rethinking of traditional left assumptions? What is the place of socialism in a postindustrial world? What caused the decline of the left in Europe? How can poststructuralist theory contribute to progressive political struggles? These are just a few of the questions addressed in this collection. Authors include Stanley Aronowitz, Fred Block, Tony Daley, Gary Delgado, Barbara Ehrenreich, Steven Epstein, Jeffrey Escoffier, Donna Haraway, Paul Joseph, Esther Kingston-Mann, Daniel Lee Kleinman, Jack Kloppenburg, Jr., Ernesto Laclau, Jack Metzgar, Chantal Mouffe, Michael Omi, David Plotke, Rayna Rapp, George Ross, Carmen Sirianni, Judith Stacey, Thomas Weisskopf, Howard Winant, and Robert E. Wood.

Socialist Review can be reached at 2940 16th Street, Suite 102, San Francisco, CA 94103.

Acknowledgements

Most of the articles reprinted in this volume have been abridged and revised. *Socialist Review* would like to thank the authors for allowing us both to reprint and to shorten their pieces. We realize that on occasion this shortening may have led to some loss of nuance or qualification and, more often, to leaving out some of the necessary documentation. The articles appeared in their original form as listed below.

Stanley Aronowitz, "Socialism and Beyond: Remaking the American Left. Part II," *Socialist Review* 69, vol. 13, no. 3 (May–June, 1983), pp. 7–42.

Fred Block, "The Ruling Class Does Not Rule: Notes on the Marxist Theory of the State," *Socialist Review* 33, vol. 7, no. 3 (May–June, 1977), pp. 6–28.

Gary Delgado, "Taking It to the Streets: Community Organizing and National Politics," *Socialist Review* 63/64, vol. 12, no. 3/4 (May–August, 1982), pp. 49–84.

Barbara Ehrenreich, "Life without Father: Reconsidering Socialist-Feminist Theory," *Socialist Review* 73, vol. 14, no. 1 (Jan.–Feb., 1984), pp. 48–57.

Steven Epstein, "Gay Politics, Ethnic Identity: The Limits of Social Constructionism," *Socialist Review* 93/94, vol. 17, no. 3/4 (May–August, 1987), 9–54.

Jeffrey Escoffier, "Socialism as Ethics," *Socialist Review* 85, vol. 16, no. 1 (Jan.–Feb., 1986), pp. 117–21.

Donna Haraway, "A Manifesto for Cyborgs: Science, Technology and Socialist Feminism in the 1980s," *Socialist Review* 80, vol. 15, no. 2 (March–April 1985), pp. 65–107.

Paul Joseph, "From MAD to NUTs: The Growing Danger of Nuclear War," *Socialist Review* 61, vol. 12, no. 1 (Jan.–Feb., 1982), pp. 13–56.

Esther Kingston-Mann, "Perestroika with a Human Face?", *Socialist Review* 97, vol. 18, no. 1 (Jan.–March, 1988), pp. 7–30.

Jack Kloppenburg, Jr., and Daniel Lee Kleinman, "Seed Wars: Common Heritage, Private Property, and Political Strategy," *Socialist Review* 95, vol. 17, no. 5 (Sept.–Oct., 1987), pp. 7–41.

Ernesto Laclau and Chantal Mouffe, "Recasting Marxism: Hegemony and New Political Movements," *Socialist Review* 66, vol. 11, no. 6 (Nov.–Dec., 1982), pp. 91–113.

Jack Metzgar, "Plant Shutdowns and Worker Response: The Case of Johnstown, PA," *Socialist Review* 53, vol. 10, no. 5 (Sept.–Oct., 1980), pp. 9–49.

Michael Omi and Howard Winant, "By the Rivers of Babylon: Race in the United States. Part I," *Socialist Review* 71, vol. 13, no. 5 (Sept.–Oct., 1983), pp. 31–65.

David Plotke, "Reaganism and Neoliberalism," *Socialist Review* 86, vol. 16, no. 2 (March–April, 1986), pp. 7– 23.

Rayna Rapp, "Is the Legacy of Second Wave Feminism Postfeminism?" *Socialist Review* 97 vol. 18, no. 1 (Jan.–Feb., 1988), pp. 31–37.

George Ross and Tony Daley, "The Wilting of the Rose: The French Socialist Experiment," *Socialist Review,* 87/88, vol. 16, no. 3/4, (May–August, 1986), pp. 7–40.

Carmen Sirianni, "Production and Power in a Classless Society: A Critical Analysis of the Utopian Dimensions of Marxist Theory," *Socialist Review* 59 vol. 11, no. 5 (Sept.–Oct., 1981), pp. 33–82.

Judith Stacey, "Sexism by a Subtler Name? Postindustrial Conditions and Postfeminist Consciousness in the Silicon Valley," *Socialist Review* 96, vol. 17, no. 6 (Nov.–Dec., 1987), pp. 7–28.

Thomas Weisskopf, "The Current Economic Crisis in Historical Perspective," *Socialist Review* 57, vol. 11, no. 3 (May–June, 1981), pp. 9–53.

Robert E. Wood, "Debt Crisis Update: 1988," *Socialist Review* 88/3, vol. 18, no. 3 (July–Sept., 1988), pp. 103–15.

Introduction

Socialist Review – called *Socialist Revolution* until 1978 – emerged from the ferment and struggle of the 1960s to embrace the US left in all its complexity. Over the years, its writers and editorial collective members have retained and expanded the journal's commitment to the liberating power of debate. This anthology of articles taken from *Socialist Review* invokes a two-decade history of ideas, debates, and visions with the goals of pointing us toward the future and helping to articulate the meanings of socialism in a rapidly changing world.

At the time the journal was founded in 1970, affirming a commitment to socialism was a daring act. Even on the left, socialism was a curiously marginalized discourse: in a period when many on the left believed that revolution was imminent, it was the first word in the name *Socialist Revolution* – not the second – that struck people as controversial. Why endorse the tradition of democratic socialism, as opposed to the then more popular currents of Marxism or Leninism or Maoism?

Twenty years later socialism remains a controversial concept, but for quite different reasons. Ideologically equating it with Stalinist regimes in current popular discourse, many have roundly condemned the term and cast it onto the ashheap of history. Yet the actual ideals and aspirations of socialism survive with surprising tenacity to animate the political will of people around the globe. Given the changes that have occurred in the past twenty years both in the United States and throughout the world, a contemporary affirmation of socialism involves a commitment to the difficult, yet vital process of reconceiving socialism: of reconstructing the visions of social justice, solidarity, and

1

democracy that are embodied by the term and that would be appropriate to the world in which we now live.

By identifying *SR* as socialist, its founders were declaring a particular identity within the multiplicity of radical political positions. But at the same time, the journal began as, and has remained, a place where many different voices can speak. While making a broad commitment to democratic socialism, the journal has always eschewed any narrow "line," either about how to achieve it or what it might look like once achieved. For twenty years, the four men and one woman who have worked as executive editors of the journal, and the dozens of people who have served on its editorial collectives, have often disagreed with one another – usually fruitfully so. But what has united them are shared assumptions not only that *SR* can accommodate that diversity, but also that in a world as profoundly complex as our own, only a broad and open discussion can point us toward meaningful solutions. Rather than expecting *SR* to assert pat and dogmatic answers, the contributors, editors, and readers who collectively embody the journal have made it a place for posing difficult questions.

The Early Years

Socialist Revolution came on the scene at a critical turning point for progressive politics in the United States. To virtually everyone's surprise, the US left awakened in the early 1960s after a long period of somnolence, led by a powerful movement of racial minorities and university-educated youth. By the end of the decade the evolution of this New Left had raised as many questions as it had answered; *SR*, which was founded at this point, became the most important theoretical forum for addressing these questions.

The US "New" Left was in many ways unique. It grew out of the civil rights movement, the domestic political upheaval generated by the Vietnam War, and huge urban uprisings against racism and long-standing social divisions in the United States. The "Movement's" first wave, which dates from the early 1960s, was organized around a variety of causes, but shared a principled rejection of rule by the "power elite." "Let the people decide," read the masthead of the newspaper published by Students for a Democratic Society, one of the most important organizations of the time. This early New Left's goal of "participatory democracy" sought to empower those who had been disenfranchised in myriad ways by techno-bureaucratic control of the economy, government, and politics. The democratic promise of the United States, these early New Leftists argued, had to be redeemed. Many of the founders of *Socialist Revolution* – in particular those who originated in *Studies on the Left* – came from this early New Left.

2

By the later 1960s, a second "New Left" emerged. Overlapping the first, it was born out of events like the murders of Martin Luther King, Robert Kennedy, and Malcolm X; the Tet offensive; the police riots at the Chicago Democratic convention; and international uprisings like May–June 1968 in France. The participants in this wing of the New Left found it hard to sustain beliefs in a long and patient democratic reconstruction of US society in the face of what looked increasingly like an unmovable imperialistic system committed to domination and social inequality.

At the end of the 1960s, many came to believe that the chaotic destructiveness of the United States indicated that revolution was on the agenda. The most strident voices of the time offered essentially two scenarios. The first involved a "turn to the working class," through community and workplace organizing, to awaken the dormant proletarian vanguard of basic change in the United States. The second involved revolutionary support in "Amerika" for Third World national liberation movements, which supporters believed would at one and the same time defeat imperialism and provide new alternative models for progress. In both scenarios, the early 1960s theme of redemocratizing the United States receded. Much of the force of the first issues of *Socialist Revolution* in the 1970s grew out of questioning these tendencies within the US left. The new journal was led by former members of the short-lived journal *Studies on the Left* – James Weinstein and Anne Farrar – who were soon joined by a number of others, including John Judis, James O'Connor, and Eli Zaretsky. They made a deliberate choice to settle the new journal in the San Francisco Bay Area, in order to avoid the growing sectarianism of East Coast leftism. The original *Socialist Revolution* collective was completely white and predominantly male. This arrangement was particularly problematic given that the journal's founding coincided with the stunning emergence of the second wave feminist movement.

The journal's guiding conception was that the antiwar movement could transform itself into a mass US socialist movement, with *SR* as its theoretical journal. In and around the journal, debates flowered about appropriate larger movement organizations – debates which pointed toward the New American Movement and *In These Times*, the left newsweekly which James Weinstein left *SR* to found – and about the political and organizational possibilities of socialist feminism. This latter concern became increasingly central as the Bay Area collective gradually included more and more women. The journal's founding mission was to try to develop a democratic socialist analysis appropriate to US conditions which could help reorient the broader US movement away from models borrowed from European and Third World experiences. *SR* stressed the importance of developing revolutionary consciousness, challenging "bourgeois hegemony," and proposing new, persuasive, change-oriented perspectives. The title of an article by John Judis in the

3

journal's second issue, "The Triumph of Bourgeois Hegemony in the Face of Nothing That Challenges It," succinctly summarized these concerns.

From *Socialist Revolution* to *Socialist Review*

SR was successful enough to do more than survive. It thrived and influenced activists and left supporters about both political and ideological matters, introducing, for example, the thought of Italian theorist Antonio Gramsci to a wide and politicized audience. But given the revolutionary hopes of its founders these achievements were ironic, since no mass socialist movement emerged in the United States in the 1970s. As the ebullition of the 1960s receded, the journal had to settle down for a longer haul. And as universities and university environments became the refuge for movement participants and sympathizers, *Socialist Revolution* faced an increasingly academic audience.

The debates that the journal encouraged, which very often flowed from the internal debates of its editorial collective, addressed the changing context of the times. One area of extensive discussion in the journal was the "new communist movements," prompted by the political evolution of movement "revolutionaries" who went off after SDS's disintegration in 1969 to build cadre groups for an anticipated period of heightened struggle and direct action. Thousands of committed people chose this route, often doing extremely important organizing work in factories and neighborhoods in the process. However, these sects grew ever more isolated and self-referential. Editors and writers in *SR* quickly recognized the impasse that was developing, and debated issues of agency raised by the "party builders." A series of articles in the journal addressed problems in the delineation of working-class boundaries, for example, in an attempt to counter a romantic workerism on the left. Ultimately it became clear that no "party" would emerge from the efforts of the "party builders"; events, furthermore, undermined the appeal of various formulations of the "new communism." China's changes – the reevaluation of the Cultural Revolution, the accusation of the "Gang of Four," and Nixon's trip – made it extremely difficult to continue believing in the redness of the East. The evolution of Vietnam after the great 1975 victory was hardly more inspirational. The sad Brezhnev era saw the self-proclaimed vanguard of the "youth of the world" dominated by a repressive gerontocracy. If this was what modern revolution offered, many concluded that it might be wise to strike a different note.

In addition to questioning the "workerist" politics of left revolutionary sects, *SR* authors in the journal's early years also questioned the value of an exclusive analytical focus on social class as a way of accounting for people's behavior. *SR*'s sustained interest in the mid-1970s in issues of consciousness

4

led to a series of articles – including important contributions by Nancy Chodorow, Richard Lichtman, and Eli Zaretsky – that debated ways of joining Marxist and Freudian insights in order to analyze questions of personal motivation and radical change. Eli Zaretsky published a series of articles on capitalism and the family that were widely discussed in parts of the women's movement. Also during these years, writers such as Todd Gitlin, Bruce Dancis and Ellen Willis analyzed the workings of US culture, with the goal of exploring what motivated people either to accept or reject the dominant culture.

By the middle 1970s, *SR* had also become a major site for wide-ranging debates about the political implications of the new feminism. Many of these discussions focused on the meaning and prospects for a distinctively socialist feminism and its relation to other strains of the new women's movement. These works by feminists contributed to *SR*'s continuing concern to broaden theoretical categories, especially as they related to consciousness. *Socialist Revolution* changed its name to *Socialist Review* in 1978, after long reflection and considerable disagreement within the editorial collective about the evolution of the left and *SR*'s place within it. Part of this reflection involved concern that use of the word "revolution" could cut the journal off from part of its potential audience. The matter was more profound, however: almost everywhere the left had begun to question conventional wisdom about the relationships between revolution and basic change. Carmen Sirianni's 1981 critique of utopian dimensions of Marxist theory, reprinted in this volume, was an *SR* contribution to this debate.

The name change did not mean that the journal's editors wished to discard the goal of global social transformation, but the shift did signal *SR*'s growing interest in electoral politics and strategies for reform in the United States. The 1976 establishment of a second editorial collective in Boston made the task of constructing unity out of decentralized diversity more complex. The differences in sensibility and outlook, both within and between the two collectives, brought a vigorous pluralism as well as complex transcontinental editorial discussions.

For theoretical and strategic help, *SR*, now edited by David Plotke, shifted its eyes toward Europe. The 1970s were years of tremendous creative ferment for the European left. As the Italian, French, and Spanish Communist parties seemed to be shaking off the burdens of the Soviet model and working on innovative theories for transcending capitalism democratically, the journal aired a wide range of Gramscian and other European neo-Marxist and neo-socialist theoretical arguments. *SR* became the major forum for US reflection on the prospects and problems of Eurocommunism, seen as a "third way" between capitalism and Soviet-style "existing socialism." Eurocommunist and Eurosocialist reflection on the internally contradictory, rather than monolithic, character of the state encouraged a major debate on the theory of the capitalist

5

state. The debate is represented in this volume by Fred Block's 1977 article, "The Ruling Class Does Not Rule," which challenged prevailing instrumentalist conceptions of the relation of the ruling class to the state.

These theoretical concerns led to a discussion of strategies aimed at empowering people rather than integrating them into a national political system which, as it stood, transcended their control and worked to disempower them. *SR* published a number of articles dealing with different strategies for community organizing, including an important debate about the political meaning of populism, sparked in large part by Harry Boyte's 1977 essay, "The Populist Challenge." By the end of its first decade, *SR*, like the broader US left, had shifted its political center of gravity, looking to a cumulation of grassroots organizing efforts and electoral activity to lead to qualitative change.

The Second Decade

By the later 1970s the contours of the US left had clearly changed. The tenuously united radical front of the 1960s had become a congeries of social movements, each organizing around its own issues. With events on the traditional left having called "revolution" into question, many radical theorists and organizers grouped around *Socialist Review* saw in this more issue-oriented energy, activism, and optimism a promising and potentially more democratic replacement. Stanley Aronowitz's 1983 manifesto, "Remaking the American Left," and the 1982 interview with Ernesto Laclau and Chantal Mouffe, both reprinted in this volume, were important attempts to retool left theory to incorporate the radically democratic and pluralist insights of the so-called "new social movements." Gary Delgado's article, "Taking It to the Streets," originally published in 1982 and reprinted here, addresses these issues from a more on-the-ground political perspective. Likewise, Michael Omi and Howart Winant's 1983 essay, "By the Rivers in Babylon," reexamines the issue of US racism from the perspective of a left analysis no longer centered on class.

The most important heir – and challenge – to the New Left was the new women's movement. Throughout the 1980s, the feminist movement continued to shake the foundations of left politics and theory. Analytically and practically, both the Old and New Lefts had subordinated gender, along with other structures of oppression to the workings of economic structures (when they addressed such matters at all). But if, as feminists argued, gender-based oppression was coequal in importance to economic exploitation and inequality, then the productivist theoretical framework that resulted from these older assumptions had to be reconsidered.

Was it possible to reconcile commitments to socialism *and* feminism? Many

6

within the feminist movement didn't think so, and distanced themselves from the Marxist and post-Marxist left. But for many others, who felt both a political and intellectual imperative to synthesize the two traditions, *Socialist Review* became the major forum for addressing the theoretical and practical barriers to doing so. *SR* became the locus of an extensive theoretical debate about "dual-systems theory" – the shorthand description for attempts to simultaneously theorize the workings of capitalism and patriarchy. The new feminist politics went well beyond theory. The feminist injunction, "the personal is political," also served as a criticism of the way traditional left organizations almost always instrumentalized those they sought to mobilize, treating them as vehicles for a cause transcending their own lives.

SR also became a key arena for left perspectives on a range of central issues within the feminist movement: pornography, sexuality, the question of mothering. Barbara Ehrenreich's 1984 "Life without Father," included in this anthology, presents a critical retrospective overview of socialist-feminist politics and theory. The women's movement raised the complex matter of sexual politics and identity more generally, forcing the left to confront not only homophobia but the politics of personal life. In the new political environment, gender definitions and matters of sexual preference could no longer be kept in a repressive closet constructed by a male-dominated heterosexual culture.

The 1980s were a test for *SR* at many levels, not least of which was organizational. When *Marxist Perspectives*, a short-lived Marxist journal of more academic orientation, folded, *MP* collectives in Boston and New York joined *SR*. As a result, *SR* had to reconfigure its already complicated decentralized editorial practices to include two more collectives. It was not easy, but much was gained in the process: the New York collective contributed numerous articles on culture, and the new Boston group brought expertise and writings on international politics. The New York collective eventually disbanded, while the two groups in Boston ultimately united. The very fact of the *SR–MP* merger was sobering. Many left publications were unable to survive the fiscal problems and political pall of the 1980s, leaving *Socialist Review* as one of the few surviving theoretical journals on the US left by the decade's end. Of course, the Reagan years were a blow for the US left and the disenfranchised within US society. The devastating 1981–82 recession and the strange economic boom that followed confirmed that the US economy faced a new and dangerous situation, one that Thomas Weisskopf reflects on in his 1981 article reprinted here. The corrupting influence of a crass yuppie ethic individualized the new middle strata and the intelligentsia who had formed the left's most reliable constituency. The revived Cold War hysteria of the 1980s led both to frightening new defense and military strategies and to vigorous peace movement responses to them. Paul Joseph's 1982 article, included in this

7

anthology, analyzed the rightward shift in US defense policy and suggested more fruitful approaches to antiwar organizing. Jack Metzgar's analysis of plant shutdowns and workers' responses, which we also reprint here, shows the labor movement staggering under anti-union hammer blows from capital and governments.

News from abroad was little better. Eurocommunist and left social-democratic hopes were dashed in one country after another. In their 1986 article, "The Wilting of the Rose," reprinted here, George Ross and Tony Daley discuss perhaps the most spectacular of these failures, that of the French Socialist Party. In the later 1980s *perestroika* and *glasnost* provided welcome signs of change, provoking extraordinary upheavals in Eastern Europe; but as Esther Kingston-Mann's 1988 article on the Soviet Union shows, their immediate effect was to underline the economic inefficiency and undemocratic politics of "existing socialism."

Between the collapse of old left models and the new complexities of political and economic life in the late 1980s, *SR*'s founding mission – to provide the left "Movement" with a democratic socialist analysis of its tasks and prospects – became more difficult, if not outright impossible. The journal continued to provide valuable and insightful critiques of the rapidly changing capitalist economic system, exemplified in this volume by Robert E. Wood's 1988 discussion of the debt crisis. Yet the writers and editors of *Socialist Review*, like the rest of the US left, had to face the troubling fact that important parts of the US public supported a rightward shift in political priorities. It became very difficult to perceive *mass* support for left alternatives, at least as traditionally proposed. Thus Reaganite success tempted the Democratic Party towards self-defeating neoliberal imitation, as David Plotke's controversial "Reaganism and Neoliberalism" suggests in the pages which follow. Feminism seemed to survive these changes more successfully, despite New Right challenges, but there were nonetheless important "postfeminist" questions to be asked about the legacy of seventies feminists to the next generation, as Judy Stacey's article in this volume suggests.

Socialist Review was at the forefront in opening left discussions of gay rights and liberation during this period, led by the lucid writings of editor Jeffrey Escoffier, whose piece on the ethics of socialism in this volume provides a good summary of his broader concerns. Steven Epstein's 1987 article on gay politics, which we also include, is an excellent representative of this debate. Left movements, and *SR*'s pages, included militant opponents of apartheid, American racism, and the arms race as well. Environmentalism grew in movement significance and global appeal, as reflected in Kloppenburg and Kleinman's "Seed Wars."

Perhaps more importantly from the perspective of the journal, it became effectively impossible – and arguably undesirable – to speak any longer of a unified, coherent "left," united under the banner of democratic socialism or any other ism. The new social movements of the 1980s, whose promise and pitfalls were extensively explored in the pages of the journal, challenged such a unitary vision of "the left" as being inherently exclusionary and totalizing. With their attention to identity and difference, they provided new models for a democratic *and* plural radical politics, whose relation to traditional socialist politics, however, was neither straightforward nor clear. Donna Haraway's iconoclastic 1985 "Manifesto for Cyborgs" provided one solution, by arguing for a diffuse politics connected by "affinity" and firmly based in contemporary reality, rather than rooted in a nostalgic longing for organic unity. Jeffrey Escoffier's "Socialism as Ethics," published the following year, suggested another approach: a left politics that emphasized the emancipatory moral core of the socialist tradition, rather than an outdated and exclusionary politics based on economic class alone. At the same time as many *SR* authors and collective members welcomed these shifts as a refreshing break from dogmatisms of the past, other writers and editors from the journal found themselves increasingly troubled by the growing fragmentation of progressive movements and the enormous barriers to alliance- and coalition-building. Some felt that a postmodern politics of identity ran the risk of failing to distinguish between what was progressive and what might be parochial and serve to reinforce privatism, introversion, and the market.

SR's authors and editors struggled with these issues, trying to connect reappraisals of new social movements with discussions of changes in capitalism. At the same time, the journal never abandoned its analyses of the evolution of labor and more traditional socialist outlooks.

Two decades of *Socialist Review* have passed, and the 1990s present immense new challenges. The journal's editors and contributors refuse to accept US boosterism about the "end of history" or claims that one hundred years of struggle for a better, and socialist, society have come to an end. Instead, the time has come to devise new versions of such politics for the contemporary moment. How can the proliferation of radical issues and vital energies that underlie the US left's "politics of identity" be preserved *and* joined in a broader radical movement? What kind of socialist politics and vision are appropriate to a new era of "posts": postmodern, post-Fordist, post-Stalinist? As we enter the last years of the century, *Socialist Review* will continue to be the forum where progressive forces in the United States debate and elaborate their strategic visions. The articles in this volume are a record of the first twenty years of that enterprise. But the articles were not selected for their historical interest alone. They have been chosen, abridged, and in some cases updated because they speak to pressing contemporary concerns. And they were chosen only with great difficulty – and sometimes only after heated debate among the collective members – with the painful awareness that many equally valuable and still relevant articles would necessarily have to be excluded.

The volume is divided into four sections. The first section, "Back to the Drawing Board," illustrates just a few of the important arenas in which *SR* authors have made advances to our theoretical understandings. "Architectures of Power," the second section, offers a sampling of *SR* articles about international issues of central importance to the US left. "Reassembling Political Identities," our third section, focuses on the critical analysis of different types and methods of progressive struggle in the contemporary United States. The concluding set of articles, "Unfinished Business," reflects some of the varied visions of the future that have been presented in the pages of *SR*. Considered overall, the twenty articles in this volume constitute an unusual and provocative collection. In their persuasiveness and openness, in their analytical rigor and political acumen, they testify to the paramount importance of journals such as *Socialist Review* in encouraging thoughtful and daring reflection on progressive change.

PART I

Back to the Drawing Board

1

The Latest Economic Crisis
in Historical Perspective
(1981)
Thomas Weisskopf

The United States, and indeed much of the world capitalist system, entered into a period of generalized economic crisis in the early 1970s. This crisis had many facets, political and social as well as economic. Its three principal economic elements were a slowdown in economic growth, an increase in inflation, and an increase in unemployment.

Economic difficulties similar to those of the United States have affected virtually every other advanced capitalist country; some (for example, West Germany and Japan) suffered less, while others (for example, the United Kingdom) suffered even more. This crisis marked a sharp break with the buoyant prosperity of the earlier postwar period. In the following pages I intend to bring a historical perspective to the analysis of the economic crisis in the United States. First, I will discuss the crisis in the context of a long history of ups and downs in the development of capitalism; second, I will analyze the crisis in the perspective of the postwar boom that preceded it.

A Long-Run Historical Perspective

A look back over the history of capitalist economic development shows that major structural crises are not unprecedented. Moreover, such crises arise with almost cyclical regularity. The period since World War II has included both phases of such a cycle; the world capitalist economy first experienced a period of prosperity that lasted for approximately two and a half decades, and it then entered what we now perceive as a major economic crisis.

13

At several points in its long, turbulent history, capitalism has been in at least as much trouble as it is today, and in the past it has always recovered in one way or another. Indeed, there is much evidence in support of a very rough kind of long-wave pattern characterizing the development of capitalism.[1] If one goes back about 130 years, one can discern a period of relatively good times beginning around the middle of the nineteenth century and continuing up to the 1870s, followed by a period of relatively bad times from the 1870s to the 1890s (when there occurred what was at that time labeled the "Great Depression"). Then a renewed period of prosperity lasted from the 1890s up to World War I and (in the United States) through the late 1920s. There followed a period of serious economic difficulties, the worst of which was the Great Depression of the 1930s. But the depression and war years were followed again by the postwar boom and then the latest economic crisis. With the increasing integration of the world capitalist economy, economic booms and crises have become increasingly synchronous across different capitalist nations.

There is no single common cyclical mechanism that has generated these long waves. Rather than explaining the long waves by a common recurring cyclical mechanism, it is more accurate to argue that each wave begins on the basis of a new capitalist "institutional structure."[2] This is a set of social/economic/political institutions that provide a certain stability and thereby generate prosperity for a capitalist system. Such an institutional structure works for a while – perhaps for two or three decades, depending on various circumstances. But sooner or later, each such institutional structure begins to run into trouble, as internal contradictions develop. The very basis of the expansion becomes contradictory, in that it generates forces that restrain the expansion. I would argue that in each of the previous periods of capitalist prosperity, one can point to internal contradictions that ultimately brought the expansion to an end and precipitated a systemic economic crisis.

Compared with the endogenous nature of the crisis, the subsequent recovery is usually more autonomous. Each crisis creates conditions under which major institutional change can take place, as the classes and/or interest groups favored by the current institutional structure are weakened by its economic contradictions. The crisis poses a challenge to capitalists in particular, for they are the principal operators and beneficiaries of a capitalist system. They are challenged either to reform it in some fundamental structural ways, so as to provide the institutional basis for a new period of accumulation, or else to yield to revolutionary changes which would radically restructure the mode of production as a whole. Thus each crisis reflects the exhaustion of the particular institutional structure that characterized the preceding long-wave upswing, and it can only be resolved by some major restructuring that establishes a new and viable institutional structure for accumulation. While the

14

nature of the crisis itself circumscribes the set of possible outcomes, it does not lead inexorably to any particular one. What kind of new structure eventually gets established – and whether or not it remains consistent with the capitalist mode of production – depends to a large extent upon the political actions of different classes confronting the crisis situation.

This general model can be applied to the periods of crisis in the American economy in the late nineteenth century and in the 1930s. Each of those challenges to the system was ultimately met by major structural changes that laid the basis for a subsequent stage of accumulation. It was not that capitalists got together and acted self-consciously to restructure the system. Rather, a series of changes and reforms, sometimes even forced upon a reluctant capitalist class by political leaders and/or noncapitalist classes, gradually caused capitalists to change their way of doing business and thereby to restructure the system so as to lay the basis for a profitable new period of accumulation.

In the late nineteenth century the difficulties that American capitalism encountered had much to do with growing competition among capitalists.[3] Increasingly cutthroat competition generated economic instability and weakened capitalist control over the working classes. The shift from a predominantly competitive type of capitalism to a much more monopolistic form of capitalism ultimately paved the way for a new and more profitable period of accumulation. This structural shift was accomplished by mergers and takeovers that led to the concentration of capital into large units with a much greater ability to control labor and markets. The whole process was facilitated by the growth of governmental regulation of finance and industry, which had the effect of promoting greater business concentration and streamlining the system so it would work more effectively on capitalist terms to produce the economic growth of the early twentieth century.

That model, however, did not work forever. By the 1920s the very monopolistic structure of business that had been part of the solution to the difficulties of the late nineteenth century became the source of new difficulties. The distribution of income shifted against workers and aggregate consumption demand began to decelerate, very much along the lines suggested by neo-Marxian "underconsumption" theorists.[4] By the 1930s, the underlying consumption problem could no longer be offset by other sources of demand, and the increasing inadequacy of aggregate demand compounded itself into the Great Depression. Thus a major crisis had resulted from the growing contradictions of the monopoly capitalist stage of development

The resolution of this crisis on capitalist terms initially owed much to the boost in aggregate demand represented by massive military expenditures for World War II. But the new institutional structure on which postwar capitalist prosperity was built involved an augmented role for the state in the economy, which included the pursuit of Keynesian demand-management policies, the

15

provision of social security and social-service benefits to a substantial part of the population, and other measures enhancing the economic security of individuals and firms. Partly as a consequence of working-class struggles, partly as a consequence of capitalist initiatives, the crisis of the 1930s led to a restructuring of the system, moving it from a stage of "monopoly capitalism" to a new stage of "security capitalism" in which a significant measure of state-sponsored economic security was grafted onto the monopolistic core of the capitalist economy. This combination helped to stimulate the vigorous postwar boom of the American economy.

This whole approach to the analysis of the development of capitalism suggests that what we have witnessed in the 1970s and early 1980s is an economic crisis generated by the internal contradictions of an initially successful institutional structure established after World War II. If we want to understand this crisis, we must first analyze what made possible the prosperity of the 1950s and 1960s and then see what contradictions developed out of it.

Sources of the Postwar Boom

The period from the end of World War II to the late 1960s was one of overall economic prosperity for the US economy. Although the business cycle took its toll in a series of cyclical recessions, these recessions were relatively mild and short-lived by historical standards. The postwar prosperity of the American economy was grounded in the new institutional structure that emerged after World War II. Both domestic and international aspects of that structure contributed significantly to the long-wave upswing, and I will analyze the process in more detail below. However, certain general environmental conditions were also favorable to rapid economic growth in the postwar period.

First, this was a period in which key natural resources were available in plentiful supply both inside and outside of the United States. Second, the capacity of the earth to receive the waste products of industrial production without serious environmental deterioration had yet to be exhausted in most parts of the world. Thus productive activities in the United States were not subject to any major constraints imposed by the need to maintain ecological balance. Overall, favorable physical supply and environmental conditions, both in the United States and in the rest of the world, contributed to the favorable economic availability of energy and other key resources to the American economy in the 1950s and 1960s.

Turning now to the postwar institutional structure itself, I believe that two international elements of that structure were especially critical for the postwar boom of the American economy. First, and most important, was the international political, economic, and monetary stability that was assured by American political and economic hegemony over the world capitalist system. To consider briefly again the long-term history of capitalism, the international stability of the capitalist system has been assured only at times when a single nation has been dominant and taken responsibility for political order and monetary discipline. This hegemonic role was played by Great Britain in the nineteenth century ("Pax Britannica") and by the United States in the quarter-century following World War II ("Pax Americana"). American political and economic dominance contributed to a stable economic and political climate within which capitalist trade, investment, and output could grow very rapidly. Although the gains from this stable world capitalist economy were shared unequally, the economies of all the advanced capitalist powers were major beneficiaries.

Second, the fact that it was the United States that played the role of hegemonic power in the postwar world capitalist system meant that the American economy gained special advantages in addition to those stemming simply from the stability of the international order.[5] For example, the use of dollars as the key currency for international payments in effect forced other nations to make short-term loans to the United States: this permitted American capitalism and the government to undertake more long-term foreign investment and/or more foreign aid and/or more imports of goods and services than would otherwise have been possible. Moreover, the use of American military forces and aid to defend the "free world" (by maintaining governments friendly to capitalist enterprise) provided American capitalists with channels of influence that facilitated their access to Third World resources and markets and provided certain competitive advantages vis-à-vis capitalists from other nations. Perhaps most critical for the United States was the way in which American political and economic hegemony assured favorable terms of access to Third World mineral and energy-related raw materials (notably oil), thereby helping to keep down the real price of key raw materials relative to industrial output.

The principal domestic elements of the postwar institutional structure in the United States provide substance to the label "security capitalism." First, there was the more or less explicit agreement between organized labor and corporate capital whereby workers would get rising real wages and substantial economic security, while capitalists would get a reasonably disciplined and cooperative labor force that would not offer a political challenge to the capitalist order. The left wing of the American trade union movement was sacrificed for this truce between labor and big capital, which contributed both a substantial amount of stability and a mass consumption base to the postwar American economy. Although this capital–labor accord centered on the relations between private sector corporations and unions, it was consummated in

17

the context of a series of key government measures (such as the Wagner Act of 1935 and the Taft–Hartley Act of 1947) that set the legal framework for collective bargaining in the United States.

The second important new domestic element of the institutional structure was the commitment of the state to stabilize the macro-economy by means of Keynesian techniques of demand management. Throughout the postwar period the ability of the US government to stimulate aggregate demand has been linked to the political acceptability of high levels of government spending for military purposes. In conjunction with the rising real wages emerging from the capital–labor accord and the "automatic stabilizers" embedded in state-sponsored programs for economic security, government demand management was successful in maintaining relatively high rates of employment and capacity utilization and avoiding the waste of periodic sharp downturns that slowed down the long-run rate of growth in earlier stages of American capitalism.

Finally, the third key element of the domestic institutional structure of the postwar period was the role of the state in protecting people and businesses from the unpredictable (and often cruel) vicissitudes of the market. On the one hand, new and increasingly comprehensive government programs rendered workers less dependent for survival on their current wages. Social security (which benefits not only retired people, but also the working family members on whom they would be dependent if they did not have access to social security payments), unemployment compensation, and various other kinds of government transfers and social services all constitute a "social wage" that now supplements the "private wage."[6]

On the other hand, the US government in the postwar period has also become increasingly protective of private business constituencies. The government is extremely reluctant to allow major banks or corporations to go bankrupt because of the disruptive consequences such failures would have both for the owner, managers, and workers and for related sectors of the economy. In the contemporary era of security capitalism corporations have gained the modern capitalist state as a significant source of protection from the full impact of market forces.

Both the international and the domestic aspects of the postwar institutional structure of American capitalism represent, to a significant degree, the outcome of structural reforms that responded to the failure of the capitalist system in the 1930s. American international hegemony owed much to the emergence of the United States as the largest and economically healthiest nation on the victorious side of World War II. But the framework of the postwar world capitalist economy was established by negotiators at Bretton Woods who sought deliberately to avoid the systemic international economic problems of the interwar period of crisis.[7] The reforms that led to the capital–labor accord, Keynesian demand management, and the protective state were aimed at the most serious economic problem of the Great Depression: inadequate aggregate demand. Some of these reforms were pushed very strongly by working-class organizations, some were initiated by government officials, and many had to be introduced over the intense opposition of particular capitalists. But the end result was a new stage of capitalism that was, in fact, more conducive to capitalist growth (for a period of a couple of decades) than the stage preceding it. The overall institutional structure was converted from a depression-prone system to a new type of system that was relatively immune to that type of threat to the viability of capitalism.

All of the different factors discussed above contributed to the rapid economic growth of the American economy in the postwar period. The favorable resource availability and international institutional conditions, as well as the capital–labor accord, provided a strong impetus to aggregate supply, while the three domestic aspects of the institutional structure provided a complementary boost to aggregate demand. Economic growth itself helped in turn to contain the extent of both inflation and unemployment. A gradually increasing rate of growth in per capita output in the 1950s and 1960s provided the system with the resources to meet, in a non-inflationary manner, the growing real claims placed upon it by various classes and interest groups. Moreover, the stability of the international system – and the dominant position of the United States within it – enabled the American economy to avoid the kind of external shocks (for example, oil price increases) which have exacerbated inflationary pressures in all the advanced capitalist economies in the last decade. Finally, the rising trend in the rate of economic growth, combined with a domestic institutional structure geared to the support and management of aggregate demand, contributed to success in keeping rates of unemployment relatively low – by American historical standards – during the 1950s and 1960s.

Contradictions of the Postwar Boom

Why did the boom not last forever, as it was assumed that it could by many economists and public officials in the 1960s? In retrospect, one can see not only that the critical conditions of the postwar period turned from favorable to unfavorable, but that their metamorphosis was a natural consequence of the boom itself. In other words, like previous periods of capitalist prosperity, the postwar boom was inherently contradictory.

First, the favorable resource and environmental supply conditions were bound, sooner or later, to be undermined by sustained economic growth itself. The rapid growth of US industrial production put increasing pressure on the domestic supply of raw materials and nonrenewable resources. Similarly, the rapid growth of industrial activity began to increase environmental costs. Similar processes were at work in other advanced capitalist nations, so that Ricardian problems of natural-resource supply began to affect the world capitalist economy as a whole.

These Ricardian problems loom increasingly ominous as a long-term secular constraint on the growth potential of "spaceship earth." But their effect on the postwar American capitalist economy was limited so long as American firms had privileged access to foreign resources and capitalists could prevent the social costs of environmental deterioration from being translated into the private costs of doing business. But for reasons to be discussed at greater length below, the political strength of raw material–exporting nations abroad increased to the point where the terms of trade turned against the United States, and the political strength of the environmental movement at home increased to the point where American capitalists were no longer able to externalize the costs of waste disposal.

Turning to the international aspects of the postwar institutional structure, one can see that the favorable condition of America's hegemony was bound to be short-lived because of its very success in promoting capital accumulation throughout the world capitalist system. Thanks to the international economic stability assured by US dominance, the other advanced capitalist nations in Western Europe and Japan were able to rebuild their economies rapidly. By the 1960s they were becoming effective rivals economically as well as politically. The resultant erosion of American dominance of the world capitalist system led to the restructuring of the whole postwar international monetary system in 1971, which deprived the United States of its privileged position within the international framework.

An additional contradictory element in the postwar international hegemony of the United States developed out of American relations with Third World nations. Being the "policeman of the free world," the United States came increasingly into conflict with Third World revolutionary movements. The cost of defending the empire mounted for the hegemonic power, reaching its debilitating peak with the escalation of the war in Vietnam.

In an overall context of increasing pressure on resource supplies, diminishing American hegemony, and increasing rivalry among advanced capitalist powers, the economic bargaining power of some of the Third World raw material–exporting nations increased substantially. The successful OPEC cartel represents the most visible and most important example of this process. Its ability (in conjunction with multinational petroleum corporations) to shift the terms of trade against the oil-importing nations was enhanced by its ability to play off the oil-importing nations against one another and by the declining capacity of the US government to control Third World states. In a characteristically contradictory fashion, the huge increase in the real cost of imported oil had a particularly adverse effect on the US economy because, in their earlier state of blissful hegemony, American policymakers had allowed the economy to become geared to a continual flow of low-cost energy from abroad.

Finally, the domestic elements of the postwar institutional structure of American capitalism also generated contradictions that would ultimately render them problematical. The domestic capital–labor accord did attenuate, up to a point, the traditional and often damaging struggle between capital and labor over wages. But the fact that capitalists could provide material security and growing real wages for a substantial portion of the labor force did not do away with all sources of capital–labor conflict, for as workers solidified their gains in this domain, they became concerned about other spheres of capitalist dominance. Workers, minority groups, and local communities began to organize themselves around demands for greater workplace democracy, affirmative action, community control, etc., all of which involved an effort to limit the decision-making freedom of capitalists in the interest of broader social goals than high profits and growing real wages. These new kinds of struggles generated increasing problems for capitalists at the enterprise level; even more significantly, they resulted in increasing pressure on government to legislate restrictions on capitalist activity. All of these movements and challenges gradually undermined the relatively harmonious relations between capital and labor that had been fostered by the capital–labor accord and contributed to an increasingly contentious business climate.

The use of Keynesian techniques of demand management and military spending to stabilize the American macroeconomy also proved contradictory in the long run. The prospect of massive depression, unemployment, and financial collapse receded as a plausible threat to the economy as business, unions, and everyone else began to see that there could not be a serious and protracted downturn on the scale of the Great Depression, because the government would intervene with an expansionary macro-policy to prevent it. Periodic recessions would continue to occur, but no government could afford politically to permit a major economic downturn to destabilize the system. This meant that the lid was taken off price and (money) wage restraint. The major actors in the economic arena came to perceive that the government was guaranteeing them against economic loss, so they could, for the most part, continue business as usual rather than reforming and changing things. Thus, the classical capitalist medicine of periodic economic downturn became increasingly ineffective as a restraint on inflationary pressures and as a stimulant to economic efficiency.

The high levels of military spending that helped to stimulate the demand-constrained American economy of the 1950s and 1960s further exacerbated economic problems. First, military demand for resources added to all the other

21

claims on the economy and put growing pressure on the potential supply of goods and services as the Vietnam War escalated in the late 1960s. Second, the fostering of the military–industrial complex created a major sector of the US economy where incentives for efficient, low-cost production were particularly weak. Third, it is arguable that the national priority placed on the expansion of military capabilities resulted in an undue concentration of financial and intellectual resources on research and development activities that would promote technological progress only in the military and closely related industries.

The last key element of the postwar domestic institutional structure – the protective role of the state – contained some important contradictory elements as well. The growth of welfare-state transfers and programs, if not the protection of particular business interests, was functional for postwar American capitalism. But the development of a welfare state has a dynamic logic that leads to greater and greater economic expectations from the general public. Such expectations have been characterized by Daniel Yankelovich as a "philosophy of entitlement,"[8] which in effect continuously increases the cost of legitimating the capitalist system. For the overall vitality of the American economy these rising economic aspirations – and the rising ability of different groups to act upon them with political pressures on government – proved dysfunctional, for they led to increasingly incompatible claims on available resources. As the rising costs of state protective activities reduced the resources available for economic growth, American capitalism confronted ever more sharply the classical capitalist conflict between legitimation and accumulation.

Many of the contradictory processes I have discussed here reflect ultimately a basic contradiction of liberal democracy in a capitalist society.[9] On the one hand, the liberal democratic political framework is useful as a means of stabilizing and legitimating the capitalist system. On the other hand, liberal democracy is increasingly used by various groups in order to improve their economic and social position at the expense of the long-run capitalist interest in profitable accumulation. This contradiction was intensified during the postwar boom, for the boom itself was based on an institutional structure that relied on a greatly enhanced role for the liberal democratic state.

Sources of the Latest Crisis

The analysis in the preceding section suggests the reasons why real economic growth slowed, inflation accelerated, and unemployment rose in the 1970s. Among the causes of the slowdown in real economic growth, the reduced accessibility and increased cost of key raw material inputs and waste disposal processes had a direct adverse effect on the growth of productivity in the American economy. Likewise, the increased instability of the international economic system, and the deteriorating position of the United States within it, contributed to the difficulty of maintaining productivity growth and reduced the value of American output in terms of its purchasing power over foreign goods and services. For a flexible and resilient capitalist economy, these adverse developments would have had only a temporarily debilitating effect on economic growth. The burden of the deteriorating overall economic environment would soon have been diverted away from capitalists, who would then have had both sufficient investable resources and sufficiently profitable investment opportunities to engage in a new surge of domestic capital formation. In this process, technological advances and substitution away from scarce inputs would help to meet the challenge posed by the changes in the economic environment; a form of "reindustrialization," involving substantial changes in both the industry composition and productive techniques of the US economy, would revitalize American capitalism.

The fact that such changes did not occur, and that the American economy stagnated rather than revived during the past decade, can be attributed in large part to the contradictions of the domestic institutional structure of postwar American capitalism. First, the capital–labor accord, the avoidance of mass unemployment, and the growth of state-sponsored measures to promote economic security reduced the ability of capitalists as a class to protect their profits by shifting the burden of hard times onto others. Beginning in the 1960s a variety of noncapitalist groups – organized labor, the elderly, consumers, environmentalists, minorities, and even welfare recipients – developed an increasing ability to put political pressure on the liberal democratic state to defend their interests. At the same time the rise in importance of the social wage, as well as government macroeconomic stabilization policy, combined to restrain the disciplinary impact of the reserve army of labor;[10] the threat of unemployment was increasingly ineffective as a whip to induce greater work intensity and more moderate wage demands by unionized workers. As the growth in real income available to US residents slowed down in the 1970s, the growth in the real claims of private wages, government transfers (for example, social security), and public services (for example, health and educational programs) could not be restrained to the same extent; thus, increasing pressure was placed upon the share of national income going to profits (after taxes).

There was therefore a decline of profitability in the domestic American economy. Quite apart from any adverse impact on the rate of profit, the growth in political power of noncapitalists from the 1960s to the 1970s may also have restrained the capitalist growth process by placing increasing restrictions on capitalists' decision-making freedom with respect to the environment, worker safety, product safety, and other such social concerns. Except where they are very poorly legislated or enforced, such restrictions on capitalists generate important social gains in terms of unmeasured (and insufficiently ap-

23

preciated) benefits like environmental protection, worker health, and consumer protection. But in a capitalist society, these same progressive regulations may also impose a general cost on the public by depressing profit expectations and hence the incentive for capitalists to invest.*

There is another important mechanism by which the domestic aspects of the American postwar institutional structure seem to have ultimately slowed down economic growth. The postwar period has witnessed the development of a capitalist state that refuses to allow economic downturns to go very far, that seeks to prevent financial or business collapse (for example, by bailing out troubled companies like Lockheed and Chrysler), and that caters to a bloated military–industrial complex. As a consequence, the competitive capitalist pressures to reorganize firms and restructure the economy no longer operate as strongly, and the private enterprise system in the United States has become increasingly flaccid. Throughout the 1970s there was very little to make up for the obsolescence of creative destruction. The inflexibility of American capitalism has been especially damaging to economic vitality in recent times because of the rapid changes in the world economic environment that have occurred in the past decade.

Turning now to the second major aspect of the latest economic crisis, I believe that the accelerating inflation of the late 1970s can best be analyzed as a consequence of the growing imbalance between economic claims made upon the American economy and the economic resources it could deliver.[11] On the one hand, the real income available per working person grew fairly rapidly from the end of World War II up to the late 1960s and then slowed down significantly during the following decade. On the other hand, there has been a continual growth of claims upon the economy since the beginning of the postwar period. At the same time, government military and related programs have claimed a consistently high proportion of available GNP, contributing in particular to a surge in claims during the escalation of the Vietnam War.

As long as the overall economic pie was growing rapidly, the economy was able to satisfy the growing real claims placed upon it. But when the real value of available output per person began to slow down in the late 1960s, there was no corresponding mechanism to slow down the claims placed by the public and by the state upon the system. Quite understandably, there was considerable resistance to cuts in wages, cuts in social services, cuts in military outlays,

---

* The impact of progressive regulations on profits is, to be sure, a controversial issue. There can be little doubt that they increase business costs; the key question is whether businesses have been able to pass the higher costs on to consumers, or whether they have had to absorb at least part of them in lower profits.

and cuts in profits. Nobody was inclined to accept any decline in real income; and many were able to use their ability to press economic claims, either in the marketplace or in government, in order to try to shift the burden onto others. The end result was accelerated inflation, because if the sum total of the claims (made in dollars at anticipated prices) exceeds the total available resources (in dollars at anticipated prices), then the general price level will necessarily rise more than anticipated. This, in turn, frustrates many of the claimants, who wind up with less real income than they expected; so the whole process is set off again and continues in an upward spiral.

The same kinds of forces that stimulated inflation in the US economy operated in the world capitalist system as a whole. For example, Third World oil exporters increased their claims upon the world capitalist economy, as well as their ability to act upon those claims, because of a change in the international structure of power. Multinational oil companies, in turn, refused to absorb the burden of those claims, so they passed them on (and added some of their own) to oil consumers around the world. Thus, the whole phenomenon of rising oil prices really reflected, on an international scale, an imbalance between claims and available real output. Capitalism had been transformed from a depression-prone to an inflation-prone system by its postwar institutional structure.[12]

The third element of the latest economic crisis – the upward trend in unemployment rates – was related to the rising trend in inflation. For as inflation grows, capitalist governments come under increasing pressure to do something about it. The conventional policy prescription is to slow down the economy via fiscal and monetary restraints, and this is the policy to which the US government has regularly turned (except for the unpopular Nixon wage/price controls). The immediate consequence of such an anti-inflationary policy is a sharp rise in unemployment, followed eventually by some moderation of the rate of inflation. Since the postwar institutional structure limited the use of unemployment to combat inflation, the US government was prevented from pursuing such an anti-inflationary policy long enough to rein in all the inflationary pressures. Instead, a stop-go pattern of macroeconomic stabilization policy worsened the trade-off between unemployment and inflation, with the result that both became more serious with each successive short-run business cycle. Thus the worsening trend in unemployment rates in the early 1980s was attributable to the (relatively unsuccessful) efforts of the government to fight inflation with medicine appropriate to an earlier stage of capitalist development.

Implications of the Crisis

The long-wave historical framework developed earlier suggests that a genuine resolution of the latest crisis will have to be based on a new institutional structure. Major institutional changes will be required to overcome the contradictions that undermined the postwar institutional structure in the past decade. Depending on political struggles still to come, these changes could lead to a reformed and revitalized capitalist structure or even possibly to a fundamental transformation of the capitalist mode of production.

One point that deserves initial emphasis, however, is that some of the contradictions that have contributed to the current economic crisis are unlikely to be fully overcome under any conceivable institutional conditions. First, Ricardian constraints on the physical availability of natural resources are likely to weigh more heavily in the future than in the past: the ecological balance of the world's environment has undergone a qualitative change in the latter part of the twentieth century.

A second, related contradiction that is also unlikely to be fully overcome under any future institutional structure is the erosion of US hegemony over the world capitalist system. It is certainly possible that international economic stability may be restored under some kind of joint or supranational capitalist authority, although such a development would require a great deal of negotiation and compromise of a kind that is scarcely in evidence among the major capitalist powers today. But even if a stable international capitalist economic structure can be refashioned, it will not be one from which the American economy will draw many special privileges or economic advantages vis-à-vis rival capitalist economies. Perhaps more important, it will never again be one that will provide such favorable access to the raw materials and energy of Third World nations. Thus if the American economy is to rejuvenate itself with a new wave of prosperity, it will most likely have to do so by coming to terms with a more modest rate of economic growth than was achieved during the last long-wave upswing represented by the postwar boom.

Given the limited potential of international restructuring alone to generate a new long-wave upswing in the United States, the primary focus of a successful restructuring process will have to be on the domestic aspects of the postwar institutional structure of the United States.

Conclusion

I have argued in this paper that the postwar economy of the United States has been characterized by an institutional structure that can be labeled "security capitalism." In its heyday, security capitalism represented a viable and histori-

26

cally progressive solution to the demand-constrained crisis of prewar American capitalism. It provided simultaneously for high profits to stimulate capitalist economic growth and for a degree of economic security, protection, and income redistribution unprecedented in American capitalist history. But the postwar institutional structure of the economy contained internal contradictions that rendered it increasingly unviable and unsatisfactory. It gradually eroded the favorable environmental and international conditions on which it initially thrived; and by virtue of solving problems of inadequate demand with the provision of increased economic security, it generated growing problems of inadequate supply and economic inflexibility. Thus contradictions inherent in the postwar long-wave upswing led to the subsequent long-wave downswing – a generalized crisis in which the American economy could no longer provide for both profit-fueled capitalist growth and widespread protection from the ravages of an unrestrained capitalist engine.

It follows from this analysis that economic recovery leading to a new long-wave upswing will have to be based on a new institutional structure that can overcome the current impasse. Any new institutional structure will inevitably impose significant burdens on the American people, for resources will have to be mobilized for economic revitalization and patterns of economic activity will have to be substantially altered. How the burdens of the restructuring process will be distributed among classes and regions and other segments of American society becomes then a central focus of political struggles in the years to come.

Notes

I am greatly indebted to Sam Bowles and David Gordon for a series of stimulating discussions about most of the issues raised in this paper. I also owe a significant debt of gratitude to many constructive critics of an earlier version of this paper – including especially Jim Campen, Robert Heilbroner, Victor and Walter Weisskopf, and Joan Hannon together with the other members of the San Francisco Bay Area collective of *Socialist Review*.

1. For documentation and analysis of "long waves" in capitalist development, see Hobsbawm (1976), Gordon (1978), and Mandel (1980).
2. My concept of an "institutional structure" is similar to the notion of a "social structure of accumulation" utilized by Gordon (1978, 1980) in his analysis of capitalist long waves.
3. Arrighi (1978) advances persuasively the thesis of this paragraph in the context of a general theoretical analysis of recurring economic crises in the history of capitalism; Dowd (1974), chapter 3, describes the shift from relatively competitive to relatively monopolistic capitalism in the US.
4. The neo-Marxian theory of underconsumption has been most forcefully developed and applied to the American economy by Baran and Sweezy (1966); for a test of its relevance to the 1920s and 1930s, see Keller (1975).
5. See MacEwan (1978) for an analysis of the benefits of American hegemony for the American economy.
6. The concept of the "social wage" is discussed in detail by Gough (1979), and its empirical magnitude in the United States has been estimated by Bowles (1982).
7. For a thorough analysis of the development of the postwar international capitalist monetary system, see Block (1977).

8. This term, coined by Yankelovich, is cited and utilized by Heilbroner (1978), p. 44.

9. The fundamental contradiction between capitalism and liberal democracy is the basic theme of an article by Bowles [published in *Socialist Review* in 1982], who analyzes the issue thoroughly both in Marxian theoretical terms and in the empirical context of the United States. For an earlier, much briefer, exposition of the basic ideas, see Bowles (1978).

10. The reduced impact of cyclical downturns on the growth of both nominal and real wages in the United States is documented and persuasively analyzed by Bowles and Gintis (1981), section 6.

11. The analysis of inflation presented here is based on the approach developed more rigorously by Rosenberg and Weisskopf (1981).

12. This is precisely the same conclusion reached by Heilbroner (1979) in a perceptive analysis of contemporary capitalist inflation.

Bibliography

Arrighi, Giovanni. "Towards a Theory of Capitalist Crisis." *New Left Review,* no. 111 (Sept.–Oct. 1978).

Baran, Paul, and Paul Sweezy. *Monopoly Capital.* New York: Monthly Review Press 1980.

Block, Fred. *The Origin of International Economic Disorder.* Berkeley: University of California Press 1977.

Bowles, Samuel. "The Trilateral Commission: Have Capitalism and Democracy Come to a Parting of the Ways?" In URPE, *US Capitalism in Crisis.* New York: Union for Radical Political Economics 1978.

————. "The Post-Keynesian Capital-Labor Stalemate." *Socialist Review,* vol. 12, no. 5 (Sept.–Oct. 1982).

Dowd Douglas. *The Twisted Dream.* Cambridge, Mass.: Winthrop 1974.

Gordon, David. "Up and Down the Long Roller-Coaster." In URPE, *US Capitalism in Crisis.* New York: Union for Radical Political Economics 1978.

————. "Stages of Accumulation and Long Cycles." In T. Hopkins and I. Wallerstein, eds, *Processes of the World-System.* Beverly Hills, Calif.: Sage 1980.

Gough, Ian. *The Political Economy of the Welfare State.* London: Macmillan 1979.

Heilbroner, Robert. *Beyond Boom and Crash.* New York: Norton 1978.

————. "Inflationary Capitalism." *New Yorker,* October 8, 1979.

Hobsbawm, Eric. "The Crisis of Capitalism," *SocialistRevolution,* vol. 6, no. 4 (Oct.–Dec. 1976).

Keller, Robert. "Monopoly Capital and the Great Depression: Testing Baran and Sweezy's Hypothesis." *Review of Radical Political Economy,* vol. 7, no. 4 (Winter 1975).

MacEwan, Arthur. "The Development of the Crisis in the World Economy." In URPE, *US Capitalism in Crisis.* New York: Union for Radical Political Economics 1978.

Mandel, Ernest. *Long Waves of Capitalist Development.* Cambridge: Cambridge University Press 1980.

Rosenberg, Sam, and Thomas Weisskopf. "A Conflict Theory Approach to Inflation in the Postwar US Economy." *American Economic Review,* vol. 71, no. 2 (May 1981).

2

The Ruling Class Does Not Rule
Notes on the Marxist Theory of the State
(1977)
Fred Block

The Marxist theory of the state remains a muddle despite the recent revival of interest in the subject.[1] Substantial progress has been made in formulating a critique of orthodox Marxist formulations that reduce the state to a mere reflection of economic interests. However, the outlines of an adequate alternative Marxist theory are not yet clear. This is most dramatically indicated by the continued popularity in Marxist circles of explanations of state policies or of conflicts within the state that are remarkably similar to orthodox formulations in their tendency to see the state as a reflection of the interests of certain groups in the capitalist class. Many Marxists, for example, were drawn to interpretations of Watergate that saw it as a conflict between two different wings of the capitalist class.[2] This gap between theory and the explanation of actual historical events demonstrates that the critique of orthodox formulations has not been carried far enough. These earlier formulations – even when they have been carefully criticized and dismissed – sneak back into many current analyses because they remain embedded in the basic concepts of Marxist analysis.

This essay proposes two elements of an alternative Marxist theory of the state. The first is a different way of conceptualizing the ruling class and its relationship to the state. This reconceptualization makes possible the second element – the elaboration of a structural framework that specifies the concrete mechanisms that make the state a capitalist state, whereas other structural theories have tended to analyze structures in an abstract and mystifying way.[3]

Although these two elements do not provide a complete Marxist theory of the state, they do provide a new way of thinking about the sources of rationality within capitalism. Contemporary Marxists have been forced to acknowledge that despite its fundamental irrationality, capitalism in the developed world has shown a remarkable capacity to rationalize itself in response to the twin dangers of economic crisis and radical working-class movements.[4] Since the present historical period again poses for the left the threat of successful capitalist rationalization, understanding the sources of capitalism's capacity for self-reform is of the utmost political importance. The traditional Marxist explanation of capitalist rationality is to root it in the consciousness of a sector of the ruling class. In this light, capitalist reform reflects the conscious will and understanding of a sector of the capitalist class that has grasped the magnitude of the problem and proposes a set of solutions. The alternative framework being proposed here suggests that the capacity of capitalism to rationalize itself is the outcome of a conflict among three sets of agents – the capitalist class, the managers of the state apparatus, and the working class.[5] Rationalization occurs "behind the backs" of each set of actors so that rationality cannot be seen as a function of the consciousness of one particular group.

This argument and its implications will be traced out through a number of steps. First, I intend to show that critiques of orthodox Marxist theory of the state are flawed by their acceptance of the idea of a class-conscious ruling class. Second, I argue that there is a basis in Marx's writing for rejecting the idea of a class-conscious ruling class. Third, I develop a structural argument that shows that even in the absence of ruling-class class consciousness, the state managers are strongly discouraged from pursuing anticapitalist policies. Fourth, I return to the issue of capitalist rationality and describe how it grows out of the structured relationship among capitalists, workers, and state managers. Finally, I briefly analyze the implications of this argument for capitalism's current difficulties in the United States.

The Critique of Instrumentalism

The major development in the Marxist theory of the state in recent years has been the formulation of a critique of instrumentalism. A number of writers have characterized the orthodox Marxist view of the state as instrumentalism because it views the state as a simple tool or instrument of ruling-class purposes. First, it neglects the ideological role of the state. The state plays a critical role in maintaining the legitimacy of the social order, and this requires that the state appear to be neutral in the class struggle. In short, even if the state is an instrument of ruling-class purpose, the fact that it must appear otherwise indicates the need for a more complex framework for analyzing state policies. Second, instrumentalism fails to recognize that to act in the general interest of capital, the state must be able to take actions against the particular interests of capitalists. Price controls or restrictions on the export of capital, for example, might be in the general interest of capital in a particular period, even if they temporarily reduced the profits of most capitalists. To carry through such policies, the state must have more autonomy from direct capitalist control than the instrumentalist view would allow.

The critics of instrumentalism propose the idea of the relative autonomy of the state as an alternative framework. In order to serve the general interests of capital, the state must have some autonomy from direct ruling-class control. Since the concept of the absolute autonomy of the state would be un-Marxist and false, the autonomy is clearly relative. However, the difficulty is in specifying the nature, limits, and determinants of that relative autonomy. Some writers have attempted to argue that the degree of autonomy varies historically, and that "late capitalism" is characterized by the "autonomization of the state apparatus." But these arguments have an ad hoc quality, and they share an analytic problem derived from the phrase "relative autonomy from ruling-class control."

The basic problem in formulations of "relative autonomy" is the conceptualization of the ruling class. Relative autonomy theories assume that the ruling class will respond effectively to the state's abuse of that autonomy. But for the ruling class to be capable of taking such corrective actions, it must have some degree of political cohesion, an understanding of its general interests, and a high degree of political sophistication. In sum, the theory requires that the ruling class, or a portion of it, be class-conscious, that is, aware of what is necessary to reproduce capitalist social relations in changing historical circumstances. Yet if the ruling class or a segment of it is class-conscious, then the degree of autonomy of the state is clearly quite limited. At this point the theory of relative autonomy collapses back into a slightly more sophisticated version of instrumentalism. State policies continue to be seen as the reflection of inputs by a class-conscious ruling class.

The way out of this theoretical bind, the way to formulate a critique of instrumentalism that does not collapse, is to reject the idea of a class-conscious ruling class. Instead of the relative autonomy framework, the key idea becomes a division of labor between those who accumulate capital and those who manage the state apparatus. Those who accumulate capital are conscious of their interests as capitalists, but, in general, they are not conscious of what is necessary to reproduce the social order in changing circumstances. Those who manage the state apparatus, however, are forced to concern themselves to a greater degree with the reproduction of the social order because their continued power rests on the maintenance of political and economic order. In this framework, the central theoretical task is to explain how it is that despite this division of labor, the state tends to serve the interests of the capitalist class. It

31

is to this task – the elaboration of a structural theory of the state – that I will turn after a brief discussion of the division of labor between capitalists and state managers.

Division of Labor

The idea of a division of labor between non-class-conscious capitalists and those who manage the state apparatus can be found in Marx's writings.[6] Two factors, however, have obscured this aspect of Marx's thought. First, Marx did not spell out the nature of the structural framework in which that division of labor operated, although he hinted at the existence of such a framework. Second, Marx's discussion of these issues is clouded by his polemical intent to fix responsibility for all aspects of bourgeois society on the ruling class. Even when Marx recognizes that the ruling class lacks class consciousness, he still formulates his argument in such a way as to imply that the ruling class as a whole is in conscious control of the situation. Marx used the idea of a conscious, directive ruling class as a polemical shorthand for an elaboration of the structural mechanisms through which control over the means of production leads to control over other aspects of society.

The tension in Marx's formulations is clearest in *The Eighteenth Brumaire* when he is explaining why the bourgeoisie supported Louis Bonaparte's coup d'état against the bourgeoisie's own parliamentary representatives. He writes:

> The *extraparliamentary* mass of the bourgeoisie, on the other hand, by its servility towards the President, by its vilification of parliament, by the brutal maltreatment of its own press, invited Bonaparte to suppress and annihilate its speaking and writing section, its politicians and its *literati*, its platform and its press, in order that it might then be able to pursue its private affairs with full confidence in the protection of a strong and unrestricted government. It declared unequivocally that it longed to get rid of its own political rule in order to get rid of the troubles and dangers of ruling.[7]

Marx suggests a division of labor and a division of interest between the extraparliamentary mass of the bourgeoisie, primarily interested in accumulating profits, and the parliamentary and literary representatives of that class, whose central concerns are different. Marx uses the notion of representation as a substitute for specifying the structural relationship that holds together the division of labor.

In an earlier passage, in a discussion of the petty bourgeoisie, he states what is involved in the idea of representation:

> Just as little must one imagine that the democratic representatives are all shopkeepers or enthusiastic champions of shopkeepers. According to their education and their

individual position they may be separated from them as widely as heaven from earth. What makes them representatives of the petty bourgeoisie is the fact that in their minds they do not go beyond the limits which the latter do not go beyond in life, that they are consequently driven theoretically to the same tasks and solutions to which material interest and social position practically drive the latter. This is in general the relationship of the *political and literary representatives* of a class to the class that they represent.[8]

Marx here rejects the simple reductionism so common among his followers. For Marx, representation was an objective relationship – one did not need to be of a class to be its representative. And, in fact, representatives and their classes did not always see eye to eye, since their different positions could lead to different perspectives. In sum, representatives are *not* typical members of their classes, and it is a mistake to attribute to the class as a whole the consciousness that parliamentary or literary representatives display.

Marx's idea of representation suggests the general structural links between the capitalists and those who manage the state apparatus. Marx recognized that those in the state apparatus tended to have a broader view of society than the capitalists, although their view is still far short of a general understanding of what is necessary to reproduce the social order. After all, the state managers' preoccupation with the struggle for political power distorts their understanding. This is the source of the "parliamentary cretinism" that made Louis Bonaparte a better defender of the bourgeoisie's interests than that class's own representatives. But if neither the ruling class nor its representatives know what is necessary to preserve and reproduce capitalist social relations, why then does the state tend to do just that? The answer is that such policies emerge out of the structural relationships among state managers, capitalists, and workers.

Major Structural Mechanisms

A viable structural theory of the state must do two separate things. It must elaborate the structural constraints that operate to reduce the likelihood that state managers will act against the general interests of capitalists. An understanding of these constraints is particularly important for analyzing the obstacles to reformist socialist strategies. But a structural theory must also explain the tendency of state managers to pursue policies that are in the general interests of capital. It is not sufficient to explain why the state avoids anticapitalist policies; it is necessary to explain why the state has served to rationalize capitalism. Once one rejects the idea of ruling-class class consciousness, one needs to provide an alternative explanation of efforts at rationalization.

Both tendencies can be derived from the fact that those who manage the state apparatus – regardless of their own political ideology – are dependent on the maintenance of some reasonable level of economic activity. This is true for two reasons. First, the capacity of the state to finance itself through taxation or borrowing depends on the state of the economy. If economic activity is in decline, the state will have difficulty maintaining its revenues at an adequate level. Second, public support for a regime will decline sharply if the regime presides over a serious drop in the level of economic activity, with a parallel rise in unemployment and shortages of key goods. Such a drop in support increases the likelihood that the state managers will be removed from power one way or another. And even if the drop is not that dramatic, it will increase the challenges to the regime and decrease the regime's political ability to take effective actions.

In a capitalist economy the level of economic activity is largely determined by the private investment decisions of capitalists. This means that capitalists, in their collective role as investors, have a veto over state policies in that their failure to invest at adequate levels can create major political problems for the state managers. This discourages state managers from taking actions that might seriously decrease the rate of investment. It also means that state managers have a direct interest in using their power to facilitate investment, since their own continued power rests on a healthy economy. There will be a tendency for state agencies to orient their various programs toward the goal of facilitating and encouraging private investment. In doing so, the state managers address the problem of investment from a broader perspective than that of the individual capitalist. This increases the likelihood that such policies will be in the general interest of capital.

Constraints on State Policies

This is, of course, too simple. Both sides of the picture – constraints and rationalization – must be filled out in greater detail to make this approach convincing. One problem, in particular, stands out – if capitalists have a veto over state policies, isn't this simply another version of instrumentalism? The answer to this question lies in a more careful analysis of the determinants of investment decisions. The most useful concept is the idea of business confidence. Individual capitalists decide on their rate of investment in a particular country on the basis of a variety of specific variables such as the price of labor and the size of the market for a specific product. But there is also an intangible variable – the capitalist's evaluation of the general political/economic climate. Is the society stable; is the working class under control; are taxes likely to rise; do government agencies interfere with business freedom; will the economy grow? These kinds of considerations are critical to the invest-

34

ment decisions of each firm. The sum of all of these evaluations across a national economy can be termed the level of business confidence. As the level of business confidence declines, so will the rate of investment. Business confidence also has an international dimension when nations are integrated into a capitalist world economy. Multinational corporations, international bankers, and currency speculators also make judgments about a particular nation's political/economic climate that determine their willingness to invest in assets in that nation. This, in turn, will affect the internal level of business confidence and the rate of productive investment.

Business confidence is, however, very different from "ruling-class consciousness." Business confidence is based on an evaluation of the market that considers political events only as they might impinge on the market. This means that it is rooted in the narrow self-interest of the individual capitalist who is worried about profit. Business confidence, especially because of its critical international component, does not make subtle evaluations as to whether a regime is serving the long-term interests of capital. When there is political turmoil and popular mobilization, business confidence will fall, and it will rise when there is a restoration of order, no matter how brutal. It was business confidence that responded so favorably to Louis Bonaparte's coup d'état, because he promised to restore the conditions for business as usual, despite negative implications for the political rights of the bourgeoisie. The crudeness of business confidence makes capitalism peculiarly vulnerable to authoritarian regimes that are capable of acting against the general interests of capital.[9]

The dynamic of business confidence as a constraint on the managers of the state apparatus can be grasped by tracing out a scenario of what happens when left-of-center governments come to power through parliamentary means and attempt to push through major reforms. The scenario distills a number of twentieth-century experiences including that of Chile under Allende. From the moment that the left wins the election, business confidence declines. The most important manifestation of this decline is an increase in speculation against the nation's currency. Reformist governments are always under suspicion that they will pursue inflationary policies; a high rate of inflation means that the international value of the nation's currency will fall. Speculators begin to discount the currency for the expected inflation as soon as possible. This association between reformist governments and inflation is not arbitrary. Reformist policies – higher levels of employment, redistribution of income toward the poor, improved social services – directly or indirectly lead to a shift of income from profits toward the working class. Businesses attempt to resist such a shift by raising prices so that profit levels will not be reduced. In short, price inflation in this context is a market response to policies that tend to benefit the working class. The reformist government, faced with the initial speculative assault on its currency, has two choices. It can reassure the international and domestic business community, making clear its intention to pursue orthodox economic policies. Or it can forge ahead with its reform program. If it pursues the latter course, an increased rate of inflation and an eventual international monetary crisis is likely.

The international crisis results from the combination of continued speculative pressure against the currency and several new factors. Domestic inflation is likely to affect the nation's balance of trade adversely, leading to a real deterioration in the nation's balance-of-payments account. In addition, inflation and loss of confidence in the currency leads to the flight of foreign and domestic capital and increased foreign reluctance to lend money to the afflicted nation. The initial speculative pressure against the currency could be tolerated; the eruption of an acute international monetary crisis requires some kind of dramatic response. The government may renounce its reformism or cede power to a more "responsible" administration.

But if the government is committed to defending its programs, it will have to act to insulate its economy from the pressures of the international market by imposing some combination of price controls, import controls, and exchange controls. Escalation in the government's attempt to control the market sets off a new chain of events. These new controls involve threats to individual capitalists. Price controls mean that firms lose the ability to manipulate one of the major determinants of profit levels. Import controls mean that a firm may no longer be able to import goods critical to its business. Exchange controls mean that firms and individuals no longer are able to move their assets freely to secure international havens. The fact that assets are locked into a rapidly inflating currency poses the possibility that large fortunes will be lost.

These are the ingredients for a sharp decline in domestic business confidence. Why should business owners continue to invest if they must operate in an environment in which the government violates the fundamental rules of a market economy?

A sharp decline in business confidence leads to a parallel economic downturn. High rates of unemployment coexist with annoying shortages of critical commodities. The popularity of the regime falls precipitously. The only alternative to capitulation – eliminating controls and initial reforms – is sharp forward movement to socialize the economy. The government could put people back to work and relieve the shortages by taking over private firms. However, the political basis for this kind of action does not exist, even where the leaders of the government are rhetorically committed to the goal of socialism. Generally, the reformist government has not prepared its electoral supporters for extreme action; its entire program has been based on the promise of a gradual transition. Further, the government leaders themselves become immersed in the political culture of the state apparatus, militating against a sharp break with the status quo.

The outcome of this impasse is tragically familiar. The government either falls from power through standard parliamentary means – loss of an election, defection of some of its parliamentary support – or it is removed militarily. Military actions that violate constitutionality meet formidable obstacles in liberal capitalist nations, but when economic chaos severely diminishes the legitimacy of a regime, the chances of a military coup are enhanced. When the military intervenes, it does not do so as a tool of the ruling class. It acts according to its own ideas of the need to restore political order and in its own interests. Naturally the removal of the reformist government leads to a rapid revival of business confidence simply because order has been restored. However, it should be stressed that this revival of business confidence might not be sustained, since there can be substantial conflicts between the interests of the military and the capitalists.

The key point in elaborating this scenario is that the chain of events can unfold without any members of the ruling class consciously deciding to act "politically" against the regime in power. Of course, such a scenario is usually filled out with a great deal of editorializing against the regime in the bourgeois press, much grumbling among the upper classes, and even some conspiratorial activity. But the point is that conspiracies to destabilize the regime are basically superfluous, since decisions made by individual capitalists according to their own narrow economic rationality are sufficient to paralyze the regime, creating a situation where the regime's fall is the only possibility.

Rationalization

The dynamic of business confidence helps explain why governments are constrained from pursuing anticapitalist policies. It remains to be explained why governments tend to act in the general interests of capital. Part of the answer has already been suggested. Since state managers are so dependent upon the workings of the investment accumulation process, it is natural that they will use whatever resources are available to aid that process. In administering a welfare program, for example, they will organize it to aid the accumulation process, perhaps by ensuring certain industries a supply of cheap labor. Unlike the individual capitalist, the state managers do not have to operate on the basis of a narrow profit-maximizing rationality. They are capable of intervening in the economy on the basis of a more general rationality. In short, their structural position gives the state managers both the interest and the capacity to aid the investment accumulation process. There is one major difficulty in this formulation – the problem of explaining the dynamic through which reforms that increase the rationality of capitalism come about. Almost all of

37

these reforms involve an extension of the state's role in the economy and society, either in a regulatory capacity or in the provision of services. The difficulty is that business confidence has been depicted as so shortsighted that it is likely to decline in the face of most efforts to extend the state's role domestically, since such efforts threaten to restrict the freedom of individual capitalists and/or increase the tax burden on capitalists. If the state is unwilling to risk a decline in business confidence, how is it then that the state's role has expanded inexorably throughout the twentieth century?

Most theorists escape this problem by rejecting the idea that the capitalists are as shortsighted as the idea of business confidence suggests. Even if many members of the class share the retrograde notions implicit in the idea of business confidence, there is supposed to be a substantial segment of the class that is forward-looking and recognizes the value of extending the state's power. Theorists of corporate liberalism have attempted to trace many of the major extensions of state power in twentieth-century America to the influence of such forward-looking members of the ruling class. However, the position of these theorists ultimately requires an attribution of a high level of consciousness and understanding to the ruling class or a segment of it, and assumes an instrumental view of the state where state policies can be reduced to the input of certain ruling-class factions.[10]

There is, however, an alternative line of argument, consistent with the view of the ruling class and the state that has been advanced in this paper. It depends on the existence of another structural mechanism – class struggle. Whatever the role of class struggle in advancing the development of revolutionary consciousness, class struggle between proletariat and ruling class in Marx's view has another important function. It pushes forward the development of capitalism – speeding the process by which capitalism advances the development of the productive forces. This is conservative in the short term, but progressive in the long term; it brings closer the time when capitalism will exhaust its capacity to develop the productive forces and will be ripe for overthrow. Class struggle produces this result most clearly in conflict over wages. When workers are able to win wage gains, they increase the pressure on the capitalists to find ways to substitute machines for people. As Marx described the cycle, wage gains are followed by an intense period of mechanization as employers attempt to increase the rate of exploitation; the consequence is an increase in the size of the industrial reserve army, as machines replace workers. This, in turn, diminishes the capacity of workers to win wage gains, until the economic boom again creates a labor shortage. While this description applies particularly to competitive capitalism, the point is that workers' struggles – in Marx's theory – play an important role in speeding the pace of technological innovations. *Class struggle is responsible for much of the economic dynamism of capitalism.*

This pattern goes beyond the struggle over wages. From the beginning of

38

capitalism, workers have struggled to improve their living conditions, which also means upgrading their potential as a labor force. For example, unbridled early capitalism, through child labor and horrendously long working days, threatened to destroy the capacity of the working class to reproduce itself – an outcome not in the long-term interests of capitalists. So working people's struggles against child labor, against incredibly low standards of public health and housing, and for the shorter day, made it possible for the class to reproduce itself, providing capitalism a new generation of laborers.

In its struggles to protect itself from the ravages of a market economy, the working class has played a key role in the steady expansion of the state's role in capitalist societies. Pressures from the working class have contributed to the expansion of the state's role in the regulation of the economy and in the provision of services. The working class has not been the only force behind the expansion of the state's role in these areas. Examples can be cited of capitalists who have supported an expansion of the state's role into a certain area either because of narrow self-interest – access to government contracts, or because government regulation would hamper competitors – or because of some farsighted recognition of the need to coopt the working class. However, the major impetus for the extension of the state's role has come from the working class and from the managers of the state apparatus, whose own powers expand with a growing state.

Once working-class pressures succeed in extending the state's role, another dynamic begins to work. Those who manage the state apparatus have an interest in using the state's resources to facilitate a smooth flow of investment. There will be a tendency to use the state's extended role for the same ends. The capacity of the state to impose greater rationality on capitalism is extended into new areas as a result of working-class pressures. Working-class pressures, for example, might lead to an expansion of educational resources available for the working class, but there is every likelihood that the content of the education will be geared to the needs of accumulation – the production of a docile work force at an appropriate level of skill. Or similarly, working-class pressures might force the government to intervene in the free market to produce higher levels of employment, but the government will use its expanded powers of intervention to aid the accumulation process more generally.

This pattern is not a smoothly working functional process, always producing the same result. First, working-class movements have often been aware of the danger of making demands that will ultimately strengthen a state they perceive as hostile. For precisely this reason, socialist movements have often demanded that expanded social services be placed under working-class control. However, working-class demands are rarely granted in their original form. Often, the more radical elements of the movement are repressed at the same time that concessions are made. Second, there can be a serious time lag be-

39

tween granting concessions to the working class and discovering ways that the extension of the state's power can be used to aid the accumulation process. There might, in fact, be continuing tensions in a government program between its integrative intent and its role in the accumulation process. Finally, some concessions to working-class pressure might have no potential benefits for accumulation and might simply place strains on the private economy. If these strains are immediate, one could expect serious efforts to revoke or neutralize the reforms. If the strains occur over the long term, then capitalism faces severe problems because it becomes increasingly difficult to roll back concessions that have stood for some time.[11]

These points suggest that the tendency for class struggle to rationalize capitalism occurs with a great deal of friction and with the continuous possibility of other outcomes. Nevertheless, the tendency does exist because of the particular interests of the state managers. Where there is strong popular pressure for an expansion of social services or increased regulation of markets, the state managers must weigh three factors. First, they do not want to damage business confidence, which generally responds unfavorably to an expansion of the government's role in providing social services or in regulating the market. Second, they do not want class antagonisms to escalate to a level that would endanger their own rule. Third, they recognize that their own power and resources will grow if the state's role is expanded. If the state managers decide to respond to pressure with concessions,[12] they are likely to shape their concessions in a manner that will least offend business confidence and will most expand their own power. These two constraints increase the likelihood that the concessions will ultimately serve to rationalize capitalism.

Major Reforms

This argument suggests that while some concessions will be made to the working class, the threat of a decline in business confidence will block major efforts to rationalize capitalism. Since business confidence is shortsighted, it will oppose even procapitalist reform programs if such programs promise a major increase in taxes or a major increase in the government's capacity to regulate markets. This leaves the problem of explaining the dramatic increases in the state's role that have occurred in all developed capitalist nations during the course of this century. The explanation is that there are certain periods – during wartime, major depressions, and periods of postwar reconstruction – in which the decline of business confidence as a veto on government policies doesn't work. These are the periods in which dramatic increases in the state's role have occurred.

In wars that require major mobilization, business confidence loses its sting

40

for several reasons. First, international business confidence becomes less important, since international capital flows tend to be placed under government control. Second, private investment becomes secondary to military production in maintaining high levels of economic activity. Third, in the general patriotic climate, it would be dangerous for the business community to disrupt the economy through negative actions.[13] The result is that state managers have the opportunity to expand their own power with the unassailable justification that such actions are necessary for the war effort. Some of these wartime measures will be rolled back once peace returns, but some will become part of the landscape.

In serious depressions and postwar reconstruction periods, the dynamics are somewhat different. Low levels of economic activity mean that the threat of declining business confidence loses its power, at the same time that popular demands for economic revival are strong. In such periods, the state managers can pay less attention to business opinion and can concentrate on responding to popular pressure, while acting to expand their own power. However, there are still constraints on state managers. Their continued rule depends on their capacity to revive the economy. As government actions prove effective in reducing unemployment, redistributing income, or expanding output, the political balance shifts. Pressure from below is likely to diminish; business confidence reemerges as a force once economic recovery begins. In short, successful reforms will tilt the balance of power back to a point where capitalists regain their veto over extensions of the state's role.

The increased capacity of state managers to intervene in the economy during these periods does not automatically rationalize capitalism. State managers can make all kinds of mistakes, including excessive concessions to the working class. State managers have no special knowledge of what is necessary to make capitalism more rational; they grope toward effective action as best they can within existing political constraints and with available economic theories.[14] The point is simply that rationalization can emerge as a by-product of state managers' dual interest in expanding their own power and in assuring a reasonable level of economic activity. The more power the state possesses to intervene in the capitalist economy, the greater the likelihood that effective actions can be taken to facilitate investment. Not every extension of state power will survive beyond those periods in which state managers have special opportunities to expand the state's role. After a war, depression, or period of reconstruction, the business community is likely to campaign for a restoration of the status quo ante. State managers in these new periods will be forced to make some concessions to the business community in order to avert a decline in business confidence. However, the state managers also want to avoid the elimination of certain reforms important for the stabilization of the economy and the integration of the working class. Self-interest also leads them to resist a complete elimination of the state's expanded powers. The consequence is a selection process by which state managers abandon certain reforms while retaining others. In this process, reforms that are most beneficial for capitalism will be retained, while those whose effects are more questionable will be eliminated.[15] Again, the ultimate outcome is determined by intense political struggle.

Conclusion

The purpose of this essay has been to argue that a viable Marxist theory of the state depends on the rejection of the idea of a conscious, politically directive ruling class. By returning to Marx's suggestions that the historical process unfolds "behind the backs" of the actors (including the ruling-class actors), it is possible to locate the structural mechanisms that shape the workings of the capitalist state. These mechanisms operate independently of any political consciousness on the part of the ruling class. Instead, capitalist rationality emerges out of the three-sided relationship among capitalists, workers, and state managers. The structural position of state managers forces them to achieve some consciousness of what is necessary to maintain the viability of the social order. It is this consciousness that explains both the reluctance of state managers to offend business confidence, and their capacity to rationalize a capitalist society. However, the fact of consciousness does not imply control over the historical process. State managers are able to act only in the terrain that is marked out by the intersection of two factors – the intensity of class struggle and the level of economic activity.

This framework has implications for a wide range of theoretical and political questions. One of the most critical of these concerns capitalism's capacity to overcome its current economic difficulties. Analysts on the left have predicted that the forward-looking segment of the American ruling class will favor a further extension of the state's role in regulating the economy as a means to solve the problems of stagflation.[16] This perspective exaggerates the capacity of capitalism to reform itself in "normal" periods, and is unable to account, for example, for the inability of British capitalism to rationalize itself during the long period of decline since the 1950s. The framework developed here predicts that the whole working class and the state managers themselves might favor an expansion of state intervention, business confidence will effectively veto such changes. It is therefore quite possible that the American economy will continue in its present state of crisis for many years to come.

Notes

In addition to the *SR* collectives, I would like to thank the McNeil Marxist Group, Clarence Lo, and Theda Skocpol for their help on this article.

1. For two surveys of Marxist work on the state – one polemical and the other dispassionate – see Alan Wolfe, "New Directions in the Marxist Theory of Politics," *Politics and Society*, vol. 4, no. 2 (1974), and David Gold, Clarence Y. H. Lo, and Erik Olin Wright, "Recent Developments in Marxist Theories of the Capitalist State," parts 1 and 2, *Monthly Review* (Oct. and Nov. 1975).

2. For critiques of such interpretations of Watergate, see Steve Weissman, "Cowboys and Crooks," in Steve Weissman, ed., *Big Brother and the Holding Company: The World behind Watergate*, Palo Alto: Ramparts 1974, pp. 297–310; and Stephen Johnson, "How the West Was Won: Last Shootout for the Yankee–Cowboy Theory," *Insurgent Sociologist* (Winter 1975), pp. 61–93.

3. My analysis has been influenced by the arguments of Nicos Poulantzas, particularly in his "Problems of the Capitalist State," *New Left Review*, no. 58 (Nov.–Dec. 1969). However, my analysis differs from Poulantzas's in two important respects. He tends to attribute consciousness to particular fractions of the ruling class and he fails to explain adequately the mechanisms by which the state is structurally a capitalist state. In this regard, my position is closer to that of Claus Offe in a number of articles, including "Structural Problems of the Capitalist State," in *German Political Studies*, Klaus von Beyme, ed., Beverly Hills, Calif.: Sage Publications 1976; and Claus Offe and Volker Ronge, "Theses on the Theory of the State," *New German Critique*, no. 6 (Fall 1975).

4. By "rationalization" and "capitalist reform," I am referring primarily to the use of the state in new ways to overcome economic contradictions and to facilitate the integration of the working class. Rationalization must be distinguished from strategies of forcing the working class to bear the costs of economic contradictions through dramatic reductions in living standards combined with severe political repression.

5. Each of these categories requires some definition: "Capitalist class" or "ruling class" is used to refer to the individuals and families that own or control a certain quantity of capital. The cutoff point would vary by country or period, and it would necessarily be somewhat arbitrary, but the point is to distinguish between small businesses and large capitalist firms. The "managers of the state apparatus" include the leading figures of both the legislative and executive branches. This includes the highest ranking civil servants, as well as appointed and elected politicians. "Working class" is being used in the broad sense. It includes most of those who sell their labor for wages, unwaged workers, and the unemployed.

6. In *The German Ideology*, Marx and Engels talk about a division of labor and of interests between capitalists and the producers of bourgeois ideology: "So that inside this class one part appears as the thinkers of the class (its active, conceptive ideologists, who make the perfection of the illusion of the class about itself their chief source of livelihood), while the others' attitude to these ideas and illusions is more passive and receptive, because they are in reality the active members of this class and have less time to make up illusions and ideas about themselves" (in Robert C. Tucker, ed., *The Marx–Engels Reader*, New York: Norton 1972, pp. 136–37). This suggests an analogous division of labor between capitalists and state managers as part of the ruling class. In both cases, however, treating ideologists or state managers as part of the ruling class violates the idea that class is determined by one's relation to the means of production. In short, Marx and Engels in this passage are using the notion of the ruling class in a polemical sense.

7. *The Eighteenth Brumaire* in ibid., p. 502.

8. Ibid., p. 462.

9. It is beyond the scope of this essay to explore the dynamics of authoritarian rule in capitalist societies.

10. For a critique of corporate liberal theory, see Fred Block, *Revising State Theory: Essays in Politics and Postindustrialism*, Philadelphia: Temple University Press 1987, ch. 2.

11. An obvious example here is the commitment to maintaining "full employment." This was a concession granted to the working class in the aftermath of the Great Depression, but it has proved increasingly costly for the developed capitalist nations.

12. They also have the option of responding to pressures through severe repression. The choice between concessions and repression is made by state managers on the basis of their percep-

tions of the general environment and their political orientations.

13.   These arguments all assume that some significant degree of national mobilization has occurred. In this sense, the business confidence veto was far stronger during the Vietnam War than during the Korean War.

14.   This was the case with the New Deal. The Roosevelt Administration simply stumbled on some of the elements necessary for a rationalization of the economy. The open-ended nature of the process is indicated by the fact that full recovery was not achieved until the mobilization for World War II.

15.   This kind of selection process was carried out by the Conservative government that came to power in Britain in 1951 after Labour had presided over postwar reconstruction. The dangers involved in the selection process are indicated by the fact that Britain's long-term prospects as a capitalist nation might have been improved by the retention of more of the Labour reforms.

16.   See, for example, Stanley Aronowitz, "Modernizing Capitalism," *Social Policy* (May–June 1975), and James Crotty and Raford Boddy, "Who Will Plan the Planned Economy?" *Progressive* (Feb. 1975). Such analyses tend to assume that the contradictions of advanced capitalism can be solved or effectively eased through state action. The possibility exists that this is not the case. While it is virtually impossible to reach a conclusion on that issue, one can debate whether such expanded state intervention will even be attempted.

3

Life without Father

Reconsidering Socialist-Feminist Theory

(1984)

Barbara Ehrenreich

By the late 1970s, most socialist-feminists accepted as "theory" a certain description of the world: "the system" we confronted was actually composed of two systems or structures, capitalism and patriarchy. These two systems or structures were of roughly equal weight (never mind that capitalism was a mere infant compared to patriarchy, or, on the other hand, that patriarchy had no visible corporate headquarters). And capitalism and patriarchy were remarkably congenial and reinforced each other in thousands of ways (which it was the task of socialist-feminists to enumerate). As Zillah Eisenstein wrote in her 1979 anthology, *Capitalist Patriarchy and the Case for Socialist Feminism*, patriarchy and capitalism meshed so neatly that they had become "an *integral process:* specific elements of each system are necessitated by the other." Capitalism plus patriarchy described the whole world – or nearly: racism usually required extensive addenda – and that world was as orderly and smoothly functioning as the Newtonian universe.

It was a brave idea. Today, just a few years later, few people venture vast theoretical syntheses. In the course of time, many of the socialist-feminist system builders of the seventies have become struggling academics, constrained to publish in respectable journals and keep their noses to the empirical grindstone. No longer do people meet, as many of us did, intensely and repeatedly, with an agenda of discovering the connections between *everything* – sex and class, housework and factory work, the family and the state, race and gender, sexuality and profits. If "capitalism plus patriarchy" was too easy an answer, at least we (the socialist-feminists of the seventies) asked the hard questions.

45

In a practical sense, too, it was a good theory, because it served to validate the existence of socialist-feminism. And I do not say this to trivialize the theory as self-serving. In the mid-seventies, in particular, socialist-feminists were an embattled species. On the one hand there was cultural and/or separatist feminism, drifting off toward spirituality, Great Goddess worship, and sociobiological theories of eternal male perfidy. To these "radical" feminists, socialist-feminists were male-identified dupes of the left, which they always described as the "male left." On the other hand, there was the left, which featured at the time a flourishing Marxist-Leninist tendency, bent on self-proletarianization and the "rectification" of everyone else. To this tendency, socialist-feminists were agents of the petty bourgeoisie on assignment to distract working-class women from the main event, the class struggle. The Marxist-Leninists and separatist feminists were extremes in a much wider radical context, but they helped define a political atmosphere in which socialist-feminism was hard put to establish that it was neither an oxymoron nor a form of treason.

The capitalism–plus–patriarchy paradigm was an ingenious defensive stance. If the world were really made up of two systems that were distinct and could not be reduced to each other, it was never enough to be just a socialist or just a feminist. If patriarchy were not only distinct but truly a "system" and not an attitude (like sexism) or a structure of the unconscious (as Juliet Mitchell saw it), those who opposed patriarchy were not just jousting with superstructural windmills: they were doing something real and "material." Finally, if patriarchy and capitalism were mutually reinforcing, it didn't make any sense to take on one without the other. If "the system" were capitalist patriarchy, the only thoroughgoing oppositional politics was its mirror image, socialist–feminism.

Not all socialist-feminists were perfectly comfortable with the capitalism–plus–patriarchy formulation, however. For one thing, there always seemed to be something a little static and structuralist about it. Deirdre English and I argued, in our book *For Her Own Good*, that "patriarchy" ought to be left where Marx last saw it – in preindustrial European society – and that modern feminists should get on with the task of describing our own "sex-gender system," to use Gayle Rubin's phrase, in all its historic specificity. In addition, we were not convinced that capitalism and patriarchy were on as good terms as socialist-feminist theory demanded. If the theory couldn't account for the clashes as well as the reinforcements, it couldn't account for change – such as the emergence of feminism itself in the late-eighteenth-century ferment of bourgeois and *antipatriarchal* liberalism. The world of capitalism plus patriarchy, endlessly abetting each other to form a closed system with just one seam, was a world without change, a world without a subject.

There is another problem. Things *have* changed, and in ways that make capitalist patriarchy (or, better, "patriarchal capitalism") almost seem like a good deal. Socialist-feminists – not to mention many plain feminists and socialists – went wrong in assuming that the system, whatever it was called, would, left to itself, reproduce itself.

Woman as Domestic Worker

The linchpin of socialist-feminist theory, the factor that put women, so to speak, on the Marxist map, was domestic work. In theory this work included everything women do in the home, from cooking and cleaning to reading bedtime stories and having sex. Radical feminists were quick to point out how women's efforts, whether serving coffee in a movement office or polishing the coffee table in a suburban home, served the interests of individual men. Socialist-feminists, coming along a few years later, asserted that women's domestic work served not only men, but capital. As Zillah Eisenstein put it:

> All the processes involved in domestic work help in the perpetuation of the existing society: (1) Women stabilize patriarchal structures (the family, housewife, mother, etc.) by fulfilling these roles. (2) Simultaneously, women are reproducing new workers, for both the paid and unpaid labor force. . . . (3) They work as well in the labor force for lesser wages. (4) They stabilize the economy through their role as consumers. If the other side of production is consumption, the other side of capitalism is patriarchy.

The discovery of the importance of women's domestic work put some flesh on the abstract union of capitalism and patriarchy. First, it gave patriarchy, which had otherwise had a somewhat ghostly quality (stretched as it was to include everything from rape to domestic slovenliness), a "material base" in "men's control over women's labor power." Second, it revealed a vivid parallel between "the private sphere," where patriarchy was still ensconced, and the "public sphere," where capital called the shots. In the public sphere, men labored at production, and in the private sphere women labored at "reproduction" (not only physical reproduction, but the reproduction of attitudes and capabilities required for all types of work). Finally it showed how essential patriarchy was to capitalism: most capitalist institutions produced only things, but the quintessential patriarchal institution, the family, produced the men who produced things – thanks to the labor of women.

It was not altogether clear where one went with this insight into the centrality of women's domestic work. If what women did in the home was so critical to the reproduction of both capitalism and patriarchy, shouldn't women be advised to stop doing it? Perhaps to sabotage it? The "wages for housework" position, which surfaced in this country in 1974, provided a strategic answer and an unintended caricature of American socialist-feminist theory. American socialist-feminists had argued that women's work was "necessary" to capitalism; the Italian feminists who launched wages for housework insisted, with considerable eloquence, that domestic work actually produced surplus value for the capitalists, just as what we ordinarily thought of as "productive" work in the public sphere did. If you were going to say that women's domestic work reproduced the labor power needed by capital, you might as well go all the way and say it was part of the productive process, just as much as the extraction and preparation of raw materials for manufacturing. Thus the home was an adjunct to the factory; in fact it was part of the great "social factory" (schools and all other sites of social reproduction) that kept the literal factories running. Women's domestic activities were no longer a shadowy contribution, but a potentially quantifiable productive factor with the distinguished Marxist status of "producing surplus value." The only difference between the man laboring for Fiat or Ford, and the woman laboring in her kitchen, was that she was unpaid – a patriarchal oversight that "wages for housework" would correct.

The Obsolescence of Capitalism-plus-Patriarchy

Looking back from the vantage point of 1984, the debates of 1970s have an almost wistful quality. They (men, capitalists) needed us (women) to do all our traditional "womanly" things, and, if theory were to be trusted, they would apparently go to great lengths to keep us at it. Well, they don't seem to need us anymore – at least not that way – and if this weren't completely evident in 1975, it is inescapable today.

No matter how valuable the services of a full-time homemaker may be, fewer and fewer men earn enough to support one. The reasons for the disappearance of the male "family wage" and the influx of married women into the workforce have been discussed at length. The relevant point here is that for all we say about the "double shift," employed women do far less housework than women who are full-time homemakers, 26 hours per week as compared to 55 hours per week.[1] Other family members may be compensating in part (though most studies show little increase in husbands' contributions), but it is hard not to conclude that the net amount of housework has decreased dramatically. If women's work were as essential to the status quo as socialist-feminist theory argued, capitalism should have been seriously weakened by this withdrawal of women's labor. Yet no one is arguing, for example, that the decline of American productivity is due to un-ironed shirts and cold breakfasts. Nor has any sector of capital come forth and offered to restore the male family wage so that women can get back to their housework.

If capital does not seem to need women's domestic work as much as theory predicted, what about individual men? Mid-seventies feminist theory tended to portray men as enthusiastic claimants of women's services and labor, eagerly enlisting us to provide them with clean laundry, homecooked meals, and heirs. If we have learned anything in the last ten years, it is that men have an unexpected ability to survive on fast food and the emotional solace of short-term relationships. There are, as Marxists say, "material" reasons for this. First, it is physically possible, thanks to laundromats, frozen food, and other conveniences, for even a poor man to live alone and without servants. Second, there have always been alternatives to spending a "family wage" on an actual family, but in the last few decades these alternatives have become more numerous and alluring. Not only are there the classic temptations of drink, gambling, and "loose women" to choose from, but stereos, well-appointed bachelor apartments, Club Med, sports cars, and so forth. For these and other reasons, American men have been abdicating their traditional roles as husbands, breadwinners, and the petty patriarchs of the "capitalism-plus-patriarchy" paradigm.[2]

In a larger sense, events and some belated realizations of the last few years should have undermined any faith we had in capital's willingness to promote the "reproduction of labor power." Capital as well as labor is internationally mobile, making US corporations relatively independent of a working class born and bred in this or any one country. Furthermore, capitalists are not required to be industrial capitalists; they can disinvest in production and reinvest in real estate, financial speculation, or, if it suits their fancy, antiques, and they have done so despite any number of exhortations and supply-side incentives. In their actual practices and policies, capitalists and their representatives display remarkable indifference to the "reproduction of labor power," or, in less commoditized terms, the perpetuation of human life.

This is not to say that individual companies or industries do not maintain a detailed interest in our lives as consumers. They do, especially if we are lucky enough to be above "the buying point" in personal resources. But it is no longer possible to discern a uniform patriarchal or even pronatalist bias to this concern. Capitalists have figured out that two-paycheck couples buy more than husband-plus-housewife units, and that a society of singles potentially buys more than a society in which households are shared by three or more people. In times of labor insurgency, far-seeing representatives of the capitalist class have taken a minute interest in how ordinary people organize their lives, raise their children, etc. But this is not such a time, and it seems plain to me that the manufacturers of components for missile warheads (a mile from where I sit) do not care whether my children are docile or cranky, and that the people who laced our drinking water with toxins (a mile the other way) could not much care whether I scrub the floors.

49

With hindsight, I am struck by what a *benevolent* system the "capitalism-plus-patriarchy" paradigm implied. In order to put women's hidden and private interests on the economic map, we had to assume that they reflected some much larger, systemic need. Since these efforts of women are in fact efforts to care and nurture, we had to project the functions of caring and nurturing onto the large, impersonal "structures" governing our all-too-functional construct of the world. Capitalism, inscribed with the will to "reproduce," became "patriarchal capitalism." This suggested that, in a sense, our theory was a family metaphor for the world: capitalists were "fathers," male workers were "sons," and all women were wives/daughters, both mediating the relations between fathers and sons and producing more sons (and daughters) to keep the whole system going. The daughters had the worst deal, but at least they were members of the family, and this family, like actual ones, intended to keep on going – a motivation that is no longer so easy to attribute to the men who command our resources and our labor.

So where do we go from here? Is it possible to be a socialist-feminist without a "socialist-feminist theory"? Yes, of course it is. After all, those who are plain socialists or feminists get along – with no evident embarrassment – on just half a theory at best. The socialist-feminist project has always been larger and more daring than that of either of our progenitors, so if we have fumbled, it is in part because we attempted more.

But we do need a better way to understand the world we seek to act in. I hesitate to say we need a new "theory," because that word suggests a new set of structures and laws of mechanics to connect them. If not "capitalism-plus-patriarchy," you are probably thinking, what is it? The point is that "it" is changing, and in a more violent and cataclysmic fashion than we had any reason to expect.

"The family," so long reified in theory, looks more like an improvisation than an institution. A new technological revolution, on the scale of the one that swept in industrial capitalism (and state socialism) is transforming not only production but perception. Whole industries collapse into obsolescence; entire classes face ruthless dislocation. At the same time, the gap between the races domestically, between the north and the south internationally, widens to obscene proportions. Everywhere, women are being proletarianized, impoverished, becoming migrants, refugees, and inevitably "cheap labor." Meanwhile the great and lesser powers race to omnicide, making a mockery of all our diverse aspirations, struggles, and movements. Truly, "all that is solid melts into air" – that is, if it is not vaporized instantaneously.

I still believe that if there is a vantage point from which to comprehend and change the world, our world today, it will be socialist and feminist. Socialist – or perhaps here I should say Marxist – because a Marxist way of thinking, at its best, helps us understand the cutting edge of change, the blind driving force of capital, the dislocations, innovations, and global reshufflings. Feminist because feminism offers our best insight into that which is most ancient and intractable about our common situation: the gulf that divides the species by gender and, tragically, divides us all from nature and that which is most human in our nature. This is our intellectual heritage, and I do not think we have yet seen its full power – or our own.

Notes

1. Joann Vanek, "Time Spent in Housework," *Scientific American* (Nov. 1974), p. 116.

2. One poignant indication of this shift in male values and expectations: When I was in my early twenties (in the early sixties), it seemed to require a certain daring and resourcefulness to dodge the traditional female fate of becoming a full-time housewife and mother. Today, I hear over and over from young women that they would like to have a family or at least a child, but do not expect ever to be in a stable enough relationship to carry this off.

4

Recasting Marxism
Hegemony and New Political Movements
(1982)
Interview with Ernesto Laclau and Chantal Mouffe

The problems that together constitute the contemporary "crisis of Marxism" are often approached in terms of the problem of economism. Yet "economism" has been used to identify diverse tendencies within the Marxist tradition, and it's no longer clear what the term signifies. What does it mean to say that a theory is economist? And how do we locate economism within the Marxist tradition?

MOUFFE: I would distinguish two main forms of economism. The first concerns the *role* played by the "superstructures," which are seen as epiphenomena of the economic structure, mechanically reflecting the latter while playing no active part in the historical process. This approach can be termed epiphenomenalism. The other main form of economism, which can be called class reductionism, concerns the *nature* of the superstructures. In this case, politics and ideology are conceived as determined by the position of agents in the relations of production.

The classical form of economism – the Marxism of the Second International – combines these two forms. But even critiques of that Marxism, such as those offered by Lukács or Korsch, broke only partially with economism. While they rejected epiphenomenalism, they remained strongly class reductionist. More recently, Althusser, despite his repeated criticisms of economism, should also be seen as having failed to free himself completely from that problematic. His position in his article on the state, for instance, is without any

---

Interview conducted for *SR* in October 1981 by David Plotke.

53

doubt a class reductionist one. The dominant ideology realized in the ideological state apparatuses, according to Althusser, comes from elsewhere. This supposes that it expresses the interests of the dominant class *as a class,* and therefore rejects, at the ideological level, a certain position within the relations of production.

LACLAU: An insufficient critique of economism accepts the mechanical notion of the economy with which economism works, and tries to limit that notion's effects by introducing a certain degree of autonomy for the superstructures. This approach is very limited, because it leaves untouched the traditional notion of "the economy."

I think the critique of economism should have a much wider deconstructive effect on traditional Marxist theory. That is, we should no longer conceive the economy as a homogeneous milieu that follows its own endogenous laws of development, which could be understood in a rationalistic way as a set of logically related concepts. Today we can see that the space which traditional Marxism designated "the economy" is in fact the terrain of a proliferation of discourses. We have discourses of authority, technical discourses, discourses of accountancy, discourses of information. Even categories such as profit can no longer be accepted as unequivocal. For instance, a multinational corporation today develops complex political and economic strategies within which the search for profit certainly plays a fundamental role, but does so within a whole policy of investment which can often require sacrificing immediate profits to wider strategic aims. The functioning of the economy itself is a political functioning, and cannot be understood in terms of a single logic. What we need today – and considerable advances have been made in this direction – is a non-economistic understanding of the economy, one which introduces the primacy of politics at the level of the "infrastructure" itself.

If we conceive the economy as the site of different types of discourses, what do we understand as the economic moment within "the economy"? Does the critique of economism you propose offer simply to move the problem back one step, to the problem of defining the relations among political, economic, and other elements in discrete institutional spheres?

LACLAU: I am saying that there is *not* a single moment that can be called "the economic" as different from the political. The unity of the economic sphere in classical Marxism – especially the systematization of Marxism in the work of Engels and in the period of the Second International – was conceived in a way which today we cannot accept.

Classical Marxism conceived the economy as a homogeneous milieu. It was a "level" of society, but a level governed by a single logic which started from the category of commodity to produce out of itself all the other categories. In the end, the whole historical process was considered to be governed by the unique contradiction between forces and relations of production. I am trying to suggest that no such single logic exists. The material reproduction of society results from complex practices which are articulated in diverse ways. Thus the unity of the economic as such, as far as it is conceived as a logical postulate, should be dissolved. Of course I am not saying that the notion of "material reproduction of society" disappears. But I *am* rejecting the idea that a unique logic can explain this reproduction. I have tried, in my polemic with Poulantzas, to distinguish between two different senses of "the economic": on the one hand, the economic as material reproduction; on the other hand, the economic as the specific logic of the market. It is this second sense of the economic that we cannot accept, insofar as it pretends to explain the ensemble of the process of material reproduction. But this does not imply denying the central incidence of material reproduction in historical processes.

MOUFFE: I think it is very important to develop a conception of the economy that asserts the primacy of politics within the economy itself. If it has taken so long to put into question the idea of the neutrality of the productive forces, it is because of the idea that politics was located outside the economy. Now we have a series of studies that show how the labor process itself is the locus of relations of domination, and we cannot maintain the position that there could be something called the economy that could exist prior to and independent of specific political and "ideological" conditions and that could "determine in the last instance" the other spheres of society. The economy like all other spheres is the terrain of a political struggle, and is governed not by a single logic but by the hegemonic articulation of a complex of social relations.

Regarding your distinction between two types of economism, in recent years the critique of the cruder form — what you term "epiphenomenalism" — has gained currency not only theoretically but within political movements. But what you have described as class reductionism is still prevalent, even predominant. How does one understand the persistence of that economism, especially in politics?

MOUFFE: One reason for the persistence of reductionism at the political level has its source in the theoretical field. It comes from a serious shortcoming of Marxist theory: its lack of understanding of the nature of ideology and of the way in which we are constituted as subjects. The prevailing conception — which manifests the general problematic of class reductionism — has been that all subjects are class subjects; that each class has a paradigmatic class ideology; and that each ideological element has a necessary class belonging. This concep-

55

tion necessarily leads to seeing ideological struggle as a confrontation between two closed ideological systems completely opposed one to the other, in which victory consists in the total destruction of "bourgeois ideology." There is no space here for a process of transformation of ideological elements, of differential articulation through which new political subjects are created. Nor is there any space to understand the importance of determinants of consciousness which are not reducible to class position.

The consequences of this view for socialist politics have been disastrous. Instead of trying to create a popular socialist movement on the basis of transforming the actual consciousness of the people by articulating in a socialist project their real struggles and demands, the latter have been neglected as reformist, or expressions of "false consciousness." Explanations have been found for the fact that the workers seem unaware of their "real interest," and theories elaborated to predict when the worsening of their condition would at last dissipate the effects of bourgeois ideology and allow them to see their "true situation." It was as the result of a reflection on the mistakes made by the Italian Communist Party in the 1920s, its lack of understanding of the phenomenon of fascism, that Gramsci began to challenge that reductionism and to lay the basis for a new conception of politics.

LACLAU: Another major reason for the persistence of economism in the socialist movement has been the oppositional status of Marxism and the various working-class movements. Bourgeois hegemony is constructed through a naturalization of social relations. That is to say, the ensemble of social and cultural institutions are presented as if they were all essentially related. The socialist movements which began to fight within the framework of this bourgeois hegemony also tended to accept this articulation of elements as natural and necessary, rather than to fight to rearticulate these elements and values into a new working-class or socialist hegemony. So most socialist movements present themselves as a fully fledged counter-society which rejects the present order in toto, rather than engaging with it in hegemonic struggle to rearticulate its elements. Thus if all "war of position" is abandoned, it becomes necessary to postulate an external mechanism ensuring the advent of socialism. This mechanism was found in the notion that the capitalist economic system is advancing towards its collapse through its own internal laws. A philosophy of history lies behind this confidence in a necessary evolution of society towards socialism, due to the unfolding of the contradiction between forces and relations of production.

In other words, economism as a political force within the socialist movement has been a way of reconciling groups to an existing oppositional status while promising a future that will be realized by the movement of the economy.

LACLAU: Yes, classical economism was constituted in that way, as both the strength and the weakness of the revolutionary socialist groups. The strength, because it allowed them to close themselves around this economistic outlook and the defense of working-class values. This gave to them an identity which otherwise would have been very difficult to constitute. The weakness, because this working class was putting all its bets on the evolution of economic forces, and could not fight on other terrains. Thus in the 1920s, amidst the failure of bourgeois hegemony, when the socialist movement could have presented itself as a popular hegemonic alternative to gather together many radicalized forces in society, the persistence of this economistic class-centered outlook prevented it from effectively playing such a role. This opened the way to reactionary-popular solutions, such as fascism.

Today economism is no longer a defense in the traditional sense of protecting working-class identity, but instead poses a fundamental obstacle to the articulation of workers' struggles to the ensemble of the new anticapitalist social movements emerging at various levels of contemporary society.

MOUFFE: Economism has been a crucial shortcoming from the beginning. The first "crisis of Marxism," at the end of the last century, was provoked by economism. Bernstein put the economist vision into question because he realized that, contrary to the predictions, there was not going to be a growing polarization between the bourgeoisie and the proletariat, that the working-class movement needed a strategy with respect to those "new middle strata" created by the development of capitalism. He understood clearly that the obstacle was economism because of its denial of the importance of ideology and politics as constitutive practices. Yet since Bernstein identified Marxism with its Second International version, he thought that a break with economism was necessarily a break with Marxism. As he identified all types of determination with economic determination, he was led to the extreme position of abandoning all possible forms of determination and proposing a Kantian "ethical ideal" as the basis for the creation of a socialist movement. We can see Gramsci as one who attempted to give a Marxist answer to these problems through his concept of hegemony.

Today we face a different form of the same kind of problem. Yet it is even more complicated, because we need to elaborate a strategy to articulate the demands of those new political subjects – women, racial minorities, ecological and anti-institutional movements – which are incomprehensible within an economistic framework.

Ideology and Discourse

A critique of economism in the present period demands a non-economistic conception of ideology. You've touched on a number of themes that might contribute to such a conception, but mostly in negative terms. In more positive terms, what might such a conception be? One central problem in this regard is the relation of the concept of discourse to that of ideology.

LACLAU: Discourse is a concept which has been used very much recently, and its uses have diverged enormously. By discourse I understand an ensemble whose terms are related in a meaningful way. In a causal relation of the physical-natural type, we have a relationship among events which is meaningless. But in social life any event has a meaning. When we kick a ball in a football game the meaning of this act differs completely from kicking the same ball elsewhere. Even if the physical act is the same, it enters into two different discursive sequences dominated by different systems of rules.

To understand a social event, we do not appeal to any type of physical causality but we have to understand its meaning – the ensemble of its signifying relations. In this sense, the concept of discourse is as large as the concept of social life. There is no social practice that is not a discursive practice. Economism thought, on the contrary, that social life was the result of ineluctable laws of the same type as physical, natural laws. That is to say, the world of the discursive – the way people act and relate to each other – was seen to reflect an occult movement of history which could be detected from a privileged position. The relationship between forces and relations of production was conceived as the secret movement of history, with the character of a natural law. If there is an essential identity between society and discourse, we have to conclude that all social articulations are political. To have politics we need to have choice, that is, a situation whose outcome is open and depends on the struggle between antagonistic forces. This is compatible with a discursive conception of social antagonisms, but not with a causalist one, for which every result is determined by ineluctable aprioristic laws. For this second conception politics can only be appearance, that is, a superstructure through which the cunning of reason fulfills its task.

In your formulation, the concept of discourse seems to replace the concept of ideology.

LACLAU: I do not think that the two concepts overlap, or that one replaces the other. While "discourse" is coextensive with society, the traditional concept of "ideology" referred to one level of society. This notion of ideology was firmly rooted in the base/superstructure distinction. If the movement of the base was identified with causal natural laws, the ensemble of the signifying practices constituting the field of discourse could only be conceived, by definition, as belonging to the realm of the superstructures. "Ideology" was synonymous with "forms of consciousness," and the latter were the necessary reflection – or at least representation – of a causal movement which transcended them. Thus, we are in the domain of what could be called "topography of the social."

But if we assert the discursive nature of all social relations, the basis for the distinction between base and superstructure collapses and with it disappears the only terrain on which the concept of ideology made sense. The problem, however, is more complicated because for classical Marxism, "ideology" was not only a level of society, but also the locus of constitution of distorted representations of society as a whole. This conception of ideology as misrecognition has recently been very much under attack, insofar as it presupposes the idea of a preconstituted essential subject. I think, however, that the case has been overdrawn. An essentialist notion of the subject – traditionally inherent in concepts such as "alienation" or "false consciousness" – should be rejected. But this does not mean that a subject cannot enter into relations of misrecognition from the point of view of his or her discursively and politically constituted identity. How else are we going to understand a feminist discourse which tries to constitute "women" by showing the variety of ways in which the naturalization of meanings tends to create female subordination, which tries to deconstruct one discourse through the "effects of sense" of other discourses? A social world in which the category of misrecognition – dispossessed of its essentialist connotations – has no role would be a transparent world, in which there would be no repression, no desire.

Hegemony and Gramsci's Theory

In economist conceptions, the problem of the unity of the social formation is solved by the economy in a double way. The economy provides a determination in the last instance, and also provides the principle by which other social instances are articulated to each other. Once one abandons that notion of social unity, what alternative means of conceptualizing it are available? What does the notion of hegemony offer in this regard?

MOUFFE: In answering your question it is important to specify the meaning of the concept of hegemony in Gramsci. There are several common misleading interpretations. The main one reduces the concept of hegemony to the that of the dominant ideology. According to this view, a class is hegemonic when it has been able to impose its own paradigmatic ideology on the whole of society. Hegemony is therefore a phenomenon of "symbolic violence," of augmenting domination through ideological means. Such an interpretation can be found in many different forms; in a Lukácsian view which sees hegemony as the imposition of the class-conscious worldview of the class subject, or an Althusserian approach in which hegemony consists in the imposition of the ideology of the dominant class through the control of the ideological state apparatuses. Another type of interpretation, common among sociologists, but also to be found in Marxists such as Perry Anderson, reads the concept of hegemony through the Weberian problematic of "legitimation." This view reduces hegemony to implementing the mechanisms of legitimation of an already given class power.

Both interpretations miss the radical novelty of the Gramscian conception and fail to draw out its potential for a non-economistic conception of society. For Gramsci, hegemony is the imposition of an articulating principle upon an ensemble of social relations and practices which do not in themselves have a necessary class belonging prior to their articulation to the "hegemonic principle" of a fundamental class. Such a concept puts into question the reductionist view which postulates that all ideological and political elements have a necessary class character. I think that we have here the reason why the concept of hegemony has been so misunderstood by Marxists. It has been "unthinkable" within a dominant problematic which remains strongly reductionist.

The Gramscian concept of hegemony allows us to break definitively with the problematic of economism according to which the unity of a social formation results from the necessary effects of the infrastructure upon the political and ideological superstructures. The very distinction between base and superstructure must be abandoned, to be replaced by the concept of "historic bloc" presented by Gramsci as the fusion of these two elements into an organic unity which depends upon the articulating practices of a fundamental social force.

LACLAU: I would like to take up the problem that you posed, about the unity of the social formation, in relation to various moments in the history of Marxist theory. Here we are facing a problem which has always plagued Marxism: how to conceive the role of politics. Either historical changes are the necessary outcome of contradictions constituted at the level of the economy, or these historical changes result from the intervention of the political subject. Either we see a constitutive moment in this intervention of the political subject, or we see it as the epiphenomenal expression of an underlying infrastructural process. These two conceptions have always been present in Marxism, but the one which nullifies the role of the political subject has dominated.

In the Second International's conception, as formulated by Plekhanov or Kautsky, the unity of the social formation is constituted around a main contradiction, which develops according to a causal, nondiscursive logic. The first important break with this conception is to be found in Leninism. Leninism asserts the primacy of politics, the primacy of the intervention of the political subject. Lenin was perhaps the first Marxist thinker for whom the international economy was conceived in a political way. It was conceived as an imperialist chain. In this chain, the crisis of one or several of its links could produce a dislocation in the relation of forces at other points, at the so-called weakest link. This dislocation of forces opens the way to a political crisis in which the revolutionary subject can intervene. So we have a notion of the political which does not present the outcome of a crisis as the result of the immanent laws of the economy, but, on the contrary, as a consequence of an autonomous intervention of the vanguard party. And with this, the primacy of politics is stated: the result of the revolutionary crisis depends on some form of political mediation and intervention, that is, on discursive practices. That was the highest point of Leninism.

The limit of this conception, however, was that for Leninism and even more clearly for the whole tradition of the Comintern, this primacy of politics was limited to moments of revolutionary crisis. In periods of stability, the old logic of Kautskyism dominated almost unaltered. For Lukács, for example, the problem of the primacy of politics coincided with the problem of the actuality of revolution. In periods of stabilization, the Comintern advocated the defense of the economic interests of the workers and the preparation for the moment of the revolutionary outbreak. This search for the moment of the revolutionary outbreak dominated the whole strategy of the Comintern. With the advent of fascism, and the enormous rearticulation of the whole ensemble of the so-called superstructures in Western Europe, the socialist forces had to think and fight on a new terrain. This opened the way to a new conception of hegemony, conceived as a struggle for political rearticulation not limited to revolutionary crises but extending also to periods of stability. Gramsci's reflections take place at the epicenter of this transformation. Revolutionary struggle is conceived by him in a processual way, as a war of position. This concept meant that the relation of forces – the political articulation of society – could change through a plurality of struggles and should not be reduced to a single moment – the revolutionary crisis and the seizure of power. With this we arrive, I think, at a concept of the unity of the social formation as one which is not dictated by the simple "laws" of an infrastructure, but by a complex process of creation of new political subjects, of changing the relation of forces in society.

Following the Gramscian tradition, Togliatti conceived revolutionary strategy in Western Europe as a protracted war of position. His notions of progressive democracy, of the new party, of the national tasks of the working class, all pointed in this direction: that is, toward the constitution of a popular pole around the working class, a popular pole which could increase its hegemony through the constant expansion of the field of democratic struggles.

Political and Social Struggle

If every social moment contains a political dimension, how do we understand the relationship between that general presence of politics, and the specific institutional forms of political life, of those institutions that are primarily political?

LACLAU: To answer your question requires some remarks on the notion of power. Traditionally, power was conceived as located in determinate levels of society, in specific institutions. The classical conception of "the seizure of power," for instance, presupposed that power was concentrated in some point from which its effects spread over the rest of society. At the limit it was a building, the Winter Palace.

Today this notion of power is increasingly abandoned, and the omnipresence of power and resistance is admitted. Power is not something one can seize, because power is constitutive of the ensemble of social relations. The limitation of all vanguardist conceptions of the seizure of power is that they cannot deal with the character of a revolutionary transformation as a process with a mass character that requires a drastic change in popular common sense. This transformation, as a long and complex process, covers a whole historical period. For this reason the strategy of war of position involves a plurality of democratic struggles, aiming to change the relation of forces at all levels of society.

The rejection of the conception of power as located in one point which has to be seized means rejecting the identification of the revolutionary agent with a single political force – such as the vanguard party. On the contrary, the political protagonism of the masses requires the existence and the autonomy of a variety of social movements whose unity should be the result of a process of political construction, not an aprioristic postulate.

Having said this, I would like to add that the recognition of the omnipresence of power and of the complexity of political struggle has sometimes led to denying the importance of political struggle in the traditional sense – i.e., control of the state apparatuses. So, let's put things right. I am not saying that it is not a primary political task in Bolivia or Chile to get rid of the military dictatorships. *That* power has to be taken, given that its presence prevents the development of other democratic struggles. But we should avoid thinking that once this aim is achieved one has conquered "power" as such. No single type of political struggle will guarantee, by itself, the advent of socialism. So, what is at stake is not the abandonment of the traditional arena of political struggle but conceiving this arena as one sphere of struggle, not as the privileged location where the destiny of society is decided. If we want a truly socialist society, women should be liberated, but women are not going to be liberated as an automatic consequence of any seizure of power by a vanguard. They will be liberated only if they fight for their own liberation and organize themselves as a social force which negotiates with other social forces. And this is true for any other antagonism in society. This requires the autonomy of the social movements, which have to impose their own conditions on popular and socialist political parties. Consequently the party is not the all-inclusive form of political struggle. It has its own task to fulfill, its own sphere of action, but it is just *one* form of socialist organization, which has to coexist and to be articulated to many other forms of organization.

If the concept of hegemony is made primary for understanding the unity of social formations, how do we relate the concept of hegemony to that of class? Are you arguing that the concept of hegemony is in some sense prior to or more basic than the concept of class?

MOUFFE: First of all let us make clear what we understand by "class." In the Marxist tradition the concept of class is often used to designate places in the economy to which correspond specific political and ideological positions. This is a reductionist conception, and it must be abandoned. We must choose between two options. We can use the concept of class to designate positions at the level of the relations of production, but in that case we cannot deduce from it anything necessary concerning politics or ideology. Or, we can reserve the term to designate collectivities in struggle at the political level and whose objectives include the transformation of the relations of production. But in this case we cannot know anything necessary concerning the position of those agents in the process of production. I think that the first solution is preferable, but on the condition that one rejects completely the problematic of the "class in itself" and "class for itself." That is, we must put into question the very idea of class "interests" and accept that there is no paradigmatic form of the class struggle. The struggle of the working class may take many different forms according to the conditions of the labor process and the discourses through which it constructs its interests and organizes its objectives at a given moment. Class position is only one of the terrains where antagonisms exist and on which collectivities in struggle can organize themselves, because a society contains a multiplicity of social relations: relations between sexes, races, generations, etc. The mistake of class reductionism is to reduce all social relations to social relations of production or to their ideological and political conditions of reproduction. Each individual as participant in a series of different social relations is therefore the locus of a plurality of determinations to which correspond subjective positions constructed through discourses and practices with their corresponding "interests." Among those positionalities there is no a priori reason to attribute a special privilege to class, as the articulation principle of subjectivity and determinant of political consciousness. Which positionality

63

will play that role will depend on the discursive practices in which an individual is inserted, and the type of antagonism and of subjectivity they construct.

I am not saying that the class position never plays that articulating role, and in the nineteenth century that was often the case, but it was for historical rather than ontological reasons. Thus the concept of hegemony is more fundamental than class, since the role that class positionality plays in the constitution of political subjects depends on the type of hegemony existing in society at a given moment.

On this point, we need to go beyond Gramsci to break with the remnant of reductionism that we find in his thought, the idea that only a fundamental class can articulate a hegemony and that the working class must necessarily be the center around which a national-popular collective will is articulated in the transition to socialism. There is no way in which such an assertion can be defended once we put economism into question. Obviously I do not mean that there could be a socialist transformation without overcoming the class contradiction, but rather, such a transformation can be conceived as the result of a popular movement in which the working class might not have the leading role.

To illustrate some of these themes, how would one interpret Thatcherism and the responses to it in terms of the framework you are proposing?

MOUFFE: Since the Second World War Britain and the other advanced capitalist countries had seen the expansion of capitalist relations into most spheres of social life, and this has entailed the emergence of new antagonisms and new forms of struggle against these relations of domination. As well, the growing intervention of the state at all levels of civil society has led to an open politicization of many social relations. In all fields where the state intervenes, health, housing, education, energy, etc., social contradictions become directly political. At the same time old relations of domination, such as those based on sex/gender, have become more acute and the whole realm of civil society, of what was traditionally considered as private, is now the terrain of political struggles.

These diverse new antagonisms cannot be understood in "class" terms and this is the reason why the left has generally been unable to grasp their importance. At best they have been considered "secondary" issues when they were not simply dismissed as "petty bourgeois" demands. I think that it is in this context that we must situate the rise of the "new right" which has been able to hegemonize many popular feelings against the profound transformations of the traditional way of life. Thatcher's victory in 1979 was based on her ability to articulate the strong anti-state feeling which resulted from the bureaucratic and corporatist way in which the welfare state had been implemented. Concerning the new struggles, it seems to me that the left is far behind because the right has grasped more clearly the importance of "ideological" issues in providing a powerful factor of constitution and unification of political forces. The left generally remains very statist and tends to see state intervention as the remedy to all social evils. That is obviously a serious obstacle to the elaboration of a strategy that could articulate the potential of struggles released by the type of development characteristic of the hegemonic system installed after the Second World War. And which is now in crisis.

LACLAU: I would like to add, to that point, that the present crisis in advanced capitalist countries is reflected not only in what is changing but in the difficulties of directing change in a coherent and precise direction. If we compare the present situation with the origins of fascism, a first difference strikes us: in the 1920s the democratic demands addressed to the state apparatuses were considerably fewer than today. Fascism in its classical form was a pre-welfare state phenomenon. Because of that it was relatively easy to constitute a popular positionality – i.e., a popular identity of a sharply oppositional character which unified a variety of unfulfilled demands. In a welfare-state situation, on the contrary, a transformist process of differential absorption by the state of a variety of democratic demands makes it very difficult to construct a mass political discourse, one which addresses the "people" as such. In the British case fascism never succeeded, not even in the depths of the Depression, in spite of having such an able leader as Oswald Mosley. I am saying this to qualify some apocalyptic images of the political consequences of the present crisis. It is true that we are bearing witness to an erosion of the consensus which presided over the forms of state constituted after the Second World War. It is true also that some shifts toward more radical politics – of the right or of the left – are going to take place. But we are still far from a situation in which a total oppositional politics could become dominant. It is difficult to foresee the evolution of the present crisis, but one perspective should not be excluded: a slow decline, in which no sector has strength enough to reorient the situation in a radically new way, and in which small pendular movements after each change of government dominate the political scene.

The framework you're proposing discards the base/superstructure conceptualization, abandons or at least severely narrows the range of the concept of ideology, and designates the process of hegemony as fundamentally prior to the political emergence of classes. Taken together, this amounts to a dramatic shift away not only from the premises of orthodox Marxism, but from most neo-Marxist efforts as well. What is the status of "Marxism" in this project? How does one understand the meaning of the theoretical reconstruction you are proposing with respect to a conception of the Marxist tradition? If the aim is to continue the "Copernican revolution" within Marxism initiated by Gramsci, how would one conceptualize the aim of this revolution?

LACLAU: You are right to say that today we are in the middle of a profound transformation of Marxist theory and of the conception of socialism. This transformation is no more, to some extent, than the unfolding of the ambiguities always present in Marxist thought – especially the tension between conceiving socialism as the necessary result of capitalist development, and conceiving it as the outcome of class struggle. It is naive to postulate, or to assume, a unity of the "doctrine" of Marx which would not present contradictions and ambiguities. All orthodoxies are of course dominated by the search for an impossible unity of the text. According to a very well known view, Marx would have put together German classical philosophy, English political economy, and the French socialist tradition. If this were so, Marx would have accomplished the considerable deed of putting together three things radically incompatible with each other. But in fact Marx did quite a different thing: he created a situation of interdiscourse in which these three traditions produced effects of sense over each other, deconstructed each other, and in this way generated new and unexpected discursive forms. The orthodoxy, later, did its best to ignore the openness, the specific conditions of Marxist discursivity. This exercise of closure begins with Engels' *Anti-Dühring*. The result was the vulgata that from Kautsky and Plekhanov to Stalin presented itself as the truth of history.

But beyond those attempts at systematization, history proceeded, asserting the essential openness characteristic of all discourses of liberation. Today not only German philosophy, English political economy, and French socialism constitute the interdiscourse of radical emancipation. The struggles of oppressed peoples in the Third World, women's emancipation, antiracist demands, gay demands, and many other struggles claim as well their right to intervene in the constitution of a radically anticapitalist discourse. There is no more idealistic – I would add, ridiculously idealist – conception than one assuming that the truth of history was fully revealed to one man born in 1818 and dead in 1883, and that the course of events in the following century has been nothing but the fulfillment of his prophecies. So, my answer to your question about the status of Marxism is that its validity is not that of a "doctrine" which establishes "laws of history" sub specie aeternitatis: its validity is that of a tradition, with its limitations, its contradictions, its misrecognitions, but also with its greatness, with its proven abilities to open new avenues of history. Our identification with that tradition, not the assertion of any orthodoxy, permits us to call ourselves Marxists today. Within this tradition there are moments of deep breaks. And no doubt today we are in the epicenter of a third break, from which Marxism is going to emerge deeply transformed. Because we are aware of the internal tensions and ruptures that have characterized the history of Marxism and because we do not think it is a uniform history of monotonous mistakes, we prefer to construct our discourse as difference within the Marxist tradition, rather than to reject the latter in toto. As for the question about the moment when the "Copernican revolution" is finally won, my answer would be that it is never won, that there is no final discourse. The different interdiscourses through which a political identity is constituted have no more ending than the succession of natural numbers. Because history is not a closed universe, dominated by a pre-given finality, there are no limits to what it is possible to construct within it.

MOUFFE: Without a drastic recasting, Marxism not only is not going to be helpful in the struggle for a socialist transformation of society today, it might even become a fetter. We have stressed that economism and reductionism block the elaboration of a contemporary strategy that could unite all the fragments of the democratic movement. It is urgent to abandon the metaphysics of "scientific socialism" and "determination in the last instance by the economy," and to stop conceiving socialism as the culmination of the development of the capitalist forces of production. We need a different conception of "socialism," for so long as it is conceived only in terms of the socialization of the means of production it has very little to offer to satisfy the demands of the "new movements." The struggle must be waged at a much deeper level than is usually thought by the left, and the socialist project must engage with all the antagonisms existing in society and not only with those located in "the economy."

I know that the elaboration and implementation of such a strategy is far from easy, and I have no intention of underplaying the difficulties that need to be solved. But it is evident that it requires a theoretical framework that would allow us to pose the problems in an adequate way, and that orthodox Marxism does not provide such a framework. I also strongly believe that such a strategy requires the elaboration of a new conception of democracy that could provide the "cement" of a new collective will that could articulate the demand of the democratic subjects. Our conception of democracy is too limited. To frame a new socialist project it is urgent to reformulate liberal-democratic discourse in such a way as to allow us to advocate not only a real participation of people in all the decisions concerning the organization of social life, but also a real equality irrespective of gender, race, or sexual orientation. Such a "pluralism of subjects" is the necessary foundation on which to start building socialist hegemony today.

5

Gay Politics, Ethnic Identity
The Limits of Social Constructionism
(1987)
Steven Epstein

What does it mean to be gay? Do lesbians and gay men constitute a "deviant subculture"? A "sexual minority"? A privileged "revolutionary subject"? Is homosexuality a "preference" (like a taste for chocolate ice cream)? Or perhaps an "orientation" (a fixed position relative to the points of a compass)? Or maybe it's a "lifestyle," like being a "yuppie" or a surfer? Is being gay something that has some importance? Or is it a relatively inconsequential difference?

Most people who identify as gay or practice homosexuality adopt some variety of relatively inconsistent positions regarding their identity over the course of time, often depending on the needs of the moment. These contradictions are paralleled by the attitudes of homophobic opponents of the gay movement, which are typically even less consistent; for example, one frequently hears the belief that homosexuality is an "illness" combined with a simultaneous concern that youngsters can be "seduced" into it. The whole issue, it seems, is a terminological and conceptual minefield. Yet given the startling newness of the idea of there being such a thing as a "gay identity" – neither that term, nor "lesbian identity," nor "homosexual identity" appeared in writing by or about gays and lesbians before the mid-1970s – the confusion is hardly surprising.[1]

This article does not address the question of what "causes" homosexuality, or what "causes" heterosexuality. Instead, what I seek to explore is how lesbians and gay men, on a day-to-day basis, interpret their sexual desires and practices so as to situate themselves in the world; how these self-understandings relate to social theories about homosexuals; and how both the theories and the self-understandings can shape – or block – different varieties of political activism by gays. I take as given that power inheres in the ability to name, and that what we call ourselves has implications for political practice. An additional assumption is that lesbians and gay men in our society consciously seek, in a wide variety of ways, to *legitimate* their forms of sexual expression, by developing explanations, strategies, and defenses. These legitimations are articulated both on an individual level ("This is who I am, and this is why I am that way") and on a collective level ("This is what we are, and here is what we should do"). Legitimation strategies play a mediating function between self-understandings and political programs, and between groups and their individual members.

Existing theories of sexuality fail to address these concerns adequately. For some time now, sexual theory has been preoccupied with a debate between "essentialism" and "constructionism" – a debate which, despite its importance in reorienting our thinking about sexuality, may well have outlived its usefulness. "Essentialists" treat sexuality as a biological force and consider sexual identities to be cognitive realizations of genuine, underlying differences; "constructionists," on the other hand, stress that sexuality, and sexual identities, are social constructions, and belong to the world of culture and meaning, not biology. In the first case, there is considered to be some "essence" within homosexuals that makes them homosexual – some gay "core," of their being or their genetic makeup. In the second case, "homosexual," "gay," and "lesbian" are labels, created by cultures and applied to the self.

This debate is not restricted to the field of sexuality; it parallels similar ones that have taken place in many other domains, including gender, race, and class. For example, while some feminists have proposed that qualities such as nurturance constitute a feminine "essence," others have insisted that any differences between men and women, beyond the strictly biological, are the products of culture and history: men and women have no essential "nature."[2] But while the issues may be generalizable, they have a special salience for contemporary gay politics, because of a peculiar historical irony. With regard to sexuality, the constructionist critique of essentialism has become the received wisdom in left academic circles. And yet, curiously, the historical ascendancy of the new constructionist orthodoxy has paralleled a growing inclination within the gay movement in the United States to understand itself and project an image of itself in ever more "essentialist" terms.

As many observers have noted, gays in the 1970s increasingly came to conceptualize themselves as a legitimate minority group, having a certain quasi-"ethnic" status, and deserving the same protections against discrimination that are claimed by other groups in our society.[3] To be gay, then, became something like being Italian, or black, or Jewish. The "politics of identity" have crystallized around a notion of "gayness" as a real, and not arbitrary, difference. So while constructionist theorists have preached the gospel that the hetero/homosexual distinction is a social fiction, gays and lesbians, in everyday life and in political action, have been busy hardening the categories. Theory, it seems, has not been informing practice. Perhaps the practitioners are misguided; or perhaps there is something about the strict constructionist perspective which neither adequately describes the experiences of gays and lesbians nor speaks to their need to understand and legitimate their places in the world.

To address these questions, my analysis will proceed as follows. First, I will recapitulate the constructionist–essentialist debate and discuss why neither side proves altogether useful in understanding or guiding contemporary gay politics. Then I will argue that other theoretical perspectives on identity and ethnicity can provide valuable help in understanding recent political trends and in defending some version of an "ethnic/minority group model." In the process, I will return to the theoretical debate, examine some more subtle expressions of it, and show that the "ethnic" model is congruent with a modified constructionist position. Finally, I will explore the implications of this analysis for the future directions of gay politics.

The Debate

"Essentialism" is often equated with "traditional" views on sexuality in general, but can be linked specifically to the work of nineteenth-century "sexologists," such as Havelock Ellis and Krafft-Ebing; to certain aspects of Freud's work; and to deterministic theories such as sociobiology.[4] Essentialist views stress the "natural" dimensions of sex; and essentialist conceptions of homosexuality seek to account for such persons on the basis of some core of difference, whether that difference be hormonal, or medical, or a consequence of early child-rearing, or "just the way we are."

The constructionist critique of sexual essentialism has played an important role in debunking this traditional view. Much like essentialism, though, constructionism should not be thought of as a specific school, but rather as a broader tendency of thinking that has found representations in a number of disciplines. At the risk of oversimplifying, it can be said that recent historical and sociological work on gays and lesbians in Western societies[5] traces its roots to two schools of sociology: *symbolic interactionists,* particularly the path-breaking work of John Gagnon and William Simon on "sexual conduct" (1973); and *labeling theorists,* especially Mary McIntosh's analysis of the "homosexual role" (1968) and Kenneth Plummer on "sexual stigma" (1975).[6] To a lesser degree, analyses of sexual construction in Western societies have also been influenced by the cross-cultural work of constructionist anthropology; these studies of "sex/gender systems" trace a somewhat different history from the mid-century cultural anthropology of Boas, Benedict, and Mead.[7] Finally, in the 1980s, the work of Michel Foucault has become a new rallying point for sexual constructionism, and has served as an impetus for further investigations.[8]

In keeping with the central thrust of symbolic interactionism, constructionists propose that sexuality be investigated on the level of subjective meaning. Sexual acts have no inherent meaning, and in fact, no act is inherently sexual. Rather, in the course of interactions and over the course of time, individuals and societies spin webs of significance around the realm designated as "sexual." People *learn* to be sexual, Gagnon and Simon stress, in the same way they learn everything else: "Without much reflection, they pick up directions from their social environment."[9] As actors attribute subjective meanings to their interactions with others, they begin to develop "sexual scripts" which guide them in their future sexual interactions. Unlike "drives," which are understood as fixed essences destined to seek a particular expression, "scripts" are highly variable and fluid, subject to constant revision and editing.[10]

Central to this constructionist critique of essentialist "sexual drive theory" is a repudiation of the popular imagery of sex. In this view we tend to see sex as an overpowering, instinctual force, and social order depending on the proper channeling of sexual energy. In the left-wing version of the same ideology, "sex radicals" such as Wilhelm Reich and Herbert Marcuse have treated sexual repression as the cornerstone of social repression, hailing sex as the liberator from bondage.[11] More generally, in the popularizations of this imagery, the sex drive is treated as some sort of magical energy; hence the idea that athletes shouldn't have sex before the big game.

While symbolic interactionists debunked the notion of a "natural" sexuality, it was labeling theory that first provided the means to challenge essentialist views of "the homosexual" as a natural, transhistorical category. This challenge, which lies at the very crux of the constructionist argument about homosexuality, can be expressed in the following claim: although every known society has examples of homosexual *behavior,* only recently has there arisen a conception of "the homosexual" as a distinct type of *person*. Mary McIntosh has argued vehemently against the prevailing logic:

> Many scientists and ordinary people assume that there are two kinds of people in the world: homosexuals and heterosexuals. Some of them recognize that homosexual feelings and behavior are not confined to the persons they would like to call "homosexuals" and that some of these persons do not actually engage in homosexual behavior. This should pose a crucial problem, but they evade the crux by retaining their assumption and puzzling over the question of how to tell whether someone is "really" homosexual or not.[12]

In place of this essentialism, McIntosh argues that "the homosexual" has come to occupy a distinct "social role" in modern societies. Since homosexual *practices* are widespread but socially threatening, a special, stigmatized category of *individuals* is created so as to keep the rest of society pure. By this means, a "clearcut, publicized and recognizable threshold between permissible and impermissible behavior" is constructed; anyone who begins to approach that threshold is immediately threatened with being labeled a full-fledged deviant: one of "them."[13]

These sociological theories were employed by historians who, in empirical studies, have traced the genesis of the modern homosexual.[14] More recently, the work of Foucault has helped us to theorize a historical dimension to the constructionist arguments. According to Foucault, sexuality in the modern Western world has been the site of an explosion of discourses of power and knowledge; sexual meanings, sexual doctrines, and sexual beings have been generated incessantly by a culture that has come to be obsessed with the significance of the sexual, has elevated it to unprecedented dimensions, and has sought in it "the truth of our being."[15]

Foucault has tried to use this perspective to account for the origin of "the homosexual." In Foucault's view, the transformation from sexual behavior to sexual personhood is attributable to three factors: the increasing importance attached to sexuality in general; a more widespread transformation in structures of social control, from control that operates through sanctions against specific acts to control based on highly individualized discipline; and the growing power of professionals, and especially doctors, to define social problems and enforce social norms. In an oft-cited passage, Foucault argues:

> As defined by the ancient civil or canonical codes, sodomy was a category of forbidden acts; their perpetrator was nothing more than the juridical subject of them. The nineteenth-century homosexual became a personage, a past, a case history, and a childhood, in addition to being a type of life, a life form, and a morphology. . . . The sodomite had been a temporary aberration; the homosexual was now a species.[16]

As summarized in this brief sketch, constructionism posed a serious challenge to the prevailing essentialist orthodoxy concerning homosexuality. Where essentialism took for granted that all societies consist of people who are either heterosexuals or homosexuals (with perhaps some bisexuals), constructionists demonstrated that the notion of "the homosexual" is a sociohistorical product, not universally applicable, and worthy of explanation in its own right. And where essentialism would treat the self-attribution of a "homosexual identity" as unproblematic – as simply the conscious recognition of a true, underlying "orientation" – constructionism focused attention on identity as a complex developmental outcome, the consequence of an interactive process of social labeling and self-identification.

Unfortunately, while constituting a significant advance in our under-

73

standing of sexuality and homosexuality, constructionism also posed some inherent difficulties. However, before attempting a critique of constructionism, it is important to situate the debate within a social and political context. Rather than juxtaposing ideas in the abstract, we need to examine the politics of gay communities during the postwar period and the connection between those politics and the evolving theoretical stances.

Constructionism and Its Discontents

As Foucault notes, the labeling practices of the nineteenth-century doctors who invented the term "homosexual" created the possibility for a "reverse affirmation," by which the stigmatized could gradually begin to organize around their label and assert the legitimacy of that identity.[17] Foucault, however, neglects the material bases for these practices. As Jeffrey Weeks and John D'Emilio have argued, the medical categorization itself presupposes certain social conditions, including changes in family structure that were linked to the Industrial Revolution, and urbanization, which provided the social space for a homosexual subculture to develop.[18] By mid-century, such subcultures were firmly established in most major cities in the United States.

Homosexual politics of the 1950s and early 1960s preached liberal tolerance and stressed the goal of integration into the larger society.[19] The birth of the gay liberation movement marked a radical break with these accommodationist politics. When American gay liberation burst out of quiescence with the Stonewall riot in Greenwich Village in 1969, the politics that were espoused represented a mixture of New Left ideology and left-Freudian arguments that anticipated constructionism. Activists with groups such as the Gay Liberation Front portrayed homosexuals as revolutionary subjects who were uniquely situated to advance the cause of sexual liberation for society as a whole. However, the notion of "the homosexual" as a distinct type of person was specifically repudiated, in favor of a left-Freudian view of human sexuality as "polymorphously perverse." In utopian fashion, activists prophesied the disappearance of both "the homosexual" and "the heterosexual" through the abolition of constraining categories:

> The reason so few of us are bisexual is because society made such a big stink about homosexuality that we got forced into seeing ourselves as either straight or nonstraight. . . . We'll be gay until everyone has forgotten that it's an issue. Then we'll begin to be complete people.[20]

Or in the words of a lesbian activist:

We want to reach the homosexuals entombed in you, to liberate our brothers and sisters, locked in the prisons of your skulls. ... We will never go straight until you go gay.[21]

Perhaps the most sophisticated expression of this ideology is Dennis Altman's, whose *Homosexual: Oppression and Liberation* (1971) remains the classic statement of early post-Stonewall gay male politics. In the final chapter, entitled "The End of the Homosexual?," Altman looks forward to not only the abolition of sexual categorization but also the elimination of "masculinity" and "femininity," along with the creation of a "new human" for whom such distinctions would simply be irrelevant.[22]

While such arguments are not exactly "constructionist" – Gagnon and Simon, after all, would criticize the lingering essentialism of left-Freudians – they resonated fairly closely with the gay and lesbian constructionist history that began to be written soon afterward; this history, in fact, was inspired by the events of the early gay liberation movement, and many of the historians had been active in it from the start. What the liberationist position shared with the constructionist arguments was an insistence that sexual typologies are social, rather than natural facts; that these categories are highly fluid; and that they need to be transcended. Both shared a sense of the openness of historical possibilities that was inspired by the political climate of the day.

Needless to say, radical liberationist politics did not achieve its goals. However, the greater irony is that, to the extent that the activists did succeed in advancing the situation of gays and lesbians, they undermined the logical supports for their own arguments. That is, simply by advancing the cause of gay liberation, the liberationists helped to further the notion, among both gays and straights, that gays constitute a distinct social group with their own political and social interests. This is a familiar dilemma, and one that is by no means peculiar to the gay movement: How do you protest a socially imposed categorization, except by organizing around the category? Just as blacks cannot fight the arbitrariness of racial classification without organizing *as blacks,* so gays could not advocate the overthrow of the sexual order without making their gayness the very basis of their claims.

The 1970s witnessed a phenomenal growth in the institutionalization of a gay identity, as "deviant subcultures" gave way to "gay communities." And contrary to the "proto-constructionist" perspective that had been espoused by the early liberationists, the next generation of gay activists embraced a conception of gay identity that was significantly essentialist. To some extent, these essentialist notions had been around from the start; and in the political climate of the late 1970s, one can imagine why they would have more appeal than the utopian vision of early liberationism, with its focus on historical openness. What this meant, however, is that a disjuncture developed between theory and practice: in place of the rough congruence between early gay liberation politics

75

and evolving constructionist theory, we now find a growing tension between an evolving essentialist politics and a constructionist theory that is firmly in place.

Each variant of essentialism is based on some sort of legitimation strategy. In some cases, activists have legitimated their claims with reference to the transhistorical unity of homosexuals or their transcultural functional role. Perhaps most prominently, Adrienne Rich has proposed the existence of a "lesbian continuum" which links the resisters of heterosexist patriarchy across cultures and throughout history.[23] In a somewhat analogous vein, a male activist claimed: "We look forward to regaining our ancient historical role as medicine people, healers, prophets, shamans, and sorcerers."[24] Others have sought legitimations of a more "scientific" sort, making reference to a biological or genetic basis for homosexuality. Most typically, and far more usefully, gays and lesbians have adopted what Altman has in recent writings characterized as an "ethnic" identification.[25]

This "ethnic" self-characterization by gays and lesbians has a clear political utility, for it has permitted a form of group organizing that is particularly well suited to the American experience, with its history of civil rights struggles and ethnic-based, interest-group competition. In fact, an irony that Altman points out is that, by appealing to civil rights, gays as a group have been able to claim a legitimacy that homosexuals as individuals are often denied: "Thus for years the mayor of New York could proclaim an official Gay Pride Week while the very people being honored remained criminals under state law."[26]

Gay people's sense of themselves as belonging to a "minority group" was not altogether new; this view had been stated publicly at least as early as 1951, when Donald Webster Cory discussed the "invisible minority" in *The Homosexual in America*.[27] However, this self-conception could not really take root at a time when the institutional and cultural content of the gay subculture was so relatively impoverished. By the late 1970s, however, the "ethnic" self-understanding truly seemed to correspond to the reality of the burgeoning gay male communities, which had become, at least in New York and San Francisco, wholly contained cities-within-cities (or "ghettoes," as they were not infrequently called). There were gay churches, gay banks, gay theaters, gay hiking clubs, gay bookstores, and gay yellow pages listing hundreds of gay-owned businesses. While lesbian communities were neither as visible nor as territorially based, they, too, provided a variety of cultural supports and institutions, fostering a sense of minority-group identity that was furthered by separatist tendencies. Little wonder, then, that lesbians and gay men began to be seen as, and to think of themselves as, almost a distinct type of being, on an ontological par with "Irish-Americans" or "Japanese-Americans." Gone were the dreams of liberating society by releasing "the homosexual in everyone." Instead, homosexuals concentrated their energies on social advancement *as homosexuals.*

It should be noted that the "ethnic" self-understanding is a much looser form of essentialism than, say, a strict genetic or hormonal theory of homosexuality. Based on an analogy that is not necessarily intended literally, this form of group identification is peculiarly vague about where the essential "core" of gayness resides. Nonetheless, the notion does tend toward a reification of the category "homosexual," implying that lesbians and gay men are in some fundamental sense different from heterosexuals. Such viewpoints can be quite dangerous: they can lend support to eugenicist arguments and are also disturbingly compatible with the contemporary understanding of AIDS as a "gay disease."

Moreover, there are a number of questions that can be raised, from a progressive standpoint, about the political manifestations of "ethnicity." It would be unfortunate to reduce the politics of gay liberation to nothing more than the self-interested actions of an interest group, in competition with other such groups for various resources; such a model would imply that gays have no interests in common with other oppressed groups, and would almost entirely abandon any notion of a broader role for the gay movement in radical politics. In addition, such a move would further separate gay men from gay women, by questioning whether even they have sufficient common interests to overcome their senses of difference. Finally, as many critics have noted, the politics of gay "ethnicity" have tended to foster the hegemonic role in community-building played by white males within the gay movement,[28] and have been articulated to an uncomfortable extent through capitalist enterprise and the commodification of sexual desire.[29]

Given the problems posed by "ethnic" essentialism, one might think that the role of gay and lesbian theorists should be to continue promoting a constructionist critique. In a certain sense, I think this is true; but it is a project that needs some rethinking. Is constructionism to be defended unproblematically? If so, the defenders must grapple with the problem that their theoretical perspective is "out of sync" with the self-understandings of many gay people. From the standpoint of the defenders of constructionism, lesbians and gay men must be seen as victims of "false consciousness," unaware of the constructedness of their identities.

While it is important to challenge essentialism, particularly in its most insidious forms, we need not do so by reverting to a dogmatic constructionism. A strict constructionist position of the kind outlined above not only poses a threat to contemporary legitimations of lesbians and gay men: it is also theoretically unsound and analytically incomplete.

For all its radical potential, constructionism has trapped itself in the basic dualisms of classic liberalism. Liberal discourse goes back and forth between two extreme views of the relation between the individual and society: either it asserts that individuals are free to create themselves, rise above their environments, and take control over their lives; or it sees individuals as simply the product of their environment (or their genes, or what-have-you), molded like clay into various shapes.[30] Similarly, constructionism vacillates between a certain type of libertarian individualism (the left-Freudian variant is the best example here) in which sexual categories may be appropriated, transcended, and deconstructed at will; and just the opposite conception of the individual's sexual identity as created for him or her by the social and historical context (a strand of thinking best represented by Foucault). In either case, the "individual" is pitted against "Society"; and what is missing is any dynamic sense of how society comes to dwell within individuals or how individuality comes to be socially constituted.

Put more simply, constructionism is unable to theorize the issue of determination. This is true both on the societal level and on the level of individual lives. As Jeffrey Weeks has acknowledged, though constructionism would predict an infinite variety of sexual identities, sexual acts, and sexual scripts, practical experience indicates that only the tiniest fraction of these possibilities are realized.[31] Each society seems to have a limited range of potential storylines for its sexual scripts – and constructionists have surprisingly little to say about how that limiting process takes place. Moreover, strict constructionism implies a lack of determination in the sexual histories of *individuals* as well: their scripts are assumed to be in a constant state of revision. While this is no doubt true to a point, it would seem to belie most people's experiences of a relatively fixed sexual identity. It may be that we're all acting out scripts – but most of us seem to be typecast.

It is precisely this perceived nonvoluntary component of identity that cannot be accounted for within a strict constructionist perspective. Constructionism has no theory of the intrapsychic; it is unable to specify the ways in which desire comes to be structured over the course of people's lives. While it asserts that people are social products, it has no way of explaining how it is that social meanings come to resonate with the core of who people are. Falling into the dualistic traps of liberal theory, constructionism then lends itself to further misunderstanding on the part of those who encounter the theory. A "folk constructionism" comes to be disseminated: the view that sexual identities are willful self-creations. And in reaction against this folk constructionism, which denies the experience of a nonvoluntary component to identity, lesbians and gays operating within liberal discourse slide to the opposite extreme: they assert that there is something "real" about their identity, and then try to locate that felt reality in their genes, or their earliest experiences, or their mystical nature. In this way, constructionism becomes its own worst enemy, driving its potential converts into the enemy camp.

In order to build up a stronger constructionist position, my strategy will be as follows. First, I will examine more closely the idea of a gay "ethnic identity," exploring, from the standpoint of theories of identity and of ethnicity, the historical conjuncture in which this idea appeared. I will argue that the debates on identity and ethnicity have been bogged down by certain polar oppositions that parallel the essentialism–constructionism divide. By staking out an alternative position in these debates, I will further argue that it is reasonable, with certain qualifications, to accept the "ethnic" model – both as a relatively accurate characterization of contemporary gay identity formation, and as a politically defensible starting point from which the gay movement can evolve in a progressive direction. In the course of this analysis, I will return to the essentialism–constructionism debate and seek some way of transcending the dualisms, in a way that helps sexual theory to resonate more closely with the politics of gay "ethnic" identity.

Identity

The concept of "homosexual identity," as mentioned earlier, is a surprisingly new one; though the term is now ubiquitous, it first appeared in the relevant literature little more than a decade ago.[32] Perhaps it is not so surprising, then, that the term has been used in a consistently haphazard fashion. In her survey of the literature on homosexual identity, Vivienne Cass has found that

> in these articles it is possible to infer diverse meanings such as (1) defining oneself as gay, (2) a sense of self as gay, (3) image of self as homosexual, (4) the way a homosexual person is, and (5) consistent behavior in relation to homosexual-related activity.[33]

General definitions of identity are equally problematic. In an interesting "semantic history" of the term, Philip Gleason notes that it, too, is a new concept, having entered the general social science literature only in the 1950s.[34] Gleason observes that most definitions tend to fall toward one or the other pole of an opposition between two conceptions of identity, one a psychological reductionism, the other a sociological reductionism. The first conception of identity – which might be called "intrapsychic" – treats identity as a relatively fixed and stable characteristic of a person, which, from a developmental standpoint, more or less unwinds from within. In a word, this sense of identity is essentialist: it is the type of "identity" that we mean when we speak of identity as describing who someone *really* is. Quite distinct is the sense of "identity" which I will call "acquired." In this sense, identity is the internalization or conscious adoption of socially imposed or socially constructed labels or roles. According to the "acquired" definition, identity is not so deeply entrenched in the psyche of the individual, and can vary considerably over the course of one's life. This is the type of "identity" that we have in mind when we say that someone "identifies as" a such-and-such.[35]

Mediating between the poles of intrapsychic and acquired identity is Habermas's useful discussion of identity:

> [Ego] identity is produced through *socialization,* that is, through the fact that the growing child first of all integrates itself into a specific social system by appropriating symbolic generalities; it is later secured and developed through *individuation,* that is, precisely through a growing independence in relation to social systems.[36]

Ego identity, then, is a *socialized sense of individuality,* an internal organization of self-perceptions concerning one's relationship to social categories, that also incorporates views of the self perceived to be held by others. At its core, identity is constituted relationally, through involvement with – and incorporation of – significant others and integration into communities. The relationship of ego identity to subsidiary identities (such as occupational, class, racial, gender, or sexual identities) is an interactive one, in which all subsidiary identities are integrated into a relatively coherent and unique life history.[37]

Where then do these subsidiary identities come from, and in what circumstances can they be appropriated and incorporated? As Berger and Luckmann maintain, it is important to recognize that such identities are, at the same time, both human self-creations and constraining structures.[38] To paraphrase Marx, people make their own identities, but they do not make them just as they please.

In this regard, it is vital to note that identity has increasingly come to be seen as something quite important. In modern, fluid, "mass" society, the relationship of the individual to the social whole is rendered problematic; as part of a continual "quest for identity" we go through "identity crises"; we seek to "find ourselves." It is not surprising that group identities – occupational, racial, ethnic, sexual – become increasingly attractive, since they provide an intermediate link between the individual and the mass.[39] As we accept more and more identities, it does indeed begin to seem that they are all somewhat arbitrary, tried on like hats and discarded for next year's style. And yet the fundamental irony of this apparent freedom to define ourselves is that in a world where identity has been transformed into a problem – where identity "crises" must be resolved, and where we all search for our identities – external cues and definitions become increasingly authoritative. The more we feel impelled to discover our "true" identity, the more we are likely to grasp at the reassurance provided by the adoption of available identity types.

Gay, lesbian, and bisexual identities must be understood as arising out of this historical conjuncture. Their emergence reflects a world in which group identity has assumed paramount importance, and where sexuality has become a central dimension of identity formation in general. In addition, as already suggested, these identities constitute "reverse affirmations" of social labels, adoptive contestations of imposed stigma categories. As labeling theory indicates, deviant identities are particularly likely to assume totalizing dimensions, because *all* behavior of persons so categorized becomes interpreted by others through the prism of the perceived difference: "One will be identified as a deviant first, before other identifications are made."[40] And as Erving Goffman points out, the need for the stigmatized to "manage" their stigma in social situations – to tell or not to tell, to confront or to excuse – causes the stigma-identity to assume substantial proportions within the overall ego identity – to become, in some cases, an all-consuming preoccupation.[41]

Finally, the emergence of various types of sexual identity as important components of ego identity presumes the existence of individuals who are in some loose sense qualified to fill the categories – people who are capable of interpreting their erotic and emotional desires and actions as corresponding to their understanding of the meaning of these social terms.[42] This is the point at which both labeling theory and symbolic interactionism falter, for they have nothing to say about how such people come to exist. The rigid temporal sequence laid down by labeling theory is particularly inadequate. In that model, the individual commits an act of "primary" deviance (in this case, a homosexual act), is in consequence met with a stigmatizing label ("You're a queer"), and by internalizing this label becomes fixed in a "secondary" deviant identity ("I'm a homosexual").[43] But in the real world, the developmental sequences vary tremendously. Interview data suggest, in fact, the relationship among the processes of engaging in homosexual activity, being labeled a homosexual, and having suspicions that one is a homosexual can come in various orders; typical patterns seem to include "engaged, suspicious, labeled," "engaged, labeled," "suspicious, engaged, labeled," and "suspicious, labeled, engaged." As Plummer has pointed out in his review of several studies, some gay men and lesbians report a fixity and clarity of sexual preferences dating to early childhood; others experience several shifts in sexual identity and the structure of desire over the course of their lives.[44]

A theory of sexual identity formation, therefore, must be able to identify a wide range of potential developmental strategies by which individuals, in relation with significant others, compare (or fail to compare) their experiences and feelings against their comprehension (or lack of comprehension) of existing sexual and gender typologies. As a result of these processes, individuals arrive (or fail to arrive) at consistent or variable interpretations of their sexual identity. This is a complex and never-ending activity, involving both conscious and unconscious dimensions.

If the question is, Are sexual identities the outcome of choice or constraint?, then the whole thrust of the preceding argument is to suggest that the only possible answer is "neither and both." Choice and constraint constitute a false opposition; and the way to transcend this dualism, I think, is with some form of psychoanalytic theory. Such a perspective can account for the ways that sexual and emotional desires can be structured, developmentally, into relatively well-defined directions. In particular, the "object relations" school of psychoanalysis, with its focus on relational experience, and with its theory of the ego as possessing a "relational core," might be usefully applied to an analysis of sexual identity.[45] Object relations theory describes, in a vivid way, how from a child's earliest moments onward a sense of self is constituted through "introjections" of significant others. The child's needs and desires, which can only be satisfied externally, come to be mediated and shaped through these encounters; while aspects of these desires may remain highly fluid and subject to what constructionists want to call scripting, other dimensions may be sharply structured and come to comprise fundamental parts of the ego core. Without displacing the symbolic interactionist focus on conscious, adult experience, psychoanalysis also permits us to conceptualize the unconscious and to appreciate the formative element of early childhood experiences.

In light of this discussion, the organization of the gay community around the "politics of identity" would seem to have strong social roots. An intermediate position between the poles of intrapsychic and acquired identity allows us to recognize that these sexual identities are *both inescapable and transformable,* and are capable of giving rise to a variety of political expressions. The question that must now be asked is why the contemporary gay identity in the United States has particularly assumed an "ethnic" dimension, and what this implies for gay politics.

Ethnicity

How can we speak seriously of gays and lesbians as an "ethnic" group – or even a minority group? After all, there would seem to be some rather fundamental differences between gays and the other groups that we normally associate with these terms. In the first place, ethnic or racial identifications are normally conferred at birth and transmitted through the family. In place of this "primary socialization" into a racial or ethnic identity, the entrance into a gay community constitutes a "secondary socialization," occurring later in life.

A process of secondary socialization is typically seen as less formative than primary socialization, because "it must deal with an already formed self and an already internalized world. It cannot construct subjective reality *ex nihilo.*"[46] In particular, it is unclear what sort of coherent cultural content can be transmitted through a secondary socialization into a gay community, and whether this cultural distinctiveness corresponds with the kinds of cultural differences that we normally consider to be ethnic. This problem is compounded by the fact that individuals being socialized into a gay community will already possess a variety of cross-cutting identities – ethnic, racial, class, gender, religious, occupational, and so on – which may claim much greater allegiance and inhibit the secondary socialization process.[47]

The treatment of these objections rests ultimately on the particular definition of "ethnicity" adopted. And once again, an investigation into the existing definitional possibilities reveals a debate between two polar opposite conceptions. Lining up on one side are the "primordialists," who treat ethnicity as an inescapable given, an absolute ascription. In opposition to this traditional view has arisen the "optionalist" (a.k.a. "circumstantialist") critique, which in its most vulgar manifestations argues that "ethnicity may be shed, resurrected, or adopted as the situation warrants."[48] It should be clear that a "primordialist" conception of ethnicity implies an "intrapsychic" notion of ethnic identity; while conversely, an understanding of ethnicity in the "optionalist" sense is quite compatible with a definition of ethnic identity as "acquired."[49]

Once again, we need to transcend a false dualism: on the one hand, it seems ridiculous to claim that we can shed or adopt ethnicities as we please. Clearly, there are major constraints on this process. But on the other hand, it is quite true that racial and ethnic categories are historical products that are subject to extensive redefinition over time. Michael Omi and Howard Winant give an interesting example of the definitional crisis surrounding the influx of Mexicans and Chinese into the United States in the mid-nineteenth century. Confused over what sort of racial/legal status to accord these groups, courts eventually ruled that Mexicans were "white" but that Chinese were "Indian."[50] Even in the lives of individuals, racial designations can change. In South Africa, where race, of course, is of paramount importance, there is a special government agency responsible for adjudicating claims about one's racial classification; and each year many people officially "upgrade" their racial identity.[51] Donald Horowitz strikes a good intermediate note between primordialism and optionalism:

> Ethnic identity is generally acquired at birth. But this is a matter of degree. In the first place, in greater or lesser measure, there are possibilities for changing individual identity. Linguistic or religious conversion will suffice in some cases, but in others the changes may require a generation or more to accomplish by means of intermarriage and procreation. In the second place, collective action, in the sense of conscious modification of group behavior and identification, may effect shifts of boundaries. ... Ethnicity thus differs from voluntary affiliation, not because the two are dichotomous, but because they occupy *different positions on a continuum.*[52]

If ethnicity does not necessarily begin at birth, and if ethnicity involves some combination of external ascription and chosen affiliation, then a gay identity as described above seems not wholly unlike an ethnic identity. But we can better understand the adoption of the ethnic model by gays and lesbians if we spell out the particular ways in which ethnicity has come to be understood in the contemporary United States.

In the 1970s, social scientists announced that the United States was in the throes of an "ethnic revival" – a "resurgence" of ethnicity.[53] Though heavily influenced by the cultural and political assertiveness of racial minorities in the late 1960s, the revival was essentially a phenomenon of white European ethnic groups, manifesting a rediscovered pride in their heritage. It was quickly observed that, despite the implications of a turn toward the past, there was something quite new about this form of ethnicity. As Frank Parkin notes,

> the nature of collective action mounted by ethnic groups has undergone a significant change in recent times. Originally dedicated to fighting rearguard actions of cultural preservation, they have now adopted more combative forms of activity expressly designed to alter the distribution of rewards in their members' favour.[54]

The "new ethnicity" differs from traditional ethnicity in a variety of respects. First, as Daniel Bell points out, the new ethnicity combines an affective tie with the pursuit of explicitly sociopolitical goals in "interest group" form: ethnic groups become "instrumental" and not just "expressive."[55] Second, the new ethnicity places ethnic-group activity firmly on the terrain of the state.[56] Third, and as a corollary to the preceding arguments, the new ethnicity is "forward-looking," seeking to expand the group's social position, while the old ethnicity was "backward-looking," aimed at "preserv[ing] the past against the encroachments of centralization and 'modernization.'"[57] Fourth, as a reaction against "mass society" the new ethnicity is not so much a new form of aggregation as a "disaggregation" or "deassimilation" from the mass.[58] Fifth, lacking the type of structural power possessed by subordinate social classes (i.e., the ability to disrupt production), the new ethnic groups are increasingly inclined to press their demands by appealing to, and manipulating, hegemonic ideologies (such as "equal rights").[59] And finally, neo-ethnic politics frequently take on a localist character, organized around a specific geographic space or community, leading to a distinctively ethnic involvement in urban political affairs.[60] While to some extent a general feature of contemporary Western politics, the "new ethnicity" manifested itself most prominently in the United States, where the political possibilities for organizing around ethnicity were the greatest (and, conversely, class-based organizing had proven relatively ineffective).[61]

Of course, it would be a mistake to exaggerate the changes that have occurred and ignore either the continuities between the "old" and the "new" ethnicity, or the extent to which both varieties have always been present. Nonetheless, it seems that a somewhat new understanding of what ethnicity is all about emerged in the United States in the 1970s – that is to say, at the very same time that gay and lesbian identity was taking on an ethnic cast. And indeed, on the basis of the preceding discussion, this notion of gay ethnic identity seems increasingly comprehensible and plausible. Like the archetypal "new ethnicity," gay ethnicity is a "future-oriented" identity linking an affective bond with an instrumental goal of influencing state policy and securing social rewards on behalf of the group. Like the other ethnic groups, gay ethnicity functions typically through appeals to the professed beliefs of the dominant culture, attempting to mobilize commonly espoused American values such as equality, fairness, and freedom from persecution. And finally, in neo-ethnic fashion, gay identity (in this case, gay *male* identity in particular) operates by using the control of a specific geographic space to influence urban political decision-making.[62]

The final question that must be addressed, to understand and assess the gay community's adoption of an ethnic self-understanding, has to do with the issue of culture and tradition. On the one hand, gay communities have developed a variety of cultural forms which, despite the considerable internal variation, serve to unify those communities.[63] And on the other hand, the cultural potency of at least the European ethnic groups would seem to be much less than has often been assumed. In an interesting twist on the "new ethnicity" argument, Stephen Steinberg has characterized the recent "ethnic fever" as sort of a Freudian reaction-formation: an assertion that ethnicity is still culturally and psychologically meaningful, voiced with such rigid insistence as to imply that even the proponents themselves are not convinced.

Because ethnicity no longer provides the institutional supports capable of integrating individuals into the community and providing them with a sense of belonging, individuals futilely attempt to recreate that sense of belonging by grasping at a *psychological* affiliation. In the process, they fail to observe that the ground has fallen away beneath their feet:

> Indeed, it is precisely because the real and objective basis for ethnic culture is rapidly disappearing that identity has been elevated to a "symbolic" plane and a premium is placed on the subjective dimensions of ethnicity. People desperately wish to "feel" ethnic precisely because they have all but lost the prerequisites for "being" ethnic.[64]

Steinberg's analysis would lead one to characterize the gay community's adoption of an ethnic identity as profoundly ironic. It would seem to be precisely the fact that ethnic culture has been *evacuated of content* that has permitted the transposition of the category of "ethnicity" onto a group that, in the traditional sense of the term, clearly would not qualify for the designation. Thus it is true that lesbians and gay men don't really fit the original definition of what an ethnic group is: but then, neither really do contemporary Jews, or Italian-Americans, or anyone else. In this way, the decline of the old ethnicity permits and encourages new groups to adopt the mantle and revive the phenomenon.

Conclusion

In making sense of the notion of "gay 'ethnic' identity," I have deliberately steered clear of both the strict essentialist and the strict constructionist understandings of ethnicity as well as identity. The constitution of a gay identity is not something that simply unwinds from within, nor is it just an amalgam of roles that proceed according to scripts; only an intermediate, and dialectical, definition makes sense in this case. Similarly, if "ethnicity" is to serve even as an analogy for comprehending gay and lesbian group identity, then ethnicity must be understood as something that is neither an absolutely inescapable ascription nor something chosen and discarded at will; as something neither there from birth, nor something one joins like a club; as something that makes one neither fundamentally different from others, nor fundamentally the same. It is in the dialectics between choice and constraint, and between the individual, the group, and the larger society, that "identities," "ethnic identities," and "gay and lesbian identities" emerge.

The fact that, in seeking to transcend these oppositions, I have ended up quoting the arguments of many constructionists, is not incidental. Constructionists have become increasingly aware of the complexities of these debates, and have continued to provide the most insightful analyses of the changing character of the gay community and gay identity. But what constructionists have failed to acknowledge are the ways in which their own observations are increasingly at odds with the basic premises of the theoretical perspective. Plummer, in an interesting article aimed at a "synthetic" position, has gone so far as to embrace the possibility of the existence of fixed sexual "orientations" – while carefully skirting the question of how such a concept accords with his general theoretical stance.[65] Altman, one of the most subtle chroniclers of the gay ethnic experience, can never seem to quite escape his own suspicion that ethnicity rests on an illusion that is also a trap. Weeks, who is perhaps the most sensitive to the theoretical limitations of strict constructionism, and who provides the most insightful discussions of both the limitations and the possibilities inherent in gay identities, is also capable of lapsing into the most utopian constructionist arguments about the abolition of sexual categories. The hold of strict constructionism remains tenacious; and its expositors seem unwilling to clarify their relationship to the doctrine.

Clarification would require a number of modifications to strict constructionism, yet would in no way amount to an endorsement of essentialism. First, there is a need to understand the issue of determination: out of the range of potential forms of sexual expression, how are limitations created on that expression, both socially and within the individual psyche? On the individual level, this implies the systematic introduction of psychoanalytic conceptions of needs and desires and of the development of the self in relation to others. On the social level, it implies a more comprehensive understanding of power, and of the dialectical relationship between identities as self-expressions and identities as ascriptive impositions. Anthropological analyses of "sex/gender systems" in kinship-based societies have something to offer here. As Harriet Whitehead has pointed out, "To say that gender definitions and concepts pertaining to sex and gender are culturally variable is not necessarily to say that they can vary infinitely or along any old axis." Analyses such as hers have attempted to connect cultural meanings about gender and sexuality with specific social-structural relations, so as to show how culture can structure the possibilities for personhood in distinctive ways.[66]

Beyond the issue of determination, a second requirement for the reinvigoration of constructionism is a better understanding of the "collectivization of subjectivity." We must be able to speak of sexually based group identities without assuming *either* that the group has some mystical or biological unity, *or* that the "group" doesn't exist and that its "members" are indulging in a dangerous mystification. "Ethnicity" is a metaphor; but the relationships that it entails can come to be internalized as a fundamental part of the self. To the extent that this is consciously recognized – to the extent that "ethnicity" can be seen as both strategy and reality – then the dangers of it being misunderstood in a rigidly essentialist sense become greatly reduced.

A modified constructionist perspective of this sort would address the deficiencies of constructionism that were noted earlier in this paper. Not only would it permit a fuller description of the complex experiences of being homosexual, but it might also permit lesbians and gay men to feel that constructionism described the world and themselves as they experience it, rather than inducing them to flee from constructionism and into the arms of essentialism.

A modified constructionism could also allow theory to play a more helpful role in the analysis of the contemporary political expressions of gays and lesbians. In fact, the preceding analysis of the complexities and ironies of gay identity and ethnicity raises several important political dilemmas. The first of these has to do with the political manifestations of ethnicity. As I indicated, the gay movement's (and in this case, particularly the gay male movement's) subscription to the tenets of pluralism – its attempt to simply get its "piece of the pie" by appealing to hegemonic ideologies – raises questions about its potential (or desire) to mount a serious challenge to the structural roots of inequality – whether that be sexual inequality or any other kind. Despite the adoption of a goal of civil rights, gay collective identity is at present closer in form to that of the white ethnic groups than to those of racial minorities. Movement away from a political consciousness based on white "ethnicity" and toward a "sexual minority" self-understanding might increase the gay movement's capacity to pose a more fundamental challenge to the socio-sexual order.

This, however, raises other dilemmas, regarding both the internal composition of the gay movement and its leadership, and the relationship of the gay movement to other social movements. The adoption of a "white ethnic" model, in other words, is not unexpected in a movement dominated by white, middle-class males. The gay movement will never be able to forge effective alliances with other social movements unless it can address the inequalities that plague its internal organization. In this light it is worth noting a peculiar paradox of identity politics. While affirming a distinctive group identity that legitimately differs from the larger society, this form of political expression simultaneously imposes a "totalizing" sameness *within* the group: it says, this is who we "really are."[67] A greater appreciation for internal diversity – on racial, gender, class, and even sexual dimensions – is a prerequisite if the gay movement is to move beyond "ethnic" insularity and join with other progressive causes. The obvious first step in that direction would be improved understandings between lesbians and gay men – and a better articulation of feminist theory with theoretical perspectives on sexuality.

Finally, in considering the political dilemmas confronting lesbians and gays, it is vital to discuss the most serious crisis that the movement has yet faced, namely, AIDS. The "moral panic" surrounding AIDS demonstrates some of the inherent fragility of identity politics. By hardening a notion of group difference, identity politics present a highly visible target. Those social groups who see their understandings of the world as called into question by changing conceptions of sexuality, gender, and morality more broadly defined, have found in the consolidated notion of "gayness" a potent and available symbol upon which they can easily discharge their anxieties – and vent their wrath. And if there is perceived to be such a thing as a "homosexual person," then it is only a small step to the conclusion that there is such a thing as a "homosexual disease," itself the peculiar consequence of the "homosexual lifestyle."[68]

Thus the ideological and practical consequences of a complete solidification of identity into a reified notion of "the gay person" would seem to be quite grave. But to reiterate, this is not an argument for the maintenance of a strict-constructionist pose; for both the "politics of constructionism" and the "politics of essentialism" present legitimating possibilities as well as dangers of delegitimation. The task of melding theory with practice will involve creatively capitalizing on the most effective legitimations of the moment, while still remaining true both to theoretical insights and to the contemporary self-understandings of the women and men who populate the movement.

Notes

This paper could not have been written without the encouragement, advice, and criticisms offered by a good number of people (many of whom, it should be said, do not agree with aspects of my argument). I would like to thank Jeffrey Escoffier, Tomás Almaguer, Jeanne Bergman, Alan Bérubé, Ellyn Kestnbaum, David Kirp, Lisa Orlando, Gayle Rubin, Arlene Stein, Indi Talwani, Jackie Urla, Carole Vance, Chris Waters, Jeff Weintraub, and the members of the Bay Area SR collective.

1. Vivienne C. Cass, "Homosexual Identity: A Concept in Need of Definition," *Journal of Homosexuality*, vol. 9, nos 2/3 (Winter 1983/Spring 1984), p. 105.

2. See Nancy Chodorow, "Feminism and Difference: Gender, Relation, and Difference in Psychoanalytic Perspective," *Socialist Review*, no. 46 (July/August 1979), pp. 51–69.

3. See, in particular, Dennis Altman, *The Homosexualization of America*, Boston: Beacon Press 1982.

4. Gay and lesbian exponents of essentialist positions include John Boswell, *Christianity, Social Tolerance, and Homosexuality: Gay People in Western Europe from the Beginning of the Christian Era to the Fourteenth Century*, Chicago: University of Chicago Press 1980; and Adrienne Rich, "Compulsory Heterosexuality and Lesbian Existence," in Ann Snitow et al., eds, *Powers of Desire: The Politics of Sexuality*, New York: Monthly Review Press 1983, pp. 177–206.

5. Prime examples of this scholarship are Jeffrey Weeks, *Coming Out: Homosexual Politics in Britain, from the Nineteenth Century to the Present*, London: Quartet Books 1977; and John D'Emilio, *Sexual Politics, Sexual Communities: The Making of a Homosexual Minority the United States, 1940–1970*, Chicago: University of Chicago Press 1983.

6. John Gagnon and William Simon, *Sexual Conduct*, Chicago: Aldine 1973; Mary McIntosh, "The Homosexual Role," *Social Problems*, vol. 17, no. 2, pp. 262–70; Ken Plummer, *Sexual Stigma*, London: Routledge & Kegan Paul 1975.

7. The phrase "sex/gender system" is from Gayle Rubin, "The Traffic in Women: Notes on the 'Political Economy' of Sex," in Rayna Reiter, ed., *Toward an Anthropology of Women*, New York: Monthly Review Press 1975, pp. 157–210.

8. Michel Foucault, *The History of Sexuality*, vol. 1, New York: Vintage 1980.

9. John Gagnon, quoted in Kenneth Plummer, "Symbolic Interactionism and Sexual Conduct," in Mike Brake, ed., *Human Sexual Relations*, New York: Pantheon 1982, p. 226.

10. Gagnon and Simon, *Sexual Conduct*, p. 19.

11. Wilhelm Reich, *The Sexual Revolution*, New York: Farrar, Straus & Giroux 1969; Herbert Marcuse, *Eros and Civilization*, Boston: Beacon Press 1966.

12. McIntosh, "Homosexual Role," p. 182.

13. Ibid., pp.183–84.

14. See note 5 above.

15. Foucault, *History of Sexuality*.

16. Ibid., p. 43.

17. Ibid., p. 101.

18. Weeks, *Coming Out*, p. 2 and parts 1–3; John D'Emilio, *Sexual Politics*, pp. 9–22.

19. Jeffrey Escoffier, "Sexual Revolution and the Politics of Gay Identity," *Socialist Review*, nos. 82–83 (July–October 1985), pp. 119–53; D'Emilio, *Sexual Politics*, chs 5–7.

20. Carl Witman, "Refugees from Amerika: A Gay Manifesto," in Joseph A. McCaffrey, ed., *The Homosexual Dialectic*, Englewood Cliffs, N.J.: Prentice-Hall 1972, p. 159.

21. Quoted in Barbara Ponse, *Identities in the Lesbian World: The Social Construction of Self*, Westport, Conn.: Greenwood 1978, p. 95.

22. Dennis Altman, *Homosexual: Oppression and Liberation*, New York: Avon 1971.

23. Rich, "Compulsory Heterosexuality."

24. Quoted in Altman, *Homosexualization of America*, p. 161.

25. This is one of the prime arguments made by Altman in *Homosexualization of America*, written a decade after his earlier "liberationist" book.

26. Altman, *Homosexualization of America*, p. 9.

27. Donald Webster Cory [pseud.], *The Homosexual in America*, New York: Castle Books 1951. It is interesting to note that while the term "minority" is indexed frequently, "identity" does not appear in the index.

28. Tomás Almaguer, "Conceptualizing Sexual Stratification: Notes toward a Sociology of Sexuality" (unpublished essay, 1986), p. 25; Frances Fitzgerald, *Cities on a Hill: A Journey through Contemporary American Cultures*, New York: Simon & Schuster 1986, p. 58.

29. Jeffrey Weeks, *Sexuality and Its Discontents: Meanings, Myths & Modern Sexualities*, London: Routledge & Kegan Paul 1985, pp. 21–35; Altman, *Homosexualization of America*, ch. 3.

30. On the dualisms of liberal thought, see Roberto M. Unger, *Knowledge and Politics*, New York: Free Press 1975, esp. ch. 5.

31. Jeffrey Weeks, "Discourse, Desire, and Sexual Deviance: Some Problems in a History of Homosexuality," in Ken Plummer, ed., *The Making of the Modern Homosexual*, London: Hutchinson 1981, pp. 94–95.

32. Cass, "Homosexual Identity," pp. 107–8.

33. Ibid., p. 108.

34. Philip Gleason, "Identifying Identity: A Semantic History," *Journal of American History*, vol. 69, no. 4 (March 1983), pp. 910–31.

35. Ibid., pp. 918–19.

36. Jürgen Habermas, *Communication and the Evolution of Society*, Boston: Beacon Press 1979, p. 74.

37. Ibid., pp. 90–91; Cass, "Homosexual Identity," p. 110; Unger, *Knowledge and Politics*, p. 195; Chodorow, "Feminism and Difference," p. 60.

38. Peter L. Burger and Thomas Luckmann, *The Social Construction of Reality*, New York: Anchor Books 1967.

39. Kenneth Plummer, "Homosexual Categories: Some Research Problems in the Labelling Perspective of Homosexuality," in Plummer, ed., *Making of the Modern Homosexual*, pp. 60–61.

40. Howard Becker, *Outsiders: Studies in the Sociology of Deviance*, New York: Free Press 1963, pp. 33–34.

41. Erving Goffman, *Stigma: Notes on the Management of Spoiled Identity*, Englewood Cliffs, N.J.: Prentice-Hall 1963, pp. 14, 88.

42. Cass, "Homosexual Identity," pp. 110, 114.

43. See, for example, Becker, *Outsiders*.

44. Plummer, "Homosexual Categories," pp. 66–72.

45. See Nancy Chodorow, *The Reproduction of Mothering: Psychoanalysis and the Sociology of Gender*, Berkeley: University of California Press 1978.

46. Berger and Luckmann, *Social Construction of Reality*, p. 140; Escoffier, "Sexual Revolution," p. 127.

47. Almaguer, "Conceptualizing Sexual Stratification," p. 27.

48. Peter K. Eisenger, "Ethnicity as a Strategic Option: An Emerging View," *Public Administration Review*, vol. 38 (Jan.–Feb. 1978), p. 90. The terms "primordialist" and "circumstantialist" are used by Nathan Glazer and Daniel P. Moynihan in their introduction to *Ethnicity: Theory and Experience*, Cambridge: Harvard University Press, 1975, pp. 19–20. "Optionalist" is used in place of "circumstantialist" by Eisinger and by Gleason.

49. This point is made by Gleason, "Identifying Identity," pp. 919–20.

50. Michael Omi and Howard Winant, "By the Rivers of Babylon: Race in the United States (Part I)," *Socialist Review*, no. 71 (Sept.–Oct., 1983), p. 52. Their article is reprinted in this anthology on pp. 221–38.

51. Ibid., p. 47.

52. Donald L. Horowitz. "Ethnic Identity," in Glazer and Moynihan, eds, *Ethnicity*, pp. 113–14; emphasis added.

53. Glazer and Moynihan, eds, *Ethnicity*.

54. Frank Parkin, *Marxism and Class Theory: A Bourgeois Critique*, New York: Columbia University Press 1979, pp. 33–34.

55. Daniel Bell, "Ethnicity and Social Change," in Glazer and Moynihan, *Ethnicity*, pp. 169–70.

56. Glazer and Moynihan, eds, *Ethnicity*, pp. 9–10; Parkin, *Marxism and Class Theory*, p. 95.

57. Eisinger, "Ethnicity as a Strategic Option," p. 90.

58. Glazer and Moynihan, *Ethnicity*, p. 9.

59. Parkin, *Marxism and Class Theory*, pp. 85–86.

60. Ira Katznelson, *City Trenches: Urban Politics and the Patterning of Class in the United States*, New York: Pantheon 1981.

61. Ibid.

62. On this last point, see Manuel Castells, *The City and the Grassroots*, Berkeley: University of California Press 1983, ch. 14.

63. Michael Bronski, *Culture Clash: The Making of a Gay Sensibility*, Boston: South End Press 1984.

64. Stephen Steinberg, *The Ethnic Myth: Race, Ethnicity, and Class in America*, Boston: Beacon Press 1981, p. 63.

65. Plummer, "Homosexual Categories," pp. 71–72.

66. Harriet Whitehead, "The Bow and the Burden Strap: A New Look at Institutionalized Homosexuality in Native North America," in Sherry B. Ortner and Harriet Whitehead, eds, *Sexual Meanings: The Cultural Construction of Gender and Sexuality*, Cambridge: Cambridge University Press 1981, p. 110.

67. Escoffier, "Sexual Revolutions," pp. 148–49; Weeks, *Sexuality and Its Discontents*, p. 187.

68. See Steven Epstein, "Moral Contagion and the Medicalizing of Gay Identity: AIDS in Historical Perspective," *Research in Law, Deviance, and Social Control*, vol. 9 (1988), pp. 3–36.

PART II

Architectures of Power

6

From MAD to NUTs
The Growing Danger of Nuclear War
(1982)
Paul Joseph

With the possible exception of 1962, the outbreak of nuclear war is more likely now than at any other time over the 35-year existence of nuclear weapons. Several factors account for this dangerous situation, most notably the dramatic changes in technology associated with the production and delivery of nuclear weapons and the steady growth in size and influence of right-wing political forces within the United States. In addition, the instability of the international situation and the uncertain position of the United States within it have exacerbated current tensions and increased the number of potential crisis points in which nuclear weapons might be used.

The purpose of this essay is to give some idea of these technical changes and to focus in more detail on the rightward shift in doctrine governing the use of nuclear weapons. That shift is represented by the growing influence of nuclear-use theorists (NUTs) over officials who believe in mutual assured destruction (MAD). The first group thinks that the United States must prepare itself to fight a nuclear war. Such a war will have winners and losers, they believe, and it is important for the United States to win. The second group believes that it is ridiculous to think of winners and losers in a nuclear war and that nuclear weapons should be deployed in a manner that deters such a conflict.

We have reached the point where the technical features of nuclear weapons systems are sustaining illusions that help undermine the rough stability formed by a "balance of terror." Instead we confront a much more fragile situation in which the temptation to strike first in the hope of winning a nuclear exchange is growing. And in the future it may be that an American president will think

95

that the only hope of survival will be to go first. The explosion of these weapons against human beings is not inevitable. But only a peace movement in the United States can stop it. Despite a range of views within the policy-making elite, some of whom would genuinely prefer to reduce, it not eliminate, the prospect of nuclear war, the danger of war can be lowered only by building a popular antiwar movement; that is, by building pressures outside of the existing government structure. Without such a movement we will make little progress towards peace. On the other hand, that movement must learn to make compromises with certain elements of the national security apparatus. I will return to the political ramifications of this analysis in the concluding section.

Mutual Assured Destruction

Whatever their differences, members of this school of thought regarding strategic doctrines agree that a nuclear war cannot be fought and won. Each side, the United States and the Soviet Union, possesses enormous stockpiles with great destructive power. In this view, decision-makers must confront two facts: first, that the offensive is overwhelming and no effective defense is possible; and second, that despite this destructive capacity neither side can attack without being demolished in return. The result is mutual assured destruction. This is a dangerous situation to be sure, but advocates of this position feel that it is also one of rough stability that cannot be escaped. The mutual recognition that a nuclear war could have no winners deters each side from launching an attack against the other. Deterrence is in fact the key word in this school of thought.

The earliest exponent of the logic underlying mutually assured destruction was Bernard Brodie. His *Absolute Weapon: Atomic Power and World Order,* published in 1946, anticipated many of the specific tenets of a nuclear standoff even before this situation was achieved in fact by the deployment of nuclear weapons by the Soviet Union during the 1950s. "Everything about the bomb," Brodie argued, "is overshadowed by the twin facts that it exists and that its destructive power is fantastically great."[1] Brodie also pointed out several other crucial – and unique – features of the new weapons that were later accepted by the strategists of mutually assured destruction. The first was that it would be impossible for a nation to win a nuclear war, even for the aggressor. The country initiating the attack might succeed in destroying the other side's cities and industrial base but would not escape the same destruction in return. There would be no point in attacking, since the consequences for the aggressor would be precisely the same as for the defending country. Each side would be deterred from striking first by the "unacceptable level of damage" that it would receive no matter how effective its initial attack.

The next tenet of MAD was that American bombs should be targeted against Soviet population and industrial centers (countercity targeting). At first glance it might appear that it would be safe to target an opponent's military centers and especially its retaliatory missiles (counterforce targeting). In this way the damage to one's own population and industry would be minimized. But in the topsy-turvy logic of nuclear strategy, countercity targeting is less provocative and less likely to lead to nuclear war. The thinking is that countercity targeting will deter an enemy attack since the opponent will reason that there is no possible way to escape unacceptable damage. Counterforce targeting is dangerous on two grounds: it lowers the threshold of nuclear war by raising the possibility of a "limited" nuclear exchange involving "surgical strikes" against military targets, and it raises the prospect of a successful first strike in which the initial salvo against an opponent's retaliatory forces is so devastating that a second strike in response is no longer feasible. Countercity targeting reflects an understanding that it is not possible to fight and win a nuclear war.

MAD theorists also believe that once a nuclear exchange is initiated there can be no avoidance of general holocaust. War games conducted in the 1960s involving a limited nuclear response to a Soviet invasion of Europe with conventional forces indicated that there would be little hope of restraint. Even if the war was fought initially within clear ground rules there would be little incentive to prevent the side losing at a particular level of exchange from moving up to the next level of response. "Even under the most favorable assumptions," argued two of Secretary of Defense Robert McNamara's aides, "it appeared that between 2 and 20 million Europeans would be killed, with widespread damage to the enemy in the affected area and a high risk of 100 million dead if the war was escalated to attacks on the cities."[2] McNamara himself concluded that "there is little chance of limiting a conflict that has already seen the . . . widespread use of tactical nuclear weapons to tactical nuclear weapons. I think that such a conflict would almost certainly evolve very rapidly into a full nuclear exchange between the Communist bloc and the West.[3]

In general, members of the MAD school believe that nuclear weapons have qualitatively changed the conduct of war. It is no longer possible to conceive of war in terms of traditional strategy. This can be seen most clearly in the widespread recognition among MAD adherents that it is not possible to build an effective defense. For a long time it appeared that there were only two possible forms of defense: an antiballistic missile system (ABM) and civil defense. Both were rejected primarily on grounds of their technical infeasibility.

An effective ABM system would destabilize the nuclear balance by raising the possibility that a country could launch a first strike, shoot down incoming retaliatory missiles, and thus escape significant damage. In 1972 each side tacitly agreed to leave itself vulnerable to attack by signing a formal treaty that greatly restricted the number of ABM sites that each would deploy. This permanent vulnerability, it was hoped, would effectively deter attack.

In theory, an effective system of civil defense capable of limiting the damage imposed by the attacking power could also destabilize mutual assured destruction. No such system has been devised and, despite the fact that many of us received ideological training in the form of diving under wooden desks in elementary school, Americans have never been convinced that such a system is possible. The recommendation by an official government committee that each family build a fallout shelter was met with mass indifference. And while a civil-defense program exists in name, its low budget allocations reflect official recognition that defense and protection of the population during nuclear war are impossible. McNamara concluded that "it is not practical to think of protecting our population against thermal effects and blast effects for all conceivable forms of nuclear attack." When asked what current plans are in the case of a nuclear attack, American public health officials respond, "Take some bulldozers, plow a big trench, push the dead into the trench, cover them with lye and shove the dirt back over."[4] The plan is optimistic, if only because it assumes operating bulldozers and someone to operate them.

Amendments to MAD

The overwhelming destructive power of the offensive (but never to the point of wiping out an opponent's retaliatory or second-strike forces), the impossibility of creating an effective defense, the stability that results from counter-city targeting, and the difficulties of containing "limited" nuclear war formed the mainstays of an idealized policy of mutual assured destruction. However, the actual behavior of the Kennedy, Johnson, and Nixon Administrations deviated from the basic premises of the position in important ways.

At this point it is useful to distinguish between declaratory policy, that which is announced publicly, and operational policy, that which is followed in actual practice.[5] Until very recently, Washington's declaratory policy was deterrence. Operational policy has been something quite different. Here is where secrecy is so important. A secretary of defense can officially declare that we are aiming at cities so that Moscow will never think of initiating a first strike and deterrence will be preserved. In the meantime, civilian strategists, military officers, and high-ranked defense officials may make decisions on an entirely different basis. In particular, they may develop a counterforce strategy. In some cases the reasons for the difference between doctrine and actual decisions are bureaucratic in origin. For example, in theory, the United States did not have to build more bombs than necessary to achieve the official definition of unacceptable damage. In practice, the United States stockpiled far more. Interservice rivalries contributed to the decision to have *each* leg of the strategic triad (missiles, submarines, and "manned" bombers) capable of delivering unacceptable damage.[6] And top policymakers preferred to set as their real goal staying ahead of the Soviet Union, even though it was not apparent what benefit could be derived from this quantitative advantage. Postwar presidents also knew that Soviet improvements leading towards strategic parity would be leaked to the press in exaggerated form by elements hostile to mutual assured destruction and that both sides would become politically vulnerable as a result. No president was willing to fight these political forces head on (each in fact chose among his key advisors individuals who favored counterforce).

In addition, these presidents and their secretaries of defense made important compromises in order to blunt opposition to arms control talks with the Soviet Union. These compromises, usually on the order of giving the go-ahead to weapons systems that were thought to have little significance, had an unfortunate tendency to backfire, leading – after technical breakthroughs – to new systems that threaten MAD once again. For example, McNamara's efforts to avoid an ABM system encountered significant political opposition within the defense establishment. To minimize the costs of his decision to deploy only a scaleddown version of the ABM, McNamara approved Air Force requests to begin MIRV-ing American missiles (placing a number of different warheads on the top of each missile so that many different targets could be hit from one launcher). By proliferating the number of warheads, MIRV technology has once again raised the possibility of a first strike. In other words, to protect the MAD premise that neither side should offer an effective defense, McNamara approved of programs to develop an offensive sufficiently overwhelming that it could potentially wipe out the entire Soviet retaliatory force. In a similar manner, President Carter, to appease opposition to his decision to delay production of the B-1 bomber and deployment of the neutron bomb, permitted the Air Force to experiment further with air-launched cruise missiles (ALCMs) and to develop the MX systems that have now become threats in their own right. This tendency to trade off one weapons system for another, found even among those committed to MAD premises, injects a dangerous degree of uncertainty.

Bureaucratic impulses do not exhaust the reasons for the contradictions within MAD. Each administration refused to renounce explicitly the first use of nuclear weapons. To do so, it was thought, would be to give up a negotiating advantage over the Soviet Union. And in the case of a regional war in Europe, it is the declaratory policy of the United States to use nuclear weapons in response to a conventional invasion by the Warsaw Pact. For its part, Moscow *has* renounced the first use of nuclear weapons.

Some policy advisors also believed that stockpiling nuclear weapons beyond the level necessary to achieve unacceptable damage would result in greater leverage in direct negotiations with Moscow over non-nuclear issues, and that it would deter the Soviet Union from supporting revolutionary movements in the Third World. The American nuclear arsenal, under this "Type II deterrence," was supposed to prevent the Soviet Union from supplying or coming to the aid of opponents of the United States in underdeveloped countries, even after Washington intervened militarily.

Even more dangerous is the fact that the Standard Integrated Operating Plan (SIOP), or list of targets to be struck during a nuclear war, reflected a war-fighting strategy of hitting Soviet military bases rather than cities. In this respect, Carter's Presidential Directive 59, which announced a counterforce posture, was only a public and formal statement of a policy that had been enacted years before. Even McNamara, in a 1962 speech, stated a counterforce position that was presented as a humanitarian effort to limit the number of deaths in the event of a nuclear exchange. (The new targeting policy required the Soviet Union to cooperate and also aim at United States military targets, since it would make no sense for the United States to shoot only at Soviet missiles if Moscow continued to aim at American cities. In this case, the Soviet Union refused to accept these new ground rules – rules that appeared to make a nuclear exchange more likely in the first place. Nikita Khrushchev immediately termed McNamara's speech "monstrous.") It may not be a coincidence that Moscow's introduction of missiles into Cuba in 1962, leading to the October missile crisis later that year, came from a reading of US intentions as newly belligerent, with some response necessary in order to establish a modicum of credibility.

In the final analysis, those officials believing in MAD used the bomb as deterrence in two distinct ways. One was to deter nuclear war. The other was to deter the expansion of socialism and to prevent an increase in Soviet global influence. There is a tension between these two senses of deterrence, with aggression in pursuit of the second threatening to undermine the first. Despite this important consideration, the general acceptance of mutual assured destruction provided a base, not only intellectually but roughly in practice as well, that stabilized the strategic balance with Moscow. Some degree of safety was the result; not absolute, of course, but some minimal protection. It is that tentative stability that is being eroded today.

The Impact of Technological Improvements

Over the 1970s, dramatic improvements in technology and engineering, centered more on delivery systems than on nuclear warheads themselves, have helped alter the terms in which nuclear war is being discussed.

Two new developments, both initiated by the United States, are particularly ominous: first, increased accuracy in the delivery of warheads increases offensive capacity; and second, improvements in both anti-submarine warfare and space-based lasers capable of destroying Soviet satellites and missiles enhance defense. The general significance of these technical changes has been to increase the possibility of a first strike, by making it seem feasible that one side could launch an attack effective and accurate enough to wipe out virtually all of an opponent's retaliatory force, while its improved defenses could minimize the damage resulting from missiles escaping the initial salvo. If each side achieved a first-strike capacity, at least in the minds of top leaders, then the pressure, in a crisis, to strike first would be immense, since the consequences of waiting for the other side to go first would be the destruction of one's own society. Instead of each side being deterred by the recognition that the other side would destroy it, one side would have to strike first in order to ensure its own survival. Rather than survival through a balance of terror, the only hope for survival would come by pulling the trigger first.

Are these technical changes actually on the order of creating a first-strike capacity? No. The premises of mutual assured destruction have not been contradicted. Military equipment has not exactly established an unblemished reputation for reliability. The consequences of just normal levels of malfunctioning would be catastrophic. Thus it is unlikely that the current ability of each side to wreak unfathomable damage on the other, no matter what the circumstances, will be changed. No one would win. But technology is slowly changing the perceptions of the leadership of each side, moving each closer to the trigger. Technology by itself, however, is not the threat. It is the shifts in strategic doctrine accompanying these changes that pose the real danger.

The NUTs

Nuclear-use theorists (NUTs) believe that a nuclear war will not inevitably escalate to a full exchange with each side serving up everything that it has at the other. Further, they think it is possible to conceive of different types of nuclear war, encompassing different levels of hostility, and that it is important for the US to be superior at all levels. In fact, because it is dependent upon counterforce weapons, nuclear-use theory is an extremely aggressive stance which, if accepted by an American president, may mean the end of all of us.

101

Three distinct contexts should be kept in mind in assessing the strength of the NUTs. The first is the rapidly maturing technology that is making the idea of fighting and winning a nuclear war conceivable – given a particular myopia. The second context involves important changes in the international situation. The dangers here reflect the fact that the United States is a declining power that nonetheless seeks to retain its influence over the political and economic future of much of the world. That influence is no longer structured through a system, such as the monetary arrangements established at Bretton Woods at the end of World War II. Tensions have appeared with the "natural" allies of the United States, such as the countries of Western Europe and Japan. Some of these tensions involve military issues, but new directions can be seen most clearly in the failure of summit meetings among these industrialized countries to establish coordinated economic policies, and in the importance that Europe attaches to burgeoning trade with Eastern Europe and the Soviet Union. To partially compensate, and to build up a new set of local regional powers, Washington has negotiated new bilateral ties with Egypt, China, Pakistan, Chile, Israel, Morocco, Saudi Arabia, and a number of military dictatorships in Central and South America. In general, relations with these countries are less the product of similar social systems than of common security concerns.

This is not to exclude economic concerns entirely, but to note that military assistance has become the cutting edge in establishing these new allies. At the same time, each of these regional powers is involved in new areas of instability frequently caused by revolutionary movements. There has been a marked tendency on the part of the United States to respond with policies that intensify a military definition of the situation and to hold the Soviet Union and what are perceived to be its regional allies – Cuba, Vietnam, Syria, Nicaragua – responsible for the trouble. The NUTs have concluded that diplomacy and conventional weaponry have accomplished little in defusing these crises and in many cases have only served to exacerbate local and international tensions. The United States is thus faced with an unstable world situation, with many nations undergoing dramatic realignment or experiencing new political pressures. All of this is occurring without a coherent policy response on the part of the United States, save that of spending more on the military budget and blaming the trouble on Moscow. Foreign policy, as traditionally conceived, has enjoyed fewer successes. It is in this context of declining world power for the United States that strategic doctrines concerning the use of nuclear weapons are becoming more belligerent.

A third context is the history of hostility towards the Soviet Union, a factor that is not appreciated by many on the left who have come of age politically since the 1960s. That generation focused on US intentions in underdeveloped countries, on "counterrevolution," rather than on the enmity that has been directed against Moscow. Within a general stance of belligerence towards the

Soviet Union, political leaders in the United States fall into two camps. Each has a particular view of Soviet society, the nature of competition between Moscow and Washington, and what should be the proper response from the United States. Advocates of MAD belong to one group; the NUTs to another.

Implicit in the deterrence position is the notion that the USSR has legitimate national security concerns, especially given the hostility between Moscow and Peking. In this view, the Soviet economy has weaknesses, particularly its dependence on foreign assistance in both agriculture and technology. But these weaknesses are not so severe that the economy will collapse from within. The Russian people and the different nationalities are not overjoyed with the Soviet state, but they will support their country when provoked by threats from the West. The competition between the United States and the USSR can be regulated and channeled into non-war-threatening forms. And civilians still control the Soviet governing apparatus, even though the military has come to take a larger percentage of the budget.

None of these tenets is accepted by the NUTs, who have a very different view of the Soviet Union. They see it as inherently expansionary and militaristic, but at the same time as a peculiarly fragile state. The NUTs think that the nationalities and Eastern Europe are on the verge of revolt against the Soviet state, and that the Soviet governing apparatus is dominated by the military. The fabric of Soviet society is brittle and the proper combination of economic, political, and military pressures will create a breakdown. For example, Richard Pipes, a Harvard historian, believes that "militancy, a commitment to violence, and coercion [are] as central to Soviet communism as profit is to a market-oriented society."[7] As a result, attempts to limit arms will fail to produce a corresponding response from the Soviet Union. Arms control should be subordinated to the greater goal of reducing the role of the Soviet state in the world arena. The United States must respond with superior forces – politically, economically, and morally.

How does this general stance towards the Soviet Union become transposed in the specifics of nuclear strategy? The current generation of NUTs feels that developing a "menu of options," a list of different targets, makes sense only in the context of a clearly enunciated will to victory. There must be a plan.

While there is some internal disagreement among the NUTs over details, all agree that the United States should target the military, the state, political command centers, and the KGB. Here a connection can be drawn between the target list and the general perception that the Kremlin is ready to crumble at a moment's notice. In this view, a limited nuclear war would knock off the head of the monster, and the various nationalities and Eastern Europe would finish the job. Colin Gray, for example, argues that the "United States and its allies probably should not aim at achieving military defeat of the Soviet Union, considered as a unified whole; instead it should seek to impose such military stalemate and defeat as needed to persuade disaffected Warsaw Pact allies and ethnic minorities that they can assert their own values in very active political ways."[8] Other NUTs argue that it is important to target the recoverable economy of the Soviet Union so that military defeat in the traditional sense can be achieved.

Besides developing a different list of targets, one of the programs most favored by the NUTs is command, control, and communication, or C^3 (sometimes intelligence is added to the list in which case the notation is C^3I). C^3 is important because any scenario that assumes that a nuclear war can be fought also must assume that communications still exist, that command centers are still around so that decisions can be made, and that control lines are intact so that, once made, these decisions can be implemented. If we are in the middle of a scenario of "exchanging" Houston for Kiev, we have to know if the former has in fact been attacked, whether or not the attack missed, and whether or not we managed to hit Kiev. Then somebody has to be around to assess the outcome and damage, make an assessment as to what Moscow is likely to do, and then tell the military what to do.

This scenario assumes that nuclear war would be something like World War II. There are many things wrong with this view, however. One of the most important is virtually unrecognized: the effects of electromagnetic pulse (EMP) on vital communication and control capacities. Nuclear explosions set off above the United States may bathe command transmissions with EMP and render inoperative efforts to coordinate a controlled attack. EMP reduces controlled response under conditions of nuclear war to a huge unknown. Chaos would reign. Needless to say, these possible implications of EMP are not discussed by nuclear-use theorists.

The NUTs think that the Soviet Union plans to win a nuclear war. They point out that 20 million Russians died during World War II, the implication being that the Kremlin would not mind expending that many people again in order to dominate the world. In the meantime, they argue, the Soviet Union is actively developing its civil defense effort. T. K. Jones, a former consultant to the Boeing corporation and now Deputy Undersecretary of Defense for Strategic and Nuclear Forces, has argued that the Soviet Union has dispersed its population, hardened its protection of industrial sites, and prepared blast and fallout shelters so that Soviet leaders can expect that they will lose "only" 10 million people.[9] General Daniel Graham, a former director of the Defense Intelligence Agency, explains the situation that, in his mind, an American leader would then confront: "The Soviets evacuate their cities and hunker down. They then move against NATO or Yugoslavia or China or the Middle East with superior conventional forces. The United States is thus faced with the demand to stay out or risk a nuclear exchange in which 100 million Americans would die, as opposed to 10 million Russians."[10] To counter Soviet efforts and to develop American determination to win, the NUTs lay great emphasis on "damage-limitation" programs. Civil defense and the ABM are two examples.

The NUTs also have an extremely harsh judgment of even the idea of arms control. For them, the SALT process has given MAD theory and strategic stability a legitimacy that they do not deserve. One NUT has argued that SALT "enshrined mutual assured destruction and strategic parity; it made challenges to these *idées fixes* illegitimate, irresponsible, and beyond the pale of responsible debate."[11] Arms control efforts have the effect of distracting officials from developing long-term strategy as well as much-needed weapons systems to match that strategy.

In thinking about nuclear war, the NUTs argue that nuclear weapons do not represent a "great divide," a qualitative shift in war or international politics. War with nuclear weapons is different only in degree from war without nuclear weapons.[12] International politics has not changed much either. "Statecraft with nuclear weapons," says one representative, "looks very much like statecraft without nuclear weapons. Wars are fought, force is threatened, crises are waged, arms races are run, territory is coveted and allies are hoarded. The 'rules of the road' in international politics are more restrictive than previously was the case, but the same activities are pursued; the basic competitive character of international politics has accommodated nuclear energy."[13] It was thoughts like these that provoked Albert Einstein to remark, "Nuclear weapons have changed everything except how people think."

One of the scariest aspects of this position is that the target is the American president as much as it is Moscow. Confronted with an actual crisis, the NUTs know that the reaction of most presidents is to avoid pushing the button. Colin Gray argues that "one function of nuclear doctrines and the evolution of strategies is to make sure that political leaders in a crisis should not shy away from employment options and fall back upon instinctive deterrence actions. The defense community has to design clear options so that a reasonable leader would not ever be self-deterred."[14]

One step towards this goal is a harsh attack against the doctrine of mutual assured destruction on moral grounds – claiming that MAD holds civilians hostage, that it has no plan for civil defense and damage limitation, and that there is no difference between levels of nuclear war. There is a difference, NUTs counter, between 10 million and 100 million dead. A president, claim the NUTs, "should feel less inhibited over the prospective dispatch of (say) thirty (or even 130) reentry vehicles, than he would over the dispatch of one to three thousand bombs particularly when the targets for those thirty to 130 reentry vehicles [have] been chosen very carefully with a view to inflicting the minimum possible population loss on the Soviet Union. . . ."[15]

Possible Explanations

How can we explain the persistence of these dangerous views, the expansion of the defense budget, and the renewed commitment to new strategic programs? First there is the economic explanation: that behind the large defense budget lie the interests of large corporations. Individual firms profit from contracts that are delivered on a cost-plus basis from the Pentagon. Other firms benefit by manufacturing products that are civilian spinoffs from research originally conducted for the military. The Boeing 707 airliner from the B-52, freeze-dried food, and paints with special properties are examples. Advanced capitalism, the argument continues, suffers from a lack of effective demand. Unlike social programs, the stimulus provided by military spending does not interfere with the dominant priorities of the economy. The result of this "safe" form of government spending is lower unemployment and a "multiplier effect" in which the effects of defense spending spread from contractors to layers of subcontractors. Representatives of the capitalist class indicate their general approval of high levels of defense spending privately, through speeches, and by their direct participation in policy groups such as the Council on Foreign Relations, the Trilateral Commission, and the Committee for Economic Development.

Whether or not this form of "military Keynesianism" existed in the past, such a motivation is not behind increases in the defense budget during the last two years of the Carter Administration and the still further increase due to follow under Reagan. The dominant economic philosophy is for a diminished role for the state. Wall Street is nervous about high levels of military spending. Moreover, military spending is extremely capital-intensive; it produces fewer jobs than does government spending in the civilian sector. What is often not appreciated in this regard is the difference between spending on strategic and conventional weapons, the economic impact of the former being yet again more restricted. The nature of military technology has become so esoteric that the trickle-down effect that was once present has become attenuated. Profits and economic gain on the part of some firms clearly play a background role in explaining the growth of the defense budget and nuclear weaponry. But it is equally clear that the main explanation must be sought elsewhere. The NUTs do not represent the business community.

The second reason is a special application of the theory of the military-industrial complex to the field of nuclear weapons. In this view, militarism is a powerful force in its own right, dominating capital investment and research and development funds, and spreading a "military definition of reality." Foreign policy by diplomacy, carried out by an independent and professional foreign service, has declined. In its place are military alliances and the techniques of "crisis management," in which the armed forces exert an inordinate influence. Defense contractors are part of this establishment, relying on state spending for profits that are both high and secure. In addition, scientists and engineers are attracted to the military or to defense contractors by high salaries and by the prospect of working on projects that are the "state of the art." New weapons are the product of several pressures within the military–industrial complex: scientists who push their particular programs, different agencies contending for larger shares of the budget; and interservice rivalries that produce an arms race within an arms race. In addition, a technological imperative contributes a steady, irresistible push to the accumulation of more weaponry. One consequence of all this is that modernization of the traditional industrial sector lags behind, leading to a decline in productivity. (Currently one-half of all capital investment is devoted to the military and more than a third of all the physicists, mathematician and engineers are employed in arms-related production.) Corporations and state enterprises in Japan and Western Europe invest more in new plants and equipment and secure a competitive advantage as a result. The dismal performance of the American steel and automobile industries vis-à-vis their foreign counterparts is a case in point. In this view, both the American people and most corporations suffer from this encroaching militarism.

Closely identified in the United States with the work of C. Wright Mills and Seymour Melman, the military–industrial complex thesis has won new adherents from the socialist tradition – those who used to believe that the benefits of military spending trickled down to the capitalist class as a whole. In particular, E. P. Thompson has recently argued that the vast stockpiles of nuclear weapons, and the accompanying pressures for modernization of the delivery systems, represent a "mode of exterminism."[16] The bomb is a weapons *system* with an accompanying social structure, an organization of labor, a hierarchy of command, research and development, and specific rules. "Exterminism," Thompson concludes, has as its institutional base "the weapons-system, and the entire economic, scientific, political and ideological support system to that weapons-system – the social system which researches it, 'chooses' it, produces it, polices it, justifies it, and maintains it in being."

One consequence of the development of nuclear weapons and plans for their use is further centralization of power in the executive branch of government, and in particular in the presidency. Indeed, an important aspect of nuclear weapons is that they further not only the interests of the national security apparatus but specifically those of the presidency. Control over strategic policy becomes a convenient mechanism to shape foreign policy, including relations with the Soviet Union and the European allies, while remaining comparatively immune from popular pressures, or even the influence of lobbies and interests located within the elite. In turn, strategic policy helps the president to define national security in ways that amplify his own power to control domestic debate on the issue. It helps to define what the "threats" are to the United States and what should be the appropriate response. Presidents are attracted to nuclear weapons because the special qualities of these weapons grant them additional political leverage. This observation probably applies to all executive authority of the modern state no matter what the economic system.

Economic interests, the organizational interests of the military-industrial complex, and presidential interests form a background within which the nuclear arsenal has grown to such enormous proportions. But these reasons do not explain the specific right-wing cast to the current debate, particularly the resurgence of nuclear-use doctrines.

Ultimately, the existence of the NUTs can only be understood within the context of the political current that remains so hostile to the Soviet Union. Since 1917 one faction of policymakers has persisted in seeing the Soviet Union as a revolutionary state committed to ideological warfare and world domination. There is no chance of compromise, no room for détente or any form of peaceful coexistence. The reason, in this view, for the tension between the Soviet Union and the United States is the very character and nature of the Russian state. The behavior of the Kremlin is firmly rooted in Russian history and cannot be changed by American diplomacy. Indeed, efforts to achieve diplomatic settlements between the two countries, including arms control, have been extremely dangerous. The Kremlin has been encouraged by these actions and interprets them as expressions of political weakness. Diplomacy only redoubles their efforts to expand their influence. The only proper response on the part of the United States is military pressure.

The Peace Movement

How does one respond to the "debate" between the advocates of MAD and the NUTs? One understandable reaction, certainly, is that both sides are absolutely insane. To any person with a shred of human decency, politics through the threatened use of nuclear weapons is deeply reprehensible. What a danger to life from both sides! A peace movement must shout it loud and clear: we are against a world in which the accumulated means of destruction threaten the very existence of the human race. Only a strong peace movement with its own identity and organization can prevent the day when, during a crisis, both sides will confront the possibility that the only chance for survival will be to push the button first. The question is the character of that peace movement, and the strategies that it should adopt. A successful movement will have to be totally opposed to the arms race in general and nuclear weapons in particular. At the same time, that movement will have to be aware of the differences between MAD and the NUTs and will have to make pragmatic compromises with the first camp. Finding the proper balance between these two stances is admittedly difficult and will undoubtedly be a source of serious tension in the peace movement. But the first question is: Why do we need a peace movement to block the dangers of nuclear war?

It could be argued that the mainstream economic and political elites will check the NUTs. There is, after all, no conceivable class interest in destroying the planet. Corporations have an interest in expanding trade with the Soviet Union, not in demolishing it. Corporate leaders do not desire an overly military definition of US–Soviet relations. Détente could be of enormous economic benefits – as already proved in Europe. Nuclear-use theorists threaten the stability that corporations need to plan future growth. As a result, over the postwar period, leaders in the business community who have taken a position on strategic issues have generally endorsed mutually assured destruction. This is because MAD creates a *regulated* competition that neither eliminates nuclear weapons nor poses a realistic first-strike opportunity. The existence of nuclear weapons helps contain socialism and structures a bipolar world that the United States dominates. Supporters of MAD say privately that the nuclear weapons are not to be used. At the same time, it is thought that the huge American arsenal limits the political influence of the Soviet Union. MAD supports the general interests of the economic and political elite without threatening a conflagration that would destroy the capitalist as well as the socialist world.

Yet, when measured against the goal of creating enduring world peace, elite opposition to nuclear war is extremely weak. Why? A SALT treaty based on MAD continues to concentrate power in Washington and, to a lesser extent, Moscow, leaving other world tensions unresolved. Our security, in the sense of lowering the chances for nuclear war arising from a direct conflict between the two major powers, might be improved. But world politics would remain volatile and the threat of war stemming from regional conflict would continue. SALT has not checked technical advances in the realm of nuclear weapons and delivery systems, thus leaving open the possibility that some combination of elements would, at some time in the future, coalesce into a new first-strike capacity. In addition, the elite supporters of MAD have never, by themselves, been able to achieve a treaty that *unambiguously* reflected the logic of deterrence. In their details the two SALT agreements leave loopholes subject to exploitation by the NUTs.

Finally, elite support for MAD preserves the possibility of presidential manipulation of nuclear weapons for partisan benefit and accomplishes little towards the goal of penetrating the atmosphere of secrecy that restricts public knowledge and debate. One danger is that presidents who attempt to use nuclear politics to create coalitions, or to send political signals, can be duped and used. This happened to Jimmy Carter when he attempted to use an arms-control proposal to secure support from both the dovish and hawkish wings of the Democratic Party. Thus, to overcome a variety of elements – the reticence of the elite, the trade-off dynamic among different constituencies of the military establishment, the attempt to control weapons systems, the atmosphere of secrecy, a foreign policy based on a bipolar view of the world – and to build political momentum capable of pushing beyond the limits of a balance of terror, a peace movement is necessary. That movement will have to demonstrate once again that people can change history, that we are not helpless victims before the bomb. Existing political elites will not end the danger of nuclear war on their own.

The next question is, what kind of politics should the peace movement present? Here one is tempted to argue that the stance should be outright opposition. Pushed initially by the NATO decision to deploy American Pershing II and cruise missiles, Europeans are now calling for disarmament, nuclear-free zones, and a weapons freeze – all with good effect. Demonstrators number in the hundreds of thousands. There is a clear feeling that Europe should not be the battleground for the two superpowers. While the final outcome is not clear, one can already detect the dramatic impact of the peace movement upon decision-makers now backpedaling away from their original decision.

Can the same process be duplicated in the United States? I don't think so. The European example is inspirational and will certainly help the development of our own movement. But the circumstances and the position of Europe and the United States in the world arena are very different. More specifically, the demand for complete disarmament is, in the American context, premature. Within the United States, an effective long-run attack will best develop by combining the impulse that nuclear weapons are horrible monstrosities with a more pragmatic view which attempts to understand and affect the more immediate debate, even if the parameters of that debate appear hopelessly skewed in favor of the military establishment. The peace movement cannot afford to ignore developments within the political world of nuclear weapons. Nuclear weapons are power, not just to destroy, but to exercise foreign and even domestic policy. The much-needed moral outrage at the prospect of demolishing the world, the fear that emanates from their threatened use, needs to be supplemented by an equally vital sensitivity to debates within the national security apparatus itself. The peace movement needs two fronts: efforts to reduce and finally eliminate the vast stockpile of nuclear weapons, and direct engagement with the politics of the arms race.

In the short run, the success of that peace movement will be consolidated in specific arms-control treaties that are negotiated and signed by individuals who have traditionally represented MAD. These interim agreements will in a limited but nonetheless real sense decrease the chances for war. These agreements also carry the danger that political momentum towards the ultimate goal of disarmament might be lost. Some, for example, may accept the interim agreements as victory. We will have to learn the political skill necessary to balance the need for continued popular pressure against the need to consolidate that pressure into arms-control agreements that may continue to legitimate dominant governing groups.

Why? "Pure" oppositional pressure – that is, pressure from outside the existing arena of political debate – carries the danger, even where it is successful, of allowing those on the inside to wriggle off the hook. President Nixon, for example, was able to rededicate Washington's commitment to a noncommunist Indochina, at terrible cost to both Americans and Vietnamese, even after the antiwar movement blocked the introduction of additional ground troops in 1968 and forced the abdication of Lyndon Johnson. Decision-makers may be forced to choose a policy that is different from what they want to do; but, in the absence of specific alternatives, they may be able to reestablish their preferred political direction in new form.

Let me continue to use the movement against the war in Vietnam as an example. At specific points in the history of the war, the movement was able to prevent Washington from undertaking significant escalation. The antiwar movement also prevented the Johnson Administration from passing tax measures that would have reduced the inflationary impact of the war. Finally, the movement left an important legacy, the so-called "Vietnam syndrome," or fear on the part of American policymakers that domestic opposition will be provoked once again by American military intervention in underdeveloped countries. In these ways, the antiwar movement was an enormous success.

But the antiwar movement did not lead to a fundamental change of foreign and military policy. The movement never really moved from opposition to the war to a much-needed, full presentation of the ways that the United States might change its economic and political relations with Third World countries and how we should respond to revolutionary movements within those countries. The need to provide a full *critique* of American policy was recognized by some participants in the movement. But the typical method of acting upon this need was to give speeches denouncing American intervention and seeing that intervention as an outgrowth of imperialism. By the end of the war, demonstrations would normally include a speaker who would present this point of view (rather than criticizing the war because it was a "mistake"). But a speaker at a demonstration is not a substitute for a full political position. In the absence of a well-developed *alternative,* the continued existence of the movement was dependent upon the war itself. Once again the movement recognized this, at least implicitly. As the war came to an end, some participants complained that "our issue is being taken away." In fact, there were plenty of issues. But the antiwar movement could not survive beyond Vietnam because it was based on opposition to Vietnam, and not on developing the political alliances and specific alternatives that could fundamentally restructure our foreign and military policy.

Thus, the argument for engaging the existing debate and the existing political establishment is *not* one for a single-minded emphasis on peace to the exclusion of every other social concern. Nor is it an argument for socialists to be content with liberal reform. It is a more offensive strategy, one that recognizes that significant change in our nuclear policies will not take place unless there is significant change in political forces within the United States. The question becomes one of creating the specific context in which opposition to the growing threat of nuclear war can develop. That context is a call to politics, not only in the sense of opposing existing madness, but in presenting specific alternatives that would begin to change the bipolar world, and would raise deeper issues concerning the place of militarism in our society and the general direction of our foreign policy.

We need to elaborate a critique of how "security" has been used and abused to protect the international interests of American business and the state, and to explain how current policies, taken in the name of "national security," are actually undermining it. But we shouldn't shy away from explaining how an alternative set of policies would actually increase our security. We need to be able to explain to skeptics that our policies will promote a more peaceful world and will encourage countries that are perceived to be our "enemies," particularly the Soviet Union, to behave in ways that bolster faith and confidence. We must be able to answer questions regarding the nature of the "Soviet threat" no matter how much that term has been manipulated for right-wing purposes. For how socialists and the peace movement handle the question, "Are the Russians coming?" will certainly remain the most important foreign policy issue for the rest of the decade.

By offering proposals for converting useless and dangerous military programs to civilian purposes, and by pointing out that our domestic interests lie with promoting an international New Deal, and not in attempting to exploit the Third World, a peace movement could begin to change two of the most damaging elements of the American economy. Ultimately our security lies in siding with movements for progressive change and with reordering global economic inequalities, and not in perfecting weapons systems. Only a movement with an eye on the structure of future peace can lower the dangers of war that loom so ominously in the present.

Postscript

Since this article was written in 1981, many changes have taken place, most notably the dramatic political transformations of Eastern Europe and the Soviet Union. These changes have affected the intra-elite debate over nuclear doctrine, public opinion on the nuclear arms race, and the peace movement.

First, in the struggle between the advocates of deterrence and nuclear war-fighting, it is now clear that the MAD position has won out. One of the most significant developments of the decade has been the gradual acceptance by nuclear strategists of many of the tenets of the peace movement. The degree to which the majority of civilian professional strategists have rejected the possibility of fighting and winning a nuclear war is quite remarkable. Indeed, many professionals are now skeptical of a military and political role for nuclear weapons and are moving towards the endorsement of a posture of minimal deterrence in which each side would have fewer than 1,000 warheads.

Second, the chances for significant nuclear arms control are now reasonably good. "From MAD to NUTs" argued that much arms control preserved the possibilities for nuclear modernization and continued competition between Moscow and Washington. The Intermediate Nuclear Forces (INF) Treaty, while not eliminating this pattern, was nonetheless significant in its removal of an entire category of weapons after they had been deployed. INF also provided for on-site inspection to verify several of its provisions. In fact, over the past five years the entire process of verification has undergone significant development both conceptually and in technique. Future arms control measures will constrain nuclear weapons development and provide added stability. (Of course, as long as nuclear weapons exist, the possibility of their use can never be totally eliminated.) While the political will to enact their recommendations is not yet present, it is still significant that strategists in both the USSR and the US are now modeling minimal deterrence. These projects are cooperative – experts visit each other's institutes – and reflect the most important premise of the nuclear age: that security cannot be achieved unilaterally.

Third, the NUTs have not disappeared but their influence is very much on the wane. True, we still have the Strategic Defense Initiative (SDI) and other nuclear modernization projects such as the Stealth bomber and the Trident II missile, but these reflect more inertia and the steadfast defense of parochial self-interest rather than strategic design. SDI is a terrible waste of $4 billion. But nobody really believes that it will lead to an effective defense against nuclear warheads. Military planners continue to plan for nuclear war in much the same way as they have done for most of the nuclear age. But the surrounding circumstances are making their efforts obsolete.

Fourth, US public opinion on security issues has changed drastically since

113

the early 1980s. The public is now much more willing to cut the defense budget, minimize the role of nuclear weapons and engage in cooperative ventures with the Soviet Union and other countries to combat terrorism, AIDS, nuclear proliferation, and environmental decay. Domestically, the need to pay more attention to public education, industrial performance, and social service is now more recognized. What we are missing is a presidential candidate who is willing to articulate these positions.

The final point concerns the role of the peace movement. "From MAD to NUTs" argued that the movement had to bridge the gap between seeking to influence the immediate intra-elite debate and presenting a long-term view of security that was based not on nuclear deterrence, but on international cooperation. The importance of that priority is still with us. The article maintained that it was important for the movement to embrace the term "security" even while giving it a different meaning than that offered by the supporters of nuclear orthodoxy. I still believe that to be the case. The present period offers a fantastic opportunity for the cause of peace. Nuclear tensions and the Cold War between East and West are losing their grip. But Washington continues to persist in Cold War attitudes in its posture towards regional conflicts in Central America and Asia. And, needless to say, the Bush Administration will not take advantage of the new situation to revitalize a progressive political agenda within the United States. The task of developing that agenda, both as a vision and in its practical details, and of providing the drive to enact it, will come, as it always has, from the mobilization of popular movements.

Notes

1. Quoted by Michael Mandelbaum, *The Nuclear Question,* Cambridge: Cambridge University Press 1979, p. 19.

2. Ibid., pp. 102–3.

3. Ibid., pp. 103–4.

4. Ibid., p. 122.

5. In addition, nuclear strategists refer to "hardware" policy, or that which their actual weapons systems will be able to achieve.

6. Kevin Lewis, "The Prompt and Delayed Effects of Nuclear War," *Scientific American* (July 1979).

7. Richard Pipes, "Militarism and the Soviet State," *Daedalus* (Fall 1980).

8. Colin Gray, "Nuclear Strategy: The Case for a Theory of Victory," *International Security* (Summer 1979), p. 80.

9. Jones's estimates are extremely dubious. The Arms Control and Disarmament Agency, for example, has concluded that even after a Soviet initial strike, the United States could still inflict 100 million deaths if the Soviet Union took no defense precautions, and, if it did take precautions, 70 to 85 million deaths if we aimed at evacuation centers. The Defense Department has estimated likely Soviet casualties at 55 million despite civil-defense efforts. See James Fallows, *The National Defense,* New York: Random House 1981, p. 161.

10. Ibid., p. 146.

11. Joseph Kruzel, "Arms Control and American Defense Policy: New Alternatives and Old Realities," *Daedalus* (Winter 1981), p. 140.

12. Colin Gray, "Across the Nuclear Divide: Strategic Studies Past and Present," *International Security* (Summer 1977).

13. Ibid., p. 32.

14. Gray, "Nuclear Strategy," p. 57.

15. Ibid., p. 64.

16. E. P. Thompson, "Notes on Exterminism: The Last State of Civilization," *New Left Review*, no. 121 (May–June 1980), pp. 3–31.

7

The Wilting of the Rose

The French Socialist Experiment

(1986)

George Ross and Tony Daley

Spring 1981 brought a glimmer of hope to progressive forces everywhere when the French left came to power. The victory of François Mitterrand in the presidential elections in May brought an overwhelming majority of left deputies in the subsequent parliamentary elections in June 1981. With five years of secure power, the French Socialists and their Communist allies embarked on a journey that promised a true social transformation. The left victory seemed all the more remarkable given the apparent tide of support for the right in most industrial countries where high unemployment rates in most national contexts forced labor on the defensive. The postwar settlement was being challenged in most of the advanced countries. Here was a left which had been excluded during the entire postwar boom and had yet to make any compromises with the seductive comforts of consumer capitalism and the Keynesian welfare state. It promised to transform society through fundamental reforms and the introduction of a Gallic version of workplace democracy, *autogestion*. Might it be the bearer of the long elusive "third way" between traditional social democracy and communism?

Almost five years later the left majority was politically defeated. Unable to retain its old constituencies and incapable of appealing to new ones, the left lost the parliamentary elections of March 1986. Yet the defeat did not chastise the left or revive left values. Moreover, when Mitterrand engineered his reelection to the presidency in May 1988, he did not revive the left, which is more divided now than at any other period in the last forty years. The largest component of that left, the Socialist Party, has clearly given up on socialism.

The story of the left experience in France is a sad one of economic "realism" and political malpractice. The new left government came out of the 1981 elections with all reformist guns ablaze. For one year it worked hyper-energetically to humanize France's legal system, redistribute income, replenish the welfare state, promote economic growth, and implement three major sets of structural reforms (decentralization, industrial-relations reforms, and nationalizations). If the Mitterrand regime had stopped there, it would now be remembered as the most radical interlude in advanced capitalism since the immediate postwar period. In response to adverse economic circumstances only partially of its own creation, however, it beat a very hasty retreat away from radicalism. Beginning in 1982 it adopted centrist austerity policies, cutting back growth, consumption, and social services to stabilize France's international economic situation. Then, from 1984 onwards, it moved towards what it called "modernization," a euphemism for urging capital to accumulate and rationalize in classic ways at the expense of workers and dramatically rising unemployment.

By the 1986 elections most observers agreed that the French left had succeeded in sanitizing the French economy and society such that, after a decade of deep crisis, new profitability had become possible. Since these policies also involved retreating from the left's own promises and dashing the hopes of its original supporters, "success" came at the cost of substantial political failure. The French left experiment seemed to have admirably remade the twin beds of French capital and the French right.

From Radical Reform to Retrenchment

The Year of Living Dangerously: 1981–1982

François Mitterrand's presidential election manifesto contained a number of radical proposals. The Socialist–Communist government wasted little time implementing its most controversial provisions. Using redistributive measures aimed to benefit lower income groups, it sought to stimulate domestic demand. It then passed a series of important legal reforms, including the abolition of the death penalty, the institution of *habeas corpus*, and new restraints on the police. Within the realm of social policy, the government decreed a fifth week of paid vacation, reduced the length of the legal work week (to 39 hours, a first installment in the goal of 35 hours), proposed retirement at 60, and pushed forward a series of smaller measures to increase the minimum wage, to raise state pensions, and to share out work and thus prevent new unemployment.

After only a few months in office, the government began to implement the "big three" structural reforms of the presidential electoral program. First,

118

governmental decentralization sought to break the long-standing stranglehold of Parisian bureaucrats over regional and local life. Next came the most extensive program of nationalizations which Western capitalism had seen since the immediate post–World War II period. The state did not simply socialize failing industries, although it took control of the ailing steel industry. It brought major parts of the electronics and telecommunications industries as well as the major investment banks within the public domain.[1] Finally, major legislation reformed the hyperconflictual system of industrial relations. Workers and their unions received new rights and channels of representation.

With a flurry of major reforms plus innumerable minor laws and decrees, the new French left regime thus qualified as one of the busiest and most energetic left governments of modern times. Such haste, of course, was deliberate, striking while the political iron was hot, passing the most controversial reforms while the left had a maximum of political resources. The rapid implementation of Keynesian demand-stimulation techniques would serve as a macroeconomic policy prelude to the moment when the left's structural reforms would bring sustained new growth. In the short run, an internationally contagious American recovery would sustain the French economy. In the medium term, the left had confidence that increased research and development as well as the expanded public sector would enable France to "reconquer the domestic market" and find new beachheads in international markets. Sustained economic growth would result in the long run.

The Ambiguities of Structural Reform

The determination to implement major structural reforms – decentralization, industrial-relations changes, and nationalizations – represented the most extraordinary aspect of the left's five years in power. Given their far-reaching scope, these reforms will not show their full effects for a much longer period. Still, enough evidence – to which we now turn – exists to know what they are not.

France has long been administratively and politically overcentralized. Colbertiste visions of statist economic promotion, Jacobin political traditions, and Napoleonic administrative ideas had merged historically to create a social order which made much of France look like a colony run by Parisian imperialists. A caste of elite bureaucrats, trained at a select number of schools and convinced of their capacities to decide for others, ran these "colonial affairs." Local government had limited autonomy from Paris over budgets, taxes, and the definition of its own development.

Before 1981 some consensus had developed that the heavy hand of Paris over the provinces should be lightened. Center-right governments had broached the matter at various points with little success. The newly elected left

119

added its own values to this consensus. According to the Socialists, decentralization ought not only to loosen Parisian control. It should empower ordinary people, enhance democracy, and promote self-management. In contrast to center-right proposals for administrative rearrangement, decentralization would be the first step toward *autogestion*. The decentralization reforms of Year I were substantial.[2] They severely diminished Parisian control by removing many of the powers of the prefect, who had been Paris's agent in the provinces. They also established new regional parliaments and imbued them with electoral legitimacy. New jockeying between center and periphery over local powers and prerogatives, however, provided no clear winner. Decentralization devolved some spending burdens to local levels. Fiscal crises have already confronted numerous local authorities, and public administration job creation ended by 1983. Greater local autonomy has accentuated regional imbalances, given the substantial variations in resources between different areas. Moreover, the adaptive capacities of Parisian administrations to reestablish lost control indirectly cannot be underestimated. Nonetheless, stemming the hypercentralization has made a great difference. Local and regional political life has become more lively. New elections have taken place and new political actors have emerged, reinforcing local identities and often benefiting the right.

However, positive, decentralization was not a particularly *left* step. The left implemented what had already become consensual about decentralization before 1981. The devolution of power represented more a reform for elites than a reform of society to increase participatory democracy. The reform merely codified many of the informal evolutions which had already shifted political control to political bosses, integrating local elites into the central machinery of the state while marginalizing dissent. Instead of bringing government closer to the governed, decentralization has made the machinery heavier. Most importantly, *autogestion* cannot be found in either the spirit or the letter of the reforms.

The reform of the French system of industrial relations also failed to introduce *autogestion*. Virtually alone among capitalist countries, France never had major regulations – similar to the Wagner Act – governing relations between labor and capital. Instead, employers, unions, and workers interacted in a jungle-like environment. Collective bargaining worked feebly. Employers and unions both challenged existing arrangements when the balance of power shifted. Contracts were not legally binding and could therefore be signed one day and denounced the next. This kept French labor free from many of the bureaucratic entrapments that have snared other labor movements. It also meant a situation of constant warfare. Moreover, both unions and employers tended to seek remedies through the state instead of dealing with each other. Consequently, industrial relations became statized and union and employer

120

actions politicized.

No consensus existed about how to reform French labor relations. Only the left and labor favored major changes. At the core of the Auroux Laws (named after the minister responsible for their passage) were provisions to establish new habits of negotiation between capital and labor.[3] Wage bargaining became both annual and compulsory. Workers received new "rights of expression" within the firm. Company health and safety committees received greater prerogatives in production supervision. Unions gained more access to company information concerning decisions and strategies. Nationalized companies even admitted workers to their boards. These measures constituted the "catch-up" phase of the left's reforms. The left envisioned a second "go-ahead" phase of reforms that would further strengthen unions and workers, provided only that these same actors proved resourceful enough to seize and use them. These openings were to be of an *autogestionnaire* kind. Still, although the left sought a new industrial citizenship, it explicitly refrained from challenging fundamental management prerogatives, such as investments, product development, and hirings and firings, at least in the private sector.

The final outcome of the Auroux reforms will depend on the relative strength and intentions of labor and capital over the long run. Since 1981, however, the effects of economic crisis, union decline, and the particularly divisive mood of French organized labor have put unions and workers in a weak position vis-à-vis capital, *despite* left political power. Employers have adapted well to plant-level struggle for control under the new reforms. This evolution has had its ironies. Employer associations vigorously opposed the new reforms. However, bargaining with labor when it is historically weak and when little exists in company coffers to concede has posed few difficulties for capital. New obligations to consult with workers have meshed with new neo-Japanese managerial strategies of the "quality circle" type. By dealing directly with workers, employers have frequently used the "rights of expression" to exclude unions on the shopfloor and to increase productivity. The reinforcement of representative institutions in the workplace enmeshed union militants in deeper levels of bureaucracy, sapping labor's mobilization potential, already at historical lows because of high unemployment. This labor market weakness began well before 1982. Still, the Auroux laws, like decentralization, fit well into an emerging centrist consensus among French elites over capitalist reproduction.

The nationalization of many of France's multinational oligopolies as well as the remainder of the banking sector was a bold step. It also cost a hefty sum in public funds since compensation to former owners was extravagant. Of all the left's reforms, nationalizations addressed most directly the aspirations of the "Old Left." Public ownership had entered the left agenda during the 1930s and had been reaffirmed by both the Socialists and the Communists in the

1940s. It was the cornerstone of the Common Program that cemented the left alliance in 1972. Thus, it served as much a mobilizational as a policy tool.

If by 1981 nationalization had become totemic, its meaning varied widely. One interpretation held that because nationalizations dispossessed capital, they would be the first step towards socialism and social justice. Changes in property ownership would engender miraculous outcomes, in other words. A second interpretation held that since the French bourgeoisie was especially backwards, nationalizations would beget more enlightened management, a second type of miracle, this one in the workplace. A third vision, not exclusively of the left, could be labeled *colbertiste*. Here the state assumed the role of economic initiator because French capital was risk-aversive and incompetent. Economic progress required energetic public intervention. Nationalizations, usually coupled with planning, constituted the most appropriate instruments. The success of Renault served as quintessential evidence. In this third conceptualization, miracles of economic success would follow from the actions of farsighted civil servants.

These visions competed with each other after the left assumed power.[4] The first fell quickly by the wayside. As a lever for a "transition to socialism," nationalization might necessitate the withdrawal of France from international capitalist relations, a dramatic step for which domestic support did not exist. The second vision died a slower death. The notion of disinterested and public-spirited management persisted through Year I given government pressure on the public sector to maintain levels of employment. However, the adoption of "modernization" meant a strict adherence to market forces which drastically curtailed public enterprise enlightenment. State firms had to embrace new technologies and shed labor like other capitalists. The *colbertiste* vision triumphed. French industrialists were condemned as inept and replaced in the public sector by both French technocrats and previously "successful" (and sympathetic) industrialists. Nationalizations became flagships for left plans to adapt the French economy to the new international arena. Increased spending on research and development would result in new products. The public sector would serve as the locomotive to increase overall industrial investment. Nationalized industries would find new niches in the international market while "reconquering" the domestic market.[5]

Even this road to "success" contained roadblocks. First, many of the newly nationalized companies, especially in steel, were already in the red. Bailing them out took initial precedence over greater industrial policy ambitions. These subsidies, in addition to the costs of compensation to former owners, consumed most of the funds which the government had envisioned for new investments. Second, the state restructured the new public firms only after considerable delay. New managers needed to learn their companies. Because of initial confusion over industrial policy goals, plans for industrial reorganization were delayed such that when restructuring came the state found itself in a budget-tightening mood. Delayed reorganization had another, more ironic, result. The left had condemned many of the firms that it would later nationalize for being too aggressively multinational at the expense of domestic investment. Yet, after the nationalizations in 1982, the government, for political reasons, did not want to take anything else into public ownership. Thus, it counseled nationalized firms not to look for investment opportunities in France. This obliged the firms to look *abroad* for merger opportunities. Third, because of the austerity after Year I, sales on the domestic market sagged while the availability of investment capital shrank. If many of the state firms started turning profits by 1984–85, they were in no position to spearhead growth.

Nonetheless, nationalization turned out to be marginally positive for French industry. In social terms, the public sector has always been more progressive than private industry toward its workers and unions, although the Auroux laws narrowed the gap. The influx of new technocratic blood into French managerial elites shook management circles considerably and in a positive way. *Colbertisme* paid off in small but undramatic ways. The *left* content of nationalization, however, remained problematic. A slight change in the composition of French economic elites to benefit non-property-owning technocrats may have contributed to international competitiveness, but it hardly represented a step toward socialism. Moreover, no consensus was ever built around the nationalizations, leaving the way open to extensive privatizations after 1986.[6] The largest uncertainty involved the initial obsession with the "commanding heights." Like previous French governments, the Socialists believed that only giant firms would compete effectively in international markets. Yet the introduction of new computer-based technologies has increased process flexibilities.[7] Thus, small and medium-sized firms, to the extent that they invest in these new technologies, now spearhead growth. If the future excludes the large oligopolies, the French left's nationalizations will look obsolete. If not, large corporate entities will have to introduce greater flexibilities into their production. French state enterprises will then need to act more like their private competitors, nullifying the advantages and accentuating the drawbacks of state-centered production. Even progressive state-enterprise social policies may not be tenable in volatile international markets that demand labor force flexibility.

Two Years of Prudence: 1982–1984

The short-term scenario of the left contained serious flaws. The forecasted American economic locomotive remained in the station far longer than anyone expected. Other advanced countries followed the American lead and deflated their economies. In stimulating its economy after 1981, therefore,

France stood out as the only major dissenter within the international political economy. The left's pump-priming proved especially dangerous given the underlying structural weaknesses in France's international competitiveness which had been overlooked in the electoral euphoria.

As a medium-sized country, France did not have the capacity to create painlessly its own destiny. The balance sheet quickly turned disastrous during the left's first year in power. Rather than generating new activity for French industry, Socialist Keynesianism flooded the domestic market with imports, created large trade imbalances, and caused international payments problems. Historically high American interest rates attracted foreign – including French – capital to the United States, and the skyrocketing dollar that resulted raised the costs of French imports. Although real oil prices were declining in terms of dollars, for example, they increased in francs. Moreover, the existing inflation differentials between France and its major trading partners grew even wider. The government had to devalue the franc in October 1981 and June 1982. The second devaluation brought austerity.

International trade and monetary problems forced an important turning point. The French Socialists faced two major choices after Year I: a continuation of redistributive reformism, which implied protectionism; or a halt to the reforms, austerity, and strict observance of the rules of the international economic game. Reformism lost out in two installments – June 1982 and March 1983. Policy and the effective political balance within the left government then shifted to the center. A third devaluation, exchange controls, higher taxes, price increases for public services, and a new budgetary stringency lowered French purchasing power to correct the massive trade imbalance. France thereby belatedly joined international deflationary trends. This U-turn occurred ironically at the very moment when other countries loosened up their own austerity. France could not enjoy the Reagan recovery.

After June 1982, the left undertook measures that the right had always wanted, but had been afraid to afraid to try. A brief wage-price freeze and subsequent wage guidelines effectively deindexed wage growth. This reduced a comparatively high level of inflation, but it also undercut earlier trade union victories. The government next began to trumpet the need for new entrepreneurial energy and for the profits necessary to encourage it. In a society whose businesspeople tended towards Malthusianism, this proved to be a novel approach, hardly what one might have expected from the left. Parts of the new left strategy "worked." Wages as a percentage of national income had risen through the 1970s, and slightly more rapidly during Year I. Beginning in 1982–83, the left reversed that tendency.[8]

The attack on wages and social transfers, however, failed to achieve the government's stated purpose of increasing French investment, even if it did stimulate the most profitable boom in the history of the French stock market.

By 1984 it had also reversed initial efforts at redistributing income to lower income groups. Nonetheless, the left controlled the effects of austerity in at least one area. The government sought to prevent a sharp increase in unemployment from 1982 to 1984 by using a battery of programs and its discretionary power, including the power to prevent employers from laying people off. By lowering the retirement age to sixty in 1982, the left sought to create more job vacancies for younger workers. It also continued in quiet ways to pursue a number of smaller positive programs, especially in the areas of legal reform, reorganization of public broadcasting, and women's rights.

"Breaking with capitalism" was forgotten and left voluntarism gave way to centrist realism – managing capitalism better than the capitalists. The new structural reforms remained, although they figured less prominently in governmental discussions and no new ones were envisioned. Beginning in 1984 whispers even arose in government circles that parts of the new public sector were perhaps better off in private hands. If account balancing and austerity were the first symptoms of the new conversion experience of the French left, the second consisted of what has come to be known as "modernization."

Modernization: 1984–1986

"Modernization" began in late 1983 and lasted through the 1986 elections. It had a simple meaning: the old industrial past could no longer be retained. French industry needed to become more competitive in international markets. New efficiencies and new technologies would push France forward into the twenty-first century. Unfortunately, the first major practical consequence of Socialist "modernization" was rising unemployment as the government began to show new tolerance toward labor force reductions. Official levels of unemployment shot up from 8 percent in 1983 to nearly 11 percent in early 1986. Business failures skyrocketed. Industrial giants in the steel, automobile, engineering, and shipbuilding sectors suffered particularly brutal reorganizations.

Continuous austerity and new modernization would have resulted in a French version of Anglo-Saxon neoliberalism without serious and compassionate efforts to deal with hard-hit groups. In particular, the government subsidized retraining programs at almost full compensation for redundant workers in the steel and shipbuilding industries. A youth employment program hired teenagers and young adults in public works at sub-minimum wage, thereby removing them from unemployment rolls. Moreover, while other countries were choosing between defense expenditures and social transfers, the left government lowered both in attempting to stimulate domestic investment.

Modernization had the political result, however, of tearing the left governmental coalition apart. The appointment of Laurent Fabius as prime minister in July 1984 confirmed that the reform experiment was over. If his predecessor Pierre Mauroy represented the "Old Left," the 38-year-old Fabius epitomized the young modernizing technocrat *par excellence*. The Communists – concerned above all with stemming their own decline – quit their ministries at this time and turned rapidly towards militant opposition. Their own working-class base was especially hard hit by policy changes, creating an impossible situation for the party in its accelerating decline.

Economics and the Triumph of the Technocratic Impulse

How can we explain the left's U-turn? A naive optimism on economic matters accompanied the left's assumption of power. Despite a menacing international environment, the left felt that France had enough room for maneuver to permit a stimulation of growth after May–June 1981. Keynesian growth would have its own virtuous circle. Demand stimulation would raise incomes and consumption, which in turn would create new investment, new jobs, and lowered unemployment. Economic growth would also increase tax receipts and relieve initial budget deficits, thus lowering inflation and making new and better social programs possible. In the middle run, of course, the virtuous circle would be reinforced by the effects of nationalizations and other reforms, allowing France to leap forward.

The left, at least initially, was the prisoner of Fordist-Keynesian assumptions about the economic world which had been rendered obsolete by the coming of crisis. It believed that domestic deals between labor and capital trading productivity increases for rising wages could be rejuvenated. It also believed that conditions could be promoted to sustain consensus around expanding the welfare state and promoting countercyclical growth-oriented macroeconomic policies. Finally, the left presumed that the international economic environment still allowed enough space for ambitious domestic goals.

These assumptions had become problematic by 1981.[9] Productivity growth had slowed dramatically everywhere, making the postwar labor–capital deal difficult to maintain. As investment needs and wage demands began to conflict, consensus in the labor market frayed. Slower growth turned domestic social policy discussion towards zero-sum confrontation. Income transfers and social insurance payments came less and less from increased productivity and more from other taxpayers. The breakdown of the Bretton Woods monetary system, oil shocks, new competition in the developing world, and market saturation made the international trade and monetary environment treacherous.

The left lacked a sufficiently coherent analysis of the new international political economy and its articulation with the French economy. French development in the 1970s, which both the French left and right misunderstood equally, was a major part of the problem.[10] Recently and incompletely modernized, much of French industry was internationally uncompetitive. French international trade was weakest with the more advanced economies which counted most, and strongest with Third World partners. The policy choices of the right in the 1970s had made the situation even worse. Because of its perilous electoral situation, the right had not been able to make the kind of welfare state cutbacks and wage reductions that it really desired. As a result, firms went into debt while profits and investment declined. When the right confronted inflation and trade deficits with a strong franc policy, it further eroded the competitiveness of French industry in international markets. Virtually all advanced industrial economies had trouble coping in the 1970s. France, however, fell behind.

The year following the left's victory in 1981 would have been difficult, no matter who had won political power, since France had very few sectors in international trade surplus and disinvestment was proceeding apace. The left's reflation simply made things even worse, leading to an invasion of imports from stronger industrial traders. Faced with such a situation, the left had only painful options. How could such a group of brilliant, highly trained, and skillful politicians – many of whom had advice from clued-in high civil servants with access to the necessary information – have so misunderstood the world around them? Left politicians seem to have had inordinate confidence in their own capacities to resolve conflicts between desires and realities through fervent voluntarism.

The left in power could see only two courses of action – Keynesian reflation, ultimately "salvaged" by a resort to protectionism, or submission to the liberal international political economy with austerity. This conventional dichotomy clearly betrayed the lack of imagination which, in France, and elsewhere, has inevitably spelled defeat for the left. France might have little influence over, and a small margin of maneuver in, the international economy. However, the left could still have sought new resources in France by attempting to create new forms of domestic consensus, for example, by carrying through the logic of *autogestion*. Since French industry needed to increase productivity in any case, the left could have taken the larger risks of rebuilding decision-making processes at plant and local levels with the goal of sharing the burden of labor displacement in the short run and providing new employment possibilities in the longer term.

Instead, when Keynesianism in one country proved difficult, conflict merely sharpened among left leaders around traditional options. Those furthest left – the Communists and the CERES group[11] within the Socialist Party – advocated protectionism and greater *colbertiste* zeal to allow the left to stay its

127

original course. Socialist technocrats backed by state funds would make the correct choices and point the French economy, driven by the newly nationalized locomotives, towards new world leadership, provided that the domestic market had not been flattened by austerity. Realists, however, argued that protectionism would inevitably cause further French decline; the moment allowed no hesitation in balancing France's books. This second group triumphed and brought with it familiar centrist economic management and a newly humble vocabulary regarding the problems which France faced. Traces nonetheless remained of social democratic reformism. The sacrifices were to be shared equitably, so that lower income groups would not suffer disproportionately.

During Year I, virtually the entire left saw voluntarism and mobilization as resources for bridging the gap between desire and constraint. Afterwards, perceptions of constraint overruled assertions of will. Prudent austerity served as an intermediary stage in which the left abandoned its earlier illusions and began to adopt an internationalist and neoclassical economic perspective. The victory of centrist social democracy constituted a victory for conventional political wisdom. Yet, this was also a victory by default. Although the more radical elements within the left coalition had good intentions, they did not have the political muscle or imagination to win.

The government did not immediately abandon its commitment to what the French call the "people of the left," progressive elements of the new middle strata, workers, and the nonworking poor. That had to wait until the turn towards modernization, which brought together international neoclassicism and a French neoliberalism. The Socialist task turned from solidarity to encouragement of entrepreneurial energy. Rebuilding an internationally competitive industrial base assumed priority over reconstructing French society on more equitable grounds. The older social democratic insistence on responsibility to the less favored in society ceded to new arguments about the peculiar suitability of high-powered center-left technocrats to the task of regenerating French capitalism.

In terms of the classic variables of economic performance, the Socialists have certainly not failed. By 1986, inflation receded to a level unmatched since the 1950s, making French exports more competitive. The balance of payments, while not positive, reached a manageable level that did not threaten the integrity of domestic policymaking. The stock market boomed for the three years before 1986. Profits increased and even many state enterprises find themselves in the black. The *bête noire* of Socialist modernization has been the high and stable level of unemployment, close to 11 percent.

The Socialists proved themselves considerably more willing than their center-right predecessors to "bite the bullet" on important economic policy issues – disinflation and the deindexation of wages, for example. After the first year,

French business leaders frequently praised the government for its realism.[12] However, because this record of solid adaptiveness emerged after a brief flirtation with quite radical policies, successes rarely received acclaim from the promoters of a more energetic, internationally integrated French capitalism. After 1983 everyone assumed that the right would return to power, and big business saw no need to endanger its political future. The right, especially given its own conversion to Anglo-Saxon liberalism, still remained closer to the values and aspirations of the corporate community. More importantly, the short period of radical policies and their abrupt termination meant that the left's own supporters were dramatically deceived.

Political and Social Disaster

The French Socialist Party (PS) led the left toward victory in the 1970s by gluing together a number of constituencies with a variety of messages. "Old Left" talk consisted of "breaking with capitalism" with a "class front" of militant workers. "New Left" rhetoric envisioned decentralization and *autogestion*. Five years in power fundamentally exhausted both vocabularies. Technocratic *colbertiste* rhetoric and substance filled the consequent vacuum. Socialist civil servants became the vanguard for the restructuring of French capitalism. Internal political developments had led the PS – for the Communists (PCF) jumped ship when it sped toward modernization – to attempt shifting the basis of its legitimacy. The technocratic self-presentation of the Socialists was a short-term political loser. The left had won the presidency in 1981 as much by right disunity as by left mobilization.[13] Despite the apparent existence in the 1970s of a "left sociological majority" based upon changes in French class structure, it never materialized at the polls until 1981.

After a determined campaign to unify left strength in the mid-1970s, divisions between Socialists and Communists, reproduced in organized labor, reared their politically destructive heads in 1977–78. These divisions, along with an unfavorable labor market, made the three years prior to 1981 particularly painful for the left. Mitterrand's considerable skill in 1980–81, at the very last moment, consolidated the traditional left vote and attracted new categories of workers. He also won – by an unspectacular shift between left and right of only 2 percent – because the center-right coalition was falling apart. The subsequent Socialist landslide in the legislative elections was more a vote of confidence for the new president than the result of any determined political shift.

If gaining power requires political mobilization, sustaining power demands the maintenance of that mobilization. The latter has been difficult for the French left. The left has seldom rallied other social classes to the working class.

Tensions between Socialists and Communists combined with a divided labor movement have made mobilization difficult to prolong beyond isolated points in history. As the Socialists gained dominance over the Communists within the left in the 1970s, any mobilization that occurred assumed a more political than social form. By French standards the PS has been a mass party, but it hardly holds the popular presence of other left parties in Europe, and it enjoys no structural relations with a large and unified labor movement.

Thus, mobilization for social change by 1981 was neither strong nor completely promising. The Socialists and the Communists conceived of social change as passing through "capturing state power." This connoted an obsession with electoral success and mobilization for it. Despite the 1981 victory, the Socialists and the left had not really built a stable majority electoral coalition, let alone a majority of allies willing to undertake a long and complex process of social change. Such coalitions would have had to have been built after 1981. The history of the left's policy accomplishments, as checkered as it is, looks like an honor role of extraordinary success when compared to the left's strictly political record. The left's position in opinion polls steadily declined over the five-year period. After the second year, both Mitterrand and Mauroy set records for unpopularity in public opinion polls. The Socialists' standing among intellectuals, not terribly high to begin with, also plummeted. The results of periodic local and partial elections were similar. Mitterrand's "state of grace" fell in front of the temple of austerity. Consolidating a majority meant in the first instance nailing down the segments of the traditional and new middle strata that had abandoned Giscard. The reforms of Year I frightened certain floating middle-class groups – in particular those involved in private-sector administrative work. The right's relentless baying about the "Socialo-Communist" threat to Western Civilization undoubtedly took its toll. The right also seized upon an apparent increase in terrorism and criminal delinquence to denounce the government's "laxity."[14] The non-devaluation of the "green franc" squeezed farmers, whom the right championed. The shift to austerity provided support for the right's allegations about the incompetence of the left in power. Emergency taxes, exchange restrictions, and other deflationary measures struck hard at middle-income earners. Ill-conceiv.ed and poorly timed attacks on strongly entrenched interest groups – farmers, doctors, police, and advocates of private parochial schools – elicited powerful anti-left protest movements which swayed centrist voters.

The manner in which the school issue got out of hand indicated a growing Socialist isolation from potential social allies.[15] The government's bill on public funding of private (Catholic) schools not only angered left constituencies (who sought a more secular system) but also Catholic school supporters backed by the political right. Two years of demonstrations by both sides evidenced a Socialist incapacity to steer policy between conflicting social interests. Catholic school advocates won the numbers game when they brought out over a *million* supporters to the streets of Paris in June 1984. The PS had lost many of the groups that had migrated from the right in 1981.

The shift to austerity and later to modernization hit hardest "the people of the left." Decades of left promises that a change in society would follow left victory were dashed. More importantly, the left failed to restore economic growth and employment. Then it turned towards policies which even the right had been unwilling to try. It presided over the first decline in wage-earner income since the mid–1970s. It engineered the rise in the share of profits in national income. It reversed its own redistributive policies. Only the left could claim that deindustrialization and high unemployment constituted "modernization." Consequently, organized labor, the left's most promising generator of mass support, became increasingly critical and angry.

Inept political communication made a bad situation worse. Well into the shift to austerity, Socialist leaders spoke as if little had changed. They tried to mobilize support with appeals to Catholic solidarity and the fear of the right. The former had its limits while the latter fell on deaf ears as economic policy placed the Socialists increasingly in the center. When the rhetoric of tech-nocratic modernization replaced traditional left phraseology, it happened with such abruptness that it led to confusion.[16]

Mixed messages from within the left camp further intensified this con-fusion. From 1981 to 1984 the government and parliamentary majority was a Socialist-Communist coalition. The internal life of the PS itself contained at least four distinct and querulous political tendencies. Public contradictions within the government represented the struggle between "voluntarists" and "realists." The French labor movement, the left's major source of extrapar-liamentary support, had never reconciled its differences after the left came to power. The exhilaration of Year I masked many of the tensions among the unions and between the labor movement and the ruling Socialist Party. Even during the early period, however, quiet complaints arose that union perspec-tives were insufficiently taken into account or that one union was favored. The left has always had to bear the cross of competitive political pluralism. This configuration of forces remained after 1981.

The Communist decision not to accept the turn to modernization in 1984 transformed pluralism into fratricidal combat. The Communists opposed the Socialists every new step of the way. The historical origins of this split, of course, transcended the 1980s.[17] Still, the inability of the Socialists to conciliate their Communist allies after 1982 proved costly. This deadlock rested partially in the explicit goal of contemporary Socialist strategy to gain hegemony within the left and to destroy the PCF.

Unity of the political left served as a historical substitute for the consensual bargaining that characterizes social democracies. The Socialists needed the

131

Communists more than they ever admitted. Alliance with the PCF and a solid left program enabled the PS before 1981 to offer a clear alternative to the policies of the right. Without the Communists, and having adopted the economic tools of the center, the Socialists could no longer promise an alternative to the current sacrifices imposed in the name of modernization. Afterwards, the Socialists failed to develop a new political vision.

Socialist strategy accelerated the continuing decline of French Communism. The PCF lost 50 percent of its voting strength from 1979 to 1986 – from a respectable 21 percent to less than 10 percent.[18] It lost much of its local political power, a hefty percentage of its membership, almost all of its ideological appeal, and a good part of its trade union leverage. The ambiguity of their years in sharing power – from 1981 to 1984 – positioned the Communists between a rock and a hard place.[19] After Year I the party swallowed increasingly bitter policy pills that contradicted both its program and its practice. Until 1984 the PCF calculated that remaining in government was more profitable than the alternative. It sought to resolve the conflict by speaking out while its four ministers intoned hymns of governmental solidarity. Instead of the best of both worlds, the PCF appeared schizophrenic. Confronted with this multiplicity of caving roofs, the Communists preferred to hide behind overdriven restatements of workerist and pro-Soviet politics of the past, accelerating their decline. The Communist downfall affects the entire left. The PCF long served as the major voice for a certain kind of radical politics. Its ideological militancy – and the organizational skills to back it up – long sustained the left against French capital. The electoral destiny of voters lost by the PCF seems uncertain. The previous left mathematics of voting success involved the addition of Communist supporters to those of the Socialists to bring the left within sight of a majority. Swing votes from a floating (but assuredly sympathetic) middle class would then be factored in to predict victory. The electoral decline of the PCF renders this equation obsolete. The future of organized labor seems equally problematic. French unions had begun to decline in terms of membership and mobilizing power several years before 1981.[20]

Deindustrialization hit at the "smokestack" heart of organized labor. Technological change reorganized the labor process and created uncertainty even for the employed. Unemployment made workers reluctant to engage in militant action. As a result, American-styled "business" unionism developed to protect individual and group interests, making class solidarity more difficult to achieve. The competitive pluralism of the multiple organization union movement reinforced these tendencies. The French left was strongly pro-labor, and its program sought to strengthen workers and their unions. Instead, the weakening of French labor has continued.

Dashed expectations and prolonged austerity opened new space for the radical right. Racist mobilization emerged in consequence. The left cannot be held responsible for the existence of the National Front (FN). Enticed to France during the postwar boom, often from former colonies, immigrants were silently tolerated. Without that economic growth, immigrant services and presence have both become undesirable, at least to a vocal segment of the urban lower middle class. Austerity after Year I intensified such feelings. The parliamentary right partially encouraged the development of the FN. Its refusal during the first three years to grant legitimacy to the "Socialo-Communist" government polarized the political sphere and popularized simplistic "law and order" solutions. Opposition intransigence on virtually every major issue contributed to a climate of refusal within which the FN represented only the most extreme position. The "respectable" right first began the major public ranting over immigration during the municipal elections in 1983. The first electoral breakthrough for the FN occurred a few months later in a partial election.

If the left cannot be blamed for its existence, the Socialists' hands were still not completely clean. With the electoral situation turning against the left after 1984, the Socialists changed the rules for the 1986 legislative elections. The government instituted a system of proportional representation to replace the previous double-ballot, single-district system. The previous electoral system placed a premium on political alliances, at least for the second ballot, and it marginalized extremes. PR enabled parties to run on their own. Thus, the new law gave the FN enough seats to form a parliamentary group, thereby granting it another public platform. In the 1986 elections, the FN won the same number of seats (35) as did the Communists.

The Socialists reasoned before 1986 that the FN represented a particular brand of bigotry, reaction, and hypernationalism that had always been part of the French right, even in its respectable forms.[21] They calculated that the FN would tease out a sufficient number of racists, bigots, and chauvinists from the two "respectable" right parties to prevent a clear majority in the future National Assembly. This would enable the Socialists to serve as broker in a game in which the FN became the joker. This strategy only partially worked. While the PS remained the largest political party in France after the 1986 elections, the left as a whole – PS, PCF, and smaller political formations – found itself with a clear minority of seats (43). Moreover, since the majority of the "respectable" right was so slim – only 2 seats – the presence of the FN in the legislative chamber enabled the radical right to exercise influence on key votes.

The French Left: Autogestion or Autodestruction?

The left assumed power in 1981 burdened with a large number of historical handicaps which it could not have reasonably been expected to overcome.

Unfortunately, this meant that the left found itself unprepared for the kinds of environments within which it had to act. Virtually all observers would agree that the program of 1981, largely formulated in 1972 before the economic crisis, was obsolete. In fact, the left brought to power in 1981 an accurate reproduction of what it had proposed *four decades earlier,* since the 1972 Common Program itself was consciously patterned on Popular Front and Liberation approaches. These programmatic elements combined the familiar staples of the "Old Left" – nationalizations, planning, strengthening of the labor movement, the centralized welfare state, and Keynesian demand stimulation – which took little account of the changes in the French and international political economies.

The left might have pursued different governing strategies given the variety of forces within the governmental majority. Socialist technocracy triumphed because the other perspectives were both weaker and divided. Behind this triumph lay a profound cultural problem. Both Socialists and Communists espoused an exaggerated statism, combining the centralizing reformism embedded in European left history with the Jacobinism of the French political tradition. French reformism throughout the twentieth century has been heavily vanguardist. Small activist groups conceived the proper paths of social change. Then they would persuade ordinary people to share these conceptions. Finally, they would seek state power to push society along these paths. Such vanguardist notions have been challenged, particularly in the last two decades, as the idea of *autogestion* – connected to May–June 1968, left Catholicism, and left Eurocommunism – spread. However, the official French left used such ideas merely as window dressing. The predominance in the PS itself of high-powered state officials, who believed that state action constituted the most effective lever to change society, contributed to this statism. Finally, the left clung tenaciously to beliefs in the pre-eminence of electoral conflict, failing to complement electoralism with grassroots activism. Voluntaristic and statist approaches to politics became "fudge factors." Energy and will developed into substitutes for knowledge of what was really happening to different groups and precise mobilization around social concerns.

The emphasis on state power and implementation of reforms from above nullified the search for renewed understanding of the changing labor process and its effects on the stratification of the labor force. Organizing towards *autogestion* in the sense of the construction of progressive new beachheads of democratic control in civil society, and most importantly in the workplace, was the missing link between the use of state power and social transformation already taking place independent of left control. Beyond this, issues of base-level democracy, control, and challenge to elitist decision-making of all kinds never assumed equal stature with bread-and-butter issues. Statism and economism became logical partners.

Because no "cultural revolution" had succeeded on the French left prior to 1981, no real foundation existed for an alternative kind of strategy and mobilization based on grassroots intervention and democracy with the left in power. The left's nearly exclusive focus on seizing state power and concentrating mobilizational efforts towards this end led to a neglect of the primordially important task of democratizing and changing "civil society" as well as empowering the working class and other subordinate groups in the very places where they were most pertinently exploited and dominated. The left's persistent statism and economism weakened the kinds of energetic grassroots social movements which one found elsewhere – environmentalism, peace, feminism, gay rights, regionalism, etc. As the left moved towards power, it drained such decentralized sources of new energy as did exist into its own orbit, where they were transformed or undercut.

Focus on the state as the ultimate lever had even more unfortunate implications after the left succeeded in capturing state power. In pressing circumstances of economic crisis and given the absence of prior preparation, the initiation of changes in state–society relations to empower ordinary people in multifaceted *autogestionnaire* ways would be a rude task. Nothing demobilizes more than unemployment. It thus seemed logical to run away from that task toward technocracy. Yet, the use of state power to prod change forward in a number of areas in a top–down manner eventually alienated the very people in whose name this same state power was being exercised.

The left did not know how to respond to the needs of different groups in French society in ways which would have elicited energy and enthusiasm. The left's unwillingness to bargain in a "democratogenic" way with its constituents reinforced the social demoralization of crisis. Political life became atomized and personalized. Such a situation might have worked worked well for a right which feared collective action. It could only harm a left which claimed to desire change. Thus, French politics since 1981 has become "Americanized." The Socialists have relied upon the media and image-making to overcome their deficiencies in policy-making. Substituting image for substance in this way reinforced the technocratic impulse.

What emerged within both the Socialist Party in and out of government as a consequence of the events we recount has been a fundamentally new form of theoretical reasoning, the "leftism is exhausted" school. Passion which had once been devoted to radical hopes has turned 180 degrees towards denouncing them as utopian and wrong. A new discourse of center-left "realism" – only marginally different from its center-right counterpart – has followed. "Constraint" has become the key. International markets and diplomatic structures constrain France's room for maneuver. Domestic constraints dictate that civil society evolves according to its own logic to be interfered with politically only at great peril and as a last resort. The linkage between the domestic and international settings constitutes the most important arena for action.

This "new realism" is even more deterministic and economistic than some versions of old leftism. It not only recognizes but embraces the constraints of market forces. Making French industry internationally competitive has assumed top priority. If profit, even at the expense of wages, makes the world turn, then enabling French capital to make as much of it as possible will make France succeed in this world. The "new realists" see the social and economic spheres as beyond the capacities of politicians to change, except on the margins. "Good politics" has assumed a new meaning. Instead of social change, it now denotes the recognition of constraint and the best use of the small room for maneuver. The new realists are foremost good managers. Within this now-dominant discourse, the left can be distinguished from the right by its capacity for better management and for its marginally greater sympathy for the victims of this constraining world. The triumph of such views within French Socialism constitutes an important consequence of the left experiment.

The years after the electoral loss of 1986 brought no major rethinking of the governmental experience. The Socialists focused on the presidential elections in 1988 and the left content of their program became even less important. The Socialist aspiration to gain hegemony within the left, while apparently successful for the Socialists, weakened the left as a whole. The left resembles the American Democratic Party more than any of its French predecessors. This did not prevent new electoral successes in 1988 and a return to power. But the left which did return to power had the palest of managerial goals and no transformative ambitions.

The French left has not led the workers to unite, throw off their chains, and create the cooperative commonwealth. No other left has accomplished this either. Breaking with capitalism remains a theoretical possibility, but no one has yet satisfactorily outlined how to do this in a non-authoritarian manner. The French left governed somewhat more radically, at least in the initial period, than most lefts. Left governance during an economic crisis is not easy, as the German and Swedish Social Democrats and British Labourites can attest. Adapting creatively to constraints appears to be the norm for the left in the advanced industrial countries as the year 2000 approaches. From this point of view the French left governed as "competently" as other lefts.

The French left sought a third way between ameliorative social democracy and illiberal neo-Bolshevism. Both represented past left approaches to the inequality created by a particular stage of industrial capitalism. The third way of the French also spoke more to the past than to the future. As a result, French Socialism failed as other lefts had before it. The future appears uncertain without a new vision as dynamic as the capitalism it seeks to replace.

Notes

1. Most of French commercial banking had been nationalized after 1944.

2. See Mark Kesselman, "The Tranquil Revolution at Clochemerle: Socialist Decentralization in France," in Philip G. Cerny and Martin A. Schain, eds, *Socialism, the State and Public Policy in France*, New York: Methuen 1985, pp. 166–85.

3. Duncan Gallie, "Les Lois Auroux: The Reform of French Industrial Relations?" in Howard Machin and Vincent Wright, eds, *Economic Policy and Policy-Making under the Mitterrand Presidency, 1981–1984*, New York: St. Martin's 1985, pp. 205–21.

4. Some of the competing conceptualizations of nationalization are developed in Lysiane Cartelier, "Intervention de l'état et politique industrielle: Les enjeux des nationalizations," *Les Temps modernes*, April 1983, pp. 144–55.

5. For an example of this thinking, see Christian Stoffäes, "The Nationalizations: 1981–1984," in Machin and Wright, eds, pp. 144–69.

6. In a world full of ironies, the nationalized investment banks have acted the most similar to their private counterparts. State investment bankers still extend loans to their large preferred customers at the expense of innovative ventures that the left had originally sought to stimulate.

7. See, for example, Michael J. Piore and Charles F. Sabel, *The Second Industrial Divide*,New York: Basic Books 1984.

8. See Michel Beaud, *La Politique économique de la gauche*, 2 vols, Paris: Syros 1983, 1985.

9. Much of this section is informed by the path-breaking work of the French economist Robert Boyer. See, for example, Boyer and Jaques Mistral, *Accumulation, inflation, crises*, 2d edn, Paris: PUF 1983. A shorter version of Boyer's argument about the consequences of the French insertion in the international political economy (and its effects on French labor) can be found in "Wage Labor, Capital Accumulation, and the Crisis, 1968–82," in Mark Kesselman and Guy Groux, eds, *The French Workers' Movement: Economic Crisis and Political Change*, London: Allen & Unwin 1984.

10. See Alain Fonteneau and Pierre-Alain Muet, *La Gauche face à la crise*, Paris: Presses de la Fondation Nationale de Sciences Politiques 1985.

11. CERES stands for Center for Socialist Studies, Research, and Education. It was on the left wing of the old SFIO and has continued to be on the left in the reconstructed PS. Its principal leader has been Jean-Pierre Chevènement.

12. See *Business Week*, January 10, 1983, for equally favorable assessments of Socialist economic management.

13. See the special issue of *Pouvoirs*, "La Gauche au pouvoir," no. 20 (1982). For an insider perspective, see Stephane Denis, *La Chute de la maison Giscard*, Paris: Lattes 1981. The politics leading to the left victory are also analyzed in Tony Daley and Jonas Pontusson, "The Left Victory in France," *Socialist Review*, no. 60 (Nov.–Dec. 1981), pp. 9–55; and Pontusson, "Apropos Mitterrand: State, Power, Class Coalitions, and Electoral Politics in Postwar France, *Kapitalistate*, no. 9 (1981), pp. 123–39.

14. The focus on personal insecurity was particularly powerful for the right in 1982 and 1983, although statistics on violent crime from the Ministry of Justice showed no dramatic increase in violent crimes. Yet perceptions count, and the French felt (and continue to feel) insecure.

15. On the school issue, see John Ambler, "French Education: The Socialist Record," *French Politics and Society*, no. 7 (Sept. 1984), pp. 11–18. See also the coverage in *Le Monde*, May–June 1984.

16. George Ross and Jane Jenson, "Political Pluralism and Economic Policy," in John Ambler, ed., *The French Socialist Experiment*, Philadelphia: Institute for the Study of Human Issues, pp. 25–59.

17. For some sense of this, see Jenson and Ross, *The View from Inside: A French Communist Cell in Crisis*, Berkeley: University of California Press 1984.

18. The 9.79 percent that the party won on March 16, 1986, represents its lowest nationwide score since 1932! The Communists now have deputies in less than one-quarter of the *departements*.

19. See Ross, "French Communism with Its Back to the Wall: The Twenty-Fourth Congress of the French Communist Party," *Socialist Review*, no. 65 (Sept.–Oct. 1982), pp. 85–120; and "The Dilemmas of Communism in Mitterrand's France," *New Political Science*, no. 12 (Winter 1983).

20. Ross, "The Perils of Politics: French Unions and the Crisis of the 1970s," in Peter Lange,

George Ross, and Maurizio Vannicelli, eds, *Unions, Change and Crisis: French and Italian Union Strategy and the Political Economy, 1945–1980* , London: George Allen & Unwin 1982, pp. 13–93.

21.   See Lionel Jospin, "Le Socialisme français, defenseur et garant de la republique," *Revue politique et parlementaire,* no. 915 (March–April 1985). Jospin was the First Secretary of the PS after 1981.

8

Seed Wars

Common Heritage, Private Property, and Political Strategy

(1987)

Jack Kloppenburg, Jr., and Daniel Lee Kleinman

If plant agriculture is one of the material foundations of society, the seed is the material foundation of plant agriculture. As such, plant germplasm – the genetic information encoded in the seed – is a resource of tremendous value. And access to, control over, and preservation of plant genetic resources have now emerged as fields of international concern and conflict.

In the capitalist world economy today, extracted natural resources are treated as commodities. Plant germplasm is a notable exception. For over two centuries scientists from the advanced industrial nations have freely appropriated plant genetic resources from Third World nations for use in the plant breeding and improvement programs of the developed world. The unrecompensed extraction of these materials has been predicated on a widely accepted ideology which defines germplasm as the "common heritage of mankind."[1] As "common heritage," germplasm is looked upon as a public good for which no payment is necessary or appropriate.

But as the private seed industries of the North have matured over the last decade, they have reached out for global markets. In order to facilitate this expansion they have sought international recognition of patent-like "plant breeders' rights" for the plant varieties they develop. With these developments, the developing nations began to see something of a contradiction in the status of their genetic resources as freely available "common heritage" and the status of seed companies' commercial varieties as "private property" available by purchase. That such commercial strains might be based on plant genetic resources originally obtained at no cost from the Third World added insult to injury.

139

Mounting Third World dissatisfaction with this and other asymmetries found expression at the 1983 biennial conference of the Food and Agriculture Organization (FAO). At that time, an International Undertaking on Plant Genetic Resources was passed amid acrimonious debate and the vehement opposition of the capitalist nations of the industrial North. The Undertaking asserts the noble principle that "plant genetic resources are a heritage of mankind and consequently should be available without restriction." However, it goes on to specify that under the rubric of plant genetic resources is included "special genetic stocks (including elite and current breeders lines)."[2] That is, the Undertaking claims what are now proprietary materials as no less the common heritage – and therefore common property – of humanity than the peasant-developed land races of the Third World. Such an arrangement is patently unacceptable to those advanced capitalist nations with powerful private seed industries. The Undertaking is viewed as nothing less than an assault on the principle of private property.

The global strength of capitalism imposes important limits upon what constitutes viable and progressive political action. Actions that appear progressive may, given the political-economic context in which they are undertaken, actually serve to reinforce existing relations of power and patterns of inequity. At this conjuncture, we do not believe that the achievement of "common heritage" in plant genetic resources would result in more equitable relations of exchange between nations or benefit the mass of the world's people. Recognition of national sovereignty over plant genetic resources would better serve the nations and peoples of the Third World.

Germplasm: The Fourth Resource

Soil, air, and water are regarded as Earth's fundamental natural resources. And germplasm, the hereditary material contained in every cell, must be counted as a fourth resource of prime importance. The term "plant genetic resources" encompasses the total range of plant germplasm available in the global gene pool. While it is really the genetic information contained in the plant cell which is the resource of interest here, it is convenient to think of plant genetic resources as seeds, for that is the form in which plant genetic information is embodied and in which it is usually collected and stored.

The vagaries of natural history have resulted in the uneven distribution of plant species over the face of the globe. The northern hemisphere lost much under the grinding impact of the last glaciation. Consequently, biotic diversity is concentrated in what is now the Third World. Moreover, it is in the Third World that the domestication of plants first occurred and systematic crop production was first initiated.

In the process of domesticating and maintaining crops over the millennia, peasant farmers developed thousands of "land races" within any one species. Land races are genetically variable populations which exhibit different responses to pests, diseases, and fluctuations in environmental conditions.[3] The genetic diversity in these land races was, and remains, a form of insurance for peasant cultivators. By planting polycultures comprising genetically diverse varieties, peasant farmers made certain that, whatever the year might bring in the way of weather or pests, some of the seed sown would grow to maturity and provide a crop. The objective of these early breeders was not high yield but consistency of production. And the result of their efforts was the development of great inter- and intra-specific genetic variability in particular and relatively confined geographic regions.

The existence of such areas was first recognized in the 1920s by the Soviet botanist N. I. Vavilov. He identified a variety of these areas, which he considered to be the centers of origin of the crops with which they are associated. They are located principally in what is now called the Third World. But subsequent research has shown that centers of diversity are not necessarily coterminous with the area in which a crop originated, and that both crop domestication and the subsequent patterns of development of crop genetic diversity were more dispersed in time and space than Vavilov realized. There has emerged a general preference for a conceptual and schematic terminology that uses "regions of diversity" to account for the genetic variability generated as crops spread from their points of origin.[4]

The empirical analysis in this article builds upon this regional schematization. We divided the nations of the globe into ten regions on the basis of current scientific understanding of the location and extent of plant genetic diversity. The boundaries of our regions are indicated in Figure 1. We then selected the twenty food crops and twenty industrial crops that lead global production in tonnage and identified their respective regions of diversity.[5] This information is also provided in Figure 1.

It is clear from Figure 1 that the regions containing all of the advanced industrial nations except Japan are the source of few of the world's leading crops. The Australian region has contributed none of the top forty crops, North America only the sunflower, the Euro-Siberian region only oats and rye. Besides the sunflower, the complement of crops indigenous to the United States includes the blueberry, the cranberry, the Jerusalem artichoke, and the pecan. An "All American" meal would be somewhat limited. Northern Europe's contribution to the global larder is only slightly less meager: currants and raspberries in addition to oats and rye. The crops that dominate the agricultural economies of the North – corn, wheat, soybeans, and potatoes – are not indigenous species at all. Rather, they have been introduced from elsewhere, principally from the South. Necessarily, then, the development of

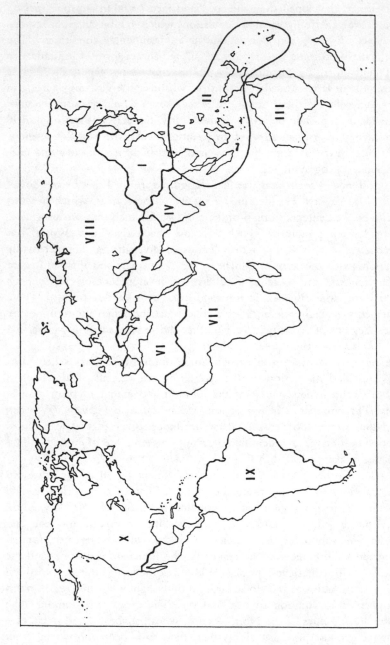

FIGURE 1: Regions of Genetic Diversity and Their Associated Crops (legend on facing page).

the rich but "gene poor" nations of the North has been predicated on transfers of plant genetic resources from the poor but "gene rich" nations of the South. The historical process by which this has occurred provides an important context for the current controversy.

Germplasm Appropriation

The spread of cultivated plants to new areas has been a constant feature of human history. But such processes were long characterized by slow extensions at the margins of ecological adaptation. By 1300 Europe had added barley, wheat, alfalfa, and a variety of vegetables to its original complement of crops. But the discovery of the New World touched off a dramatic and unprecedentedly widespread movement of plant genetic resources.

When Columbus returned from his voyage of exploration in 1493 he brought not only news of his discovery, but also maize seeds. The next year he was back in the New World carrying planting material for wheat, olives, chickpeas, onions, radishes, sugar cane, and citrus fruits with which he hoped to support a colony. Thus was initiated the great "Columbian Exchange": maize, the common bean, potatoes, squash, sweet potatoes, cassava, and peanuts went east, while wheat, rye, oats, and Old World vegetables went

---

LEGEND FOR FIGURE 1 *(facing page)*

I. CHINO-JAPANESE
 soybeans
 oranges
 rice
 tea*

II. INDOCHINESE
 banana
 coconut (copra)*
 coconut
 yam
 rice
 sugar cane*

III. AUSTRALIAN
 none

IV. HINDUSTANEAN
 jute*
 rice

V. WEST CENTRAL
 ASIATIC
 wheat
 barley
 grapes
 apples
 linseed*
 sesame*
 flax*

VI. MEDITERRANEAN
 sugar beet*
 cabbage
 rapeseed*
 olive*

VII. AFRICAN
 oil palm (oil)*
 oil palm (kernal)*
 sorghum
 millet
 coffee*

VIII. EURO-SIBERIAN
 oats
 rye

IX. LATIN AMERICAN
 maize
 potato
 sweet potato
 cocoa*
 cassava
 tomato
 cotton (lint)*
 cottonseed (oil)*
 seed cotton (meal)*
 tobacco*
 rubber*

X. NORTH AMERICAN
 sunflower*

 *industrial crops

west. Germplasm transfers of staple food crops were undertaken as a matter of course principally by sailors and settlers interested in subsistence production.

Maize and potatoes in particular had a profound impact on European diets. These crops produce more calories per unit of land than any other staple but cassava (another New World crop which spread quickly through tropical Africa). As such they were accepted, though often reluctantly, by a growing urban proletariat and by peasantries increasingly pressed by enclosures.[6]

In addition to new food staples, the New World offered new crops of great medicinal and industrial significance such as cocoa, quinine, rubber, and tobacco. The Americas also provided new locales for the production of the tropical crops of Asia and Africa (spices, bananas, tea, coffee, sugar, indigo). While food-crop germplasm moved in all directions, the tropical nature of many plantation crops meant that their germplasm tended to move laterally, among colonial possessions, rather than from the colonial periphery to the imperial center. The banana, originally from Southeast Asia, was transferred to Central and South America as well as to the Caribbean and Africa. Coffee from Ethiopia made its way to the Caribbean, South and Central America, and Asia. Sugar cane from Southeast Asia was transferred to East, North, and Southern Africa as well as to Central and South America and the Caribbean.[7]

As the commercial value of plant products increased, germplasm was recognized as a resource of tremendous strategic importance. European governments went to great lengths to prevent their competitors from obtaining useful plant genetic materials. The Dutch, for example, destroyed all the nutmeg and clove trees in the Moluccas except those on the three islands where they had established plantations. And the French made export of indigo seed from Antigua a capital offense. In the young United States the need to collect both food- and industrial-crop germplasm was particularly acute given the North American continent's relative genetic poverty.[8] By 1878, germplasm collection activity accounted for one-third of the Department of Agriculture's annual budget.

Such germplasm collection efforts on the part of the advanced industrial nations of the North have continued, indeed even accelerated, up to the present time. Although North American and European powers had by 1900 appropriated the plant genetic material that enabled them to become the breadbaskets of the globe, achievement of agricultural hegemony has been genetically precarious. The germplasm transferred from the source areas of genetic diversity constituted only a small proportion of the total genetic variability available there. Although the plant breeders of the North have worked this material into extremely productive "elite" varieties, this process has further narrowed the genetic makeup of advanced industrial agriculture. The commercial plant cultivars developed in the North are high-performing but also exhibit "genetic uniformity" and consequently suffer from "genetic

144

vulnerability."[9] Biological populations are dynamic and malleable entities. As pests and diseases mutate and as the environment changes, crop varieties are faced with new challenges to their survival. Genetically narrow cultivars have, by definition, limited genetic capabilities with which to respond to such challenges.

The classic illustration of the perils of genetic uniformity and vulnerability is the "Great Hunger" visited upon Ireland in 1846–1847 by the failure of the potato crop. In order to maintain productivity in the face of such vulnerability, plant breeders must continually incorporate new genes into elite cultivars in what has been aptly termed a "varietal relay race" that maintains a steady flow of lines into and out of production.[10] The source of many of these genes is the lower yielding but genetically variable land races and other materials that are located in regions of diversity in the Third World. Since World War II, the nations of the advanced industrial North have been collecting germplasm not for the purpose of adding new species or new varieties to their agricultures, but to accumulate material from which specific genetic characters may be extracted for incorporation into existing cultivars as they are rendered vulnerable by the changing nature of pests, disease, and environmental factors.

Contemporary Plant Genetic Dependence and Interdependence

Inter- and intra-hemispheric transfers of germplasm have created a world in which domestic agricultures are often based on, and continue to benefit from, genetic materials with origins well beyond domestic borders. Any assessment of the political economy of plant genetic resources must take into account this "genetic geography." Our melding of regions of genetic diversity with political boundaries, as illustrated in Figure 1, permits us to address the question of the plant genetic contributions and debts of particular geopolitical entities in an empirical fashion.[11]

Using production statistics from the FAO's *1983 Production Yearbook,* we calculated two types of measures for each of the ten regions of genetic diversity specified in Figure 1. First, we calculated the proportion of global production of the leading crops that is accounted for by species for which each region is the locus of genetic diversity. This figure, expressed as a percentage, is a measure of the *genetic contribution* of each region to world agriculture.

Second, for each region we calculated the proportion of production in that region accounted for by species introduced from the other regions of diversity. This figure, also expressed as a percentage, is a measure of the *genetic debt* owed by each region to the others. Moreover, to the extent that plant-breeding improvement in any crop depends on continued access to the genetic resources in that crop's region of diversity, this measure provides an index of what can be termed the plant genetic "dependence" of a region on non-indigenous sources of genetic diversity.

We performed these calculations for the twenty leading food crops and for the twenty leading industrial crops.* The results of these calculations are displayed in Figures 2 and 3. The most general conclusion to be drawn from Figures 2 and 3 is that, in plant genetic terms, the world is strikingly interdependent. With regard to food crops, only three (Indochinese, Hindustanean, West Central Asiatic) of the ten regions defined in this study have indices of dependence of less than 50 percent. With reference to industrial crops, only one region (Indochinese) shows a dependence index less than 70 percent. The world's regional agricultures are characterized not by crop genetic self-sufficiency but by substantial, and often extreme, dependence on "introduced" genetic materials.

There are important patterns of variation within this broad structure of interdependence. Figure 2 shows three distinct clusters of points. The Latin American and West Central Asiatic regions have made particularly significant contributions to global food-crop production, and are also among the most genetically self-reliant of regions. A second cluster includes the Indochinese, Chino-Japanese, and Hindustanean regions. These share a moderate level of dependence and a lower, but significant, level of contribution to the crop genetic base of global agriculture. These five regions contain nearly all of the Third World nations (with the exception of African countries), and *they have provided the genetic material that undergirds fully 91.7 percent of global production of food crops.*

The final set of points is associated with the regions that contain (with the exception of Japan) all of the world's advanced industrial nations. These regions are characterized by very high, even absolute, dependence indices and by minor, and even null, genetic contributions. Ironically, the agricultures of the advanced industrial breadbaskets of the world are almost completely based on plant genetic materials derived from other regions. At least in food crops, there is empirical justification for the characterization of the North as "rich, but gene-poor," and the South as "poor, but gene-rich." And the former has clearly benefited from the genetic largesse of the latter. While no single region can claim genetic self-reliance, and while the South is not uniformly "gene-rich" (witness the case of Africa), a clear differentiation of North and South is apparent in Figure 2.

---

* Calculations for food crops are based on metric tons. However, becasue of the skewing introduced by tremendous differences in weight among some industrial crops (for example, sugar cane and cotton), we calculated industrial crop figures on the basis of hectares in production rather than tonnage.

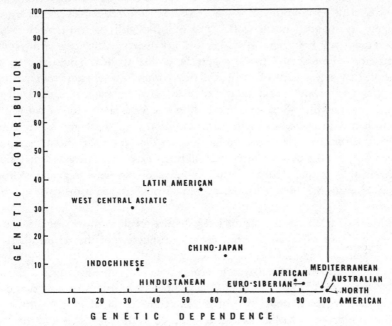

FIGURE 2: Plant Genetic Contribution and Dependence, Food Crops

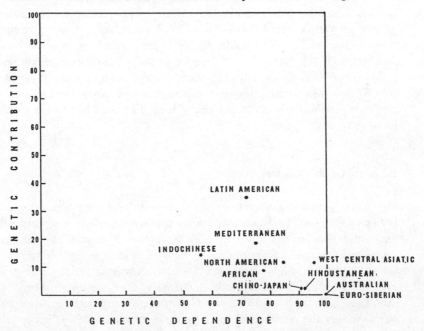

FIGURE 3: Plant Genetic Contribution and Dependence, Industrial Crops

147

The data on industrial crops in Figure 3 reinforces our overall vision of a genetically interdependent world. The North–South relation characteristic of food crops still holds, but is weaker and involves a greater degree of regional and crop specificity. With 30.4 percent of the world's industrial crop area devoted to descendants of Latin American origin, that region retains its position as the prime global donor of plant genetic material. But while the Australian and Euro-Siberian regions do not serve as the region of diversity for a single industrial crop, over 10 percent of world industrial crop area is planted with the sunflower, a species indigenous to the North American region. An even higher 18.2 percent of world industrial crop area is planted in varieties originally from the Mediterranean region. And in general, regional contributions of industrial crops are more evenly distributed than is the case with food species.

More detailed calculations of interregional relations show that it is the interdependence of regions within each hemisphere, not the relation between the developed and underdeveloped regions, that is the important feature in the global patterns of industrial crop production. For instance, over a third of Mediterranean industrial crop land is planted in North American sunflower. Similarly, nearly a third of North American industrial crop hectareage is planted in crops of Mediterranean origin such as the sugar beet and the olive.

In the South, as in the North, intrahemispheric relationships are most significant. These patterns are in large measure the product of lateral transfers of germplasm that occurred during the colonial era. Over 50 percent of the industrial crop hectareage in Latin America, for instance, is accounted for by sugar cane (30.4 percent), which originated in the Indochinese region and by coffee (25.7 percent), which originated in Africa. And despite the fact that over 35 percent of world industrial crop hectareage is planted in crops of Latin American origin, less than 30 percent of Latin American hectareage is planted in indigenous species.

Genesis of the Controversy

By "plant genetic resources," plant scientists have conventionally meant primitive cultivars, land races, and wild and weedy relatives of crop plants. Such materials have long been objects of collection and have been appropriated principally from the South for preservation in gene banks and for use in plant breeding programs.[12] Despite their tremendous utility, such materials have been obtained free of charge as the "common heritage," and therefore common good, of humanity. On the other hand, the elite cultivars developed by the commercial seed industries of the North are accorded the status of private property. They are commodities obtainable by purchase. A number of factors have combined to galvanize the emergence of global political conflict around this apparent asymmetry.

Over the last fifteen years there has been a growing awareness that global processes of industrial and agricultural development have often resulted in substantial environmental externalities. One of the most serious of these has been the accelerating destruction of biological diversity. The most visible and well-publicized example of such biological impoverishment is the destruction of tropical rainforests by timber and mining companies and by megaprojects such as the TransAm highway or the Jari paper plant in Brazil. General concern over the broad problem of biological destruction helped focus attention on the question of plant genetic resources in particular.[13]

It is now recognized that one of the consequences of the Green Revolution has been the gradual displacement of the traditional land races upon which the development of high-yielding Green Revolution varieties has been based.[14] The 1970 corn blight epidemic in the United States brought the consequences of this genetic erosion home to the developed nations. Processes of concentration and internationalization in the seed industry have also proved to be catalysts for the emergence of the current controversy. Since 1970, a wave of mergers and acquisitions which has still not run its course has swept virtually every American or European seed company of any size or significance into the corporate folds of the world's industrial elite. Many of the acquisitions have been made by transnational petrochemical and pharmaceutical firms with substantial agrichemical interests. The seeds gatherers of today are the Monsantos, ICIs, Pfizers, Upjohns, Ciba-Geigys, Shells, and ARCOs of the world. And these companies have marketing ambitions for their seed subsidiaries that match the global character of their other product lines.

Attention to questions of value and property rights in germplasm have been further emphasized by the emergence of the cluster of new genetic technologies commonly referred to as "biotechnology." Germplasm is the fundamental raw material of the genetic engineer. As the transformed seed industry pushed for the recognition of the monetary value and proprietary status of "elite" cultivars, plant germplasm as "common heritage" was brought into unambiguous and contradictory juxtaposition with plant germplasm as a commodity. Global patterns of germplasm exchange came to seem doubly inequitable to some Third World observers since the commercial varieties purveyed by the seed trade have been developed out of germplasm initially obtained freely from the Third World.

As a result of this constellation of factors, there was by 1980 a growing unease with the global germplasm system among some Third World politicians, diplomats, and scientists. Third World resentment and disaffection with the international "genetic order," informed and encouraged by the activities of activist groups, culminated in political action at the FAO. This action took concrete form in Resolution 8/83, which mandated the inclusion of the elite and proprietary varieties of the North under the rubric of human-kind's common heritage in plant genetic resources. This enlarged conception of what constitutes common heritage is opposed by those nations with highly developed private seed industries, which are engaged in breeding proprietary crop varieties for commercial sale. Australia, Canada, and the United States have indicated that they will not adhere to the Undertaking, and Belgium, Denmark, Finland, France, the Federal Republic of Germany, Ireland, Israel, the Netherlands, New Zealand, Norway, Sweden, and the United Kingdom have agreed to do so only with restrictions. Conversely, virtually every non-aligned or Third World member nation of the FAO that has provided an official response has expressed "support without restriction" for the Undertaking.[15] And in the almost four years since the passage of the Undertaking, movement towards accommodation or agreement has been slow.

The Politics of Common Heritage: North

There are four principal arguments made to justify the appropriation of certain categories of plant genetic resources as a common good. First, it is asserted that "raw" germplasm cannot be given a price because of the indeterminacy associated with the usefulness of any particular germplasm accession. The argument is not that the genetic materials collected in the Third World have no *use-value*, but that this utility cannot and should not take on *exchange-value*.

It is true that genetic materials present the market with some unique problems in pricing. But the inability to set a price through the "natural" operation of the market is not in itself justification for failure to assign some sort of exchange-value to something with recognized utility. There are a variety of nonmarket strategies that could be used to establish compensation schedules for appropriation and use of raw genetic materials if there were a willingness to do so.

A second principal justification for the position taken by the advanced capitalist nations is that "raw germplasm only becomes valuable after considerable investment of time and money, both in adapting exotic germplasm for use by applied plant breeders and in incorporating the germplasm into varieties useful to farmers."[16] This argument relies implicitly on a labor theory of value. It is asserted that only the application of scientists' labor adds value to the natural gift of germplasm. But most plant genetic resources are not simply the gift of nature. Land races and primitive cultivars have been developed by peasant farmers; they are the product of human labor. Nor is the labor contained in such materials only historical. Plant genetic diversity, which is the

150

real resource of interest, is even now produced and reproduced through the day-to-day activities of farmers throughout the world.

A third principal line of argument defends the appropriation of plant genetic resources as a public good by claiming that "collection [of germplasm] does not deprive a country of anything."[17] When plant collectors sample a population they acquire only a few pounds of seed or plant matter. The vast bulk of the material is left untouched and in place. Unlike the extraction of most natural resources, it is argued, the "mining" of plant germplasm results in no significant depletion of the resource itself. With most natural resources (e.g., minerals, timber, fish) use-value is appropriated in direct proportion to the volume of the resource extracted. But with plant germplasm the entire utility of the whole is in the part, and this masks the magnitude of the transfer of use-value which is nevertheless occurring. The donor nation, in supplying germplasm as a common good, is forgoing the opportunity to receive a reciprocal flow of benefits in return for its contribution – that is, it is forgoing the opportunity to charge a pure economic rent. Moreover, the alienation of germplasm can ultimately result in damage to the economy of those nations that practice genetic largesse. Industrial plant tissue culture – the growing of plant cells in a nutrient medium for the extraction of phytoproducts – threatens to eliminate Third World markets for a wide variety of drugs, spices, flavors, dyes, and even such high-volume commodities as sugar, cocoa, and coffee. Thus it is highly misleading to suggest that nations which permit free appropriation of their germplasm suffer no loss of any kind.

Finally, it is often claimed that adherence to the Undertaking is precluded by existing law. Such laws would have to be rescinded or altered to allow for the operationalization of the concept of "common heritage" for all types of plant germplasm. But the mere existence of such laws does not in itself justify the differential treatment of peasant land races and elite commercial varieties. Law is a social creation, not an immutable reflection of the natural order.

The arguments put forward by the seed industry and by representatives of the advanced capitalist nations to justify distinguishing some germplasm as exchange-valueless (and therefore free) common heritage and other germplasm as a valuable commodity and private property are baseless. That such a distinction exists has nothing to do with the essential character of the germplasm itself and everything to do with social history and political economy.

The Politics of Common Heritage: South

The nations of the Third World thus have legitimate grounds for demanding to have all types of plant germplasm treated similarly. But, given the contemporary structure of the world economy, is the designation of all plant genetic resources as freely available common property an appropriate strategy? If the objective of the nations of the South is the achievement of a truly "new international economic order," we think not. While the concept of "common heritage" certainly has an intuitive appeal for progressives, the material consequences of the "decommodification" of all plant germplasm might, given the realities of the world capitalist economy, actually work to the detriment of the nations of the South.

Global acceptance of the principle of common heritage for all plant germplasm would actually alter existing patterns of plant genetic resource use and exchange very little. Equality of access to this particular natural resource does not necessarily imply equality in the distribution of benefits. Given the genetic vulnerability of their high-performing agricultures, the advanced capitalist nations have a greater need to utilize plant genetic diversity than do the countries of the Third World. They also have a much greater financial and scientific capacity to do so. Formal institutionalization of common heritage will simply legitimate the differential abilities of North and South to appropriate, utilize, and benefit from plant genetic resources. Implementation of the principle of common heritage would not only allow the advanced capitalist nations to "mine" plant genetic resources with increasing intensity, it would also preclude donor nations from realizing any return benefit – financial or in-kind – from the extraction of the genetic information contained within their borders.

Under a regime of common heritage the South would gain access to genetic material it previously has been unable to obtain. But is access to advanced breeding lines and other elite germplasm developed by commercial seed firms in the industrial North actually a benefit? Such lines are developed for use in industrialized, capital-intensive, energy-intensive agricultural production systems and will not be appropriate to the needs of the bulk of Third World farmers. The FAO's Undertaking on Plant Genetic Resources does in fact constitute a direct challenge to private property and the commodity-form. The designation of proprietary breeding lines as common heritage would actually reverse the thrust of capitalist development. Yet the desirability and ultimate effectiveness of such an unambiguously confrontational strategy are not entirely clear. What makes the Undertaking a challenge of unique potential is the broad support it has garnered among Third World nations and the more or less unified front they have so far posed to the advanced capitalist nations. Maintaining such unity is already difficult. The terms "Third World" and "South" do not necessarily imply unanimity of interest on all matters. The developing nations are a very diverse set of countries with heterogeneous economic systems and ideological orientations. It is by no means clear that the political will exists for a sustained international assault on private property in plant germplasm.

What is clear is that the elite and breeders' lines of private-sector seed companies are now private property and that capital intends to do all it can to ensure that they remain so. There is no indication that the advanced capitalist nations are willing to begin dismantling the institutional arrangements that confer proprietary rights to genetic information. Given the uncertain unity of the South on the issue and the tenacity with which capitalist interests are likely to defend the sanctity of private property, the prospects for actually achieving common-heritage status for all types of plant germplasm are not bright. The South's demands are legitimate, but misplaced. The real problem for the South is not access to the elite lines of the North, but establishing control over and realizing some benefit from the appropriation and utilization of its own resources. We believe that this requires a political strategy other than common heritage.

National Sovereignty as a Political Strategy

Ironically, the FAO Undertaking on Plant Genetic Resources conflicts not only with "plant breeder's rights" legislation, but also with the right to "national sovereignty over natural resources" guaranteed by the United Nations itself.[18] Third World nations have little to gain from quixotic pursuit of common heritage in plant genetic resources. But they have a great deal to gain through international acceptance of the principle that plant genetic resources constitute a form of national property. Establishment of this principle would provide the basis for an international framework through which Third World nations could be compensated for the appropriation and use of their plant genetic information.

Codification of the status of plant genetic resources as national property has a clear basis in international law. Moreover, while capitalist interests are unalterably opposed to decommodifying their breeding lines, there are indications that they would be willing to provide compensation for use of plant genetic resources. On the whole, the recognition of exchange-value in land races will prove more palatable for private companies than continued conflict and possible restrictions on the flow of what is, for them, an essential raw material.

A national property initiative is by no means an ideal solution to the plant germplasm controversy. A principal problem with establishing a compensatory framework for plant genetic resources is that plant genetic resources are distributed unequally within the Third World as well as between North and South.[19] A multilateral approach might avoid such competition and could be built upon the current willingness of most Third World nations to confront the issue of plant genetic resources as a North–South issue. The FAO's International Undertaking on Plant Genetic Resources appears to provide a useful institutional framework for preserving Third World unity on the matter.

Although mitigating the centrifugal pressures of nationalist interests will be difficult, there are some indications that arguments for a multilateral approach are not unrealistically utopian. The second meeting of the FAO's Commission on Plant Genetic Resources took place in March 1987 with some interesting developments. In an effort to break over three years of impasse over implementation of the Undertaking, the CPGR agreed that a "contact group" comprising representatives of both the developed and developing nations should be established. This contact group will explore the possibilities of a rapprochement, "on the basis of three principles: acceptance of free exchange of plant genetic resources; recognition of plant breeders' rights; and recognition of farmers' rights so as to acknowledge the work carried out by previous generations of cultivators."[20] This straightforward mandate signals a major shift in the terrain of debate and embodies some far-reaching implications.

The principles are, *prima facie,* contradictory. Recognition of plant breeders' rights necessarily implies that at least some plant genetic resources – i.e., protected and patented varieties – will not be available for free exchange. Balancing this concession to the advanced industrial nations is the principle specifying that "farmers' rights" will also be recognized. The CPGR coined the new concept of farmers' rights expressly to parallel the established concept of plant breeders' rights. Just as plant scientists are entitled to a reward for their labor in creating breeding lines and elite varieties, so farmers have a right to a reward for creating and maintaining land races and other "raw" plant genetic resources. Further, just as the reward for plant breeders is not moral but material, so should farmers be entitled to material reward for use of the fruits of their labor. In order to provide a mechanism for the realization of such reward, members of the CPGR noted that an "international fund could be a means to compensate farmer communities *through support to the countries concerned*" (emphasis added).[21]

We believe that such movement is, on balance, in an appropriate direction. Of course, many difficulties remain to be overcome. The question of farmers' rights will be of pivotal importance. Structuring some compensatory framework will require much negotiation and compromise, both within the Third World and between the developing nations and the industrialized countries. The objective of the initiative in FAO must be to achieve a real redistribution of the flow of benefits between North and South, not to gain mere verbal recognition of "rights." Arrangements need to be made for the advanced industrial nations to make payments to the proposed fund in return for access to global collections of plant genetic materials collected and stored by national governments in cooperation with the FAO.

Realization of an effective "International Plant Gene Fund" of this type will require a high degree of cooperation among the nations of the South.

One way would be to negotiate with the North not for cash compensation, but for scientific assistance and technology transfer in support of plant genetic conservation, construction of gene banks, and the training of plant breeders in the FAO system. Such an arrangement also has the advantage of placing the determination of compensation in a political rather than market setting. This provides the basis for "noncommodified" political struggle which is not necessarily reproductive of capitalist social relations.

The current impasse benefits no one and threatens the world's food supply. National sovereignty, not common heritage, supplies the potential solution to the current geopolitical deadlock. It provides a viable means by which the current conflict can be resolved in a manner that enhances the position of the nations and peoples of the Third World.

Notes

The research on which this article is based was supported by a Resources for the Future Dissertation Fellowship, and by a Hatch Grant from the College of Agriculture and Life Sciences, University of Wisconsin-Madison. The authors would like to acknowledge the comments provided by participants in the Social Organization Training Seminar and the Sociology of Economic Change Training Seminar, Department of Sociology, University of Wisconsin-Madison, and by the editorial collective of *Socialist Review*.

1.   Norman Myers, *A Wealth of Wild Species*, Boulder, Colo.: Westview 1983, p. 24; Garrison Wilkes, "Current Status of Crop Germplasm," *Critical Reviews in Plant Sciences*, vol. 1 (1983), p. 156.

2.   Food and Agriculture Organization of the United Nations, "International Undertaking on Plant Genetic Resources," Resolution 8/83, C 83/REP/8, Rome: FAO 1983.

3.   J. G. Hawkes, *The Diversity of Crop Plants*, Cambridge: Harvard University Press 1983.

4.   Jack R. Harlan, "Agricultural Origins: Centers and Noncenters," *Science*, vol. 174 (1971), pp. 468–74; Hawkes, *Diversity of Crop Plants*.

5.   Our source of data is the Food and Agriculture Organization's *1983 Production Yearbook* (Rome: FAO 1984). We distinguish between food and industrial crops in order to capture an elusive but meaningful distinction. We define food crops as those that feed people more or less directly and are frequently grown by subsistence farmers around the world. Industrial crops are those that feed people indirectly after industrial processing, are often grown on plantations or large-scale farms, or are grown and processed for non-food purposes.

6.   Fernand Braudel, *The Structures of Everyday Life: The Limits of the Possible*, New York: Harper & Row 1979.

7.   David B. Grigg, *The Agricultural Systems of the World: An Evolutionary Approach*, London: Cambridge University Press 1974; Lucile H. Brockway, *Science and Colonial Expansion: The Role of the British Royal Botanic Gardens*, New York: Academic Press 1979.

8.   For a comprehensive historical analysis of the role of the plant sciences in the development of American capitalism, see Jack Kloppenburg, Jr., *First the Seed: The Political Economy of Plant Biotechnology, 1492–2000*, New York: Cambridge University Press 1988.

9.   See Wilkes, "Current Status of Crop Germplasm," for a full explanation of these terms.

10.   Donald L. Plucknett and Nigel J. H. Smith, "Sustaining Agricultural Yields," *BioScience*, vol. 36 (1986), pp. 1, 40–45.

11.   The methodology and empirical analysis upon which this article is based are more fully described in Jack Kloppenburg, Jr., and Daniel Lee Kleinman, "The Plant Germplasm Controversy," *BioScience*, vol. 37, no. 3 (1987), pp. 190–98.

12. Otto H. Frankel and Erna Bennett, *Genetic Resources in Plants: Their Exploration and Conservation*, Philadelphia: F. A. Davis 1970; Wilkes, "Current Status of Crop Germplasm."

13. See, e.g., United States Department of State, *Proceedings of the US Strategy Conference on Biological Diversity*, Washington, D.C.: Department of State 1982; Edward C. Wolf, "Conserving Biological Diversity," in Lester R. Brown, ed., *State of the World, 1985*, New York: W. W. Norton 1986.

14. See, e.g., Otto H. Frankel, "Genetic Dangers in the Green Revolution," *World Agriculture*, vol. 19 (1970), pp. 9–13; Jack R. Harlan, "Our Vanishing Genetic Resources," *Science*, vol. 188 (1975), pp. 618–21; Garrison Wilkes, "The World's Crop Plant Germplasm: An Endangered Resource," *Bulletin of the Atomic Scientists*, vol. 33 (1977), pp. 8–16.

15. Food and Agricultural Organization of the United Nations, "Country and International Institutions Response to Conference Resolution 8/83 and Council Resolution 1/85," CGR/85/3, Rome: FAO 1985.

16. Pioneer Hi-Bred International, *Conservation and Utilization of Exotic Germplasm to Improve Varieties*, Des Moines, Iowa: Pioneer Hi-Bred International 1984.

17. William Brown, "The Coming Debate over Ownership of Plant Germplasm," in *Proceedings of the 39th Annual Corn and Sorghum Research Conference*, Washington, D.C.: American Seed Trade Association 1985, p. 46.

18. United Nations, Resolution 3281 (XXIX), Sixth Special Session of the United Nations General Assembly, 1974.

19. See Kloppenburg and Kleinman, "Plant Germplasm Controversy."

20. Commission on Plant Genetic Resources, "Commission on Plant Genetic Resources, Second Session, Rome, 16–20 March 1987, Draft Report Part 1," CPGR/87/REP.I, Rome: FAO 1987, p. 5.

21. Ibid., p. 3.

9

"Perestroika with a Human Face?"
(1988)
Esther Kingston-Mann

Soviet officials, artists, scholars, and journalists are facing up to the problems of their present and their past in a manner which may be unprecedented in modern times. In post-Nazi Germany, or, for that matter, in post-Vietnam America, one searches in vain for Western political leaders willing to subject themselves to such painful and searching questions about national policy and values. With a certain degree of complacency, most Western observers concentrate their attention on the evidence that the Soviets are recognizing the virtues of capitalism and the utter bankruptcy of communism; commentators to the left of the political spectrum have been relatively silent on the subject of the Soviet economy and its critics. But within the Soviet Union itself, economic debates are more complex than Western writers have so far indicated. Alongside the widespread and widely publicized desire for freedom from intrusive state control and anger at mounting shortages of consumer goods, there exists a quite different, underreported, and at least equally powerful set of expectations which shape the behavior of Soviet experts and ordinary citizens.

Ever since 1917, material guarantees of health care, employment, and education have been a central economic priority of the Soviet state. For more than seven decades, political leaders, schoolteachers, and artists have encouraged the Soviet people to consider employment, health care, and shelter as obvious and quite uncontroversial human rights. While such ideological traditions and realities have in no sense created either a nation of altruists or of materially well-cared-for citizens, they have generated attitudes which deserve more serious examination than they have yet received. It is striking, for ex-

157

ample, that Soviet discussions of health care focus only on deficiencies in the quality and delivery of services and on the evils of privileged treatment for bureaucrats and officials. The universal right to health care has never been and may well *never be* called into question.

Along similar lines, popular distrust of economic polarization, described by some Soviet and American economists as "mindless envy" of the talented, and by others as revulsion against profiteering and dishonesty, constitute an equally important aspect of the current scene. In the summer of 1989, a poll conducted by the reform-oriented *Moscow News* provided results inconceivable within the American context, where "doing the best for one's self" is a sacred principle and egalitarianism is suspect in any sphere of economic activity. Of the Muscovites queried on the topic of economic inequalities, 8 percent supported the growth of income differentiations if declared "legal" by the government. A substantial 42 percent approved the growth of differentiation which was not "excessive," while 50 percent supported the principle of a more egalitarian distribution of wealth. In other words, 92 percent of those interviewed rejected the principle of unlimited acquisition of wealth.

According to *Moscow News* editor I. S. Kuteinikov, the most serious obstacle to the expansion of private enterprise in the Soviet Union is not the party bureaucracy, but the negative weight of public opinion. As "cooperatives" (limited private partnerships) increase from 13,000 in April 1988 to 133,000 in July 1989 and now employ almost 3 million people, ordinary citizens and many of their newly elected representatives in the Congress of People's Deputies denounce them as a source of high prices, unemployment, violent crime, and threats to the material security of ordinary Soviet citizens. The Boston *Globe* reported in December 1989 that Soviet shoppers attributed the emptiness of grocery shelves during the holiday season to the greed of "cooperatives" which were buying up food at low prices, stockpiling it, and reselling it at enormous profit to themselves. According to the outspoken reform economist N. Shmelev,

> You Americans need to understand our social traditions. If Gorbachev himself said to me, "set up a privately owned factory. Do it tonight, and I will support you," I tell you that working people would come from the streets that very night and burn the factory down!

In a speech at Harvard's Russian Research Center in 1988, Shmelev went on: "Unless you Americans understand our traditions, you will not understand the choices which we will make." Both the reality and significance of such popular sentiments have been neglected by Western observers, or dismissed as a sign of the backwardness of Soviet workers and peasants. As an American member of Shmelev's Harvard audience commented, "Hasn't anyone ever explained to the Soviet people what the benefits of private enterprise are? Why can't they seem to understand it?"

The following discussion of *perestroika* will examine these issues, placing special emphasis on one of its most neglected features – the attempt to consider economic growth as a social question. In the process, I will try to confront some of the reformers in their own terms, instead of concentrating only on the market-oriented features of their arguments.

The Soviet Economy in Perspective

The defects of the Soviet economic system are familiar to most Americans. The recent work of Marshall Goldman (*Gorbachev's Challenge,* New York 1987) provides a particularly eloquent discussion of the scandals and shortcomings which afflict Soviet management, production, and distribution processes. According to Robert Kuttner, it was the "utter failure of communist economic production that forced Mikhail Gorbachev to tolerate, and then instigate, reform"(Boston *Globe,* December 29, 1989). But a number of surprising anomalies exist in the midst of the Soviet Union's bleak economic picture of shortages and production failures. The Soviet Union is the world's leading producer of machine tools, tractors and combines, and electric power equipment. Western commentators give high marks to the achievements of Soviet energy technology and to the current level of research and development in the field of chemistry. The Soviets possess the largest microbiological industry in the world, with a level of expertise and a productive capacity approaching world-class status. At a time when the National Science Foundation is predicting an American shortage of 540,000 engineers by the year 2000, the Soviets already possess far more PhD-level engineers than the United States. During the Brezhnev era, the growing number of Soviet engineers was a source of concern to Western technology experts; in the age of *perestroika*, it is triggering investment ventures and a rising level of curiosity and interest on the part of Western entrepreneurs (in *Forbes* magazine's stirring call to action: "Capitalists of the world, awake!"). A striking feature of Soviet technological expertise is that over 50 percent of Soviet engineers are women, in comparison with an approximately 6 percent level documented in the latest US statistics (*Forbes,* January 8, 1990; Michael Berry, ed., *Science and Technology in the USSR,* London 1988; and John Kiser, *Communist Entrepreneurs,* New York 1989).

Between 1950 and 1983, Soviet agricultural output increased at a relatively steady 3 percent per year, which is higher than in the United States during the same period, and its industry outproduced the United States by 80 percent in steel and by 42 percent in oil. Recent CIA computations indicate that the

Soviet Union has maintained an average growth rate in real gross national income for the past fifteen years which is about equal to that of the United States. In 1985–86, the economy registered a spectacular increase in the gross national product, the highest growth rate achieved in the past ten years. According to the economist Stuart Anderson (*Bloc: The Soviet Union and Eastern European Business Journal,* vol. 5, no. 1, 1989, and *Global Finance,* January 1989, p. 55), Western banks, taking into account Soviet gold reserves and other assets, rate the USSR's credit worthiness equal to Australia's. In both 1987 and 1988 the USSR had a manageable debt-service ratio of approximately 25 percent.

As we attempt to sort out such disparate economic evidence, it becomes clear how misleading comparisons between the United States and the USSR can be. Our evaluation of the Soviet economic record depends upon our criteria, and upon whether we compare it to the pre-Soviet period, to the Soviet Union's neighbors to the South and East, or to the United States in 1990. In terms of its own past, a centralized and repressive Soviet economic system has created a situation in which each succeeding generation since 1917 has lived better in material terms than the one which preceded it. When the Bolsheviks came to power in 1917, infant mortality rates were about 250 per 1000. Today they are close to 30. To the South and East, the infant mortality rates in Turkey are currently 187 per 1000, in Pakistan 113 per 1000, and in Afghanistan, 236 per 1000. In the United States, the infant mortality rate is about 14 per 1000 and rising. According to many scholarly estimates, the Soviet living standard today is about 60 percent of ours.

If we consider seriously the fact that the USSR has achieved successes which have so far eluded the populations of Turkey, Iran, Afghanistan, and many other regions of the Third World, it becomes easier to understand how Gorbachev's call for far-reaching economic change may coexist with the claim that "in the eyes of the world's progressive public, the Soviet Union has been and remains the embodiment of people's age-old social hopes." Today's Soviet "conservatives" emphasize a traditional public self-image of the Soviet Union as a Third World model of immense success in raising material living standards for the majority of the population. According to the writer M. Antonov,

> Only naive people and wretched economic science could conclude that if we create a new economic mechanism and appoint literate managers everywhere, everything will be okay and His Majesty the Ruble will take care of the rest (*Moskva,* no. 3, 1988).

Gorbachev and his supporters insist on the need to balance traditional social welfare guarantees with greater economic efficiency and scope for individual and local decision-making. Boris Yeltsin, one of the most popular of

Gorbachev's critics, seems equally insistent on the need for both economic decentralization and social justice, and attacks Gorbachev for failing to move rapidly enough in both directions at once. At the other end of the "economics" spectrum are those who consider themselves "progressives" and concern themselves more with the positive benefits of a freer market than with the issue of balancing market and welfare concerns (although, as we shall see, in comparison with American economists, Soviet "progressives" are less able to ignore social questions).

Why Perestroika?

> A revolutionary situation has truly been created in our country. The "heights" can no longer rule, and the "lower parts" do not want to live as before.
>
> – N. Shmelev, *Novy mir,* no. 4, April 1988

Ever since 1917, the Soviet economy and society have been held together by a social contract seldom fully articulated, but nonetheless powerful and long-lasting. In return for the acceptance of one-party rule and a willingness to close ranks against a variety of internal and external threats, Lenin and his successors promised to prevent foreign military conquest, guarantee economic and social security to the majority, and eliminate starvation and illiteracy. A constant state of emergency was invoked during the first 50 years of Soviet power – and all too often, the emergencies were not fabricated but real. As civil war and foreign intervention followed three years of world war and a year of revolution, a backward economy repeatedly assaulted the hope of Soviet men and women that their children would survive disease and hunger and grow to adulthood. In the decades which preceded the Nazi invasion, Stalin argued that Soviet weakness invited foreign attack, and called for ever greater economic discipline. In World War I as in World War II Soviet losses were greater than those of all the rest of the combatants combined (20 million Soviet lives were lost in each conflict). According to B. P. Kurashvili (head of the theory sector of the Institute of State and Law of the USSR Academy of Sciences), socialist production relations in the Soviet Union and elsewhere have always varied according to whether the society is experiencing normal or emergency conditions. In times of crisis, unlimited centralization and "militarization" of the economy is fostered by officials and accepted by a fearful populace.

By the 1980s, Soviet citizens – unlike their Indian, Afgani, or Pakistani counterparts, were no longer dying of malnutrition and starvation. A generation far healthier and far better educated than their parents and grandparents has begun to indicate in no uncertain terms that the restrictions of a hierarchical, "command" system will not be accepted for the sake of the security goals which have already been achieved. *Perestroika* itself may well represent a rejection of the freedom-restricting terms of the post-revolutionary social contract. In a sense, its every feature is embodied in the "success story" of Gorbachev himself. Born on a collective farm and raised by his grandparents after losing his father in World War II, Gorbachev began work at fourteen as assistant to a combine harvester operator. When he was able to make the leap from a north Caucasus secondary school to acquire a law degree at Moscow University and advance to the height of the party hierarchy, Gorbachev was taking advantage of the kind of opportunity for achievement that Soviet society offered. Within the Soviet system of guarantees and restrictions, he began to make a name for himself as a proponent of incentive-based projects for raising agricultural production in the 1960s and 1970s. And in the 1980s, he began to speak out in the name of others like him for greater freedom of action within a system which had secured on a minimum level the health, basic livelihood, and educational opportunity of its citizens.

In the Cold War which followed World War II, fears for the long-term survival of the Soviet state and social system functioned to sustain earlier management strategies. As before, enterprises were instructed what and how much to produce, and who their suppliers should be. The central administration continued to set prices, wages, and capital expenditures, and to determine the level of profit (the difference between costs and revenues) which could be retained by a particular enterprise. A large proportion of such profits became state revenue in the form of taxes and compulsory levies, so that factory profits would benefit the economy as a whole and not any single enterprise.

It was only after a postwar military buildup which succeeded in convincing enemies, potential enemies and the Soviets themselves that their country could no longer be invaded with "impunity"[2] that Soviet economists first began to openly raise the possibility that old policies of emergency and "crisis" planning were out of date. In 1965, a confidential report by the economist A. Aganbegyan of the famed Siberian think-tank at Novosibirsk argued that Soviet rates of economic growth were slowing due to the disproportionate share of national resources committed to defense and the extreme centralization and lack of democracy in the management structure of the economy. Aganbegyan was not alone in his concerns; contemporaries like E. Liberman also put forward proposals for economic reforms which eventually resulted in new legislation sanctioning the formation of labor brigades. Small work teams, or "brigades," were granted the right to sign contracts with a state enterprise, define production objectives, organize their own work, and recruit and pay collective members, with individual wages and bonuses depending on the group's success. This system began first in the building trades and spread to some other sectors of the economy in the 1970s.

According to Kurashvili, such indications of the need for a more flexible, incentive-based system reflected a transition to "normalcy" in the sphere of economic management. But change was not widespread. Although Brezhnev himself told the 25th Congress of the CPSU that radical changes were needed in the style and method of economic activity, no clear criteria for decentralized decision-making or any other aspect of economic restructuring were spelled out. It was not until the 1980s, and more specifically after the 27th Party Congress of 1985, that "economic restructuring" was proclaimed as a way to satisfy some of the economic, social, and human needs which were not on the agenda when the Soviet Union was still suffering the penalties of backwardness in the form of malnutrition and foreign invasion. In Kurashvili's terms, the hard-won achievement of a degree of "normalcy" led Soviet leaders "to rethink ideas about the nature of the forms of planning and economic accounting established during the extraordinary conditions of our country's development."

As Soviet economic debates have widened and deepened in the Gorbachev era, economists have called into question the very principles of economic management which were previously credited with the elevation of the USSR to the level of an industrial superpower. In leading economic journals, it is being argued that Stalin's policies did not constitute an economic miracle with some "unfortunate excesses," but were instead a human and economic disaster which wiped out some of the most productive of the Soviet Union's much-needed agricultural producers. The outcome of these debates remains very much in question; but it is significant that they did not surface until after the Soviet Union had become a military superpower.

With an outspokenness which Americans are accustomed to hear only from politicians who are out of office, Gorbachev has held the current executive bodies of the party and the state responsible for economic waste, corruption, rigidity, and abdication of responsibility. Meeting the nation's economic needs becomes impossible, he argues, when state plans fluctuate and are corrected downward to the level of their actual fulfillment and economic enterprises work only to meet minimum quotas, while entirely neglecting the question of production quality.[4]

As Gorbachev sees it, the very advantages of socialism – especially its emphasis on planning – have functioned to limit and restrict rather than to encourage creative and flexible responses to the economy's problems. Overcentralization, limits on the exercise of individual and social initiative on the grassroots level, and restrictions on the rights and responsibilities of enterprises are not only reprehensible because they inhibit economic growth. Gorbachev argues that bureaucratic privilege and the failure to involve working people in the process of economic decision-making have generated cynicism, obsession with personal gain by any means, drunkenness, drug addiction, and crime – a situation of contempt for law, of bribes and servility, and the proliferation of fraudulent claims of economic success.

Thus, agricultural specialists in the Fergana region who worked to expose a director whose policies were ecologically ruinous had to "fear for their lives" (*Moscow News,* June 5, 1987). A Ukrainian reporter is fired (*Pravda,* June 6, 1987) for writing about community dissatisfaction with an incompetent factory director. Despite promises of "new and democratic" factory elections, a worker from Kherson complains to Gorbachev himself that the district Party committee simply introduced a new boss, and then went on to warn those present against putting up their own candidates. In the words of the factory worker A. Artemenko, "Everyone in our organization feels awful and is talking about nothing else" (*Moscow News,* May 1987). According to Gorbachev, too many Soviet promises have not been kept: "The world of day-to-day realities and the world of sham well-being have increasingly diverged from each other" (speech to plenary session of the Party Central Committee, January 1987).

Implementing Perestroika

As we have seen, the Soviet economic reform debates have a history which goes back at least to the late 1960s, and it was in recognition of such continuities that Gorbachev summoned the economist Aganbegyan from Novosibirsk in 1985 as his personal adviser. Now one of the most influential economists in the Soviet Union, Aganbegyan has helped Gorbachev to define "economic restructuring" as a policy which links economic incentive, democratization, and what he calls "respect, raised on high, for the value and worth of the individual" (*Pravda,* January 28, 1987). In concrete and specific terms, the new strategies for economic growth and development are intended 1) to grant economic enterprises the freedom to draw up their own plans for work, to choose the parties they will contract with, and to decide the content of their contracts in accordance with broadly conceived and stable, long-term state plans;[5] 2) to permit the development of individual, family, and small group firms (cooperatives) outside of state institutions, collective farms or other social enterprises; and 3) to emphasize labor as the source of increased private as well as social benefits.

Enterprise Self-Management. One of the most publicized success stories of *perestroika* comes from Togliatti, the "Detroit" of the Soviet Union, where the Volga Automotive Plant Association (Avtovaz) has transformed its system of management, production, and distribution of income. According to Peter Katsura (*Izvestiia,* July 28, 1985), "economic restructuring" was based upon the "Three Pillars" of "independence, paying our own way, and full economic accountability." Katsura, the plant director in charge of economics and planning, emphasizes that the original impetus for change came from within the enterprise itself, when association members rather than state planners drafted decisions for the intensive development of machine-tool construction, welding robots, and automation lines for machining parts. Taking advantage of the new rights granted in 1985, the plant went on to take responsibility for issuing bonuses and premium pay for engineering-technical personnel and office employees who increased output or devised strategies for the conservation of labor time. Funds for social and cultural measures are no longer allocated to the plant from the state budget; Avtovaz workers voted to establish their own funds and priorities on the basis of their own increased output. After deductions for the state budget, taxes, and research and development, they did not allocate the savings achieved in the unit cost of vehicles, fuel consumption, electricity, and heat only for the benefit of individual "achievers." Instead, they used their funds to build new kindergartens and preventive health centers, to obtain sports gear, to subsidize meals at the plant cafeteria, etc. According to the new management arrangements, 50 million rubles in profits in 1986 went into the enterprise development fund, and 65 million into the fund for social and cultural measures and housing construction.[6]

Nevertheless, even with this sort of success, the current director of Avtovaz denounced the "bureaucratic caution" and "foot-dragging" of various government officials. In 1986, so many ministries failed to meet state production deadlines that Avtovaz was forced to take thousands of automobiles off the production line: necessary components were not available to complete them. Despite repeated requests and applications, the State Ministry of Power and Electrification refused to erect a building for a planned new model automobile without a special government resolution; its reluctance to take action is blocking the whole process of enterprise reconstruction and retooling. It turns out, as the plant director complained in the March 10, 1986, edition of *Pravda,* that "in order to exercise its rights, the Association must continually appeal to the higher authorities." Such criticisms, coming from an innovative and productive enterprise, are evidently being listened to. In September 1986, the Party Central Committee and the Council of Ministers passed a series of resolutions specifically aimed at facilitating the reconstruction efforts of Avtovaz.

Individual Enterprise. On May 1, 1987, a much debated Law on Individual Enterprise went into operation. In part an attempt to free up the economy, the new legislation also represents a determined government effort to channel the profitable activities which have historically occurred within the Soviet Union's "shadow economy." For many decades, a wide range of private and illegal service stations, foodstands, and repair shops functioned to make up for the inadequacies of the Soviet retailing system. At the same time, profits accumulated by black marketers reveal the extent to which increased real incomes were burning holes in the pockets of a populace frustrated by a lack of goods and services. According to *Izvestiia*'s low estimate, the shadow economy generated some 7 billion rubles a year in the 1980s.

It is in this context that the new law on enterprise grants a number of freedoms within the framework of social norms which have been in place ever since the Revolutions of 1917. All citizens of legal age may now engage in licensed, "socially useful activity," with legal preference given to war and labor veterans, to those performing work in remote areas, to those with a reduced ability to work, and to all those who conclude contracts with state enterprises and institutions. Licenses are granted on payment of charges set according to the average annual income of people engaged in an analogous activity for a state or social enterprise. Local soviets are legally obligated to help licensees obtain raw materials and tools, and to facilitate market access. In Moscow, for example, the city's Individual Enterprise Commission in Sokolnicheskii District is currently attempting to provide workshops and stores for people interested in providing services which are most in demand – furniture and house repair, photography work, plumbing, and shoe repair.

Interviews with the first licensees carried out by *Moscow News* revealed both enthusiasm for new opportunities and expectations of continued social security support. Before the advent of *perestroika,* Helmut Lumi, a forty-year-old Estonian from Tallinn, worked as a taxi driver and took on another job at a youth football-training school to meet the rising cost of raising his two children and maintaining his house. While working at the school, he got the idea of starting an automobile repair shop; this seemed to him a good plan because the few which existed in Tallinn always seemed to be overcrowded. When he obtained his enterprise license in May 1987, the local soviet provided him with capital to build his workshop. On the day of the *Moscow News* reporter's visit to Lumi's place of business, a half-dozen cars were lined up and waiting. Nevertheless, despite Lumi's hopes for the future, he does not plan to give up his school job because he wants to hold on to his paid health care, sick leave, and pension. In general, despite the upsurge of national independence movements in Estonia and elsewhere, there have been no documented popular demands for "freedom" from paid health care or other social security benefits.

Seitker Meideubayev, a fifty-year-old veterinary research institute employee from Kazakhstan living with his wife, mother, and the youngest of his six children, seems equally eager to make good. For years, he had enjoyed spending his evenings and holidays making comfortable yet intricately ornamented traditional Kazakh saddles and harnesses. When he found that the area shepherds (who still spend from ten to twelve days in the saddle) were eager to buy whatever saddles he had on hand, he began to set up a real saddle-making business. Eventually, the workshop he constructed in his country house became so noisy that the neighbors complained, and the district soviet found him another place to set up and extended financial assistance to facilitate his move to the new location.

Concessions to Capitalism? Incentives, Differential Wages, Unemployment, Bankruptcy, and Competition

Although economic differences in the USSR are far less extreme than they are in the United States, debates over economic reform are particularly sensitive when they touch on this issue. In discussing income incentives and the negative impact of "leveling," Gorbachev is particularly careful to refer as well to the planned increases in social and collective benefits provided to cities, districts, and communities in the form of better health care facilities, sports clubs, gymnasia, and theaters. In general, the task of generating incentives is not considered as a simple issue of wages and economic accountability. By far the most exciting mind currently at work on the social basis of incentives is the sociologist Tatyana Zaslavskaia, a disciple of the economist Aganbegyan. According to Zaslavskaia, the Soviet Union is decisively moving away from the model of the "economic man," sensitive only to material stimuli and administrative bans.[7] Instead, she argues, the willingness of individuals to work to the best of their abilities in economics, politics, and cultural pursuits depends upon the extent to which they believe that basic principles of social justice operate in their daily lives and in the broader activities of society and the state.

According to Zaslavskaia, individuals will seek fulfillment in creative and productive work if they know, for example, that children from families of differing social status, females as well as males, from the provinces as well as from Leningrad and Moscow, are granted roughly equal starting conditions in life. Despite the existence of universal, free, and compulsory secondary education, she notes that the recognition of individual potential in children, adolescents, and adults is often a question of whether he or she comes from Moscow or Alma Ata or a village on the Aral Sea. Girls rather than boys from rural schools become dairymaids; men in mining settlements become miners regardless of the range and variation in their abilities and interests. People work harder, she insists, if their life chances are more fair, and if they know that the results of their labor depend upon their own "knowledge, abilities and will." On the other hand, if the lives of working people are pervaded by empty promises, powerlessness to affect change, and the repeated subjugation of the weaker and less prestigious by the strong, they will not work harder for themselves, their families, their community, or their nation. Social justice is thus not simply a desirable goal; it possesses real economic, social, and political utility.

Zaslavskaia argues that proponents of change, and members of her own profession of sociology first of all, should set themselves the task of investigating the ideas actually held by the principal social groups and strata in Soviet society on the subject of social justice. What do factory workers and collective farmers consider appropriate standards for housing priorities, school admissions, job promotion, and wage differentials? Opportunities need to be provided for people to discuss and defend their interests at the highest levels and to receive clear answers to their requests and demands. In Zaslavskaia's words, "Confidence in the progressive nature and justice of the social system is a highly important source of creative energy, labor activity, and economic initiative, and of the acceleration of social and economic development."

The promotion of incentives, if successful, is likely not only to accelerate economic growth but to exacerbate existing income inequalities. Gorbachev insists in this connection that egalitarian principles were never intended to reduce everyone to precisely the same level. The "radical" economist Popov of Moscow University proposes that the pay of the best employees should be increased and the pay of the worst should be lowered, with the employees themselves given the right to decide on a democratic basis how earnings should be redistributed. According to this line of argument, plants which always honor their delivery commitments and produce the highest quality goods should receive recognition in the form of social or wage benefits; prices for good and bad quality products should not be undifferentiated. As Gorbachev sees it, belief in the value of labor itself is undermined when no material or social recognition is given to those who perform efficient, high quality, and creative work. The hoped-for relationship between wage differentiation and the question of security was clearly spelled out in Gorbachev's speech to the plenary session of the Party Central Committee of June 25, 1987:

> We take pride in the high degree of social protection given to people in this country. This is what makes socialism, a system of working people and for working people. But work and work alone should be the basis of a person's material and moral standing in socialist society.

Arguing that a worker's wages should be closely linked to the personal contribution made to the end result, Gorbachev insisted that the only criterion should be whether the wages are honestly earned.

Although there is general agreement that material rewards should be more clearly linked to labor contributions, "conservatives" continue to fear that unequal distribution of wealth might enable an enterprising minority to acquire wealth and power beyond its numbers and subvert the social guarantees provided to the majority of the population. Like most successful politicians, Gorbachev has tended to give priority to immediate issues – in this case, incentives – and to assume that the social norms of Soviet society are so powerful that the formation of "inordinately" wealthy elites cannot become a problem.[8] Many Soviet proponents of increased economic opportunity argue that "excessively" high income that is "economically questionable" or "capable of destabilizing the market" should be moderated by a progressive tax.

Predictably, it is the sociologist Zaslavskaia's discussion which is the most probing and complex. It is her view that all those who work in social or state enterprises should receive a guaranteed equal minimum of housing, education, and medical services. Everything beyond the minimum should be paid for from the labor income of the household/family unit. At the same time, she looks not to the market but to a wide range of social criteria as the appropriate determinants of wage levels. According to Zaslavskaia, wage rates should be based upon a job's difficulty, the degree of physical and nervous strain involved, the social importance of the task, its harmfulness to the health of the worker, the remoteness of the work area, and the acuteness of the area labor shortage.

While those working at personal or family enterprises deserve rewards measured according to their labor contribution as well, Zaslavskaia warns against the acquisition of unlimited income by this element. In her judgement, an income which is two, three, or even four times higher than the level permitted in social production might be appropriate – a level ten times higher is in her view "too much" and could in no sense be justified in human, social, or political terms. Along these lines, the staff of the world-famous Moscow Institute for Eye Micro-Surgery has organized for themselves a kind of "social justice" wage scale. The paramedicals are the lowest paid staff; a head surgeon cannot make more than three times a paramedical. The general director can only make four and a half times a paramedical wage. This system was designed to recognize more sharply than the traditional Soviet norm the notion that those with greater knowledge and skill should receive higher wages, while preventing the differentials from becoming "excessive" (Kiser, p. 168). It is not yet certain whether such efforts to establish social criteria for income differentiation will become widespread. However, they represent a sort of "middle ground" between "progressives" who argue that given the continued shortages few limits should be set to the opportunity for individual enrichment based on quality and quantity of output, and "conservatives" who believe that permitting more inequality has not only solved no problems but has instead exacerbated the old ones.

The *perestroika* linkages between social and economic factors are particularly evident in current discussions of profit, bankruptcy, pricing, unemployment, and competition. Reformers demand that unprofitable enterprises be eliminated and ridicule earlier policies which maintained an enterprise to save jobs or in order to vindicate a powerful bureaucrat's faulty planning strategies, regardless of the quality, quantity, or social utility of the product. According to the economist Otto Lacis (*Moscow News*, January 25, 1987) the "price-fixing" which is openly implemented by the state in socialist economies is more covertly imposed under capitalism, where markets are "fixed" in order to maintain artificially high prices. In the context of either economic system, Lacis argues that bankruptcy may represent a realistic response to continuing failures in production quality or supply. In such cases, the Avtovaz economist Peter Katsura argues that when an enterprise fails, socialist systems possess a greater range of options than narrowly profit-driven capitalist firms, which resort to wholesale layoffs. In contrast, socialist states provide other jobs for workers at the bankrupt enterprise, or attempt, in the words of the 1986 draft Party program, "to use the possibilities that are being opened up for shortening the working day and increasing the length of paid vacations for the working people." As N. I. Pyzhkov notes in this connection, the current Five Year Plan grants mothers with children under the age of one year an extension of workleave to eighteen months, and promises that the number of laborers who must perform heavy, monotonous work will be reduced by 20 million.

Problems of inequality and "leveling" in housing have been incisively analyzed by the economist N. Shmelev (*Sovetskaia kultura,* March 20, 1986) who criticizes the unfair practice of providing free housing to families of high income. In his view, socially acceptable criteria need to be applied more consistently, with first consideration given to low-income families, those with numerous children, disabilities, long-time service, or special contribution to society. Shmelev, who has been described by Western reporters as the Soviet Union's Milton Friedman, has attracted much foreign attention, although his attempts to define the social criteria for housing distribution are not what have interested reporters the most.

Like Professor Popov of Moscow University, Shmelev has been called a "voice of reason" in Soviet economics because he calls for the introduction of planned unemployment at a rate of 2.5 to 3 percent as one of the best ways to render enterprises and individuals more efficient and accountable. Shmelev has argued that in the Soviet Union, shoddy workmanship is due to "excessively full employment." He goes on: "We must consider fearlessly and in a business-like manner, what can be gained by us from a comparatively small reserve army of labor," replacing "administrative coercion with economic coercion."

It is revealing, however, that Shmelev hastens to add that no Soviet state would permit "American-style" solutions which left unemployed laborers to the mercy of fate. It would be cheaper, he argues, "to pay temporarily unemployed workers an allowance sufficient for a few months" rather than maintain idlers in the factory who know that their jobs cannot be taken away no matter how irresponsible or lazy they may be. Reflecting the impact of an ideological tradition which has always emphasized issues of social justice in the evaluation of economic policy, even Shmelev feels constrained to argue that labor inefficiency is not only expensive and unprofitable but *immoral* – an unconscionable assault upon the well-being of the nation as a whole (*Novy mir*, no. 6, 1987; *Nedelia*, Sept. 26–Oct. 1988).

While Gorbachev has praised Shmelev's economic critiques, he has explicitly and firmly rejected the "unemployment option." But the issue remains both controversial and disturbing. When the economist V. Kostakov wrote an article in *Sovetskaia kultura* on job reductions due to hoped-for increases in efficiency and productivity, reader protest led him to explain that as the number of industrial jobs decreased, social and cultural services could become the new growth sector of the economy. Jobs could be created by expanding the number of preschools, mandating smaller class sizes with more teachers, and by a step-by-step extension of maternity leave to a term of years. Kostakov attributes some of the Soviet Union's worst economic problems to the apathy of the male segment of the population. In his words,

> For the overwhelming majority [of the males], the inclination to drink is a kind of compensation for the undeveloped state of their cultural needs, for the monotonous, dull way in which they spend their days off and evenings, and for their not knowing what to do with themselves, with their time and with their money. Two million workers in culture and the arts is an extremely small number for such an enormous country as ours. The comprehensive program for the development of goods and services envisages a substantial expansion in the system of cultural services.

The question of job reduction remains a difficult issue both in practice and in principle. But in general, it still seems fair to say that unemployment as a solution is at odds with the general *perestroika* effort to link economic growth with democratization and social security rather than with job insecurity and the unlimited enrichment of more enterprising individuals. In December 1989, to the enthusiastic applause of delegates to the Congress of People's Deputies, Prime Minister Ryzhkov announced not only a major shift of national economic resources toward the consumer sector, but a plan to limit the rapid expansion of cooperatives in the name of a more equitable distribution of available goods and services.

Gorbachev and his supporters repeatedly make the argument that neither wage differentiation, bankruptcy, reduction of jobs, or competition are necessarily incompatible with socialism. According to the economist D. Palterovich of the USSR Academy of Sciences, competition is too frequently identified in the minds of the Soviet public with "Western-style" anarchy in production, with unemployment, and with the destruction of output to keep prices high. Yet, he argues, in a Soviet economy within which much needed fruit rots in collective farm orchards and industrial machinery makes its way to designated factories at a snail's pace, the prevalence of rigid state planning and monopolistic markets create as much damage as the Western willingness to destroy

171

"surplus" agricultural produce while the poor go hungry. According to such arguments, a greater measure of "healthy" competition can serve a useful purpose, and is not incompatible with socialism. Palterovich argues that competition is simply a means to achieve a desired economic goal, which may be used for either destructive or constructive purposes. In his words,

> Socialism's basic difference from exploiter systems lies not in organizational techniques and economic methods, not in the means it uses but in its objectives and in those interests which social production serves. It takes exception solely to [the use of] inhuman means.

Like Kurashvili and Gorbachev himself, Palterovich argues that it is not competition, but the "inhuman cruelty" of unemployment and the general eagerness to place private profit over all other considerations which are the *inherently* capitalist practices which are alien to socialism.

The distinctively "social" component of *perestroika* emerges quite clearly in the numerous complaints which pack the letters columns of *Pravda* and *Izvestiia*. Let us look, for example, at a complaint (*Pravda,* June 5, 1987) by the employees of a poultry plant in the Chebarkul region of Cheliabinsk in Western Siberia. Plant members had decided to construct a new village for themselves. They were determined that this project would be different from the usual construction efforts which completed buildings at breakneck speed with little attempt to "consider people and the stability of their lives." The workers who were to be the future residents of the village decided that before they put up any structures, all the pipes and cables would be laid, with no wires above ground "to offend the sky." Working after hours with materials provided by the poultry plant, they constructed stone-paved storage areas and a blacktopped driveway behind every building.

But as the project proceeded, a series of unforeseen problems arose to impede their efforts, even as *Pravda* and *Izvestiia* sang the praises of openness and honesty, individual and group initiative, "restructuring," etc. Building materials suddenly became impossible to obtain; it turned out that the Poultry Industry Trust of Cheliabinsk had a construction project of its own and had taken all of the materials for itself. Chebarkul director P. Chaika was told that after the Trust's project was finished, his plant would be sure to get its materials. At the same time, the Road Construction Trust demanded apartments in the new settlement in return for telephone and road service – no apartments, no telephones or new roads! Is this what *perestroika* means, demanded Chaika?

In *Pravda* (June 5, 1987), the World War II veteran Stepashkin of the city of Voronezh bitterly pointed out that in 1980 he was ninety-eighth on the list of families slated for improvement in living conditions; by 1987 he had only managed to advance to fiftieth place. His letter ended with the following words: "This is an appropriate place to mention social justice. Why do we war and labor veterans haunt the doors of the Soviet executive committee for years on end trying to get the priority improvement in living conditions available in the law?" Why, he went on, do some neighbors have the same size apartment for two persons as his eight-person family? Why is it that a life-long resident whose children were born, educated, and still live in Voronezh has not "had a chance to live in an apartment that meets the established public health standards?"

Together with a common disgust for pervasive corruption and bureaucratic incompetence, ordinary Soviet citizens seem to share a number of common values which emerge with particular clarity if we consider what they might mean in an American context. In December 1989, as the United States Council of Mayors reported that in twenty-seven American cities, 22 percent of those seeking shelter were turned away, the Chebarkul workers, the war veteran Stepashkin, and even the supposedly Milton Friedman-like Shmelev take it for granted that the right to shelter is unconditional, and that society and government share responsibility in this area. While some Americans accumulate unprecedented amounts of wealth, the Census Bureau reported in 1989 that 37 million Americans (22 million of whom are employed) possess no health insurance, 1 million have been denied health care, and 14 million report that they do not seek it because they cannot afford to pay. Such figures suggest that while the United States imposes no ceiling to impede the rise of profit-seeking individuals to ever greater heights, it also provides no effective "floor" to impede the downward spiral of those in need. In contrast, Soviets seem to believe that they possess a floor of bad quality and a ceiling which is far too low. But so far, at least, many of them continue to believe in the need for both floors and ceilings.

Wherever *perestroika* may lead, it is essential that Western observers take more seriously than they have thus far the deeply held and widely shared social values which establish the Soviet context for the current reform process. The concern for social security and a measure of equality evident in popular expressions of frustration both with *perestroika* and with the restrictions of the pre-Gorbachev era require further examination. The extent of Western "silence" on these issues may well indicate the extent to which the very concept of social justice has disappeared from America's own economic debates. The characteristic blindness of American journalists to this issue was strikingly evident in a confrontation between CBS correspondent Ed Bradley and Gennadii Gerasimov on the CBS TV show "Seven Days in May." At one point Bradley asked Gerasimov, "Is there anything that the United States can learn from the Soviet Union?"

Gerasimov replied, smiling, "We can learn from you how to do away with lines" [so that we don't have to wait forever for goods which are often of poor quality, etc.]. "And you can learn from us how to do away with slums."

Bradley, who is black, and had just finished describing his personal triumph over the slum conditions and poverty of the South Bronx, found this an uninteresting response. Frowning, he asked the Soviet commentator, "But isn't there anything *else* we can learn from you?"[9]

Notes

1.   Two of the most valuable recent books on the origins of this and later movements for reform are Martin Walker's *The Waking Giant,* New York 1986, and Moshe Lewin, *The Gorbachev Phenomenon,* Berkeley, Calif. 1988.

2.   Throughout the 1930s, Stalin appealed to popular fears of renewed foreign attack by claiming that the Germans were certain that Russia could be invaded with "impunity."

3.   *Ekonomika i organizatsiia promyshlennogo proizvodstvo,* May 1985, no. 5, pp. 59–79.

4.   The poor quality of goods available is quite frequently a subject for ridicule. For example, a recent cartoon in the satirical journal *Krokodil* contained the following dialogue:

Customer: I like the texture of this material, but I don't like the design very much.

Salesperson: Oh, don't worry. Just wash it once or twice and the design will disappear!

5.   New opportunities for private enterprises are accompanied by greater demands for both individual and collective responsibility for economic successes and failure. According to a resolution approved by the Party Central Committee and the Council of Ministers in July 1986, research organizations are to be held accountable for fulfilling long-term demands for improvements in quality when they design or substantially modernize machinery, equipment, and technological processes. If "improved" goods are of consistently low quality, the user may unilaterally cancel any agreement with the supplier. In such cases, suppliers must suspend or cease production of the given product and reimburse users for losses due to cancellation. Executives at fault are to be subject to legal action.

6.   In similar fashion, the world-famous Moscow Institute for Eye Micro-Surgery saved 12 million rubles in 1986. The whole staff, or the *collective* in Soviet terminology, placed 300,000 rubles into a material incentive fund, spent 500,000 rubles on the purchase of new equipment and allocated over 11 million to various social benefit programs for workers.

7.   See Zaslavskaia's views and writings, as expressed in *Sovetskaia kultura,* January 23, 1986; *Pravda,* February 6, 1987; *Moscow News,* March 8–15, 1987.

8.   Gorbachev has seemed particularly sensitive to attacks which focus on this issue. According to the widely published news reports of November 1989, he went so far as to threaten to resign when critics accused him of "bowing down" before the wealthy capitalist nations of the world and turning his back on socialist values.

9.   Media indifference to such issues extends to the East bloc as well. In October 1989, in the midst of the East German upheaval leading to the destruction of the Berlin Wall, Christopher Lydon, a WGBH (Boston) TV commentator, interviewed an East German official. At one point, he asked her, "Is there anything that you *like* about East Germany?" The official replied, "Yes, there is. There is no homelessness, and medical care and education are free." Lydon looked at her in silence for a moment, waiting to see if she had anything more interesting to add, and then went on to ask questions about civil liberties and human rights.

10

Debt Crisis Update: 1988

Robert E. Wood

The debt crisis in the Third World reminds one of the French proverb about things changing and not changing at the same time. New crises constantly appear, followed by self-proclaimed bold new initiatives and pronouncements of breakthroughs, followed by new crises. Critics keep expecting a collapse of the system, yet it endures. Is anything fundamental changing? Can the crisis extend into the indefinite future? Let us start with four observations that stress the containment of the debt crisis to date, then look at how the strategy that has achieved this has become increasingly unglued, and finally take a brief look at the most likely future scenario.

1. *Not a single penny of debt has been repudiated by Third World debtors since 1982.* Massive debts – accumulated more often than not by unpopular military dictatorships, often due to military expenditures, luxury consumption, and capital flight – have been universally honored, at least in principle. In every case where individual countries have fallen behind in their debt service payments or have imposed unilateral moratoria, the governments involved have reiterated their commitment to pay in the long run. Indeed, the first formal declaration by the commercial banks that a country was in default occurred only on August 17, 1987 – almost five years to the day after Mexico announced its need to reschedule – and the relatively small debtor involved, North Korea, quickly backed down and came to terms with its creditors.

2. *Despite close to 200 debt-restructuring agreements with both official and private creditors since 1980, Third World countries have consistently paid out more in debt*

service each year than before the advent of the crisis — about $100 billion annually. Since 1984 the Third World as a whole has been a net exporter of capital on an ever-increasing basis. In 1986, and again in 1987, developing countries paid out about $30 billion more in debt service than they took in as new loans.[1] For Latin America alone, the net capital outflow between 1982 and 1987 came to $125 billion.[2]

3. *By any reasonable standard, the Third World has already repaid its debt in full — yet its outstanding debt has risen dramatically.* Using World Bank data, *South* magazine has pointed out that Third World debt service since 1980 has not only been equivalent to its outstanding 1980 principal in full but has provided for a "reasonable" rate of interest payments (at 6 percent) as well. The *South* report noted: "One small fact has gone unnoticed — that the debt has already been fully repaid."[3] The creditors don't see it that way, of course. They have demanded interest rates much higher than that, even as prices of primary commodities have collapsed to the lowest levels since the Great Depression. They have made new loans to cover debt service of about $50 billion a year, and they have insisted that governments take responsibility for unguaranteed private sector debt. The result of this has been that developing-country debt has almost doubled since 1980, reaching an estimated $1.2 trillion in 1988. Yet so wedded have the creditors been to the idea that new debt must be incurred to service old debt that when the growth of new debt slowed slightly in 1986 and 1987, World Bank officials found this a cause for despair, not joy: "The fact that debt did not increase much . . . is not a good thing in these current circumstances."[4]

4. *These three facts — the absence of repudiation or default, the continuation of massive debt service, and the rise in total indebtedness — testify to the success of a creditor strategy that identifies "success" with the narrow short-run interest of creditors.* As Richard Erb, the US "point man" at the IMF, summed up in 1987, the five years since Mexico's rescheduling:

> First, the crisis was contained. . . . Second, disruption of the world's financial system was averted. . . . Third . . . most developing countries have embarked on programs of economic reform. . . . But collaboration has not been easy. . . . Given the stakes involved and the number of participants, what I find surprising is that the stresses have not been more severe.[5]

Erb is right. In the face of the extraordinary misery it has wrought in the Third World, the success of the creditor strategy has indeed been remarkable. The basic ingredients of that strategy have varied little — rescheduling, new lending, and increased conditionality — although the mechanisms for delivering them have been continually reformed. The strategy has indeed contained the banking crisis, averted disruption of the capitalist world's financial system, and imposed the burden of adjustment ("economic reform") almost entirely on developing countries.

From the vantage point of the Third World, of course, this "success" has been an almost unmitigated disaster. The burden of debt service has drastically lowered investment and growth, contributing to absolute declines in income in most of Latin America, Africa, and parts of Asia. In the first four years of the debt crisis after Mexico rescheduled, average incomes dropped in twenty-two of twenty-five Latin American countries and in thirty-one of forty-six Sub-Saharan African countries. Per capita incomes in much of Africa are back to what they were in 1960, and in much of Latin America, back to the levels of the mid-1970s. Long-term positive trends in health and education have been reversed, as per capita expenditures have fallen to levels one-quarter to one-half of what they were a decade ago.[6] All-out efforts to follow the creditor advice to export their way out of debt have run aground on First World protectionism, declining commodity prices, and continuing high interest rates.

The Unravelling of the Baker Plan

Since the IMF–World Bank meetings in Seoul in 1985, the centerpiece of the creditor strategy has been the Baker Plan, a loose collection of proposals put forth by US Secretary of the Treasury James Baker. Its heart was the promise of new financing, from both official sources and the commercial banks, to generate the export growth necessary to repay Third World debts. The implicit assumption was that those debts should and could be paid in full without fundamental change. The Baker Plan came apart in 1987, but it was in trouble from its inception. While the Baker Plan prescribed exporting one's way out of debt, it was predicated on substantially increased capital flows in the meantime, both to pay immediate debt service obligations and to finance the necessary investments for export growth. By 1987, it was clear that this new lending was not forthcoming, from either commercial or official creditors.

Official aid provided some breathing space at the beginning of the debt crisis, but it too has been increasingly overtaken by accumulated debt. Loans from Western aid and export credit agencies, mainly because of cutbacks in new export credits, plummeted. The major multilateral institutions also became agents of capital export from the Third World. Given that the main incentive to cooperate in the creditor strategy was future access to renewed financing, these trends were doubly threatening: not only was private lending exposed as a chimera, but official sources could no longer be counted upon to

177

provide a positive transfer of resources to offset loan repayments to commercial banks. The incentives to observe the rules of the game were clearly disappearing.

Sheer necessity, combined with the reduced potency of the sanction to withhold financing that didn't seem to be forthcoming anyway, resulted in a record fifty-seven countries being officially behind in their debt-service payments at the end of 1986, half of their arrears owed to official creditors.[7] Seven countries were effectively in unprecedented default to the IMF, to the tune of $1 billion.[8] Most of these arrears had accumulated without official announcement, but in 1987 two of the debtors generally perceived to be the politically safest and most cooperative – Brazil and Ivory Coast – unilaterally announced suspension of most of their debt servicing. Ecuador, hitherto also considered one of the safer debtors, also announced limits on its debt-service payments in early 1987. No longer were the delinquents "radicals" like Peru or Nicaragua or "basket cases" like Zambia, Bolivia, or Zaire. Furthermore, the withholding by Brazil, one of the two largest debtors, was costing the banks half a billion dollars a month in interest. The Brazilian context was undoubtedly crucial in Citicorp's announcement in May 1987 that it was adding $3 billion to its loan-loss reserves against possible future losses on its loans to the Third World, a move copied in varying degrees by most of the other major banks. It is important to recognize what this did and did not do. Contrary to the language of the popular press, the banks did *not* write off any loans; they all reiterated their intention to collect their loans in full.

The Citicorp action provoked a controversy among political and financial analysts, some arguing that it was an inevitable step towards write-offs or significant rescheduling concessions and others arguing that by removing the debtors' ability to harm the banks' sacred quarterly profit reports, it would allow the banks to take much tougher negotiating stances. The reality was somewhere in between.

In late 1987, a new scheme for dealing with debt that symbolized both the unraveling of the Baker Plan and the narrow limits of reform still acceptable to creditors was created. Morgan Guaranty Trust negotiated a proposal with the US Treasury and the Mexican government for trading outstanding Mexican debt for newly issued Mexican bonds, whose value would be backed by US Treasury bonds purchased in turn by Mexico. The proposal involved only one country, Mexico. Even if it were to be extended to other countries, its costliness to the debtors and its questionable advantages to the banks over their other options meant that its implementation and impact were likely to be very limited. But the US government's involvement appeared to signify the end of even a formal pretense that the Baker Plan was still alive.

Looking Ahead

In attempting to look ahead, it is necessary to locate the debt crisis in a longer term perspective. A myriad of studies have documented the importance of a variety of historical events – the OPEC price increases, the end of the Bretton Woods system, and so forth – but here I refer to two basic longer term processes.

The first is the globalization of production and exchange: the ongoing expansion and deepening of the capitalist world system. The relationship of the accumulation of Third World debt to this system was complex – sometimes a passive reflection of the evolving structure of that system, sometimes a means of challenging it – but the periodic outbreaks of debt crises are clearly systemic phenomena. And while the current crisis has disrupted the process of globalization in certain ways, in the long run it is likely to be a major factor in carrying it forward. We can see this trend already in the policy "conditionality" imposed across the Third World in exchange for rescheduling agreements or more aid.

The second is the ascendancy of finance capital in this capitalist world economy. In this age of greenmail, junk bonds, MBAs and discounted cash flows, golden parachutes, currency speculation, *futures* in treasury bonds, and so on, it is faintly amusing to recall that Lenin thought that 1916 was the highpoint of finance capital. As Howard Wachtel observes, the ascendancy of finance capital has turned the international economic order into a "supranational" one, in which the major banks can "make end-runs around governments and then leverage their influence to promote the same deregulated and privatized environment within nation-states that they have been able to create for themselves supranationally."[9] Bank lending represented the privatization of international liquidity creation in the 1970s. Those loans then constituted a major vehicle by which the deflationary impulses of US macroeconomic policies were transmitted to the Third World, and now those debts are prying open domestic financial and productive sectors to foreign penetration.

But while the debt crisis has in some ways hastened both processes, the success of finance capital in blocking any real resolution of the debt crisis – which requires either debt forgiveness or debt repudiation – has become an increasing drag on the system as a whole. The disaster that the crisis has represented for the manufacturing sector in the United States is well known – US exports to Latin American countries fell 26 percent between 1981 and 1986, from \$42.1 billion to \$31.1 billion, and by 1984, it was estimated that the debt crisis had cost over half a million US workers their jobs.[10] The very institutionalization of the power of finance capital on a world scale is thus holding back the capacity of the capitalist world economy to move onto a new wave of accumulation.[11]

Stagnation and the Blurring of Default

Ironically, what dynamism has existed in the world economy since the outbreak of the debt crisis has been largely based on the geographical shift in the flow of global finance capital to the United States and the resulting rapid buildup of external debt there. The US is now the world's largest debtor nation, and in another year or two its debt will surpass that of all Third World nations combined. The October 1987 stock market crash almost certainly signified that the limits of this debt-based growth were being approached, although it has probably not yet run its full course. In the meantime, however, economic growth not only in the Third World but in other advanced capitalist countries, particularly Japan, has been based almost entirely on the expansion of the US consumer market – and hence is more than ever vulnerable to a downturn of that market. Even without an immediate global downturn, the rest of the 1980s is likely to see increasing challenge to the present debt-containment strategy. The creditors, divided in their interests, show no capacity to formulate any comprehensive policy in the wake of the Baker Plan's demise. Collectively they continue to squeeze debtors to the brink and then to make the minimally necessary concessions; this applies to both the "middle-income" clients of the commercial banks and the "low-income" clients of governments and multilateral institutions.

Debtor governments, on the other hand, almost universally face: 1) limits on or worsening of their exports prospects; 2) increasing domestic political pressures for expansionary growth policies and for tougher negotiating stances; and 3) continuing decrease in their prospects for new financing, both private and public. Indeed, as we have seen, even "aid" is increasingly becoming a matter of net capital outflow.

It is possible that creditor states will at the last minute pump enough money into the system to maintain the incentive to cooperate. The US government has finally come around to backing a capital increase for the World Bank which would allow the Bank to raise its lending by $75 billion, and the IMF has succeeded in creating two new facilities in the past few years to exchange short-term IMF debt for long-term IMF debt and to provide in the process a certain amount of new financing to low-income countries. Japan is increasing its aid, and a certain amount of debt forgiveness for low-income countries has been provided on a unilateral basis by Canada and some European countries. Proposals abound, some working their way through Congress, to provide various degrees of debt relief.

At the same time, however, the US has preferred to block a capital increase for the Inter-American Development Bank rather than give up its insistence on virtual veto power over new lending, and the US has refused to contribute to the new IMF facility. Overall, disarray in the creditor camp makes it unlike-

180

ly that the actions likely to be taken will fundamentally reverse the tendency towards negative transfers and global stagnation.

In theory, the stage might seem set for the scenario cherished by the left from the beginning of the crisis: domestic radicalization, an international debtors' cartel, debt repudiation, and the use of the potential "power of debt" to achieve long-sought reforms in the international economic order, reforms that would deepen domestic processes of transformation and development.

It is a vision worth fighting for, but current trends do not provide grounds for optimism about its realization. The domestic political impact of the debt crisis has proven to be highly complex, partly because of the left's historic confusion of socialism with a statism discredited across the political spectrum. Despite calls for unity at conferences in Cartagena, Havana, and elsewhere, collective resistance remains only a dream. Despite interests and publics in the North which would benefit from a restructuring of North–South relations, prospects for meaningful global negotiations seem dimmer than ever. And the increased importance of access to US markets constrains both domestic and foreign policies in Third World countries.

In this context, the history of the changing relations between Third World states and multinational corporations may provide a better sense of what is likely to happen in the medium-term future. In a useful study, Charles Lipson has shown how, in a situation of declining international constraints and increasing state capabilities, Third World states were able in the 1960s and 1970s to institute an array of measures which, while often stopping short of formal expropriation, would in the previous era have elicited strong punitive counter-measures. New policy tools permitted states to manipulate investments in a number of ways. "The distinctiveness of expropriation [was] lost, its meaning blurred."[12] This weakened the ability of multinational corporations to respond coherently, or to mobilize their home states in their defense.

Although it has remained in its early stages, a parallel process of the blurring of default has characterized the debt crisis of the past five years. No debtor country (including North Korea, which protested its designation of being in default and promptly came to terms with its creditors) has said it was defaulting, and yet a variety of debtors have found that increasingly bold unilateral actions – from the accumulation of arrears to caps on debt service – have failed to elicit declarations of default by the banks. Even the World Bank and the IMF have been prepared to go to considerable lengths to avoid formal declarations of default. Current trends suggest that it is probably in this blurred area of *de facto* but not *de jure* default that the international politics of the debt crisis will be played out over the next few years. We will almost certainly see a wide range of states, representing considerable ideological diversity, press the limits of default, and by and large both the banks and official agencies will be forced to adjust. The banks are under pressure to do so by their home governments, as in US Treasury Secretary Baker's call for a "menu" of options to reduce debt and encourage new lending. Almost surely this menu will involve the banks' taking some losses, although many of these losses will be absorbed by governments, and hence by taxpayers. Smaller banks will trade discounted debt for long-term "exit bonds" in exchange for being relieved of pressure to come up with new money. Larger banks will trade some debt for equity and commodities and may be forced to lower interest rates further. If the adaptations of the multinationals are a guide, however, the banks will at the same time find new ways to make profits in new circumstances, redefining their roles in ways parallel to what the multinationals did in the 1960s and 1970s.

The debt crisis does appear to be moving into a new phase, one in which some form of debt relief will finally have to be put on the agenda. But if recent history is a guide, the left in both the advanced capitalist countries and the Third World cannot expect the crisis by itself to reverse the powerful process of the internationalization of capital that has defined the past three decades. The danger of current trends is that the debt burden will be lightened just enough to keep the system going, but not enough to remove its oppressive and distorting effects.

Notes

1. For net transfer data through 1987, see World Bank, *World Bank Tables: Volume I. Analysis and Summary Tables,* Washington, D.C. 1988, pp. viii, xii. Net transfer figures are for long-term debt only.

2. Editorial: "Pay Up and Pay Again," *South,* vol. 85 (Nov. 1987), p. 4.

3. Ibid.

4. Statement by the head of the World Bank's economic analysis and projections department. "Poor Lands' Debt Up 1 Percent," *New York Times* (Feb. 21, 1987), p. 35.

5. *IMF Survey* (July 13, 1987), p. 210.

6. Yukon Huang and Peter Nicholas, "The Social Costs of Adjustment," *Finance and Development,* vol. 24, no. 2 (June 1987), p. 22.

7. *IMF Survey* (July 27, 1987), p. 232.

8. *IMF Survey* (April 20, 1987), p. 115.

9. Howard M. Wachtel, "The Global Funny Market Game," *The Nation,* vol. 245, no. 22 (Dec. 26, 1987/Jan. 2, 1988), p. 786. See also his *The Money Mandarins: The Making of a New Supranational Economic Order,* New York: Pantheon Books 1986.

10. In addition to an estimated 560,000 jobs lost due to the decline of US exports to the Third World between 1980 and 1984, a further 800,000 jobs would have been created if Third World growth rates of the 1970s had been maintained. *Overseas Development Council Policy Focus,* no. 7 (1985), p. 2. The United Nations Conference on Trade and Development estimates that over one-quarter of the US trade deficit stems from the Third World debt crisis.

11. For an important elaboration of this argument in a broad historical context, see Ulrich Pfister and Christian Suter, "International Financial Relations as Part of the World System," *International Studies Quarterly,* vol. 31, no. 3 (Sept. 1987), pp. 239–72.

12. Charles Lipson, *Standing Guard: Protecting Foreign Capital in the Nineteenth and Twentieth Centuries,* Berkeley: University of California Press 1985, p. 182. Although Lipson' is more complete, a useful survey of these changes is also found in Stephen D. Krasner, *Structural Conflict: The Third World against Global Liberalism,* Berkeley: University of California Press 1985, ch. 7.

PART III

Reassembling Political Identities

11

Plant Shutdowns and Worker Response

The Case of Johnstown, PA

(1980)

Jack Metzgar

On February 6, 1979, Bethlehem Steel Corporation announced its intention to eliminate over 1,000 jobs at its Johnstown, Pennsylvania, plant. Since Bethlehem had already cut nearly 4,000 from its 1977 Johnstown payroll, this meant that the Johnstown operation would be reducing its work force by more than 40 percent – from a peak of 12,000 in early 1977 to a projected 7,000 by 1982. These cutbacks have devastated this steel town of 41,000 people in a larger metropolitan area of scarcely 250,000. When their effects on suppliers, retail stores, local taxes, and property values are added up, the social and economic situation in Johnstown is truly grim. So grim, in fact, that Bethlehem's cutback announcement was greeted as good news. The local newspaper described the community's reaction with the headline: DECISION RENEWS HOPE. As the Very Reverend Monsignor John Yurcisin explained, "It's not as bad ^s it could have been. People had been guessing there would be only 4,500 jobs remaining." Given the history of Bethlehem's announcements and the state of the American steel industry within a troubled national economy, most people in Johnstown realize that this final cutback, the "worst case scenario," might still occur. But Bethlehem's announcement of a further cutback was greeted as a decision to *save* 2,500 jobs. Johnstown and its people are eager to hope, and for now they are pinning their hopes on Bethlehem Steel and the American economy.

What is most remarkable in Johnstown is the almost total submission of the steelworkers and their community to the will of Bethlehem Steel. There has been no organized effort to stop the cutback, no plant occupations, no protest demonstrations. Since 1973, when the first cutback announcement was made (later to be temporarily rescinded), no one has suggested that Bethlehem Steel has any less than an absolute right to decide the fate of this western Pennsylvania community.

The docility of the Johnstown working class is based in specific historical circumstances, some unique and local, but its apparent helplessness in the face of such economic disaster is neither unique nor atypical in the United States. The industrial Northeast, from Maine to Illinois north of the Ohio River and Maryland's southern boundary, lost more than 1.5 million manufacturing jobs from 1967 to 1976. Virtually none of these job losses was challenged. The valiant effort since 1977 by steelworkers and their community to reopen the Campbell steel mills near Youngstown, Ohio, is a rare case, the exception that highlights the rule. Their efforts failed, and additional cutbacks and closings have followed in the Youngstown area. What is distinctive about the "Youngstown Plan" is the *attempt* to challenge the decisions of the steel companies, and the mobilization of the working class around this attempt. Unfortunately, the response in Johnstown is much more typical of how workers and their communities have responded to shutdowns, runaways, and cutbacks.

Thus, what happened in Johnstown is worth study. We need to understand the social and historical basis for this political and economic helplessness. By understanding why there was no challenge to Bethlehem in Johnstown, we can understand more about how and why shutdowns and cutbacks occur, and why they are so difficult to challenge.

I will recount the events in Youngstown in order to suggest why the shutdown there resulted in such an atypical worker–community response. By comparing events in Youngstown with those in Johnstown, we can lay the foundation for understanding the lack of a worker–community response in the latter. And, paradoxically, it is only by studying a situation such as that in Johnstown that we can fully grasp the significance of what happened in Youngstown.

The Youngstown Story

In 1969 a small ocean shipping company, the Lykes Corporation of New Orleans, decided to become a conglomerate. Though it was doing well in its own business, Lykes thirsted for the greater possibilities of the high-growth, high-technology electronics industry. Lykes did not have the big money necessary for entry into electronics, however, and in order to get this money, it bought a steel company almost six times its size, Youngstown Sheet & Tube. Most people think of a steel company as a collection of grimy mills with thousands of people working amidst fire and smoke. Lykes thought of it as a cash box. The government allows big tax write-offs to steel companies as their plant and equipment is used up; the idea is that the extra cash which this depreciation allowance gives a steel company each year will be reinvested on a regular basis in modernizing and replacing existing plant and equipment. Lykes had another idea. It would use this cash to finance its entry into the electronics industry. Meanwhile, it would invest no more in Youngstown Sheet & Tube than was absolutely necessary to maintain existing operations. Sooner or later, of course, Sheet & Tube would no longer be able to produce steel profitably, but by then Lykes would be swimming in profits from electronics.

Frank A. Nemec, who engineered this operation, was named president of Youngstown Sheet & Tube. After two years amid the smoke and grit of Youngstown, Nemec decided he could run the steel company better from New Orleans, where there are no steel mills. This is understandable. People in Youngstown didn't like Nemec much. They said he didn't know much about the steel industry, and the steelworkers could see what he was doing (or rather, not doing) to their mills. Nemec, after all, was slowly sucking the life out of a company on whose fortunes thousands of families depended for their livelihood.

Nemec's bold strategy appeared to be working for a while, but as hard times hit the steel industry in the middle seventies, Lykes's financial scheme became unworkable. In September 1977 Lykes announced that it would shut down Youngstown's Campbell Works, throwing 5,000 steelworkers out of work. This was not a cutback, not even a phaseout over several months or years. It was, as *Business Week* described it, "a huge pink slip for an Ohio city" – a simple, brutal shutdown.

A group of Youngstown-area clergy and steelworkers were not satisfied to rail against Lykes, foreign imports, and the Environmental Protection Agency – which was the line adopted initially by local politicians, district and international officials of the United Steelworkers of America (USWA), and by many of the steelworkers and people of the Mahoning Valley. Led by this group of clergy, the Ecumenical Coalition to Save Mahoning Valley was formed and the coalition began to work for a community takeover of the shutdown mill. They organized steelworkers and community residents to pledge portions of their savings accounts to purchase stock in a communityowned steel company, if and when it should come about. The coalition then persuaded the US Department of Housing and Urban Development (HUD) to grant $300,000 for a detailed study of the feasibility of such a worker–community takeover.

The National Center for Economic Alternatives (NCEA) was commissioned to do the study: it, in turn, subcontracted specialists to investigate every aspect of a possible takeover. NCEA's emerging plan received encouragement and support not only from HUD but from elements within the Department of Commerce as well. The Labor Department and the USWA international, however, were relatively cool to the coalition and NCEA's efforts. In September 1978 NCEA released its report, arguing that a community takeover was feasible if it were initially supported by $15 million in federal grants and $394 million in federally guaranteed loans.

Prior to the release of NCEA's plan, however, Attorney General Griffin Bell had effectively scotched the coalition's chances for winning government money. On June 21, against the advice of the Justice Department's antitrust division, Bell approved the merger of Lykes and the LTV Corp. This meant that Jones & Laughlin Steel Corporation, an LTV subsidiary, would get Sheet & Tube's customer list as well as its intracompany sales, which by themselves amounted to a market of 1.1 million tons of steel a year. The list of Sheet & Tube's former customers and the sales to remaining Sheet & Tube operations in Youngstown and Chicago had been crucial to the worker–community takeover plan. NCEA's final report argued that even this loss could be overcome, but in the summer of 1979 a special team appointed by President Carter rejected the plan's grant and loan proposals.

The coalition failed to reverse the shutdown of Campbell Works, but by the time its plan was finally rejected it had mobilized the steelworkers and the community around a carefully reasoned challenge to the "economic inevitability" determined by the decisions of private corporations. The steelworkers themselves reacted slowly to the challenge, and their international union took no part – it didn't even grant official approval of the takeover plan until April 1979, after all the work had been done and when the chances for government support were slim. There was little direct action in Youngstown – no factory occupations and weak public demonstrations. The coalition's efforts neither resulted in nor were supported by any broader political movement.

In comparison with Johnstown (and with Lackawanna, New York; Conshohocken, Pennsylvania; and other steel towns where shutdowns and cutbacks occurred in 1977, amounting to 22,500 jobs lost), Youngstown's response was vigorous and aggressive. But Youngstown had its advantages. First, it had villains: Lykes and Nemec, who had coldly sucked the life's blood out of a community, and Griffin Bell, who in just as clear and calculating a way decided that the financial viability of an adventurist corporation was more important than the social and economic life of a community. Second, it had a rather unusual group of clergy and the remnants of a radical tradition in the community and among some of the steelworkers: longtime activist Staughton Lynd was the coalition's lawyer, and among the coalition's supporters were Ed Mann, president of USWA Local 1462 at Sheet & Tube's Brier Hill plant, and other USWA dissidents. As in the Steelworkers District 31 in the Chicago-Gary area, the existence of even a modest socialist tradition should not be underestimated, for it is from that tradition (completely absent in Johnstown) that much of the will to fight often emerges. Youngstown's advantages were not enough to make any difference between it and other steel towns in the final result. In fact, by the end of 1979 another 1,000 jobs were eliminated at another mill, now owned by LTV, and US Steel had announced it would close two Youngstown-area plants, eliminating 4,000 more steel jobs. But Youngstown's challenge is important nonetheless. Gar Alperovitz, co-director of the NCEA, reports: "I get calls all the time from Michigan, Indiana, Illinois: 'I heard about those guys in Youngstown buying the factory out. Can we try it?' Two years ago the idea wasn't possible to think."

The Johnstown Story

One place where it wasn't possible to think that idea is Johnstown. The cutback there has a more complicated history. And the Bethlehem Steel Corporation is no Dickensian villain thoughtlessly ruining communities as it plays financial tricks. The contrast with Lykes could not be more vivid. Bethlehem is not a conglomerate, it is a steel company pure and simple. Its non-steel operations are pretty much confined to steel-related activities such as mining iron ore and coal, and shipbuilding. It has been in Johnstown since 1923, and its initial announcement of a cutback projected a gradual phase-out of operations over a four-year period. At that time it paid for a study by the Urban Land Institute on how Johnstown could diversify its economic base, and it provided seed money for an economic development agency which attempted to attract new industry to the area. And though Bethlehem was not exactly philanthropic, it did provide its employees with early pensions, a severance pay option, some transfer rights, and continuance of coverage for life and health insurance. And, not unimportant to how working people view a cutback or shutdown decision, Bethlehem's chair at the time, Lewis W. Foy, is a native of the Johnstown area who has spent his working life in the steel industry.

This is not to say that Bethlehem Steel is respected and loved by the people of Johnstown. Johnstown began as a company town in the mid-nineteenth century, and when Bethlehem bought the old company, the Cambria Iron Works, it virtually bought the town as well. Its record of oppression and arbitrary rule in Johnstown was not interrupted until the United Steelworkers won their first contract during the Second World War, and this pattern has only been modified in the decades since. Hating "the company" is still family tradition in the Johnstown working class.

But there is more than one player in the Johnstown "shutdown" story. In the Youngstown story the state does not appear until the last act, when after some hesitation, it simply declares its indifference to the fate of the community. In Johnstown the state plays a role from the very beginning. Bethlehem's role of villain in the Johnstown story is shared by the federal Environmental Protection Agency (EPA) and the Pennsylvania Department of Environmental Resources (DER).

Johnstown's is an old plant, much of it originally built in the nineteenth century, and the town is no longer a good location for an integrated steel mill. Except for metallurgical coal (which it has in abundance), Johnstown is no longer close to the raw materials necessary for making steel. Nor is it close to the expanding steel markets, which are principally in the West. Neither of these disadvantages would be significant, however, if it were close to a water transportation system or to a viable system of railroad transportation. But Johnstown is landlocked, nestled in a series of bowls in the Allegheny Mountains, and the rail system (the main line of the former Pennsylvania Railroad), which used to serve it so well, has been allowed to deteriorate. Finally, its location among the mountains allows little room for building new facilities or for reorganizing the existing ones to put them in a better relationship with one another.

Johnstown's principal advantages are its knowledgeable and skilled steelworkers and the fact that the plant and the work force are already there. In its investment decisions a corporation has to weigh the increments in production of brand-new plants against the smaller but more predictable increments of investments in older plants. When the quality and stability of the work force are weighed in the balance, old mills are not at as great a disadvantage as might first appear.

The Johnstown plant has been profitable, but with so many long-term disadvantages, each investment in updating its plant and equipment must be carefully weighed. Big investments in new plant can only be justified if it is reasonably certain that the entire operation will remain profitable not only for two or three years but often for ten or twenty. When in such a situation a company is forced to invest in nonproductive environmental controls, additional investment capital is needed simply to maintain its existing plant, and investments in new facilities (such as the "greenfield plant" Bethlehem built at Burns Harbor, Indiana, in 1965) become that much more attractive. In Bethlehem's total capital investment budget, pollution controls may only represent from 10 to 15 percent per year (the industry average was about 12.5 percent in the 1970s), but at older plants like Johnstown's, this 10 or 15 percent can be the difference between a viable operation and a shutdown. When Bethlehem initially announced a cutback in 1973, it estimated that without the cutback it would have to invest $300 million to comply with all federal and state environmental regulations. This $300 million would make the Johnstown plant no more economically viable than it had been. In contrast, the modern furnaces which Bethlehem had promised in 1976 would save steelmaking in

Johnstown had an estimated cost of $70 million.

Bethlehem's estimate of what it would have had to spend on pollution controls is probably exaggerated, perhaps by as much as 50 percent, but the basic point is correct: environmental regulations place additional burdens on the productivity and profitability of older steel plants. *Any* expenditure for pollution controls makes investments in altogether new facilities or in other industries (like petrochemicals) more attractive for a profit-maximizing steel company.

Even this added burden might not have been insupportable, however, if a clear plan had been adopted which recognized both the economic and environmental necessities. Instead Bethlehem and the EPA/DER fought it out like a couple of boxers. The EPA/DER focused only on the point at which the "social costs" of pollution visibly begin – on emissions. It set specific standards on emissions, with deadlines for compliance, rather than involve itself with the production process or with the larger economic context of the steel industry. Bethlehem, in turn, held the community up for ransom at every opportunity, seeking to stretch out the life of its existing polluting equipment.

The offending equipment consists of the coke ovens and blast furnaces necessary to turn iron ore into pig iron and the open-hearth furnaces which turn the pig iron into steel. Open hearths are no longer the most cost-effective way to produce steel; basic oxygen furnaces (BOFs) are. BOFs make a better quality steel because the chemical process can be more precisely controlled, and a BOF can produce the same quantity of steel in forty-five minutes that it takes the most advanced open hearth four to six hours to produce. BOFs are also dramatically cleaner than open hearths, but like the open hearths they require pig iron which in turn requires the dirty coke ovens and blast furnaces.

But just because one process is more efficient and cleaner than another, you don't necessarily simply tear out the old and replace it with the new. Many of Johnstown's open hearths had a life expectancy of eight to twelve years when the EPA/DER said they had to stop polluting. Bethlehem never had any intention of spending millions of dollars to clean up open hearths only to replace them a few years later with BOFs, especially when it wasn't sure it would continue full operations at a facility with the long-term disadvantages of Johnstown's. There was another alternative, however: electric furnaces. Electric furnaces "produce" steel from steel scrap, and thus do not require coke ovens and blast furnaces to make pig iron. Their environmental advantages are great, but they are feasible only for small facilities (called "mini-mills") because they are dependent on a volatile scrap market.

The story of the Johnstown cutback actually begins, then, in March 1972, when the state's new air quality regulations went into effect. The Johnstown plant did not measure up to the new "get tough" DER standards. In fact it did not even come close to meeting the standards, and the DER said it had only six months in which to comply. Recognizing the comical, Falstaffian courage of this DER demand, Bethlehem waited until the final day for complying and then requested several variances on its polluting facilities (basically the coke ovens, blast furnaces, and open hearths) and asked for several additional years to bring itself into compliance. DER granted the variances and gave Bethlehem additional time to prepare a plan for attaining compliance.

In June 1973 Bethlehem announced its plan. To meet DER requirements it would eliminate its polluting coke ovens, blast furnaces, and open hearths, replace them with electric furnaces, and in the process eliminate some 4,500 jobs. Johnstown was stunned. Besides the direct impact on the laid-off steelworkers, the area would lose $40 million in annual payroll from Bethlehem and more than $4 million in Bethlehem's purchases from area suppliers. Retail sales would be cut by $20 million. And the result of all this would be another 3,000 jobs lost. Which would result in additional lost payroll . . . and so on.

Bethlehem's plan envisioned a gradual transition over a four-year period, however, and it never actually started construction of the electric furnaces. In 1974 demand for steel blossomed unexpectedly and Bethlehem needed all the production capacity it could muster. In May it announced a new decision about Johnstown. It would maintain existing production and employment in Johnstown by building BOFs instead of electric furnaces. It would install some pollution controls on the coke ovens and blast furnaces, but would also need some variances from EPA/DER standards on these facilities. By this time Johnstown-area businesspeople and politicians had effectively mounted a hate campaign against the DER, and Pennsylvania governor Milton Schapp was happy to twist the necessary arms to obtain the variances.

The next two years were boom times for Johnstown and by January of 1976, with the BOFs under construction, the general manager of the Johnstown plant was predicting the "dawning of a new steel era in Johnstown." Once the BOFs were in place, Johnstown's future would be assured for the next three or four decades.

With things so apparently rosy, the DER saw its chance to hit back at the giant steel corporation. In February of 1976 the DER filed suit against Bethlehem, charging that its pollution was causing lung cancer and that it had willfully violated its agreed-upon schedule for reducing the pollution from its coke ovens. The DER tagged benzo(a)pyrene (BAP) as the carcinogen being emitted from the coke ovens and found it in the Johnstown Air Basin in amounts twenty-five to thirty times greater than "the average urban concentration." Once supporting documents were released, however, it turned out that Johnstown was the first area extensively tested for BAP and that there was thus no basis for comparison. BAP, in fact, occurs wherever there is fire, and cancer mortality rates of US counties did not show the Johnstown area (Cambria County) as particularly high; New Orleans, it turned out, had the highest incidence of lung cancer (and no coke ovens). Bethlehem *was* cheating on its pollution abatement schedules, though, and the DER was able to force it to shut down two of its seven open hearths. More often, however, the courts stayed the DER's orders to shut down other facilities, like the coke ovens.

As Bethlehem was predicting a new steel era for Johnstown, however, the international demand for steel was beginning to weaken. By 1977 the American steel industry was in the midst of a crisis the likes of which it had never seen before: demand for steel was nowhere near the capacity of the steel industry to produce it. In May 1977, an internal study by Bethlehem recommended the elimination of steelmaking in Johnstown, doing away with all furnaces and leaving only some rolling mills and fabricating units and only 4,000 out of 12,000 jobs. Bethlehem had not acted on this recommendation when in July a freak series of summer thunderstorms caused a major flood which devastated the Johnstown valley, killing seventy-seven people and doing some $300 million in property damage.

Now Johnstown was on its knees, its downtown business district almost wiped out, its largest retail outlet never to open again, hundreds of houses destroyed, families searching for loved ones and others searching for a place to stay. And all of it televised nightly on the network news. Bethlehem clearly didn't want to be the lone villain in the final denouement, but it was in the midst of losing $448 million on the year (only $41 million of which was attributed to the flood in Johnstown). It had already decided to cut its production capacity, and Johnstown was one of the places to cut.

Lewis Foy, Bethlehem's chair, called a meeting in Washington, D.C., attended by the governor of Pennsylvania, the state's two United States senators, the Johnstown area's congressperson, and a special assistant to President Carter. Foy announced that Bethlehem was scrapping its construction of BOFs in Johnstown (which were 60 percent completed at the time and virtually undamaged by the flood). Expressing concern about the town in which he was born and raised, he further announced that unless the EPA and the DER granted a two-year moratorium on all pollution controls at the Johnstown plant, Bethlehem would cut its work force there from 12,000 to 4,000. If it were allowed this unprecedented moratorium, Bethlehem would maintain approximately 8,000 jobs (and its basic steelmaking capacity) for the two years of the moratorium and would then announce "final" plans for its Johnstown plant by September 1979. The politicians gathered for Foy's announcement fell over themselves getting to microphones to demand that the EPA and the DER save Johnstown from becoming a ghost town. This, with minor modifications, the environmental agencies did two days later.

Lost in all this drama was the fact that Bethlehem had held an entire community up for ransom and that the flood very probably saved Johnstown from a quick one-shot shutdown of two-thirds of its capacity and employment. In any case, a good portion of Johnstown's coke ovens, blast furnaces, and open hearths kept on producing steel (and bad air) while Johnstown went about the business of trying to recover from its third major flood since 1889. Meanwhile Johnstown waited on a decision from Bethlehem about the future of its remaining facilities, which finally came in February 1979. The announcement was "good news" because Bethlehem had not chosen its 4,000 job plan. Its projection of 6,900 jobs with electric furnaces was pretty much the same as it had planned for Johnstown in its 1973 announcement. What was then described as a disaster now renewed people's hopes.

The Worker–Community Response in Johnstown

The emotional rollercoaster the people of Johnstown have been riding since June of 1973 has come to rest basically where it began. The ride has left them weary and resigned. At no point, however, was a challenge to Bethlehem's rule mounted, or even suggested. The local steelworkers have been passive spectators for the most part; their union's district and international officers have done little beyond stating their concern. Insofar as there has been an active response to Bethlehem's cutbacks it has come from the local business community – a fairly typical collection of bankers, retailers, and small business owners closely coordinated with the local media. Bethlehem, in fact, set the initial direction of the response. It provided leadership and money in setting up an areawide development agency which tries to attract small manufacturing and service industries to the area.

Insofar as anger, that most basic of political emotions, has been expressed, it has been directed at the DER, not Bethlehem Steel. Local political representatives have confined their efforts to lobbying for Bethlehem's pollution variances. The only organized activity among local steelworkers in 1973 involved a petition demanding that "the State of Pennsylvania and the Federal Government revise environmental control laws so that Bethlehem Steel Corporation will reconsider its decision to curtail steel production in Johnstown." One of the petition's sponsors, Roy Sell, a welder at the Johnstown plant, explained: "We ask that the State of Pennsylvania and the federal government have as much compassion for a steelworker as they apparently do for a fish or a sparrow. . . . We want our jobs and, if it means breathing the air that already is much cleaner than the air that our parents breathed, we are willing to take that risk." By 1977 some of Johnstowners' anger and frustration focused on foreign imports, which was a major theme in the steel industry's refrain at the time. John Murtha, the area's US Representative, was active in the Congressional Steel Caucus and helped rally the community around the steel industry's efforts to establish "trigger pricing" for imported steel.

The steelworkers' union also followed Bethlehem's leadership. USWA policy in Johnstown was consistent with its actions in Youngstown: it oversaw the enforcement of contract provisions for the laid-off steelworkers, but otherwise echoed the industry's demands for greater profits and for government policies to encourage greater profitability. In 1977 many employed steelworkers' homes had been destroyed or damaged by the flood, and they needed to know if they would have jobs two or three years hence in order to decide whether to rebuild or make arrangements to leave the area. The international pressed Bethlehem for an early decision on the future of the Johnstown plant; Bethlehem responded by taking a year and a half instead of the full two years to make up its mind.

Though the USWA can be faulted for a failure of leadership (it certainly hasn't attempted to broaden anyone's horizons), its passive response has basically reflected the attitude of local steelworkers. In 1977 a group of steelworkers formed "The Fight for Jobs Committee," which could mobilize only fifty people for a demonstration protesting Bethlehem's layoffs; USWA subregional director Ernest Wadsworth denounced this group and most local steelworkers were indifferent to it at best.

Thus, through it all Bethlehem was in a command position. Not only did it provide leadership to the local community; it was able to mobilize the steelworkers, the political representatives, and the community at large to support its position against government policy, whether this involved pollution controls, steel prices, or foreign imports. At no point did Bethlehem have to explain or defend its investment or other policy decisions. The company does not report information on the profits or losses of specific facilities. It simply declares that this or that operation is or is not "profitable," and it does not define what it means by "profitable." And no one in Johnstown was asking questions.

The Steel Industry and Government-Regulated Free Enterprise

The submission of the Johnstown working class to the will of Bethlehem Steel as these events unfolded is remarkable, but it is apparently typical of worker–community responses to shutdowns and cutbacks in the United States. The character and origins of this submission must be carefully analyzed if we are to understand the possibilities for an alternative response. Things are changing, but they are not changing rapidly. And as they change, the Youngstown story is not an adequate model for understanding that change. The Johnstown story, with all its specific and local characteristics, provides a better picture of the dangers and possibilities of the current wave of shutdowns and cutbacks.

Why was there no challenge to Bethlehem's cutbacks in Johnstown? First, the causes of the cutbacks were complex and difficult to focus on; without a coherent conception of the problem, action was impossible. At a deeper level, there was no challenge because the system of negotiated class struggle established since World War II prohibits such a challenge. In discussing the causes of the Johnstown cutback, one thing should be clear – for it was clear to the steelworkers and people of Johnstown: despite the age of its plant and other disadvantages, Johnstown came close to remaining a major steelmaking center into the twenty-first century. Had steel demand held up for another year or two, had imports been 2 or 3 million tons less in 1976 and 1977, or had there never been laws passed to protect the environment – Johnstown would have had its BOFs by 1978 and would then have been a viable steel plant through 2010 or 2015.

The perception of these facts and possibilities, more than any other immediate cause, explains the lack of worker–community challenge to Bethlehem's decisions. The fate of the local community was clearly being determined outside the local community, and not simply by Bethlehem Steel but by the national and international situation in the steel industry, and by the federal government's response to this situation.

Steel in the United States is a sick industry. Why it is sick is the subject of a vigorous debate, in which I cannot fully participate here. But from the perspective of Johnstown certain aspects of the situation are visible which are not likely to be seen in broader approaches to the industry and its problems. The industry argues that because of government regulation (of prices and of pollution) and because of lack of government support (both in the form of investment incentives and other subsidies and in enforcing "fair" competition with foreign steel industries), it has become a low-profit industry which has not been able to compete effectively in the international market for steel. According to its spokespersons, the industry has not made enough money to allow it to expand and modernize its production capacity to keep pace with steel demand and with foreign industries' more modern plants. The industry's critics, on the other hand, argue that the industry's problems derive from its own shortsightedness and complacency in the years when it accounted for a majority of the world's production of steel (in 1947, for example, the American industry produced 60 percent of the world's steel, while in 1977 it produced less than 17 percent). A classic oligopoly, the industry was able to set its own prices in a noncompetitive fashion and did not have to worry about foreign competition until the mid-1960s. During this period of noncompetition, the American industry failed to invest in the new steel technology – BOFs and the continuous casting process – which it had itself developed and which would have ensured its international competitiveness. The industry was still putting up open-hearth furnaces in the late 1950s when the Japanese were already building their steel industry around BOFs. And even today, while Japan uses continuous casting for 50 percent of its production and Germany uses it for 38 percent, the American industry is using the process to produce less then 17 percent of its steel. During most of this period, the steel companies' dividend payouts were high in relation to their retained earnings; even in the past five years, during its worst time of troubles, Bethlehem Steel, for example, paid out 83 percent of its earnings. Thus, according to its critics, the industry's problems are the result of its own policies and priorities.

The federal government does not, of course, take an official position that coincides with the industry's critics, but in each of the important public policy areas – prices, pollution, and imports – the state has based its actions on the critics' analysis. The capitalist state has consistently defined its mission as representing the system as a whole ("the public interest") and not the interests of particular corporations or even of entire industries.

In the case of steel, the federal government realized that it was faced with a powerful oligopoly in a crucial sector of the economy and that if this oligopoly were unchecked by state power, it could have disastrous political and economic consequences for the system as a whole. Thus, the situation of the American steel industry cannot be understood in isolation from federal intervention in the industry. The critics of the industry almost always make this mistake. The people in steel-dominated communities (along with the steel companies themselves, of course) never do.

In the three crucial areas of public policy, government–industry relations have been bitterly and publicly antagonistic. The people of Johnstown, unlike the people of Youngstown, have not witnessed a private corporation greedily undermining their social and economic life. Instead, they have witnessed a series of fights between "the company" and "the government," fights in which both fighters claim to be representing their interests, but in which they have been the principal losers. Though there is no love for Bethlehem Steel in Johnstown, people there have clearly sided with the company. They are not stupid in this. They realize that Bethlehem has no real concern for them or their community, that profits and profitability are Bethlehem's only goal. They realize too that the government is attempting to represent "the public interest" (with the basic conception of which they do not radically disagree), but in their eyes the government's actions have clearly undermined Bethlehem's profitability and thus their own ability to survive as a community. As involved but powerless witnesses in these fights, Johnstowners often take satisfaction from the government's punches to Bethlehem's head and heart; but they also realize, except perhaps during the flushest of times in the industry, that only they will ultimately be damaged by these blows. Either the government succeeds in enforcing its regulation of the industry, in which case profits deteriorate and the future of Johnstown is put in question, or Bethlehem and the industry effectively retaliate and the people of Johnstown end up with bad air and higher priced automobiles and other made-of-steel consumer products.

The crucial fight for the Johnstown cutback was over air pollution, but a brief look at the issues in the fights over prices and imports shows the same structure of government–industry relations. Prices have never been "regulated" in the technical sense in the steel industry. Except for brief periods of economy-wide price controls, the government has relied on a series of "jawboning" techniques to keep the price of steel within reasonable limits. During most of the years since World War II there has been no other way to restrain steel prices. Given sufficient overall demand and a lack of foreign competition, the steel companies can pretty much charge whatever they can agree upon among themselves. Through a system of price leadership by US Steel and Bethlehem, the steel oligopoly publicly "discusses" the price of specific raw steel products by having one company announce a price increase and then adjusting it as other companies announce their prices. All have a basic interest, of course, in the highest possible price. The government realizes that as steel prices escalate, so do the prices of an entire line of capital goods and consumer products. This escalation not only gives the economy a steady inflationary bias, it acts as a "tax" on consumers' disposable income, thus ultimately restraining economic growth in both the consumer and the capital goods sectors. "Jawboning," while not ineffective from the steel industry's perspective, has not been a very powerful weapon. The federal government simply denounces the steel companies in public, detailing the public effects of the companies' pricing decisions and sometimes threatening direct public action. From Truman to Kennedy and since, the effect of jawboning has steadily diminished. The companies routinely announce higher prices than they know they can get away with and then partially roll back the prices when the government complains, thereby allowing the government a "victory" while taking the opportunity to state their needs for greater profits and profitability.

Because of the ineffectiveness of jawboning, the government looked the other way as imported steel began to invade the American market in the sixties. In the absence of domestic competition, foreign competition has the effect of restraining steel prices much more effectively than direct government action. In crisis, the industry demanded protection from imports which, it said, were unfairly competitive. The industry had no difficulty in mobilizing broad public sentiment (and not only in steel towns) in 1979.

The pattern of government–industry relations on prices and imports is the same as the pattern we saw in the EPA/DER–Bethlehem struggle over air pollution in Johnstown. For larger social, economic, and political reasons the state cannot allow private corporations to operate in complete freedom, unconstrained by the needs of the system as a whole. But in the United States the

198

state, while it can harass corporations and *influence* their policies, does not have the *power* to enforce its version of the needs of the system. Thus, in a show-down the private corporation or industry association has the edge, because its independent decisions can affect the lives of thousands directly and it can therefore mobilize public opinion against the government. Also, while a cor-poration or an industry presents a united front and has a deep commitment to winning the fight, the level of commitment within different parts of the state varies greatly. Thus, the fight is often reproduced *within* the state – e.g., be-tween the Department of Commerce and the Department of Housing and Urban Development, between the executive and the legislative branches, or between federal and state governments – because different departments and levels have different constituencies. Furthermore, this system of interest-group government often allows one agency of the state to establish policy in one sector (as the EPA did for many years) in almost complete disregard of the policies and programs of other agencies.

The major premise of this system of private-public decision-making by legal and bureaucratic fist-fight is that private corporations retain their ultimate right and ability to make the decisions that shape social and economic life. In the United States the state pursues "the public interest" without its big stick: it cannot nationalize those key industries that dominate the economy, but it must nonetheless concern itself with these industries' ability to make satisfactory profits and with the social consequences of their attempts to maximize profits.

Bethlehem Steel, therefore, rightly contends that "government regulation" is responsible in great part for the deplorable condition of the American steel industry and for the resulting troubled circumstances of steel towns in Pennsyl-vania, Ohio, and elsewhere. While restraining steel prices, the government has increased the costs of steel production through environmental controls. And it has done so in an arbitrary and ill-organized way.

But the problem with government regulation is not that it hampers the pursuit of profits by private corporations (which in the steel industry it un-doubtedly has done), but that it is ineffective in achieving its stated goals. The Johnstown story shows this clearly. In Johnstown the Department of Housing and Urban Development has expressed its concern about (and, in fact, has been active in trying to improve) the economic and social viability of the community. Likewise, the EPA has concerned itself with Johnstowners' health. And the price of steel, as I have explained, is also a legitimate concern of government because of its economy-wide effects, felt in Johnstown as else-where. Finally, it is in the national, as well as the local, interest that there be a viable steel industry able to produce quality steel. In the system I have sketched, these goals conflict with each other, and in Johnstown the inde-pendent pursuit by government and private industry of these ad hoc goals has resulted in the achievement of none of them.

Though I do not have a cure for the sickness of the American steel industry, study of the Johnstown story reveals the path toward such a cure. For in Johnstown there was a realistic solution to all, or most, of its problems. Had basic oxygen furnaces been installed in the mid-sixties, say, the local economy would be alive and well because it would have been able to produce more and better steel at a lower cost. Because the costs of production would have been reduced, the price of steel could have been lower. And Johnstown's air, though it would still not be very healthful, would have been considerably cleaner by 1969 than it is eleven years later.

To achieve this result in Johnstown, the government would have had to have power over Bethlehem's basic investment decisions. To extend such achievements to other steel towns, a coordinated industry plan and public investment capital would have been necessary. Neither of these possibilities necessarily requires nationalization of the steel industry, but they do require a government power over corporate policy that is now prohibited. Nor is it clear that even nationalization would cure the steel industry's sickness without some cutbacks and shutdowns of existing facilities. What is clear is that Johnstown and other steel towns are presently being undermined not simply by greedy corporations or by misdirected government bureaucrats, but by both – or rather by *the system of government-regulated free enterprise.*

What is also frustratingly clear is that this system is not visible *as a system.* Its invisibility frustrates any possibility of an effective worker–community challenge to shutdowns and cutbacks. Thus, most Johnstown steelworkers blame the EPA and DER for their problems, while others blame Bethlehem. In the national debate, one side takes up the industry's point of view while the other defends the EPA or the Department of Commerce and attacks the industry. The debates are fruitless, and solutions are not forthcoming, because all involved accept the system as given. The corporations' right to make economic life-and-death decisions is not in question, and, therefore, discussions focus almost entirely on the narrow range of issues left to government policy.

The United States has the only steel industry in the advanced industrial world which is neither state-owned nor subject to state planning. Yet for all the industry's present troubles and the social and economic reverberations of these troubles, virtually no one has even broached the possibility of nationalization or of a national system of economic planning and public investment. The veils of American free-enterprise ideology distort the reality to such an extent that even the American left, such as it is, does not challenge the system; with its anti-corporate, pro-government outlook, the left has fallen into the trap of rooting for one side against the other. That the state is relatively more humane and democratically representative makes it no less culpable – and steelworkers and their communities know this, even if they don't see the whole system in which government culpability is only one part.

Thus, the specific character of the system of government-regulated free enterprise is the principal cause not only of the Johnstown cutback but of the lack of a worker–community challenge to that cutback. Though I have arrived at this conclusion by studying a specific town dominated by a specific industry, its basic outline applies to other shutdowns and cutbacks in key industries. Many autoworkers, for example, blame the loss of thousands of their jobs on government auto pollution and safety regulations, many of them ill-conceived and ill-timed; but in the same breath they do not hesitate to excoriate the auto companies for their venality, short-sightedness, and mismanagement. These dual perceptions appear contradictory only within a national debate that pits industry against government and insists that we must choose one side or the other. The same ideological veil hangs over much of the national energy debate: are the oil companies and utilities to blame or is it the government? Such questions merely confuse the issue and violate the valid but unsystematic perceptions of workers and citizens.

Writing about government housing and health care programs, Paul Starr and Gosta Esping-Anderson find the debate over "government intervention" debilitatingly narrow and misconceived:

> The problem has nothing to do with *amount* of government intervention, but rather with its *nature*. Or to put it another way, the problem is not too much governmental activism, but too much passivity. Political compromise in America has repeatedly produced a type of policy that might be called *passive intervention:* typically, there is enough support to get social programs passed, but not enough to challenge established interests. The results are expensive.

There is little hope that this systematic passivity can be overcome unless a more ambitious form of class struggle emerges in the years ahead. For, as I said, the major premise of the system of government-regulated free enterprise is the inviolability of private corporations' right to make the basic decisions that shape our social and economic lives while pursuing the maximization of their profits. The results, in every aspect of our lives, are expensive.

Postscript

This article was written in 1980, just two years before the US economy experienced its worst recession of the postwar period. In the last ten years, the American steel industry has been cut in half and more than 2 million manufacturing jobs have been permanently lost. The overall response was consistent with that witnessed in the late 1970s in Johnstown: passive and resigned.

Though hundreds of towns and communities like Johnstown were devastated with unemployment in the 1980s, nary a political ripple was generated on a national level. There were, however, a number of labor–community fights to save plants, some which were even successful – in New Bedford, Massachusetts; Seymour, Connecticut; and Van Nuys, California, for example. The USWA, after Lloyd McBride died and Lynn Williams took over as president, adopted a "Youngstown-style" of resisting plant closings and has been successful in a couple of instances with worker-ownership. Labor–community coalitions dedicated to fighting the loss of industrial jobs and the deterioration of industrial communities have sprung up in two dozen cities from Massachusetts to California. These permanent coalitions have joined together in a national network – the Federation for Industrial Retention and Renewal – to share tactics and strategies and to push a national agenda if ever a political opportunity presents itself.

As for Johnstown, it is now the "ghost town" that people feared in 1973. Of the 12,000 steel jobs it had in 1977, only 2,500 remain – and steep wage concessions were required to save many of those. Dozens of small fabricating shops disappeared, followed by a wave of closings of department, furniture, and appliance stores. Health care is now the principal industry in Johnstown, with heart disease and alcoholism fueling the local economy. A common saying among young people is, "Life sucks, and then you die."

A Note on the Sources

The original *Socialist Review* article contained nearly four pages of notes on sources, which were of three sorts: national newspapers and magazines, with a heavy reliance on *Business Week* and *In These Times*; systematic review of the clippings and files of the Johnstown *Tribune-Democrat*, the area's only daily newspaper; and formal interviews and informal personal observation and experience as a resident and then as a frequent visitor during the period studied. These sources are now dated, and would be of little relevance to reproduce here. More relevant are a number of books and periodicals that give a picture of how both "the Youngstown story" and "the Johnstown story" were continued in other locales in the 1980s:

Bensman, David, and Roberta Lynch. *Rusted Dreams: Hard Times in a Steel Community*. Berkeley: University of California Press, 1989.
"Labor Tackles the Local Economy: Reindustrialization from Below," *Labor Research Review*, vol. 9 (Fall 1986).
Lynd, Staughton, *The Fight against Shutdowns*. Youngstown, Ohio: Singlejack Books 1982.
Mann, Eric. *Taking on General Motors: A Case Study of the UAW Campaign to Keep GM Van Nuys Open*. Los Angeles: Institute for Industrial Relations, UCLA 1987.
"Mismanagement & What Unions Can Do about It," *Labor Research Review*, vol. 10 (Spring 1987).
Swinney, Dan, and Jack Metzgar. "Expanding the Fight against Shutdowns," in *The Imperiled Economy: Book II, Through the Safety Net*. New York: Union for Radical Political Economics 1988.

The Federation for Industrial Retention and Renewal (FIRR) has offices at 3411 W. Diversey, Chicago, IL 60647.

12

Taking It to the Streets
Community Organizing and National Politics
(1982)
Gary Delgado

From 1976 to 1980 the Association of Community Organizations for Reform Now (ACORN) sought to expand from three to twenty states and consolidate itself as a national organization by waging a protracted confrontation with the Democratic Party.* It was able to grow and consolidate itself by increasing ideological unity among its membership; by building alliances with other progressive groups; and by attempting to effect meaningful change within the Democratic Party. This rendering of the facts is in no way non-partisan. As one of the initial organizers of ACORN, I had a long-standing relationship with the staff and membership and was responsible for the planning and implementation of a number of tasks in the 1980 campaign. At that time, and still today, many progressives advocated reclaiming the Democratic Party. It is my hope that this article will serve to point out some of the problems and possibilities of this strategy.

ACORN's Transition from Local to National Politics

In 1970 the Association of Community Organizations for Reform Now began in Arkansas as an experimental project of the National Welfare Rights

---

* Many important details of political analysis and strategy have had to be omitted for reasons of space from this version of this article. A more complete presentation of those details can be found in the author's book *Organizing the Movement: The Roots and Growth of ACORN*, Philadelphia: Temple University Press 1986.

Organization. The project was part of NWRO's "Southern Strategy," an attempt to expand its organizational base, mostly northern and urban, to the South and, through ACORN, to expand the organization's constituency to non-welfare poor and working-class people. Arkansas was chosen for the organizing project for three reasons. First, 70 percent of the state's population had incomes below $7,000 per year. Second, the state had a liberal Republican governor, Winthrop Rockefeller, which made reform efforts around issues of concern to low-income people potentially feasible. Third, there was a small welfare rights core group in Little Rock that encouraged NWRO to send an organizer to Arkansas.

Wade Rathke, a 22-year-old organizer who was then head staffperson for the Massachusetts Welfare Rights Organization, headed the effort. In moving to Arkansas, Rathke was interested in keeping what he perceived to be good in the welfare rights model: the membership base, use of a replicable model and strategic manipulation of the press. He incorporated some parts of the old Alinsky model: strong ties with existing organizations (especially unions and churches) and experimenting with electoral politics as a way to consolidate organizational victories.

ACORN first ventured into electoral politics in 1971, when seven ACORN leaders registered with the state legislature as special-interest lobbyists to represent poor people. Advocating the group's first political platform, ACORN put forth a legislative package calling for the establishment of a public defender system, elimination of state income taxes for people with incomes of less than $3,000 annually, an expanded collective bargaining law, free medical care for low-income persons not currently eligible, and a measure to lower the voting age to eighteen. By 1972, ACORN had plunged directly into politics by electing a Little Rock school board member committed to free textbooks, abolition of school fees, progressive special education, and more funding allocated for eastern and central Little Rock – the low- to moderate-income areas. In 1974 ACORN's venture into the political arena reflected a different approach; the organization was no longer satisfied with a "voice" in the political process. Discovering an antiquated form of local government authorized under the 1872 Arkansas Constitution which called for 1 justice of the peace for every 200 electors in each county, ACORN organized to elect 195 of the 467 members of the Pulaski County (Little Rock) Quorum Court and, through the Court, managed to direct the distribution of funds and services destined for low-income neighborhoods in the county. In response, in 1976 the state decided to "streamline" the Court, and reduced the membership to fifteen.

Up until ACORN's experience on the Quorum Court in 1974–75, the organization's attitude toward the role of the state was consistent with the strategic thrust of the National Welfare Rights Organization: the state could be manipulated on two levels. First, fiscally – the state could be held fiscally responsible for all benefit programs, and organizing efforts were directed towards increasing benefits through welfare reform and expanding state welfare programs to larger constituencies. Second, it was the organization's task to hold the state accountable in fairly enforcing laws and regulations for poor and working-class people. Therefore, in line with this thrust, ACORN initiated a tax assessment campaign that forced county assessors to reassess properties in low-income neighborhoods by publishing a table of comparative assessments in low-income and downtown neighborhoods. This approach allowed ACORN members to demand accountability from state institutions and, at the same time, educated them through direct action that the state could be held accountable, although without a people's organization it would be more responsive to other class interests.

However, 1975 marked a shift in thinking within the organization. The Quorum Court experience gave the staff and membership a view of an important difference: the difference between forcing a state institution to be accountable and actually controlling the institution. As ACORN organizer Steve Kest wrote:

> The state might be dominated or even controlled by powerful economic institutions, but if the low- to moderate-income majority is ever able to take control of the state, there's a good chance that the lines of power between the state and the economic institutions will begin reversing themselves.

This potential was enhanced by ACORN's transformation from an Arkansas statewide organization to a multi-state association with operations in nine Arkansas cities and beginning organizations in Sioux Falls, South Dakota, and the Dallas-Fort Worth area in Texas.

In 1976, Wade Rathke produced an ambitious document entitled "The 20/80 Plan." On six single-spaced, mimeographed pages, Rathke made a series of arguments for expanding ACORN's organizational base from three to twenty states over the next four years, focused in part on expanding to states where there was a Democratic primary or statewide caucus. Rathke argued that it would be possible to use the "event" of the presidential campaign to build ACORN's national power and prestige. Identifying four electoral arenas as opportunities, the memo pointed out that, if ACORN were to run a presidential candidate in 1980, the next election year, the organization could capitalize on federal campaign financing resources, the Voting Rights Act, state delegate selection processes, and the party platform procedures.

The 1976 campaign plan would therefore potentially include a number of elements: the expansion of ACORN to twenty states by 1980 with an emphasis on caucus states, the creation of an ACORN platform, and the running of delegates for the Democratic convention – a campaign aimed directly at provoking issues and candidates within the Democratic Party. It was an opportunity that would potentially transform ACORN-the-organization into ACORN-the-social-movement of low- and moderate-income people.

In a somewhat more visionary reflection, Rathke added, "ACORN has an organizational and professional responsibility to demonstrate the potential of community organization as a mechanism for social change." In defining a new direction for ACORN, Rathke was breaking with the "hands-off electoral politics" position taken by most community organizations in the Alinsky and other traditions. He was redefining not only the future of ACORN, but the shape of community organization in this country.

The introduction of the memo met with mixed reactions. While many organizers and leaders supported the 20/80 plan, a number were concerned by the potential for intraorganizational conflict. To address these concerns, Rathke developed the following guidelines: 1) ACORN's platform would be forged from existing and common organizational issues (borrowing from the Non-Partisan League); and 2) ACORN would "run the organization rather than candidates" and would therefore run on ACORN's record in each of its states. Since there was still internal opposition to the development of the campaign, it was agreed in early 1976 that the 20/80 plan would be evaluated at the end of the year against two criteria: 1) an analysis of the 1976 presidential campaign; and 2) the progress of ACORN's state expansion plan.

In exhaustive staff discussions in December 1976 and January 1977, a number of key senior organizers argued that the campaign would be too much of a resource drain and that "taking over the Democratic Party is not the business of a community organization." Essentially, there were two factions supporting this view. Most of the opposition argued for "maintenance over expansion," reasoning that if ACORN's ability to mobilize resources remained constant, the financial and personal stress within the organization would necessarily lower the quality of organizing throughout the association. Others contended that pursuing electoral politics, given the existing party structure, was strategically incorrect because no amount of work would reform the Democratic Party. The very process, they argued, would potentially co-opt ACORN leadership. Although the issues were debated, the points of contention were not resolved and, as the campaign evolved over the next four years, these questions of resource mobilization and potential cooptation continued to be the bottom-line positions that informed strategic discussion.

One of the initial questions of internal conflict was quelled with an amended plan (January 1977), which called for running uncommitted delegates to both the Democratic and Republican conventions. In addition, ACORN leadership decided to frame the campaign totally in terms of the issues of low-income people rather than endorsing a candidate.

Action in Memphis: Setting the Stage

Although ACORN had expanded into and was working in twelve states by the end of 1978, the organization was still seen by most activists as a southern organization. As a first step in testing the organization's ability to mobilize nationally, the ACORN leadership decided to challenge the Democrats in their Memphis mid-term convention. ACORN brought together 1200 members and supporters from twelve states in a freezing rain to march on the Democratic Mid-Term Convention in December 1978. Foreshadowing the 1980 campaign, ACORN members demanded platform changes and representation for low- and moderate-income people.

The Memphis action helped to concretize the 1980 campaign in a number of ways. It demonstrated ACORN's ability to organize and mobilize people from all over the country, and bolstered the internal organizational spirit. The Memphis action was also the site of the first ACORN national convention, and, for many ACORN members, was their first opportunity to meet members from other states. It was also the galvanizing impetus for ACORN to develop another expansion strategy – affiliation agreements with three statewide community organizations – Georgia Action, Carolina Action in North Carolina, and the Citizens' Action League in California. By February 1979, all of these organizations had agreements with ACORN. Another set of negotiations had earlier brought *Just Economics,* a national magazine for organizers, and its talented editor, Madeleine Adamson, under the aegis of the tax-exempt Institute for Social Justice, ACORN's education and training arm.

The affiliation of four states, *Just Economics,* and, in December 1979, the Jobs and Justice staff in Boston, allowed ACORN to reach the organizational goal of operating in twenty states without overextending its own staff and financial resources. The affiliation strategy was therefore viewed as a concession to the maintenance faction in the expansion/maintenance fight.

Yet ACORN was beset with problems. The expansion into sixteen states in four years had indeed taken its organizational toll. Many key organizers were tired and emotionally drained. Additional problems emerged from the centralization of the growing organization. It was not clear, for instance, how much direction ACORN head organizers, much less staff and leadership in "affiliate" states, would take from the national "Association" staff. And organizationally ACORN was beginning to develop other problems. First, there was wide variation in the quality of work performed in ACORN cities. Second, while many senior staff members had come through the Quorum Court experience, that experience had not been successfully communicated to ACORN's membership outside of Arkansas. Third, many ACORN campaigns reflected local conditions.

In a memo prepared in the summer of 1978 entitled "20/80 (Apocalypse or

207

Long March?)," the campaign was seen as a necessary next step – an oppor- tunity to use both the Democratic and Republican conventions as forums for raising the issues of low-income people. Reasoning that presidential election years are times when "issues are on the people's minds," It asserted that ACORN could use the election year to identify crucial national issues; to present its vision of a worthwhile America; to raise the nation's consciousness about power relationships and what organized people can achieve; and, by these means, enhance ACORN's impact.

The emphasis in the memo was on the strategy and tactics of raising issues at the Democratic National Convention, with an optional scenario for running ACORN delegates sub rosa or as "out-front uncommitted." By 1979 other oppositional forces had begun to show an interest in electoral politics. In New York a group of left/liberal foundation people interested in the potential for a third-party effort invited ACORN and the New York–based Women's Action Alliance to discuss the potential of a "citizens' party." Representing ACORN, Rathke was asked to write a memo exploring the trade-offs between two options: "building a party (an organization) versus developing a campaign (running a candidate for president)." He noted that there was no pre-existing party, no mass movement from which a candidate and organization could spring. Without an organized constituency, a top-down national campaign would be forced to make compromises based on the candidate's need for alliances and support. In view of the nature of American politics, more money would be spent for media than building organization. Further, the new party's candidate would necessarily have to be a "big name" and would thus neces- sarily be "non-indigenous." On the other hand, a "party-first strategy" would offer the advantages of organizational permanence, indigenous leaders, local issues, local alliances, and a concentration of resources based on the likelihood of success. Such a strategy, he concluded, would allow one to build a mass base. Eventually, the group decided to establish the Citizens' Party, with Barry Commoner as its candidate. ACORN and the Women's Action Alliance elected to organize their respective campaigns locally.

Developing the People's Platform

The reasons why it was necessary for ACORN to develop a platform to challenge the Democrats were internal. Primarily, the membership's ex- periences with the organization were different. For instance, some groups in Arkansas were all black and some in South Dakota were all white. Groups had initially organized around different issues. The process through which the platform would be developed would be used to consolidate and collectivize the membership's positions on key social issues, thereby beginning the forging of ideological unity within ACORN. Second, the process would, if successful, purge nonprogressive elements within the organization. Third, the experience of the platform would give the staff and membership of the organization an opportunity to familiarize themselves with issues on which they had not waged local campaigns. Fourth, the platform process would escalate the expectations of the organization's membership because the discussions were to be shaped so that members of ACORN would take responsibility for creating social programs instead of demanding accountability from already existing programs.

Yet there were two limitations in achieving these objectives. First, in following the conventional community organizing wisdom of "not going outside the experience of people and starting where people are at," ACORN developed platform planks in nine areas in which it had experience. These areas included taxes, jobs and income, energy, and health care, but they were not the areas in which special-interest groups, specifically racially based and women's groups, were spending their energy. The second limitation on platform development was time. Viewing the Democratic National Convention as the eventual target of ACORN's strategy, the platform had to be conceptualized, discussed, and ratified in six months in order to be used as a tool, during the fall of 1979, to build ACORN's alliances.

The initial platform positions were developed by the staff who prepared background papers on each of the issues, including a general definition of the issue, places where ACORN had worked on an issue, and a series of questions on the issue. These questions ran from the most generic ("If we were to put together a health care system that was really run by and for the people, what would it look like?") to fairly specific ("Should a percentage of all people who sit on governmental regulatory boards be low-income? How should they be chosen?") These information packages were sent to organizers in all cities where ACORN had local groups. The packages were duplicated and distributed to local leadership and one or more of the issues were discussed by local area boards and later at neighborhood meetings. The board meeting discussions were usually facilitated by organizers and the neighborhood meetings were led by local board members. To collect the information, the process was reversed, with some small differences. Comments and suggestions on the issues from local group discussions were funnelled directly to the Association staff in New Orleans, where positions were consolidated into preliminary versions of the platform, noting which planks came from which states, and sent out for further discussion. This cycle took place three times before ending in statewide platform conventions in which state bodies recommended final versions of the platform.

As with most attempts to initiate and implement a participatory democratic process, there were many problems. One was organizers' reluctance to initiate

209

discussions. In ACORN the role of the organizer is less an initiator of discussion than a low-key facilitator. Many organizers, therefore, were not comfortable with running discussions. Another problem was that, background papers notwithstanding, many organizers and leaders did not feel sufficiently knowledgeable in some areas and were reticent about starting discussions. There was also, of course, outright resistance to the platform process.

The culmination of the platform process was the 1979 ACORN convention in St. Louis. Two thousand delegates from nineteen states gathered at Washington University to finalize the platform. The three issues that generated the most intense conflict in the organization wear the planks on Guaranteed Income, Nuclear Power, and Rights of Workers. The Guaranteed Income plank was developed in Arkansas and was advocated by organizational old-timers who were present in ACORN when the organization was still an experimental project of the National Welfare Rights Organization. It was on this issue that the tenuous coalition of low- and moderate-income people on which the organization is built was most seriously challenged. Advocates of the plank (mostly black and low-income) argued that all families were entitled to a basic income, health care, and housing, while the opponents of the plank, the most vociferous of whom were also black but more moderate-income, argued for income based on employment. This argument, which culminated with a plank struggle in St. Louis, was the result of some fundamental differences within the ACORN constituency: the division between the low-income members, who essentially argued for guarantees from the welfare state, and the working-class constituency, who were for individual access to resources without guarantees. Although the guaranteed minimum income plank did pass, it was not without bitter feeling on both sides. There were similar divisions on the "right-to-work" question. Labor union advocates were pushing for a plank that would extend the right to organize, streamline union elections, and broaden the National Labor Relations Act to cover all workers. Not surprisingly, a strong anti-union tendency emerged from the "right-to-work" states within the Association – North Carolina, Louisiana, and Georgia – and was supported by the more conservative elements in Colorado and Arizona. Once again, the plank passed, but not without considerable internal struggle.

After nuclear power, nuclear waste disposal was a major issue in North Carolina, Arkansas, and Louisiana. Moreover, the 1979 Three Mile Island incident had motivated significant support on an anti-nuclear plank from Pennsylvania, Tennessee, and Michigan. While there were no strong pro-nuclear groups within the Association (only Arizona and Colorado had refused to approve the anti-nuclear planks in their statewide conventions), ACORN groups in Missouri and Michigan, where there were strong union ties, advocated a more moderate stand on the nuclear issue. The anti-nuclear measure passed three to one.

In all three of these areas, different factions, struggling to move their agendas through the ACORN platform process, created polarization and conflict within the organization. The victories can be attributed to the strong leadership roles of *local* leaders on *specific* issues. While few individual leaders were necessarily progressive, socialist, or even left, their experience on specific issues gave them both the perspectives and the legitimacy to push the organization to take a progressive stand. The process did develop the knowledge and skills of both the members and staff of the organization. It was not an insignificant step to get low-income people to speculate on how banking *should* be regulated or how a national health plan conceived in their interests might work. However, in terms of advancing ideological unity within the organization, the platform was at best a starting place. At worst, it represented a hodgepodge of progressive notions without an underlying ideology. Sidestepping some major social issues, it allowed ACORN members in some places to back positions that others viewed as retrograde.

Like many populist organizations, ACORN had opted to preserve class unity by developing an anticorporate political program that did not directly address salient issues of race and sex. ACORN was able to advocate one of the most progressive policy platforms written by any group, while being unable to accommodate the differences within this majority of minorities and expressing a laissez-faire ideology. President Steve McDonald said, "We're not trying to take over. The establishment has a right too. But we want our fair share." This reduction of social issues to anticorporate reforms was to have some effect in the next phase of organization – the "allied mobilization."

Grassroots Mobilization and the People's Platform

After the St. Louis convention, ACORN members began to mobilize on four fronts. As a first step, local ACORN chapters were urged to tie the positions taken in the national platform to local campaigns and to have members with other organizational affiliations (labor, church, Democratic or Republican Party) mobilize support for the adoption of the ACORN People's Platform by the Democratic Party.

This effort was necessary for the next tactical step: the allied mobilization. In this second phase ACORN began forging local coalitions in order to run ACORN-affiliated but uncommitted delegates to the Democratic National Convention. Next ACORN moved to public questioning of both the regular party platform development process and the rules through which delegates were chosen for the Democratic convention. Members also explored the possibility of gaining acceptance of ACORN platform planks in the Democratic

Party. These options were investigated by talking with local sympathetic party delegates, opportunistic candidates, and Democratic Agenda, affiliated with the Democratic Socialist Organizing Committee (DSOC). Recognition was also sought for ACORN's platform in the Republican Party. This was necessary in order to develop the bipartisan nature of the campaign and include ACORN members who were Republicans.

The allied strategy was viewed as key to success, especially for mobilizing platform support and in polarizing the issues within the Democratic Party. Danny Cantor, St. Louis head organizer, observed that "the more that Labor realizes it doesn't really have power on the Hill and the more they realize that capitalism doesn't include OSHA, then the more they are driven back to the grassroots level where militant stands might be taken."

Shift in Strategy

In attempting to carry out the platform mobilization strategy, ACORN ran into some unexpected problems. A major goal of the campaign prior to the fall of 1979 was to win platform concessions from the Democratic Party and claim any changes as an organizational victory. Assuming that there would be no serious challenge to Carter's candidacy, the platform concessions would legitimate ACORN and any fights that ACORN might make for future concessions. By September 1979, however, Edward Kennedy had decided to run for president. Not only was the drama of the campaign refocused on candidates as opposed to issues; many of ACORN's constituents favored the Kennedy candidacy and were interested in an ACORN endorsement. The second problem was even greater. The Democratic Platform Committee was chaired by one of ACORN's chief nemeses, an ex-UAW organizer who had allied himself with General Motors in his rebuilding of Detroit: Mayor Coleman Young.

Young and ACORN had, by this time, locked horns on many issues. The biggest confrontation was the 1979 struggle around the expansion of General Motors into an ACORN neighborhood. While the local group was successful in winning its demands in this instance, the organization's continued opposition to Detroit's "revitalization" without including the interests of low-income people earned ACORN Young's personal and permanent enmity.

ACORN convened a meeting in October 1979 to address questions of strategy for the campaign. Jon Kest, head organizer in Philadelphia, presented the position that the issue on which to base the campaign was representation of poor people on the party convention delegate ballot. Kest argued that the language of the Democratic Party rules gave ACORN a tactical handle with which to organize its members and other groups into pushing for the increased representation of low-income people in the party. This proposal drew majority support at the meeting. Kest recommended a shift away from work on platform or plank approval to creating a special commission within the Democratic Party to help facilitate greater participation by low- and moderate-income people.

The key rationale for the strategic shift was provided by research director Seth Borgos: "Fighting for a commission for our people to be represented within the Democratic Party is both consistent with ACORN's politics and within the experience of the members of the organization – people are less sure about their right to demand seats on corporate boards (a plank in the ACORN platform) than a seat in the government that's supposed to regulate that corporation." The decision at the October meeting was to make the commission a demand at all meetings with Democratic Party officials, and to attempt to secure support from "potential delegates and anti-Carter forces within the Party." The commission was an immediate, specific, winnable demand. The ACORN membership could be mobilized about their ability to influence Democratic Party politics.

By February of 1980, the stepped-up pledge campaign to support the ACORN Commission was opening up an organizing opportunity that had not, at least earlier, been seriously considered: the opportunity for ACORN to win victories in local units of the Democratic Party. In a *Village Voice* article entitled "It's Now or Never in Iowa: Door to Door with ACORN," Alexander Cockburn and James Ridgeway noted that ACORN produced 2,000 pledge cards and could produce 600 people at the primary caucuses in Des Moines and Davenport. Similar stories in the *Valley Tribune* (Nevada), *Tulsa World* (Oklahoma), and *Telegram* (Bridgeport, Connecticut), coupled with the triumph of Detroit ACORN in controlling a significant percentage of the votes in Coleman Young's backyard, led ACORN to be more assertive about the Commission.

These victories, coupled with Kennedy's, McGovern's, and Maynard Jackson's endorsements, made the Commission a definite possibility for the August Democratic Convention. However, the general disarray of the Democratic Party was another factor helping to advance the Commission. Later a source within the Kennedy campaign said, "Commission, hell, we were ready to do some real horsetrading."

By early July the Commission was almost in ACORN's hands. ACORN tactics in the Republican Party were similar to the episodes with Democratic Party officials: public embarrassment of Republican Party officials all over the country – however, there was one interesting difference. Since the convention was in Detroit, ACORN also used the event to embarrass the organization's old enemy, Coleman Young.

From early on, the Republican options were fairly bleak. A letter written to Republican national chair Bill Brock had received no reply and a disruption of a September 1979 Republican fundraising meeting in Memphis had produced a promise of a meeting, but the meeting had never materialized. At an ACORN executive board meeting in October 1979, the idea of getting Republican delegates to "tour the real Detroit" emerged. Board members from nineteen states voted to send up to 300 ACORN members to the convention and that ACORN would arrange for liberal Republicans to tour Detroit's worst neighborhoods "to point out the need for action on our platform planks."

After disruptions and demonstrations against prominent Republicans and at Republican Regional Platform Committee hearings in Philadelphia, St. Louis, and Davenport, Iowa, ACORN secured a commitment from Senator Tower (Texas), chair of the platform committee, that ACORN would be able to address the Republican Platform Committee in Detroit. This success, coupled with the much-publicized tour of the "real Detroit" – in which fifty Republicans, twenty-five ACORN members, and thirty reporters were given a view of the city's worst neighborhoods and estimates of how much neighborhood rehabilitation would cost compared with money spent on the convention – fired ACORN members up for the New York Democratic convention.

The Democratic Convention and Its Aftermath

By July 1980, ACORN had elected forty-two delegates and alternates to the Democratic convention in New York, had secured support for the ACORN commission in thirteen states, and was riding the crest of local activity that was mobilizing for the New York convention.

As predicted originally, the ACORN '80 Campaign with its mobilization of 1,500 ACORN members, 200 staff people, and 150 supporters put tremendous strain on the personnel and financial resources of the organization. Outlining the bleak financial situation in a memo three weeks before the New York convention, Rathke noted that transportation alone would run between $92,000 and $115,000, while operating expenses in New York could run another $40,000. Predicting a $65,000 shortfall, Rathke, in a move to avoid this situation, cut staff salaries an average of $100 per organizer per month. Balancing the potential of staff disenchantment and financial hardship against the possibility of some members being unable to attend the convention, he concluded that it was more acceptable for 200 staff to be adversely affected than for 500 members to be potentially disaffected.

This financial strain notwithstanding, ACORN planned to go to New York with two demands to be made on the Democratic delegations of twenty-four states: 1) that the delegations support the Rules Committee report which would establish the Commission on Representation of Low- and Moderate-Income People; and 2) that the Commission be fully implemented and operational by November of 1980.

ACORN's agenda for the three days people were in New York was simple. ACORN would have its own counter-convention, complete with speeches from New York city council member Ruth Messinger, Ruben Bonilla of the League of United Latin American Citizens, and Bill Lucy of AFSCME; ACORN would march on the Democratic Convention from the ACORN Convention Center in the Roseland Ballroom; and ACORN members would use the Roseland Convention Center as a base from which to sally forth into battle to confront delegates about supporting the ACORN commission.

Despite the logistical problems, the financial strains, and the ever-present humidity of a New York summer, on August 12 the Democratic National Convention voted to establish a commission to provide for the participation of low- and moderate-income people in the Democratic Party – the ACORN Commission. As in all negotiations, after pushing the Democrats to agree to a commission, the trick was to get the party to put enough resources and power into the commission for ACORN to move an agenda through the party. By March 1981, campaign coordinator Dewey Armstrong had delineated three primary demands that ACORN would attempt to wring from the party through the commission:

1. Establish lower income quotas ("minimum standards") for party conventions and central committees at all levels;

2. Create Party Organizing Councils with authority in the party structure, directly representing organized groups within the low-to-moderate-income constituency that would otherwise remain underrepresented under the present party structure and operation;

3. Once and for all, decisively remove all financial and procedural barriers that deny equal participation in party affairs to low- and moderate-income people.

The commission was to be chaired by Rep. Mickey Leland, a young black progressive from Austin, Texas, who had spoken on ACORN's behalf at the 1978 Memphis Mid-Term Convention. It was ACORN's hope that Leland's sympathy, coupled with ACORN's ability to continue to raise issues of low-income participation, would result in meaningful participation in the party.

After almost two years of agitation, the Democratic National Committee voted, on March 26, 1982, to reject the recommendations of the commission (which were essentially ACORN's demands) and, instead, accept the recommendations of the Commission on Presidential Nominating Rules and the DNC's Executive Committee to add 548 uncommitted delegates (14 percent of the total convention) who were party regulars to the number of convention delegates.

Building a National Community Organization

There are at least two levels on which the ACORN '80 Campaign can be evaluated. The first is to what extent did the campaign meet the expectations and needs of the organization? The second addresses the extent to which the experience can shed light on the potential for influence in the Democratic Party and reveal the strategic approaches that will prove most successful in carrying out these efforts.

It is clear that ACORN was successful in achieving its expansion and consolidation. This success is indicated not only by the presence of ACORN in twenty (now twenty-six) states, but also by the national press attention given to ACORN during and after the campaign. Even more important, the organization's self-image had changed. The Association staff was no longer an amalgamation of ex-lead organizers and hotshot researchers; it was a mature, battle-scarred operation that had coordinated delegate fights in over 600 precincts in twenty states.

While the emergence of regional campaigns (ACORN recently launched a multistate squatting effort) contributes to organizational unity, it does not necessarily help develop ideological unity. Work on the ACORN platform did foster internal debate and increase the knowledge within the organization on a wide range of issues. However, as previously mentioned, the platform remained an ideological hodgepodge, including demands for a guaranteed annual income and membership on corporate boards. While it is clear that tactical militancy does not necessarily relate to or translate into a progressive ideology, ACORN's squatting actions, in which low-income people in twelve cities took over abandoned houses, certainly demonstrated the organization's *attitude* toward private property and translated that attitude into action.

In building alliances with other groups, ACORN was most successful with labor and church groups and, to a lesser extent, with local Democrats. These groups, however, had problems with ACORN's refusal to endorse a candidate. A top UAW official in Missouri was alternately miffed and mystified by ACORN's position on endorsements, remarking, "We were ready to go for the Commission – but we were also committed to Kennedy." In many cases groups organized around social issues did not support the ACORN platform. Therefore, while it is true that the ACORN '80 Campaign built working alliances with many groups, the ideological stance of the organization vis-à-vis issues of race and gender did limit alliances, as did the non-endorsement of candidates.

While ACORN won the first round in trying to bring about meaningful change within the Democratic Party by getting the commission, it clearly lost the major struggle at the Democratic National Committee. ACORN was swimming upstream against an overwhelming current within the party to block "outsiders." This current was actually supported by both Douglas Fraser and Lane Kirkland, presidents of the UAW and AFL-CIO, who had approved the DNC recommendation for increased control by party regulars. Another reason has to do with the state of national politics – with Reagan's domestic and foreign policies adversely affecting low-income and Third World groups, many groups and individuals ran to embrace the Democratic Party, no questions asked. Third, many members of the DNC were not opposed to the commission recommendations in principle; they were, however, opposed to giving in to ACORN. The demands themselves were threatening to entrenched party regulars. Income quotas through organized groups are tantamount to class quotas at all levels, and party organizing councils "directly representing organized groups" could potentially shift the balance of power and accountability within the party.

Internally, therefore, ACORN was able to use the campaign to develop organizationally, creating a unifying national focus and consolidating ACORN as a national organization. The campaign, however, did not elevate ACORN into a movement.

Implications for Progressive Organizations

The Campaign raised a number of questions that are relevant to many progressive organizations. First is the question of emphasis. While ACORN had, prior to the 1980 campaign, successfully elected local candidates, there was strong feeling within the staff and leadership that support for a candidate would not build the power of the organization. This non-endorsement approach did allow ACORN to work with both Carter and Kennedy delegates within the party, but ACORN's non-endorsement strategy gave the organization minimal support. Labor allies, the UAW in particular, were less ready to "go to the wall" with ACORN. The principle of putting issues before candidates was, I believe, strategically correct, because it had the effect of forcing ACORN members and allies to address policies instead of personalities. This strategic approach is completely in line with the approach of traditional community organizations.

Another question raised by the ACORN '80 campaign is also tactical.

217

While ACORN did mobilize more than 10,000 people in the primaries, it also mobilized an equal number of people to picket, demonstrate, disrupt and generally raise hell. Clearly the slot at the Republican Convention was due not to ACORN's ability to pull Republicans to the polls but to embarrass key Republican figures – and the same is true of the Democrats. Pulling the campaign out of an arena where party politics controlled the rules of the game was a key ingredient in ACORN's successfully advancing the campaign toward the commission. Although these tactics angered many party regulars, it is clear that demonstrating the organization's ability to produce in the primaries as well as maintain hard-hitting actions kept the party, in the initial stages of the campaign, sufficiently off balance, especially in the context of a national election, to produce concessions.

Each of the aforementioned tactical points assumes the legitimacy of the ACORN campaign. The campaign built and consolidated ACORN, developing the skills and analytical prowess of the staff and leadership of the organization. This objective is in line with Gramsci's assertion that the working class must demonstrate its claim to sovereignty through its political organization prior to the actual seizure of power. By forcing the Democratic Party to say no to the recommendations of the ACORN commission, it in effect forced the party to say no to the increased organizational participation of low- and moderate-income people.

ACORN sufficiently penetrated the party apparatus to polarize the issue of low-income representation into a "we (ACORN) – they (Democratic Party regulars)" adversary relationship. The process served to delegitimate the party in the eyes of the ACORN membership and open up the possibility in the future of more militant action against the party or more interest in participating in third-party efforts. It is fortunate that the commission resolutions were not passed by the Democratic National Committee, because a "win" would have reopened the question of party legitimacy and created the potential for co-optation of ACORN members.

To what extent could ACORN really increase the power and influence of low-to-moderate-income people, or ACORN members, in the Democratic Party? This question can only be answered through the continued struggle of ACORN and other groups in the electoral arena. It is important, in my view, that the struggles that take place on this new terrain reflect the interests of non-class-based constituencies (women, people of color, lesbians and gays) as well as the interests of a disenfranchised working class. Part of the struggle to raise the question of representation and control over the political process must necessarily reflect some internal struggle among class-based groups to address the politics between them and these constituencies of new social movements.

Is struggling for power, influence, and control over a state institution a worthwhile endeavor? While it has always been the view of community organizations that the state is not a monolith and that mass-based community organizations can force the state to act in the interest of the disenfranchised, this has not been the view of most Marxist theorists or organizations. It is only recently that Gramsci's notions, elaborated by Nicos Poulantzas in *State, Power, Socialism,* have allowed us to see that the "crisis of democracy" provides the requisite conditions for struggles within the state that may shift the balance of class power within a given state apparatus and consequently effect democratic change within the society at large. It is assuredly clear that the Democratic Party is only one instrumentality of the state, but by pressing for concessions within the party – reasonable concessions that could in no way be granted – there is the possibility of creating a new terrain of struggle within the party.

ACORN had a vision in 1975 when the organization had operations in three states – a vision that not only sustained the organization for seven years but one that allowed it to expand to twenty-six states and 45,000 members. ACORN is not a socialist organization, nor is it, in the normal sense of the term, left; but neither is it mechanistic. The organization is anti-ideological, if tactically militant.

In the mid-sixties many organizers went into local communities to build what they hoped would be the backbone of a new progressive movement. Grassroots organizing around local candidates has been explored by the four major national community organizing networks: ACORN, the Industrial Areas Foundation, National People's Action, and Citizen Action. In fact, a special project of the Chicago-based Midwest Academy was training community leaders to participate in local campaigns. It may well be that progressive unions or church groups coupled with students will be able to mount the next wave of struggle that targets domestic policies, disarmament, and American intervention. In my view, however, the network of groups with the expertise, the organizing experience, and the resources and inclination to fight protracted struggles are community organizations.

And, of course, when it comes to where I'd put my money for the most radical community organizing – I'd bet on the 'CORN.

13

By the Rivers of Babylon
Race in the United States
(1983)
Michael Omi and Howard Winant

Lulled by a false sense of security, many people in the United States took little notice of race in the 1970s. The wave of urban unrest which had swept many cities from 1964 to 1969 had faded from collective memory. "Burn, baby, burn!," once the militant cry of black frustration, had been transformed by the "me decade" into the snappy chorus of a disco number. Racial oppression had hardly vanished, but it was less likely to be seen as contributing to the national malaise. Perhaps those who suggested that race relations in the United States were moving toward enlightenment, progress, and eventual assimilation were right after all. This faith was short-lived.

Racial conflict and the very meaning of race itself are becoming central political issues in the 1980s. The many newly emerging patterns of racial conflict will differ significantly from those which the nation has experienced in the past. The confrontations and reforms of the 1950s and 1960s altered the manner in which racism had operated, but these transformations were not far-reaching enough to prevent the subsequent reintroduction of various new forms of racism throughout the social fabric. The nature of this new racism will be one of the major topics of this discussion. Since the early 1970s, a reactive restructuring of the American racial order has been in progress; this process affects all major institutions and interacts with every political issue, even those such as sex/gender, nuclear power, or gun control, which seemingly have no "direct" relationship to patterns of racial oppression.

The reconstitution of racial oppression is not simply a matter of policy-making or social engineering. It can be accomplished only by society-wide political struggle. Ideologically and culturally, in the state institutions and the relationships of domination, and at the level of production relationships, a prolonged reappraisal of ideas and reorganization of social practices has been taking place with regard to race. By no means can such a process be centrally planned or controlled. Its outcome cannot be securely predicted, either by those for whom the consolidation of a new racism would be desirable or by those for whom it would be disastrous.

In many respects the reconstitution of racial oppression in the United States is an ideological process. The contemporary right has demonstrated this. The "new right" has sought to mobilize an alliance, based at least partly on race, between traditionally right-wing sectors of the populace on the one hand, and white workers and middle-class groups threatened by inflation, crime, and high taxes on the other. Right-wing ideologue William Rusher conveys the new alignment of political forces sought:

> A new economic division pits the producers – businessmen, hardhats, manufacturers, blue-collar workers, and farmers – against a new and powerful class of non-producers comprised of a liberal verbalist elite (the dominant media, the major foundations and research institutions, the educational establishment, the federal and state bureaucracies) and a semi-permanent welfare constituency all coexisting happily in a state of mutually sustaining symbiosis.[1]

Although it is presented as a "new class" alignment, we think Rusher's analysis contains a hidden racist appeal. The "semi-permanent welfare constituency" is implicitly nonwhite; the "producers" are white. The right, in grafting together issues of race and issues of class, manages to restructure American racial discourse (the framework of meaning that makes race comprehensible to us) in a way that the left is not presently capable of doing. The political agenda here is the containment and rollback of the democratic and egalitarian achievements of the social movements of the 1960s, particularly the black movement. These gains cannot be flatly opposed or easily reversed, but they can be reinterpreted. The concept of "reverse discrimination" is an excellent case in point. This phrase appropriates the demands for "equal opportunity" made by the civil rights movement and rearticulates them in a new conservative discourse which appeals to principles of "individual merit" in the allocation of scarce jobs and resources. No explicit racial discourse need be employed to accomplish this shift, and no specific racial groups need to be targeted, yet the effect of the concept's use is to justify inequality.

Much of the left in the United States has been unable to gauge the depth and appeal of a new "racial discourse" that doesn't need to make explicit reference to race. The left often misreads contemporary currents; it is encumbered with dogmatic understandings of what race and racism are, and it lacks the necessary vision to mount effective antiracist campaigns. Racism is, in fact, endemic to much of the left itself.

Such problems stem, fundamentally, from the inability of Marxist theory to grasp the breadth and depth of racial oppression. Marx and Engels believed, along with the other Eurocentrist social thinkers of their time, that the extension of capitalist social relationships would sweep away such "traditional" social distinctions as race and ethnicity. Racial identity was a remnant of the precapitalist order, and was expected to decline in importance as the "final conflict" of the two great capitalist classes loomed up. Its persistence, along with other "traditional" categories, has presented orthodox Marxists with major theoretical problems.

The Marxist analysis of race and racism confronts us with a double distortion. First, race is understood as an epiphenomenon or manifestation of class. Race is explained by reference to class and thus *reduced* to an aspect of class struggle. Second, class itself is seen in an economically determinist way. The "base" (the sphere of production) determines the "superstructure." In classical Marxism, the *objective* nature of class relationships (class "in itself") shapes the consciousness and political organization (class "for itself") required to transform society.

From such a standpoint, racism is explained as "false consciousness" – at odds with the "genuine" interests of the working class to unite against the capitalists. In one version of this approach, capitalists are thought to delude workers, creating and sustaining racial antagonisms as part of a "divide and conquer" strategy to keep wages low and the workers' movement disorganized. In another version, racism is seen as the consciousness appropriate to the economic interests of a privileged stratum of workers – the "aristocracy of labor" – whose immediate interests lie in protection of their better paid and more secure jobs at the expense of competing, lower priced minority labor.

Traditional Marxist analyses which explain racial phenomena by reference to economic interests have limited explanatory power. While class-reductionist accounts are not always wrong, it is not possible to argue a certain political strategy's effectiveness in combating racial oppression from an analytical model of economic interests. Nor is it possible to locate the origins of racial categories and meanings in such a model.

This essay explores the dynamics of race and racism in United States society, from a standpoint both conversant with and critical of existing Marxist viewpoints on race. Its perspective has been shaped by two major developments over the last few decades. The first has been the emergence of "new" social movements in the postwar years: movements largely inspired by and following upon the achievements of the black liberation movement. These movements – racial, sexual, gender-based, environmental, antimilitarist – offer new opportunities for the creation and development of oppositional politics in American society. The second development that has inspired our analysis has been the emergence of new perspectives on the meaning of class rooted in the

Italian Marxist Antonio Gramsci's conception of *hegemony*. This theoretical tool permits a break with economically determinist viewpoints in Marxist analysis, perspectives that have blocked not only left attempts to grapple with race and racism, but have also limited our understanding of the fluidity of class itself.

In the analysis that follows, we argue that race relations have the capacity to shape class relations in the United States. An important concept advanced is that of *racial formation* – the complex process, at once political, economic, and ideological, by which racial meanings are developed and applied, both to individual identities and to institutions. Racial formation is the counterpart of the *class-formation* process suggested in the Gramscian analysis of hegemony. This approach, combined with an appreciation of the potential of the "new" social movements for oppositional politics today, constitutes the two points of departure for the present analysis. It is to the problem of hegemony that we now turn.

Class Formation Processes and the Problem of Hegemony

Marxist analysis has sought to understand race in terms of class, but not class in terms of race. Our concern with the depth and significance of race in the United States, and the relationship between race and class, has led us to reappraise both traditional Marxist and "neo-Marxist" approaches to class formation and to advance an alternative conception.

The Traditional Marxist Approach to Class Formation

Despite Marx's occasional suggestions to the contrary, perhaps the most venerable orthodoxy in Marxian thought is the economic determination of classes and class relationships. Classes are portrayed as objective entities, groups united by common relationship with the means of production. Their economic conditions appear as given; these conditions set the stage for political and ideological struggle. Successful organization and "correct" consciousness are judged to exist when these correspond to "objective economic conditions." The "subjective" elements of class struggle are brought to bear because a fundamental transformation of economic conditions cannot be achieved in the economic realm itself.

Collective activity and class consciousness (which makes collective action possible for the members of a class) are essential components of class struggle because revolution is a subjective action. It is a political and ideological intervention into objective economic conditions. Class "in itself" shapes the subjective possibilities for transforming class relations through class "for itself."

There are two immediate problems with this approach. First, it defines classes solely in terms of economic relationships, thus reducing them to mere locations or positions in the production process. Such an approach says nothing about the actual occupants of these locations, their capacity for organization, or their ideology.

The second problem that limits the traditional view of class formation is its misunderstanding of economic relationships themselves. Various "subjective" factors must be present in these relationships before human beings can engage in commodity production at all; they must understand themselves as "workers," for example, and they must come to terms with the organization of the workplace. Ideologically, the very meanings of work, authority, discipline, solidarity are contested in every minute of every working day. What constitutes a "worker" is not obvious. As we shall argue below, the very term was historically applied in the United States, until quite recently, to signify "white man." If nonwhites cannot join unions, if women are excluded from various job categories, doesn't the ideological self-recognition and social significance of the term "worker" apply only to some producers and not to others?

The "Hegemony" Approach to Class Formation

Valuable insights into the relationship between popular struggles and class formation are emerging from the legacy of Antonio Gramsci, the Italian Communist theorist whose major work was done in Mussolini's prisons. Such analysts as Ernesto Laclau, Christine Buci-Glucksmann, Chantal Mouffe, Adam Przeworski, and Nicos Poulantzas (particularly in his later works) offer a new perspective on class formation based on Gramsci's notion of hegemony.[2]

Hegemony is the thoroughgoing organization of society on behalf of a class which has gained the adherence of subordinate as well as dominant sectors and groups. Often summarized as rule by means of a combination of coercion and consent, hegemony is better understood as the creation of a collective popular will by what Gramsci calls "intellectual and moral leadership."[3] The exercise of hegemony extends beyond the mere dissemination of "ruling-class" ideas and values. It includes the capacity to define, through a vast array of channels (including the basic structures of economic, political, and cultural life) the terms and meanings by which people understand themselves and their world.

From this perspective, class-formation processes continually shape and reshape classes. Classes are not economically determined. Instead they are understood as 1) *multiply-determined,* 2) *historical actors,* themselves the 3) *effects of the social struggles* in which they are formed:

1. *Multiple determination:* Political and ideological factors are recognized to constitute classes in combination with economic ones. Once the political and ideological have been released from the iron grip of the economic, the interpenetration of the three types of relationships in the concrete can be seen as a complex one. It is not possible to distinguish the economic, political, and ideological "instances" or "moments" of concrete social relationships except analytically. Even production is a fully political and ideological relationship.

2. *Historical actors:* Class relationships are never given, objective, or obvious; rather they are ongoing processes of historical conflict whose participants and outcomes are contingent. Classes are continually being created, transformed, and destroyed – organized and disorganized. Their memberships are not pre-given but to a certain extent self-selected, depending upon the particular social struggles in which the class is engaged, and its ability to link its collective interests with that of potential members.

3. *Effects of struggles:* "Class formation is an effect of the totality of struggles which organize the same people as class members, as members of collectivities defined in other terms, [or] simply as members of 'the society.'"[4] It is *never* correct to attribute an "appropriate" consciousness or political organization to a given group simply on the basis of its economic location in society. The recognition that classes are effects of struggles grasps a reality that traditional and neo-Marxist theories of class formation usually miss: each social group *interprets its own interest,* and is therefore subject to competing efforts to organize it and define its role in social struggle.

From such a perspective, classes may be understood as *political projects.* At any given historical moment, different projects are being implemented by forces seeking to organize particular classes, to interpret their interests, and to (re)define their role in production relations. The working class that Eugene Debs sought to create in 1912 was not the working class that Samuel Gompers sought to create. Alternative and competing efforts to identify and organize classes necessarily confront each other, as individuals and groups seek to understand their interests and conditions, and to act upon those understandings.

Beginning with the competing projects of various oppositional groups, the class-formation process continues with the consolidation of such groups into an oppositional or counterhegemonic bloc. The collective subjectivity of a class can only be attained when an integrative or *articulating principle* is developed to link the various groupings constituting the bloc. There is always a concrete historical process by which various social groupings move from isolated opposition, through oppositional bloc to counterhegemonic class, and finally to hegemony. This process is marked by two features that distinguish it radically from classical accounts of class-formation. First, every stage of the process is *contingent*. Objective conditions, including the economic situations of various oppositional groups, the political strategies and organizational resources available to them, their ability to identify their interests in sufficiently unified and accessible terms, and so on, combine with subjective and contingent ones, including even luck, audacity, and error, to advance the class-formation project.

Second, there is a great deal of flexibility in the *sources* of opposition. It does not necessarily spring from a core of the most exploited, or from those located nearest to the heart of production processes. Nor from disaffected intellectuals. Sheila Rowbotham has demonstrated the crucial role of women in leading upsurges of social opposition.[5] Herbert Gutman has shown the importance of displaced culturally rooted and traditional groups, in reacting to the processes of industrialization and modernization.[6] Such forces can be characterized with regard to their participants, programs, or interests at a given historical point, but they are *not fundamentally and irrevocably grouped around an economically defined "class."* The importance of this insight for a study of the role of antiracist struggle in the modern-day United States cannot be exaggerated.

Racial Formation

What Is Race?

Spurred on by the classificatory schemes of living organisms devised by Linnaeus, many scholars in the eighteenth and nineteenth centuries were consumed with discerning and ranking the variations in humankind. Race was thought of as a *biological* concept, yet its precise definition was the subject of continual debate. From Dr. Morton's studies of cranial capacity to contemporary efforts to link race with shared gene pools, the concept of race has defied biological definition. Even today the question of *how many* races there are elicits a range of popular responses.[7]

Within the social sciences, race is generally regarded as a *social* as opposed to biological concept. We share this view. Race is a sociohistorical construct which is neither objective nor static. It is a multidimensional complex of social meanings, subjectivities, practices, and institutions organized around the question of human physical characteristics. Race is constantly being reinterpreted and recreated. Examples of the diversity of racial meanings abound:

— In the United States, the black/white color line has been rigidly defined and enforced. White was considered a pure category – any black parentage made one black. Elizabeth Taylor in *Raintree County* describes the worst of fates to befall whites as "havin' a little Negra blood in ya' – just one little teeny drop and a person's all Negra."[8]

— By contrast, Brazil has had less rigid conceptions and a variety of "intermediate" racial categories exist. Marvin Harris suggests that this difference sprang from the employment of *hypodescent* as a mechanism of racial identity in the United States. Hypodescent means affiliation with the subordinate (in a societal hierarchy) rather than dominant group. No such rigid descent rule characterizes racial identity in many Latin American societies. As Harris notes, "One of the most striking consequences of the Brazilian system of racial identification is that parents and children and even brothers and sisters are frequently accepted as representatives of quite opposite racial types."[9]

— Contradictions abound in what is considered to be the country with the most rigidly defined racial categories, South Africa. The apartheid system considers Chinese as "Asians" while the Japanese are accorded the status of "honorary whites." A race classification agency is employed to adjudicate claims (particularly among the mulatto or "colored" category) for upgrading of official racial identity.[10]

Racial categories also vary between different societies and historically within a given society. The term "black" in the United States at different times and places has referred variously to non- or semi-human chattels or to the "vanguard of the proletariat" (in certain left-wing analyses). In Britain today, the term "black" is beginning to connote all nonwhites, since Asian as well as Afro-Caribbean youth are adopting it as an expression of self-identity.[11] The various meanings of "black" thus illustrate the point that the content of racial categories is shaped politically. The meaning of race is defined and contested throughout society, in both collective and personal practice. In the process, racial categories themselves are formed, destroyed, and reformed. An important part of this process is social-scientific. Since the way that race is understood theoretically has great impact on law, policy, and custom, the academic disciplines that have studied the subject might be expected to have been especially sensitive to the complexity and malleability of racial formation processes.

In reality, nearly the opposite is true. Almost every approach neglects to consider racial formation as a continuous process. There is thus a vast failure to consider not only how the meaning of race is formed and transformed, but also how racially defined individuals, collectivities, and institutions encounter racial categories, either accepting or opposing them, and thus act to shape the meaning of race themselves. Race is usually seen as a static entity, a given, even if the theory in question might abstractly recognize the possibility of the transformation of racial categories over time.

The Process of Racial Formation

In the United States, the existence of racial identity and of a racist social order is a historical fact dating from the initiation of European colonization. Every individual and social group, regardless of the contradictions or difficulties involved, and irrespective of the particular historical period in which relationships between that individual or group and the American racial order are examined, has been assigned to and maintained in a racial category: white, red, yellow, brown, and black.

Racial classification is a matter of identity. One of the first things we notice about people (along with their sex) is their race. We utilize race to provide clues about *who* a person is and to suggest how we should relate to him or her. This fact is made painfully obvious when we encounter someone whom we cannot conveniently categorize racially. Such an encounter becomes a source of discomfort and momentarily, a crisis of racial meaning. People in our culture need to clarify who people are in racial terms. Without a racial identity, one is in danger of having no identity.

"Racial etiquette" encompasses the micro-level rules that govern our perception of race in a comprehensively racial society. This etiquette is quintessentially ideological in that it is fully learned, without obvious teaching, by everybody. It becomes "common sense." Racial beliefs operate as an "amateur biology," a way of explaining the variations in "human nature."[12]

Simultaneously, racial classification is *institutionalized*. From the micro-level of individual racial identity to the macro-level of collective racial identity and conflict on the terrain of the state, a seamless continuum of racial meanings pervades society. Every institution in the United States is a *racial* institution. The churches, scientific organizations, the trade unions, etc. – all helped to define and shape, and have been shaped by, racial practices. Since a racial order is a political order, an understanding of the development and character of the racial order of American society requires an approach to the *state* as the focus of racial contradictions over historical time. Racial categories and racial conflict do not confront the human beings who must live them out as mere blind necessities. Individually and collectively, we struggle to understand (or not to understand), to accept or reject, to strengthen or to undermine, the definitions and social structures within which we discover ourselves.

Racial formation has proceeded in the United States by means of a complex interplay among these elements. It should be understood as a *process:* 1) through which an unstable and contradictory set of social practices and beliefs are articulated in an ideology based fundamentally on race; 2) through which the particular ideology thus generated is enforced by a system of racial subjection having both institutional and individual means of reproduction at its disposal; and 3) through which new instabilities and contradictions emerge at a subsequent historical point and challenge the pre-existing system once more. Racial formation processes have interpenetrated with class-formation processes in ways that have profoundly shaped the nature of political discourse and struggle in the United States.

Racial Discourse

Perhaps the most important feature of this approach is its concept of ideology. Racial ideology, as much as that of class or nation, must be constructed from pre-existing ideological elements. This is a task that cannot be carried out all at once, but requires a period of time in which competing discourses, competing projects seeking to articulate similar ideological elements differently, must be struggled with and overcome. We employ the term "racialization" to signify the extension of racial meaning to a previously racially unclassified relationship, social practice, or group. For the present, we concentrate on the creation of existing American racial *groups* over time.

The racialization process is filled with incongruities and contradictions, and varies enormously. Historically speaking, before the Civil War substantial tendencies existed that sought the classification of Southern Europeans, the Irish, and the Jews among "nonwhite" categories. This brand of nativism was only effectively curbed by the institutionalization of a racial order that drew the color line around, rather than within, Europe. By stopping short of racializing immigrants from Europe after the Civil War, by allowing their assimilation (although not without having "paid some dues" at the bottom of the free labor force first, of course), the American racial order was reconsolidated in the wake of the tremendous challenge placed before it by the abolition of racial slavery. Reconstruction was ended in 1877, and an effective set of tools for limiting the emergent class struggles of the later nineteenth century was forged: the definition of the working class in *racial terms* – as "white." This was not accomplished by any decree but rather by white workers themselves. Many of them were recent immigrants, who organized on racial lines as much as on traditionally defined class lines. In California, for example, 1877 began a period of fierce racial struggle. In that year, white workers in San Francisco rioted and attacked the Chinese quarter of the city, burning laundries, killing any Chinese they could catch, and demanding the exclusion of Asian immigrants from the West Coast.[13]

Racial formation processes are adaptive. Historically, a variety of previously racially undefined groups have required categorization to situate them within the prevailing racial order. In the United States, the racial category of "black" evolved with the consolidation of racial slavery. By the end of the seventeenth century, Africans, whose specific identity was Ibo, Yoruba, Dahomeyan, etc., were rendered "black" by an ideology of exploitation based on racial logic. Similarly, Native Americans were forged into "Indians" or the "red man" from Cherokee, Seminole, Sioux, etc., people.

Throughout the nineteenth century, state and federal legal arrangements recognized only three racial categories: "white," "Negro," and "Indian." In California, the influx of Chinese and the debates surrounding the legal status of Mexicans provoked a brief juridical crisis of racial definition. California attempted to resolve this dilemma by assigning Mexicans and Chinese to categories within the already existing framework of "legally defined" racial groups. In the wake of the Treaty of Guadalupe Hidalgo (1848), Mexicans were defined as a "white" population and accorded the political-legal status of "free white persons." By contrast, the California Supreme Court ruled in *People* v. *Hall* (1854) that Chinese should be considered "Indian" and denied the political rights accorded to whites.[14]

A vast range of similar examples could be cited. There is simply no racial order or set of racial categories that comes into being without a complex process of societal struggle, or without the ransacking of pre-existing ideologies and discursive systems for materials which can be invoked to service the "new" racial understanding. Religion, science, nationality, language, art, economics, politics, and the law all contribute to the development of ideology.

Obviously, racialization is not solely imposed by the state or by dominant social groups. Racial self-definition is an important factor in forging minority collectivity. For example, such categories as "Asian-American" and "La Raza" appeared in the sixties proclaiming a new understanding on the part of former "ethnic groups" (e.g., Chinese-Americans and Japanese-Americans) of their shared *racial* identity.

The Hegemonic Racial Order

We have suggested that the racial order simultaneously affects identity and social structure. Every individual is subjected to the particular racial order that obtains during the historical period in which he or she lives, and has a racial identity constructed for him or herself, whether the individual accepts this identity or not. Furthermore, every individual is steeped in the rules governing interpersonal racial relations and recognition of racial characteristics in others. These rules are not codified but are micro-social aspects of the "presentation of self." They are essential elements of racial ideology.

At the level of social structure, race is present in all collective relationships. In each historical period the *shape* of American society has had a distinctly racial pattern, discernible in production relations, laws, political organization, residential patterns, religion, cultural life, and all other aspects of social reproduction. Since the earliest days of the colonial system in North America, a pre-existing racial ideology has served to link the identity of the individual to the racially ordered social structure.

But even at its most oppressive, the American racial order was unable to arrogate to itself the entire capacity for production of racial ideology, of racial subjects. As scholars such as George Rawick and Herbert Gutman have shown, black slaves developed cultures of resistance based on music, religion, African traditions, and family ties, through which they sustained their own ideological project: the development of a free black identity and a collectivity dedicated to liberation.[15] Roxanne Dunbar Ortiz notes how the examples of Geronimo, Sitting Bull, and other resistance leaders of the Native peoples were passed down to children as examples of resistance, and how the Native American Church and the Ghost Dance were employed by particular generations of Indian people to maintain a resistance culture.[16] Rodolfo Acuña has pointed out how the same "bandits" against whom Anglo vigilantes mounted expeditions after Guadalupe-Hidalgo – Tiburcio Vasquez, Joaquín Murieta – became heroes in the Mexicano communities of the Southwest, remembered in folktales and celebrated in *corridos*.[17] We do not recite these examples to romanticize brutal repression or to give the air of revolutionary struggle to what were often grim defeats; we simply seek to affirm that even in the most uncontested periods of American racism, oppositional cultures were able, often at very great cost, to maintain themselves.

Without reviewing the vast history of racial conflict in the United States to determine how precisely challenges were deflected or incorporated, it is still possible to make some general statements about the manner in which the racial order is consolidated. Gramsci's distinction between "war of maneuver" and "war of position" will prove useful here. An additional element with which we must reckon, if only briefly, is the enforcement of the racial order by the state.

For much of American history, no political legitimacy was conceded to alternative racial discourses, competing racially defined political projects. The absence of democratic rights, of property, of political *space* within civil society forced racially defined opposition both outward and inward, away from the public sphere. Slaves who ran away, who took part in the subversive operations of the underground railway, who formed communities in woods and swamps; Indians who made war on the United States in defense of their land; Chinese and Filipinos who drew together in Chinatowns and Manilatowns to gain some measure of collective control over their existence – these exemplify the movement of racial opposition outward, away from a political engagement within the hegemonic racial order.

These same slaves, Indians, Asians (and many others), having been driven out of the dominant political framework and relegated to a supposedly permanently inferior sociocultural status, were forced inward upon themselves as individuals, families, and communities. The tremendous cultural resources nurtured among such communities, the enormous labors required under such conditions to survive and still further to develop elements of an alternative society, can best be understood as combining with the continuous violent resistance ("riots," etc.) which characterized these periods to constitute a racial *war of maneuver.* More recent history suggests that war of maneuver is being replaced by war of position as racially defined minorities achieve political gains within the hegemonic racial order.

Prepared in large measure by the practices undertaken in conditions of war of maneuver, minority communities were able to make sustained strategic interventions within the mainstream political process beginning with World War II. As we have noted, the black movement for a variety of historical reasons provided leadership in confronting the dominant racial order, mobilizing in the electoral sphere (and demanding the extension of the elementary democratic right of the vote to areas of the country where it was still denied), mounting marches and demonstrations, making use of the judicial system, and harking back to precedents set in those brief historical moments such as Reconstruction when racial despotism had been briefly ameliorated.

A strategy of *war of position* can only be predicated on political struggle – on the existence of institutional and ideological terrain upon which competing projects can be mounted in the face of a hegemonic order. The postwar black movement, later joined by other racially based minority movements, has sought by a strategy of war of position to transform the dominant racial ideology in the United States, to rearticulate its elements in a more egalitarian and democratic discourse. It has also sought to confront the manner in which state institutions enforce the preexisting system of racial categories and practices.

The Racial State

Race establishes the identity of human subjects, it structures social conflict and social cohesion, and it is deeply woven into every aspect of existence. Historically and contemporarily, racial categories have been determined and enforced by the state. The Naturalization Law of 1790, Congress's first attempt to define American citizenship, declared that only free "white" immigrants would be eligible. Japanese could become naturalized citizens only after the passage of the Walter-McCarran Act of 1952.*

---

* The ideological residue of these contradictions is the popular equation of "American" with "white."

Even the census is racially contradictory. Latinos were included in the census as a racial category in 1930 and surfaced as an ethnic category, "Persons of Spanish Mother Tongue," in 1950 and 1960. In 1970 they appeared as "Persons of Both Spanish Surname and Spanish Mother Tongue," and in 1980 the "Hispanic" category was created.[18] Such attempts betray institutional noncomprehension of the underlying meaning of race. They also reflect the struggles through which particular racially defined groups have pressed their demands for recognition and equality and the state's efforts to manage and manipulate those demands.[19]

The state is indeed the focus of collective demands both for egalitarian and democratic reforms and for the enforcement of existing privileges. The state "intervenes" in racial conflicts, yet it does not do so in a coherent or unified manner. Distinct state institutions often act in a contradictory fashion. Concurrent with the passage of antiracist legislation and the handing down of judicial decisions prohibiting racial discrimination in the fifties and sixties, other branches of the federal government pursued welfare and urban redevelopment policies that worked to the disadvantage of racial minorities.

It is tempting to see the state as clumsily trying to capture, steer, or organize the realities of racial identity and racial conflict. The notion of a racially interventionist state contains a measure of truth since clearly the state does organize the racial order – it does systematize and operationalize concepts of racial discrimination, for example. Yet this approach implies a state that is not inherently racial, since it is intervening in race relations from *outside* them. Such a state appears open to democratizing demands.

In contrast to this, we suggest that the state is inherently racial. Like the society it organizes, the state has been from its foundation penetrated and shaped by racial elements. Every state institution is a racial institution; the United States Constitution (as is well known) is a racial document. Far from intervening in racial conflicts, the state is itself increasingly the preeminent site of racial conflict. A more accurate model of the racial state, then, would depict a network of state institutions, each linked by history, mandate, internal composition, and constituency to the racial order existing in the United States at the historical point under consideration.

Such a model, we suggest, accounts far better than the "interventionist" one for the variations in the racial character of different state institutions, as well as for the changes in specific institutions' racial policies and activities over historical time. It suggests that state institutions and programs address particular demands as part of an overall political *trajectory*. Conflicts and demands that were previously ignored or asserted to be *outside* the proper realm of state activity are redefined as occurring *within* a given institution's mandate; new politics are developed and some demands are met as a new (temporary) equilibrium is sought; gradually the new equilibrium becomes part of the established order and is revealed to contain new conflicts as new demands are placed upon the state institutions and programs that maintain it.

Race and Class

Our conception of racial formation has stressed the political, ideological, and economic determinants of race which find expression not only in various institutional arrangements, but in the very way we live, love, breathe, and think. Such a conception is drawn from the emerging theoretical literature on class-formation processes which has prompted both a reevaluation of the concept of class and a reassessment of traditional notions of class politics. A reexamination of class and racial dynamics is crucial to fathoming current American political realities. The interpenetration of race and class needs to be considered.

In the modern world, race and class appear nearly synonymous in some societies (e.g., South Africa) while in others they seem to exist as separate axes of stratification as well as cultural and political organization (e.g., the United States). Race and class are complexly structured relationships that are given concrete meaning only by specific political projects. Race and class: 1) exist with some degree of autonomy; 2) are subject to enormous variations over time; and 3) are capable in certain historical moments of encompassing one another.

Central to our conception of race and class as evolving sets of social relationships is the notion that non-economic, non-accumulation-based factors such as ideology, organization, and strategy are crucial to the formation of both races and classes. Such political and ideological factors are not the mere reflections of objectively determined "material" (i.e., economic) interests, but are themselves forces shaping the very definition of interests. In other words, as opposed to viewing these factors as being determined by the economic location of a race or class, we assert that such factors may be crucial to establishing the economic location itself.

In the United States, capitalist development created races as well as classes. African slavery set a racially based understanding of society in motion which resulted in the shaping of a specific *racial* identity not only for the slaves, but for the European settlers as well. Winthrop Jordan has observed:

> From the initially common term *Christian,* at mid-century there was a marked shift toward the terms *English* and *free.* After about 1680, taking the colonies as a whole, a new term of self-identification appeared – *white.*[20]

The consolidation of racial slavery structured the class system as much as the class system determined the racial order.

235

The self-conscious organization of the US working class in the nineteenth century was to a large degree a *racial* as much as a class project. The legacy of racial arrangements and conflicts shaped the definition of working-class interests and in turn led to the consolidation of institutional patterns (e.g., segregated unions, dual labor markets, and exclusionary legislation) which perpetuated the color line within the working class. Alexander Saxton has noted that

> North Americans of European background have experienced three great racial confrontations: with the Indian, with the African, and with the Oriental. Central to each transaction has been a totally one-sided preponderance of power, exerted for the exploitation of nonwhites by the dominant white society. In each case (but especially in the two that began with systems of enforced labor), white workingmen have played a crucial, yet ambivalent, role. They have been both exploited and exploiters. On the one hand, thrown into competition with nonwhites as enslaved or "cheap" labor, they suffered economically; on the other hand, being white, they benefited by that very exploitation which was compelling the nonwhites to work for low wages or for nothing. Ideologically they were drawn in opposite directions. *Racial identification cut at right angles to class consciousness.*[21]

One cannot always objectively determine or disaggregate the class and racial dimensions of a specific conflict. The very *terms* of political struggle are contested by the participants themselves.

Japanese plantation laborers striking against the Hawaiian Sugar Planters Association (HSPA) in 1920 characterized their struggle as a *class conflict* and attempted to forge a class coalition with Filipino workers. Their labor organization, the Japanese Federation, changed its name to the Hawaii Laborers Association and its programs and slogans reflected the class character of its demands. The HSPA characterized the conflict as a *racial* one, emphasizing that the Japanese were seeking the political and economic domination of the islands.[22] In such a struggle, competing projects seek to organize people along distinct lines by appealing to their interests in racial and/or class terms. Consequently, the strike could simultaneously be portrayed by its participants as labor versus capital or as white versus nonwhite.

Racial categories create political subjects. One is not merely a worker, one is also white; one is not only Chicano, one is equally a worker. In the history of the United States, race has not merely been an impediment to the development of working-class consciousness. It has also shaped it. The conception of race and class as relationships shaped by political projects is crucial to understanding the historical development of American politics and political discourse. It is just as crucial, we maintain, for an understanding of contemporary politics. The profound changes brought about by racially based movements in the post–World War II period are currently being contested forcefully. The shape of the American racial order and, in important ways, of capitalism in the United States hangs in the balance as these struggles are fought out.

Notes

1. William Rusher, *The Making of a New Majority Party*, Ottawa, Ill.: Greenhill 1975, p. 31.
2. Antonio Gramsci, *Selections from the Prison Notebooks*, ed. Quintin Hoare and Geoffrey Nowell Smith, New York: International 1971; Ernesto Laclau, *Politics and Ideology in Marxist Theory*, London: Verso 1977; Christine Buci-Glucksmann, "Hegemony and Consent," in Anne Showstack Sassoon, ed., *Approaches to Gramsci*, London: Writers and Readers 1982; Chantal Mouffe, ed., *Gramsci and Marxist Theory*, London: Routledge & Kegan Paul 1979; Adam Przeworski, "Proletariat into a Class: The Process of Class Formation from Karl Kautsky's *The Class Struggle* to Recent Controversies," *Politics and Society*, vol. 7, no. 4 (1977); Nicos Poulantzas, *State, Power, Socialism*, London: Verso 1978; Bob Jessop, *The Capitalist State*, New York: New York University Press 1982.
3. Gramsci, *Prison Notebooks*, p. 57.
4. Przeworski, "Proletariat," pp. 372–73.
5. Sheila Rowbotham, *Women, Resistance, and Revolution*, New York: Vintage 1973.
6. Herbert C. Gutman, *Work, Culture, and Society in Industrializing America*, New York: Vintage 1977.
7. In the fifties and sixties, children in the United States were taught that there were three races: Caucasoid, Negroid, Mongoloid. Anthropologists have devised (in various periods) complex sets of indices (including skin color, anthropometrical data, and cultural elements) to create hundreds of "racial" categories.
8. Quoted in Edward D. C. Campbell, Jr., *The Celluloid South: Hollywood and the Southern Myth*, Knoxville: University of Tennessee Press 1981, pp. 168–70.
9. Marvin Harris, *Patterns of Race in the Americas*, New York: W. W. Norton 1964, p. 57.
10. We are grateful to Steve Talbot for consultation on this point.
11. A. Sivanandan, "From Resistance to Rebellion: Asian and Afro-Caribbean Struggles in Britain," *Race and Class*, vol. 23, nos 2–3 (Autumn–Winter 1981).
12. Michael Billig, "Patterns of Racism: Interviews with National Front Members," *Race and Class*, vol. 20, no. 2 (Autumn 1978), pp. 161-79.
13. Michael Kazin, "Prelude to Kearnyism: The July Days in San Francisco," *New Labor Review*, no. 3 (June 1980), pp. 5–47.
14. For a comprehensive discussion of racial minorities in nineteenth-century California, see Tomás Almaguer, "Class, Race, and Capitalist Development: The Social Transformation of a Southern California County, 1848–1903," (PhD dissertation, University of California, Berkeley, 1979).
15. George Rawick, *From Sundown to Sunup: The Making of the Black Community*, Westport, Conn.: Greenwood Press 1972; Herbert C. Gutman, *The Black Family in Slavery and Freedom, 1750–1925*, New York: Vintage 1976.
16. Roxanne Dunbar Ortiz, "Land and Nationhood: The American Indian Struggle for Self-Determination and Survival," *Socialist Review*, no. 63–64 (May–August 1982), pp. 105–20.
17. Rodolfo Acuña, *Occupied America: The Chicano's Struggle toward Liberation*, San Francisco: Canfield Press 1972, pp. 113–18; see also Leonard Pitt, *The Decline of the Californios*, Berkeley: University of California Press 1966.
18. Harry Pachon and Joan W. Moore, "Mexican Americans," *Annals of the American Academy of Political and Social Science*, vol. 454 (March 1981).
19. They also set the stage for tragicomic attempts to manipulate this incomprehension. In 1979, for example, an Anglo named Robert E. Lee changed his name to Roberto E. Leon in order to qualify for affirmative action programs available to those with Spanish surnames. See David E. Hayes-Bautista, "Identifying 'Hispanic' Populations: The Influence of Research Methodology upon Public Policy," *American Journal of Public Health*, vol. 70, no. 4 (April 1980), p. 355.
20. Winthrop D. Jordan, *White over Black: American Attitudes toward the Negro, 1550–1812*, Baltimore: Penguin 1969, p. 95.

21.   Alexander Saxton, *The Indispensable Enemy: Labor and the Anti-Chinese Movement in California,* Berkeley: University of California Press 1971, p. 1. Our emphasis.

22.   Alan Moriyama, "The 1909 and 1920 Strikes of Japanese Sugar Plantation Workers in Hawaii," in Emma Gee, ed., *Counterpoint: Perspectives on Asian America,* Los Angeles: Asian American Studies Center 1976, pp. 169–80.

14

Sexism by a Subtler Name?

Postindustrial Conditions and Postfeminist Consciousness in the Silicon Valley

(1987)

Judith Stacey

This essay explores a number of connections between the recent transition to an emergent "postindustrial" stage of capitalist development and the simultaneous rise and decline of a militant and radical phase of feminism in the United States.[1]

Feminism as Midwife to Postindustrial Society

Let me begin by explaining my use of the troubling term "postfeminist," a concept offensive to many feminists who believe that the media coined it simply "to give sexism a subtler name."[2] Whatever the media's motives, I find the concept useful in describing the gender consciousness and the family and work strategies of many contemporary women.* I view the term postfeminist as analogous to "post-revolutionary" and use it not to indicate the death of the women's movement, but to describe the simultaneous incorporation, revision, and depoliticization of many of the central goals of second wave feminism.[3] I believe postfeminism is distinct from anti-feminism and sexism, for it aptly describes the consciousness and strategies increasing numbers of women have developed in response to the new difficulties and opportunities of postindustrial society. In this sense the diffusion of postfeminist

---

* The author wishes to point out that the necessity of abridgment within the space constraints of this volume has meant a certain loss of nuance, qualification, *caveats*, and supporting documentation.

239

consciousness signifies both the achievements of, and challenges for, modern feminist politics.

Hindsight allows us to see how feminist ideology helped legitimate the massive structural changes in American work and family that invisibly accompanied the transition to postindustrial society in the 1960s and early 1970s. I believe this period of postindustrialization should be read as the unmaking of a gender order rooted in the modern nuclear family system: the family of male breadwinner, female homemaker, and dependent children. Family and work relations in the emergent postindustrial order, by contrast, have been transformed by the staggering escalation of divorce rates and women's participation in paid work. As the US changed from having an industrial- to a "service"-dominated occupational structure,[4] unprecedented percentages of women entered the labor force and the academy, while unprecedented percentages of marriages entered the divorce courts. Unstable, and often incompatible, work and family conditions have become the postindustrial norm as working-class occupations become increasingly "feminized."

The gap between the ideology of domesticity and the increasingly non-domestic character of women's lives helped generate feminist consciousness in the 1960s. As that consciousness developed, women launched an assault on traditional domesticity, an assault, that is, on a declining institution and culture. Therefore this feminist movement was backward-looking in its critique, and unwittingly forward-looking (but not to the future of our fantasies) in its effects.

Feminism developed a devastating critique of the stultifying, infantilizing, and exploitative effects of female domesticity on women, especially of the sort available to classes that could afford an economically dependent housewife. Although the institutions of domesticity and its male beneficiaries were the intended targets of our critique, most housewives felt themselves on the defensive. Feminist criticism helped undermine and delegitimize the flagging but still-celebrated nuclear family and helped promote the newly normative double-income (with shifting personnel) middle- and working-class families. We also provided ideological support for the sharp rise of single-mother families generated by soaring divorce rates. Today fewer than 10 percent of families in the US consist of a male breadwinner, a female housewife, and their dependent children.[5]

Millions of women have derived enormous, tangible benefits from these changes in occupational patterns and family life and from the ways in which feminist ideology encouraged women to initiate and cope with these changes. Yet it is also true that since the mid-1970s, economic and personal life has worsened for many groups of women, perhaps for the majority. The emerging shape of postindustrial society seems to have the following characteristics: as unionized occupations and real wages decline throughout the economy, women are becoming the postindustrial "proletariat," performing the majority of "working-class," low-skilled, low-paying jobs. Because the overall percentage of jobs that are secure and well-paying has declined rapidly, increasing numbers of men are unemployed or underemployed. Yet the majority of white, male workers still labor at jobs that are highly skilled and comparatively well-paid.[6] Family instability is endemic with devastating economic effects on many women. Increasing percentages of women are rearing children by themselves, generally with minimal economic contributions from former husbands and fathers.[7] Yet rising numbers of those single mothers who work full-time, year-round do not earn wages sufficient to lift their families above the official poverty line.[8]

In the emerging class structure, marriage is becoming a major axis of stratification because it structures access to a second income. The married female as "secondary" wage-earner lifts a former working-class or middle-class family into comparative affluence, while the loss or lack of access to a male income can force women and their children into poverty.[9] In short, the dramatic increase in female employment during the past several decades has meant lots more work for mother, but with very unevenly distributed economic benefits and only a slight improvement in relative income differentials between women and men.

In light of these developments, many women (and men) have been susceptible to the appeals of the anti-feminist backlash, and especially to profamily ideologies. Because of its powerful and highly visible critique of traditional domesticity, and because of the sensationalized way the media disseminated this critique, feminism has taken most of the heat for family and social crises. Feminism serves as a symbolic lightning rod for the widespread nostalgia and longing for "lost" intimacy and security that presently pervades social and political culture in the US. The past decade, during which postindustrial social patterns became firmly established, has been marked instead by the emergence of various forms of postfeminist consciousness and family strategies.

Family and Work in Silicon Valley

As the birthplace and international headquarters of the electronics industry, Silicon Valley – Santa Clara County, California – is popularly perceived as representing the vanguard of postindustrialism. Until the early 1950s the region was a sparsely populated agricultural area, one of the major fruit baskets in the United States. But in the three decades since the electronics industry developed there, its population has grown by 350 percent and its economy, ecology, and social structure have been dramatically transformed.[10]

During this period, electronics, the vanguard postindustrial industry,

241

feminized (and "minoritized") its production work force. In the 1950s and 1960s, when the industry was young, most of its production workers were men, for whom there were significant opportunities for advancement into technical and, at times, engineering ranks even for those with very limited schooling. But as the industry matured, it turned increasingly to female, ethnic minority, and recent migrant workers to fill production positions that offered fewer and fewer advancement opportunities.[11] By the late 1970s, the industry's occupational structure was crudely stratified by gender, as well as by race and ethnicity. At the top was an unusually high proportion (25 percent) of the most highly educated and highly paid salaried employees in any industry – the engineers and professionals employed in research and design. As in traditional industries, the vast majority were white males (89 percent males, 89 percent non-Hispanic whites). At the bottom, however, were the women, three-fourths of the very poorly paid assembly workers and operatives who performed the tedious, often health-threatening work assigned to 45 percent of the employees. In between were the moderately well-paid technicians and craft workers, also primarily Anglo males, but into whose ranks women and Asians were making gradual inroads.[12]

What is less widely known is that the area is also the site of a significant degree of family turbulence. For example, whereas the national divorce rate has doubled since 1960, in Santa Clara County it nearly tripled so that by 1977, divorces exceeded marriages. Likewise the percentage of "nonfamily households" grew faster than in the nation as a whole, and abortion rates were one and one-half times the national figures. And although the percentage of single-parent households was not quite as high as in the US as a whole, the rate of increase has been far more rapid.[13] During the past three years I have conducted intermittent fieldwork in the Valley, concentrating on an in-depth study of two kinship networks of people, which mainly consist of nonethnic Caucasians who have lived in the region during the period of postindustrialization. My key informant in each network is a white woman in her late forties who married in the 1950s and became a homemaker for a white man who was to benefit from the electronics industry opportunities of the 1960s. Both of these marriages and careers proved to be highly turbulent, and in response both women and several of their daughters have devised a variety of postfeminist survival strategies.

Paths to Postfeminism

Let me first introduce Pam, currently a staff analyst in a municipal agency. (I have given pseudonyms to all the individuals dscribed in this essay.) We became friendly in 1984, when I was interviewing clients at a feminist-inspired social service program where Pam was then an administrator.From various informal conversations, lunches, and observations of her work goals and relations, I had pegged Pam as a slightly cynical divorcée who came to feminist consciousness through divorce and a women's reentry program at a local community college. I had learned that Pam's first husband, Don, to whom she was married for twelve years and with whom she had three children, was one of those white male electronics industry success stories. A telephone repair worker with an interest in drafting when they married, Don entered the electronics industry in the early 1960s and proceeded to work and job-hop his way up to a career as a packaging engineer, a position which currently earns him $50,000 annually.

Don's route to success had been arduous and stormy, entailing numerous setbacks, failures, and layoffs, and requiring such extraordinary work hours that Don totally neglected Pam and their children. This and other problems led to Pam's divorce fifteen years ago, resulting in the normative female impoverishment. Pam became a single mother on welfare, continued her schooling (eventually through the master's level), developed feminist consciousness, experimented with sexual freedom, cohabited with a couple of lovers, and began to develop an administrative career in social services. Before the 1984 election Pam made many scornful remarks about Reagan, Reaganomics, and the military buildup. Therefore, I was quite surprised when, four months after meeting Pam, I learned that she was now married to Al, a construction worker. I also learned that they both were recent converts to charismatic, evangelical Christianity, and that they were participating in Christian marriage counseling to improve their relationship. Pam had been separated from, but was on a friendly basis with, Al when he had an automobile accident followed by a dramatic conversion experience. Al "accepted Jesus into his life," and Pam suddenly accepted Al and Jesus back into hers.

Pam acknowledges the paradoxes and contradictions of her participation in "Christian marriage" and Christian marriage counseling.* Pam, however, credits the conversion experience and the counseling with helping her achieve a more intimate, positive marital relationship than she had experienced before. The conversion, she claims, changed Al from a defensive, uncommunicative, withholding male into a less guarded, more trusting, loving, and committed mate.** Although Pam and Al's marriage is not as communicative, nurturant, and intimate as Pam would like, she believes that their shared faith is leading them in this direction. And she believes that "if you can work out that kind of

---

* Pam, like many evangelical and fundamentalist Christians, uses the term "Christian" to designate only born-again Christians.

** Al and Pam's children agree with this description.

relationship, then who would care who's in charge, because it's such a total, wonderful relationship?" Moreover, Pam cedes Al dominance only in the "spiritual realm"; financially, occupationally, interpersonally, and politically, she retains strong independence, or even control.

Pam's selective adaptation and blending of feminist and fundamentalist ideologies first struck me as rather unique as well as extremely contradictory. I have gradually learned, however, that a significant tendency in contemporary fundamentalist thought incorporates some feminist criticisms of patriarchal men and marriage into its activism in support of patriarchal profamilialism. Quite a few evangelical ministers urge Christian wives to make strong emotional demands on their husbands for communication, commitment, and nurturance within the framework of patriarchal marriage, and they actively counsel Christian husbands to meet these demands.[14]

Feminism served Pam well as an aid for leaving her unsatisfactory first marriage and for building a career and sense of individual identity. But Pam failed to form successful, satisfying, intimate relationships to replace her marriage. Struggling alone with the emotional and social crises to which two of her three children were prone, Pam describes herself as desperately unhappy much of the time. Although Pam received support from several intense friendships with women, neither this nor feminism seemed to offer her sufficient solace or direction. Her retreat from feminism and her construction of an extreme form of postfeminist consciousness took place in this context.

Dotty Lewison has a more complex story. Dotty was a teenager in 1954 when she met and married Lou, a sailor who had dropped out of school in the ninth grade. Although Dotty primarily had been a homemaker for Lou and their five children, she also had made occasional forays into the world of paid work, including one two-year stint in the late 1950s assembling semiconductors. But Dotty neither perceived nor desired significant opportunities for personal advancement in electronics or any occupation at that time. Instead, several years later she pushed Lou to enter the industry. With his mechanical aptitude and naval background, Lou was able to receive on-the-job training.

Dotty and Lou's marriage had been broken by numerous short-term separations, and one of two years' duration that almost became permanent. During that separation Dot too was a welfare mother, who hated being on welfare, and who had a serious live-in love affair. Dot does not repudiate very many of her former feminist ideas, but she has not been active since the late 1970s. She specifically distances herself from the "militant man-hating types."

Dotty is a feisty, assertive woman who had protofeminist views long before she (or most of us) had heard of the women's liberation movement. Yet for twenty years, Dotty tolerated a marriage in which she and her husband fought violently. Her children were battered, sometimes seriously, most often by Lou, but occasionally by Dotty as well. Before I learned about the violence, Dotty

244

and Lou both led me to believe that their near-divorce in the mid-1970s was caused by Lou's workaholicism as an upwardly mobile employee in the electronics industry. They spoke of the twelve- to fourteen-hour days and the frequent three-day shifts that led Lou to neglect his family completely. Later I came to understand the dynamic relationships between that workaholicism and their marital hostilities. Dotty had become a feminist and community activist by then, involved in anti-battering work and many other community issues. Partly due to her involvement with feminism (again, some of it encountered in a college women's reentry program), Dotty was beginning to shift the balance of power in her marriage. In this situation, I suspect Lou's escape into work was experienced more as relief than neglect on all sides. Although now Dotty blames the work demands of the electronics industry for Lou's heart disease and his early death last year at the age of fifty-two, at the time Lou's absence from the family gave Dotty the "space" to develop her strength and the willingness to assume the serious economic and emotional risks of divorce and an impoverished life as a single parent.

Dotty kicked Lou out, although she did not file for divorce. Two years later she took him back, but only after his nearly fatal, and permanently disabling, heart attack, and after her live-in lover left her. Even then she took him back on her own rather harsh terms. She was to have total independence in her time and relationships. Despite the economic inequality between them, Dotty now held the undeniable emotional balance of power in the relationship, but only because she had proven she could survive impoverishment and live without Lou. And, of course, Lou's disability contributed to the restructuring of the division of labor and power in their household. Lou did most of the housework and gardening, while Dotty participated in the paid labor force. Nonetheless, Dotty remained economically dependent on Lou, and she regrets her limited career options. Indeed, this was one crucial factor in her decision to resume her marriage with Lou.

By the late 1970s Dotty was no longer active in feminist or community causes. She says she "got burned out" and "turned off" by the "all men are evil" kind of thinking. More importantly, I believe, Dotty's life stage and circumstances had changed so that she did not feel she needed or benefited from feminism any more. In the mid-1970s, she "needed to have my stamp validated," to be reassured that her rebellious and assertive feelings and her struggles to reform her marriage were legitimate. But, partly due to the feminist-assisted success of those struggles, Dotty came to feel less need for reassurance from feminists. Dotty also finds she has no room for feminism today. She is "too tired, there's too much other shit to deal with." These days she has been trying to maintain her precarious hold on her underpaid job at a cable television service, while heroically struggling to cope with the truly staggering series of family tragedies that befell the Lewisons this year. Lou and two of the adult Lewison children died and one son spent four months in prison. Under these circumstances Dotty too has found more comfort from organized religion than from feminism.

Parallels and idiosyncrasies in the life histories just described illustrate some of the complex, reciprocal effects of the family and work dynamics and gender consciousness that I have been observing in the Silicon Valley. Pam and Dotty both were young when they married. They both entered their marriages with conventional "Parsonsian" gender expectations about family and work responsibilities and "roles." For a significant period of time, they and their husbands conformed to the then culturally prescribed pattern of "instrumental" male breadwinner and "expressive" female housewife/mother. Assuming primary responsibility for rearing the children they began to bear immediately after marriage, Pam and Dotty supported their husbands' successful efforts to develop careers as electronics engineers. In the process, both men became workaholics.

As their marriages deteriorated, both Pam and Dotty enrolled in a women's reentry program where they were affected profoundly by feminist courses. Eventually both women left their husbands and became welfare mothers, an experience each of them found to be both liberating and debilitating. Each experienced an initial "feminist high," a sense of enormous exhilaration and strength in her new, independent circumstances. One divorced her husband, developed a viable career, experimented with the single life, and gradually became desperately unhappy. The other did not develop a career, lost her lover, and only then decided to take back her newly disabled husband (with his pension). Their rather different experiences with failed intimacy and their different occupational resources, I believe, help explain their diverse postfeminist strategies.

Postfeminist Daughters

Between them Pam and Dotty had five daughters, all of whom have distanced themselves from feminist identity and ideology, in some cases in conscious reaction against their mothers' earlier feminist views. At the same time, however, most of the daughters have semi-consciously incorporated feminist principles into their expectations and strategies for family and work.

Pam's oldest daughter, Lanny, is twenty-three and is a designer-drafter who received her initial training in a feminist-inspired skills program. She is now in her second marriage, with one child from each marriage. Lanny dropped out of high school and at seventeen married a truck driver, who she describes as addicted to drugs and totally uncommunicative. Staying home with their baby, she found herself isolated and unbearably lonely. Pam encouraged Lanny's

246

entry into a drafting course sponsored by a county agency, and Lanny soon found employment in electronics via various temporary agencies. After she discovered her husband's narcotics addiction and convinced him to enter a residential detox program, Lanny spent a brief period as a welfare mother. Although she hated drafting, she job-shopped frequently to raise her income sufficiently to support herself and her daughter. She was earning fourteen dollars an hour, without benefits, in 1985 when she met her present husband, Ken, at one of these jobs where he worked as an expediter in the purchasing department for eight dollars an hour until a recent layoff.

Lanny does not consider herself a feminist and has never been active or interested in politics. She hates her work, but has no desire to be a homemaker and is perfectly willing to support her husband if he wants to stay home and take care of the children, or if, as they hope, she can afford to send him back to engineering school. She would like to become an interior designer. Although Lanny started out in a rather traditional working-class marriage, she is an authentic postfeminist. She was not able to tolerate the isolation, boredom, and emotional deprivation of that traditional marriage. Lanny's goals are to combine marriage to a nurturant, communicative, coparenting man (the way she perceives Ken) with full-time work at a job she truly enjoys. There is an ease to Lanny's attitudes about the gender division of labor at home and at work. These are not political issues to Lanny, nor even conscious points of personal struggle. She did actively reject her traditionally gendered first marriage, but without conceptualizing it that way. Lanny takes for granted the right to be flexible about family and work priorities. Remarkably, Ken appears to be equally flexible and equally oblivious to feminist influences on his notably enlightened attitudes.

The postfeminism of Dotty's oldest daughter, Lyn, however, represents a somewhat more conscious and ambivalent response to feminism. Like Lanny, Lyn was a high school dropout who took a variety of low-wage service sector jobs. But, unlike Lanny, the father of her child left during her pregnancy, making Lyn an unwed welfare mother. Lyn got off welfare by moonlighting at an electronics security job while developing her successful career in drafting. She is now a hybrid designer at one of the world's major semiconductor companies. Unlike Lanny, Lyn loves her work, although she is constantly anxious, exhausted, and deeply frustrated by her working conditions, and by their incompatibility with her needs as a single mother. There have been long periods when Lyn hardly saw her son and depended upon parents and friends to fill in as babysitters.

Lyn's desire for a father for her son was a major motive for her brief marriage to a man who abused her. She has lived alone with her son since she divorced her husband five years ago. Although Lyn is proud and fiercely independent, during the past two years she has somewhat ambivalently pursued a marital commitment from her somewhat resistant boyfriend, Tom. Tom, like Lanny's husband Ken, appears both unthreatened by Lyn's greater career drive and income and quite flexible about gender norms generally. He, however, seems much less willing or able than Ken to commit himself to marriage and parenthood.

Lyn is aware of sex discrimination at work and of issues of gender injustice generally and will occasionally challenge these by herself. Yet more explicitly than Lanny, Lyn distances herself from a feminist identity which she regards as an unnecessarily hostile and occasionally petty one: "I do not feel like a feminist, because to me my mother is a perfect feminist. . . . If someone asks her to make coffee, she first has to determine if it is because she is a woman." Upon reflection Lyn acknowledges that it is the word "feminist" that she does not like, "because of the way I was brought up with it. It meant slapping people in the face with it. . . . I do what I think is right, and if I am asked, I tell them why. . . . Honestly, I guess I am a very strong feminist, but I don't have to beat people with it."

I consider Lyn a stronger postfeminist than feminist. She cannot imagine being active politically on any issue, not even one like battering, which she experienced: "I leave them for people like my mother who can make issues out of that, because I don't see it that way. I'll help the neighbor next door whose husband is beating her to death , , . I do it my way. My way is not in a public form. I am very different from my mother." Equally postfeminist are the ways Lyn fails both to credit feminist struggles for the career opportunities for women she has grown up taking for granted, or to blame sexism or corporations for the male-oriented work schedules and demands that jeopardize her family needs. For example, she would like to have a second child, but accepts the "fact" that a second child does not fit with a successful career. Lyn shares Lanny's postfeminist expectations for family and work, that is, the desire to combine marriage to a communicative, egalitarian man with motherhood and a successful, engaging career.

The emergent relationships between postindustrialism, family turbulence, and postfeminism are nuanced and dynamic. Crisis in the family, as manifested in escalating rates of divorce and single-mother households, contributes both to the gender stratification of this postindustrial workforce, and to a limited potential for feminist consciousness. Marital instability continually refuels a large, cheap female labor pool which underwrites the feminization of both the postindustrial proletariat and of poverty. But this crudely gender-stratified and male-oriented occupational structure helps to further destabilize gender relationships and family life. Moreover, the skewed wages and salaries available to white men help to inflate housing costs for everyone, thereby contributing to the rapid erosion of the working class breadwinner and the family wage.

One consequence of family instability in such an environment seems to have been an initial openness on the part of many women, like Dotty and Pam, to feminist ideas. Neither feminism nor other progressive movements have been as successful, however, in addressing either the structural inequalities of postindustrial occupational structure, or the individualist, fast-track culture that makes all too difficult the formation of stable intimate relations on an egalitarian, or, for that matter, any other basis. Organized religion, and particularly evangelical groups, may offer more effective support to troubled family relationships in these circumstances.

I believe this explains the attractiveness of various kinds of postfeminist ideologies and strategies for achieving intimacy, or for just surviving in a profoundly insecure milieu. Postfeminist strategies correspond to different generational and individual experiences of feminism as well as postindustrial family and work conditions. For many women of the "mother" generation, feminism has become as much a burden as a means of support. Where once it helped them to reform or leave unsatisfactory relationships, now it can intensify the pain and difficulty of the compromises most women must make in order to mediate the destructive effects of postindustrial society on family and personal relationships. Too seldom today can women find committed mates, let alone those who also would pass feminist muster.

In a general climate and stage of their lives characterized by diminished expectations, Pam and Dotty have sought support for the compromises with and commitments to family and work they have chosen to make, rather than for greater achievement or independence. Without repudiating feminism, both Dotty and Pam have distanced themselves from feminist identity or activism. On the other hand, their postfeminist, oldest daughters take for granted the gains in female career opportunities and male participation in child rearing and domestic work for which feminists of their mothers' generation struggled. Lanny and Lyn do not conceptualize their troubling postindustrial work and family problems in political terms. To them feminism and politics appear irrelevant or threatening.

These diverse forms of postfeminism, I believe, are semi-conscious responses to feminism's unwitting role as midwife to the new family and work conditions in postindustrial America. Some versions are more reactionary, some more progressive, but all, I believe, differ from *anti*-feminism. They represent women's attempts to both retain and depoliticize the egalitarian family and work ideals of the second wave. This is an inherently contradictory project, and one that presents feminists with an enigmatic dilemma. Is it possible to devise a personal politics that respects the political and personal anxieties and the exhaustion of women contending with the destabilized family and work conditions of the postindustrial era? To do so without succumbing to conservative nostalgia for patriarchal familial and religious forms is a central challenge for contemporary feminism.

Notes

I wish to thank Linda Gordon, Carole Joffe, David Plotke, Rayna Rapp, and Barrie Thorne for their challenging and supportive responses to earlier drafts of this article.

1. As with the term "postfeminist," I use the term "postindustrial" with trepidation as it carries a great deal of ideological charge. I use it here exclusively in a descriptive sense to designate a form and period of capitalist social organization in which traditional industrial occupations supply a small minority of jobs to the labor force, and the vast majority of workers labor in varieties of clerical, sales, and service positions. Daniel Bell claims to have formulated the theme of postindustrial society in 1962 in an essay, "The Post-Industrial Society." See his *The Coming of Post-Industrial Society: A Venture in Social Forecasting,* New York: Basic Books 1973, p. 146.
2. Thus Geneva Overholser concludes a *New York Times* editorial opinion entitled, "What 'Post-Feminism' Really Means," September 19, 1986, p. 3.
3. My appreciation to Steven Buechler for first suggesting this analogy to me.
4. There is considerable debate among economists concerning the accuracy of labeling the US as a service economy. For example, see Richard Walker's challenge to this characterization, "Is There a Service Economy? The Changing Capitalist Division of Labor," *Science & Society,* vol. 49, no. 1 (Spring 1986), pp. 42–83. The debate involves the politics of semantics. Few disagree, however, that significant occupational changes have occurred in the past few decades, or that these involve the decline of unions and real wages and the rise of female employment.
5. "A Mother's Choice," *Newsweek,* March 31, 1986, p. 47.
6. These are among the findings of a study that attempted to operationalize Marxist criteria for assigning class categories to workers in the US. Even though the study excluded housewives from its sample, it found "that the majority of the working class in the United States consists of women (53.6 percent)." See, Erik Olin Wright et al., "The American Class Structure," *American Sociological Review,* vol. 47 (December 1982), p. 22.
7. As the much-publicized findings from Lenore Weitzman's study of no-fault divorce in California underscore. Lenore J. Weitzman, *The Divorce Revolution: The Unexpected Social and Economic Consequences for Women and Children in America,* New York: Free Press 1986.
8. Households headed by fully employed women had a poverty rate almost three times greater than husband-wife households and twice that of households headed by unmarried men. The number of female-headed families doubled between 1970 and 1980. By 1981, women headed almost one-fifth of all families with minor children: Joan Smith, "The Paradox of Women's Poverty: Wage-Earning Women and Economic Transformation," *Signs,* vol. 10, no. 2 (Winter 1984), p. 291.
9. Households with working wives accounted for 60 percent of all family income in 1985, which made it possible for 66 percent of all families to earn more than $25,000 per year, compared with only 28 percent of families who achieved comparable incomes twenty years ago. In 1981 the median earnings of full-time year-round women workers was $12,001, 69 percent of the $20,260 that men earned. That year married women contributed a median of 26.7 percent of family income. The lower the family's annual income, however, the higher the proportion contributed by women. Paradoxically, however, there is an inverse relationship between family income and the percentage of wives working. See *The Working Woman: A Progress Report,* Washington D.C.: The Conference Board 1985, and Barbara F. Reskin and Heidi I. Hartmann, eds, *Women's Work, Men's Work,* Washington, D.C.: National Academy Press 1986, p. 4. The combined effects of these trends are acute for black women, for whom astronomical divorce rates have overwhelmed the effects of their relative gains in earnings, forcing them increasingly into poverty. For data see US Department of Labor, *Time of Change: 1983 Handbook on Women Workers,* Washington D.C.: Dept. of Labor, Women's Bureau Bulletin 298, 1983, p. 29; Paula Giddings, *When and Where I Enter: The Impact of Black Women on Race and Sex in America,* Toronto: Bantam Books 1985, p. 353.
10. The county population grew from 290,647 in 1960 to 1,295,071 in 1980. US Bureau of the Census, *Census of Population: 1950,* vol. 2, *Characteristics of the Population pt 5,* California, 1952; and *Census of Population: 1980,* vol. 1, *Characteristics of the Population, General Population Characteristics, pt 6,* California, 1982.
11. For data and a superb ethnographic and analytical account of this transition, see John

Frederick Keller, "The Production Worker in Electronics: Industrialization and Labor Development in California's Santa Clara Valley," (PhD dissertation, University of Michigan, 1981).

12. For data on the occupational structure of the electronics industry, see Keller, "Production Worker in Electronics," Marcie Axelrad, *Profile of the Electronics Workforce in the Santa Clara Valley,* San Jose: Project on Health and Safety in Electronics 1979; Lennie Siegel and Herb Borock, "Background Report on Silicon Valley," prepared for the US Commission on Civil Rights, Mountain View, Calif.: Pacific Studies Center 1982.

13. For the data on divorce rates and household composition for Santa Clara County in comparison with California and the US as a whole, see Bureau of the Census, *Census of Population,* 1960, 1970, and 1980. During the 1970s Santa Clara County recorded 660 abortions for every 1000 births, compared with a statewide average of 489.5 and a ratio of less than 400 for the nation. See Bureau of the Census, *Statistical Abstract of the United States,* 1981. The most influential representative of this tendency may be James Dobson, founder and president of Focus on the Family, "a nonprofit corporation dedicated to the preservation of the home." Focus produces a radio talk show on family issues aired as much as three times daily on hundreds of Christian stations throughout the US and abroad. The organization also produces and distributes Christian films, tapes, and audiocassettes on family topics. Dobson, who served on the recent Meese Commission on Pornography, has also authored scores of advice books and pamphlets on family and personal relationships, most of which advocate the doctrine of "tough love." The uneasy fusion of patriarchal and feminist thought is marked in his advice book.

14. For a discussion of the infusion of the female sexual revolution into fundamentalist culture, see Barbara Ehrenreich, Elizabeth Hess, and Gloria Jacobs, *Re-Making Love: The Feminization of Sex,* New York: Anchor Press 1986, ch. 5.

15

Is the Legacy of Second Wave Feminism Postfeminism?

(1988)

Rayna Rapp

Judith Stacey's "Sexism by a Subtler Name: Postindustrial Conditions and Postfeminist Consciousness in the Silicon Valley" challenges us to ask some hard questions: What is the relationship between women's experiences of domestic turbulence and abuse, and their ability to transform or escape those conditions? What is the role of feminist consciousness, or its lack, in those struggles? How does a period of economic turbulence both force and foster female initiative to escape marital violence?

Family stress, fighting, battering, and addiction all play complex roles in the lives of the women of California's Silicon Valley. These women alternate between unstable marriages and times served as single heads of households, often and periodically on welfare. The legacy of family reform movements includes no-fault divorce and diminishing state entitlement act as shock absorbers to domestic unrest.

Pam and Dotty, the women Judith Stacey came to know, live lives which reflect the boomerang economy and marital patterns of the region. Judith Stacey helps us to understand the circumstances under which they came to think of themselves as feminists, and then to distance themselves from organized feminism. Pam and Dotty's daughters are recipients of feminism's strengths, although they are wary of its labels. The second generation adamantly rejects being called "feminist." Why? They are not unsympathetic toward the social transformations feminism demanded; they have benefited from the changes in education, jobs, and domestic services that feminist groups have helped to bring forth. But they are clearly concerned with questions of "personal choice" rather than politics.

Judith Stacey labels their stance "postfeminist," and provides us with a provisional definition of that painful phenomenon: "The simultaneous incorporation, revision and depoliticization of many of the central goals of second wave feminism." And, I'd add, that depoliticization often takes the form of the reduction of feminist *social* goals to individual "lifestyle." It's a process as American as apple pie, in a culture strongly influenced by a very Protestant notion of free and individual will. And Protestant Evangelism in turn responds to aspects of women's family-based dilemmas, renaming them, and offering guidance toward their individual, but not their social, resolution.

What are we to make of that vexatious term, "postfeminism"? As Judith Stacey points out, "postfeminism" must be taken as more than a media hype, for it describes the assumptions of entitlement to decent work and decent home lives of millions of American women who would be quick to distance themselves from our label of "feminist." They take our victories for granted! As well they should, as we took for granted the vote, the existence of widespread higher education for women, and the relative accessibility of divorce, when we wandered, barely historically conscious, onto the stage of women's political history as new actors in a discontinuous, but continuing drama.

Paradoxically, the "taking for granted" in Lanny and Lyn's lives constitutes our greatest victory and simultaneously poses a very large problem. It's a victory because it represents the fruition of the gains won by the feminist movement and feminist-inspired social services. Would Pam and Dotty or their daughters have their current options without programs for returning women at local community colleges, or training courses for women in the "nontraditional" skilled trades? Their consciousness is surely both transformed by and transformative of those myriad second wave institutions

But that "taking for granted" does not happen all at once, nor is it all of one piece, or even inevitable. For diverse women separated by class, race, ethnic, sex-preferential, or other divides live their history differently. We all share a chronology, but we do not live, or make, or experience the same history.

To make this point most dramatically, I want to shift my gaze from Silicon Valley back to my hometown, New York, where a group of "second wavers" has been privileged to participate in a series of women's studies conferences organized with and for trade union women. In the "progressive" unions where organizing in female sectors is a do-or-die proposition, women by the thousands struggle for goals which entail high feminist consciousness: comparable worth, childcare facilities, protection from sexual harassment, and contract language extending sick days to care for all dependents. And they simultaneously struggle against male privilege and control in their unions, while confronting sexual inequalities in the labor market.

At meeting after meeting, our team of women's studies activists witnessed important conflicts among trade unionists, some of whom claimed the label of "feminism," while others rejected it. A group of rank-and-file retail workers, who had struggled for many months to have a women's history course offered as part of their trade union education program, finally won their goal. They had no use for the word "feminist" until they actually sat in the course. Then they claimed it as their own, citing historical precedents.

A very successful organizer scorned *Ms.* magazine when we offered a reprinted article as part of an educational packet. In querying why, teeth clenched for an attack on feminism, we discovered it was the anti-union stance of some *Ms.* editors to which she objected; the magazine's definition of feminism posed no problem. Health care workers made it clear that childcare had to become a top union priority. Without it, they threatened to withdraw their time and energy from crucial union projects. "This is a woman's union, and until they make our kids welcome here, it's no home to us. Doesn't matter if we have to turn the world upside down to do it, it's got to be done," one woman told us. None of them would ever identify with the label "postfeminist." They're too busy fighting over what the initial term can bring to, or detract from, their immediate concerns.

Nor do I think we can call the divided responses to *The Color Purple* in black communities "postfeminist." The struggles of black feminists to name themselves, organize themselves, and mobilize their sisters, in spite of the perceived whiteness of the label "feminist," must be understood in its own terms. It requires confrontations with issues like domestic violence, teen pregnancy, and lesbian-baiting, all of which may reveal divisions rather than solidarities within already embattled communities. These are not easy issues to discuss in a language formulated by a movement which has often taken the experiences of white women as its point of orientation. Such struggles are not reducible to the "postfeminism" expressed (by young, predominantly white, highly privileged female doctors, lawyers, and business executives whose efforts to build integrated home and work lives are gleefully covered by the *New York Times Magazine*. Movements that may feel "dead" to second wave feminists are actually just beginning or continuing for other groups of American women, depending on the social fault lines upon which their experiences are constructed.

But how can we locate ourselves in a political era which has no unified name? Without an obvious and defined national political feminist movement, many struggles continue to bubble under the surface of daily life. But the *lack* of a unified name also points to a problem: women dispersed among men and children are not likely to constitute a self-conscious social movement without a political name.

Individuals may work for personal transformation without naming collec-

255

tive problems. The "discovery" of male violence and marital rape, like the naming of sexual harassment, or even that controversy-laden term, the "feminization of poverty," is an essential part of feminist process. And it is a process which has forever changed the ways we all think about women. While the victory of naming a problem through women's eyes is far from accomplishing the abolition of the conditions which caused the problem, it is a necessary step. If we want future generations to assume the gains second wave feminism has made, we must preserve and move forward those struggles in ways that are *social*. Does a concept like "postfeminist" help or hinder that process?

How can we insist on the social at a time of great political reaction? How can we shape collective strategies in a culture whose hegemonic values and material constraints beckon us all to enact individual, "lifestyle" solutions? Surely we must take very seriously the sobering weight of cultural individualism in response to fragmenting political economic circumstances. But just as surely, we must never wallow in the mistaken and nostalgic view that if certain aspects of organized second wave feminism are declining, *all* forms of activism which will enhance women's interests are dead. Not only are individual "postfeminists" asserting personal rights and agency, but other organized groups – like trade union women and black feminists – are mobilizing on other terrains. Women's historical agency neither began nor ended with second wave feminism, and the individualistic incorporation of some, but not all, of our goals as "postfeminism" does not speak to the contradictions most women still experience in juggling the pressures of their domestic and public lives.

Wearisome as it may be, that old Chinese curse bears repeating: "May you live in interesting times." In the central, critical task of avoiding outmoded rhetoric in favor of facing the really difficult questions that now confront us, the work of Judith Stacey offers some hard-headed and useful guidance. We can use her insights to open our understanding of feminism's influence and its limitations. We need to at least begin to chart the diverse terrain in which American women are both constructed, and are reconstructing, their lives.

Note

This brief comment grows out of a session at the Seventh Berkshire Conference of Women Historians held at Wellesley College in June 1987. In addition to Judith Stacey's presentation, "Sexism by a Subtler Name?," Linda Gordon read a chapter of her forthcoming book, *Heroes of Their Own Lives: The Politics and History of Family Violence*, New York: Viking 1988. Barri Brown presented a second comment on the meaning of feminism in "non-feminist" times. Our ideas were developed jointly, and it is impossible to separate the "mine" from the "ours" in the themes which run through this comment.

16

A Manifesto for Cyborgs

Science, Technology, and Socialist Feminism in the 1980s

(1985)

Donna Haraway

An Ironic Dream of a Common Language for Women in the Integrated Circuit

This essay is an effort to build an ironic political myth faithful to feminism, socialism, and materialism. Perhaps more faithful as blasphemy is faithful, than as reverent worship and identification. Irony is about contradictions that do not resolve into larger wholes, even dialectically, about the tension of holding incompatible things together because both or all are necessary and true. Irony is about humor and serious play. It is also a rhetorical strategy and a political method, one I would like to see more honored within socialist-feminism. At the center of my ironic faith, my blasphemy, is the image of the cyborg. A cyborg is a cybernetic organism, a hybrid of machine and organism, a creature of social reality as well as a creature of fiction.

By the late twentieth century, our time, a mythic time, we are all chimeras, theorized and fabricated hybrids of machine and organism; in short, we are cyborgs. The cyborg is our ontology; it gives us our politics. The cyborg is a condensed image of both imagination and material reality, the two joined centers structuring any possibility of historical transformation. In the traditions of "Western" science and politics – the tradition of racist, male-dominant capitalism; the tradition of progress; the tradition of the appropriation of nature as resource for the productions of culture; the tradition of reproduction of the self from the reflections of the other – the relation between organism and machine has been a border war. The stakes in the border war have been the territories of production, reproduction, and imagination. This essay is an argument for *pleasure* in the confusion of boundaries and for *responsibility* in their construction. It is also an effort to contribute to socialist-feminist culture and theory in a postmodernist, nonnaturalist mode and in the utopian tradition of imagining a world without gender, which is perhaps a world without genesis, but maybe also a world without end. The cyborg incarnation is outside salvation history.

The cyborg is resolutely committed to partiality, irony, intimacy, and perversity. It is oppositional, utopian, and completely without innocence. No longer structured by the polarity of public and private, the cyborg defines a technological polis based partly on a revolution of social relations in the *oikos,* the household. Nature and culture are reworked; the one can no longer be the resource for appropriation or incorporation by the other. The relationships for forming wholes from parts, including those of polarity and hierarchical domination, are at issue in the cyborg world. Unlike the hopes of Frankenstein's monster, the cyborg does not expect its father to save it through a restoration of the garden; i.e., through the fabrication of a heterosexual mate, through its completion in a finished whole, a city and cosmos. The cyborg does not dream of community on the model of the organic family, this time without the Oedipal project. The cyborg would not recognize the Garden of Eden; it is not made of mud and cannot dream of returning to dust. Perhaps that is why I want to see if cyborgs can subvert the apocalypse of returning to nuclear dust in the manic compulsion to name the Enemy. Cyborgs are not reverent; they do not remember the cosmos. They are wary of holism, but needy for connection – they seem to have a natural feel for united front politics, but without the vanguard party. The main trouble with cyborgs, of course, is that they are the illegitimate offspring of militarism and patriarchal capitalism, not to mention state socialism. But illegitimate offspring are often exceedingly unfaithful to their origins. Their fathers, after all, are inessential.

I want to signal three crucial boundary breakdowns that make the following political fictional (political scientific) analysis possible. By the late twentieth century in United States scientific culture, the boundary between human and animal is thoroughly breached. The last beachheads of uniqueness have been polluted if not turned into amusement parks – language, tool use, social behavior, mental events, nothing really convincingly settles the separation of human and animal. And many people no longer feel the need of such a separation; indeed, many branches of feminist culture affirm the pleasure of connection of human and other living creatures. Movements for animal rights are not irrational denials of human uniqueness; they are clearsighted recognition of connection across the discredited breach of nature and culture. Biology and evolutionary theory over the last two centuries have simultaneously produced modern organisms as objects of knowledge and reduced the line between humans and animals to a faint trace re-etched in ideological struggle or professional disputes between life and social sciences. Within this framework, teaching modern Christian creationism should be fought as a form of child abuse.

The second leaky distinction is between animal–human (organism) and machine. Precybernetic machines could be haunted; there was always the specter of the ghost in the machine. This dualism structured the dialogue between materialism and idealism that was settled by a dialectical progeny, called spirit or history, according to taste. But basically machines were not self-moving, self-designing, autonomous. They could not achieve man's dream, only mock it. They were not man, an author to himself, but only a caricature of that masculinist reproductive dream. To think they were otherwise was paranoid. Now we are not so sure. Late-twentieth-century machines have made thoroughly ambiguous the difference between natural and artificial, mind and body, self-developing and externally designed, and many other distinctions that used to apply to organisms and machines. Our machines are disturbingly lively, and we ourselves frighteningly inert.

Technological determinism is only one ideological space opened up by the reconceptions of machine and organism as coded texts through which we engage in the play of writing and reading the world. "Textualization" of everything in poststructuralist, postmodernist theory has been damned by Marxists and socialist-feminists for its utopian disregard for lived relations of domination that ground the "play" of arbitrary reading. It is certainly true that postmodernist strategies, like my cyborg myth, subvert myriad organic wholes (e.g., the poem, the primitive culture, the biological organism). In short, the certainty of what counts as nature – a source of insight and a promise of innocence – is undermined, probably fatally. The transcendent authorization of interpretation is lost, and with it the ontology grounding "Western" epistemology. But the alternative is not cynicism or faithlessness, i.e., some version of abstract existence, like the accounts of technological determinism destroying "man" by the "machine" or "meaningful political action" by the "text." Who cyborgs will be is a radical question; the answers are a matter of survival. Both chimpanzees and artifacts have politics, so why shouldn't we?

The silicon chip is a surface for writing; it is etched in molecular scales disturbed only by atomic noise, the ultimate interference for nuclear scores. Writing, power, and technology are old partners in Western stories of the origin of civilization, but miniaturization has changed our experience of mechanism. Miniaturization has turned out to be about power; small is not so much beautiful as preeminently dangerous, as in cruise missiles. Contrast the TV sets of the 1950s or the news cameras of the 1970s with the TV wristbands or hand-sized video cameras now advertised. Our best machines are made of sunshine; they are all light and clean because they are nothing but signals, electro-magnetic waves, a section of a spectrum.

The ubiquity and invisibility of cyborgs is precisely why these sunshine belt

259

machines are so deadly. They are as hard to see politically as materially. They are about consciousness – or its simulation. They are floating signifiers moving in pickup trucks across Europe, blocked more effectively by the witchweavings of the displaced and so unnatural Greenham women who read the cyborg webs of power very well, than by the militant labor of older masculinist politics, whose natural constituency needs defense jobs. Ultimately the "hardest" science is about the realm of greatest boundary confusion, the realm of pure number, pure spirit, C³I, cryptography, and the preservation of potent secrets. The new machines are so clean and light. Their engineers are sun worshipers mediating a new scientific revolution associated with the night dream of postindustrial society. The diseases evoked by these clean machines are "no more" than the miniscule coding changes of an antigen in the immune system, "no more" than the experience of stress. The nimble little fingers of "Oriental" women, the old fascination of little Anglo-Saxon Victorian girls with doll houses, women's enforced attention to the small take on quite new dimensions in this world. There might be a cyborg Alice taking account of these new dimensions. Ironically, it might be the unnatural cyborg women making chips in Asia and spiral dancing in Santa Rita whose constructed unities will guide effective oppositional strategies.

One of my premises is that most American socialists and feminists see deepened dualisms of mind and body, animal and machine, idealism and materialism in the social practices, symbolic formulations, and physical artifacts associated with "high technology" and scientific culture. The analytic resources developed by progressives have insisted on the necessary domination of technics and have recalled us to an imagined organic body to integrate our resistance. Another of my premises is that the need for unity of people trying to resist worldwide intensification of domination has never been more acute. But a slightly perverse shift of perspective might better enable us to contest for meanings, as well as for other forms of power and pleasure in technologically mediated societies.

Fractured Identities

It has become difficult to name one's feminism by a single adjective – or even to insist in every circumstance upon the noun. Consciousness of exclusion through naming is acute. Identities seem contradictory, partial, and strategic. With the hard-won recognition of their social and historical constitution. gender, race, and class cannot provide the basis for belief in "essential" unity. There is nothing about being "female" that naturally binds women. There is not even such a state as "being" female, itself a highly complex category constructed in contested sexual scientific discourses and other social practices.

260

Gender, race, or class consciousness is an achievement forced on us by the terrible historical experience of the contradictory social realities of patriarchy, colonialism, and capitalism. And who counts as "us" in my own rhetoric? Which identities are available to ground such a potent political myth called "us," and what could motivate enlistment in this collectivity? Painful fragmentation among feminists (not to mention among women) along every possible fault line has made the concept of *woman* elusive, an excuse for the matrix of women's dominations of each other. For me – and for many who share a similar historical location in white, professional middle class, female, radical, North American, mid-adult bodies – the sources of a crisis in political identity are legion. The recent history for much of the US Left and US feminism has been a response to this kind of crisis by endless splitting and searches for a new essential unity. But there has also been a growing recognition of another response through coalition – affinity, not identity.[8]

"Women of color," a name contested at its origins by those whom it would incorporate, as well as a historical consciousness marking systematic breakdown of all the signs of Man in "Western" traditions, constructs a kind of postmodernist identity out of otherness and difference. This postmodernist identity is fully political, whatever might be said about other possible postmodernisms. This identity marks out a self-consciously constructed space that cannot affirm the capacity to act on the basis of natural identification, but only on the basis of conscious coalition, of affinity, of political kinship. Unlike the "woman" of some streams of the white women's movement in the United States, there is no naturalization of the matrix.

I do not know of any other time in history when there was greater need for political unity to confront effectively the dominations of "race," "gender," "sexuality," and "class." I also do not know of any other time when the kind of unity we might help build could have been possible. None of "us" have any longer the symbolic or material capability of dictating the shape of reality to any of "them." Or at least "we" cannot claim innocence from practicing such dominations. White women, including socialist-feminists, discovered (i.e., were forced kicking and screaming to notice) the non-innocence of the category "woman." That consciousness changes the geography of all previous categories; it denatures them as heat denatures a fragile protein. Cyborg feminists have to argue that "we" do not want any more natural matrix of unity and that no construction is whole. Innocence, and the corollary insistence on victimhood as the only ground for insight, has done enough damage. But the constructed revolutionary subject must give late-twentieth-century people pause as well.

Both Marxist/socialist feminisms and radical feminisms have simultaneously naturalized and denatured the category "woman" and consciousness of the social lives of "women." Perhaps a schematic caricature can highlight both kinds of moves. Marxian socialism is rooted in an analysis of wage labor which reveals class structure. The consequence of the wage relationship is systematic alienation, as the worker is dissociated from his (sic) product. Abstraction and illusion rule in knowledge, domination rules in practice. Labor is the preeminently privileged category enabling the Marxist to overcome illusion and find that point of view which is necessary for changing the world. Labor is the humanizing activity that makes man; labor is an ontological category permitting the knowledge of a subject, and so the knowledge of subjugation and alienation.

In faithful filiation, socialist feminism advanced by allying itself with the basic analytic strategies of Marxism. The main achievement of both Marxist feminists and socialist feminists was to expand the category of labor to accommodate what (some) women did, even when the wage relation was subordinated to a more comprehensive view of labor under capitalist patriarchy. In particular, women's labor in the household and women's activity as mothers generally, i.e., reproduction in the socialist-feminist sense, entered theory on the authority of analogy to the Marxian concept of labor. The unity of women here rests on an epistemology based on the ontological structure of "labor." Marxist/socialist feminism does not "naturalize" unity; it is a possible achievement based on a possible standpoint rooted in social relations. The essentializing move is in the ontological structure of labor or of its analogue, women's activity.* The inheritance of Marxian humanism, with its preeminently Western self, is the difficulty for me. The contribution from these formulations has been the emphasis on the daily responsibility of real women to build unities, rather than to naturalize them.

Catherine MacKinnon's version of radical feminism is itself a caricature of the appropriating, incorporating, totalizing tendencies of Western theories of identity grounding action. It is factually and politically wrong to assimilate all of the diverse "moments" or "conversations" in recent women's politics named radical feminism to MacKinnon's version. But the teleological logic of her theory shows how an epistemology and ontology – including their negations – erase or police difference.

MacKinnon argues that radical feminism necessarily adopted a different analytical strategy from Marxism, looking first not at the structure of class, but at the structure of sex/gender and its generative relationship, men's constitution and appropriation of women sexually. Ironically, MacKinnon's "ontol-

---

* The central role of object relations versions of psychoanalysis and related strong universalizing moves in discussing reproduction, caring work, and mothering in many approaches to epistemology underline their authors' resistance to what I am calling postmodernism. For me, both the universalizing moves and the versions of psychoanalysis make analysis of "women's place in the integrated circuit" difficult and lead to systematic difficulties in accounting for or even seeing major aspects of the construction of gender and gendered social life.

ogy" constructs a non-subject, a non-being. Another's desire, not the self's labor, is the origin of "woman." She therefore develops a theory of consciousness that enforces what can count as "women's" experience – anything that names sexual violation, indeed, sex itself as far as "women" can be concerned. Feminist practice is the construction of this form of consciousness; i.e., the self-knowledge of a self-who-is-not.

Perversely, sexual appropriation in this radical feminism still has the epistemological status of labor, i.e., the point from which analysis able to contribute to changing the world must flow. But sexual objectification, not alienation, is the consequence of the structure of sex/gender. In the realm of knowledge, the result of sexual objectification is illusion and abstraction. However, a woman is not simply alienated from her product, but in a deep sense does not exist as a subject, or even potential subject, since she owes her existence as a woman to sexual appropriation. To be constituted by another's desire is not the same thing as to be alienated in the violent separation of the laborer from his product.

MacKinnon's radical theory of experience is totalizing in the extreme; it does not so much marginalize as obliterate the authority of any other women's political speech and action. It is a totalization producing what Western patriarchy itself never succeeded in doing – feminists' consciousness of the non-existence of women, except as products of men's desire. I think MacKinnon correctly argues that no Marxian version of identity can firmly ground women's unity. But in solving the problem of the contradictions of any Western revolutionary subject for feminist purposes, she develops an even more authoritarian doctrine of experience. If my complaint about socialist/Marxian standpoints is their unintended erasure of polyvocal, unassimilable, radical difference made visible in anticolonial discourse and practice, MacKinnon's intentional erasure of all difference through the device of the "essential" non-existence of women is not reassuring.

In my taxonomy, which like any other taxonomy is a reinscription of history, radical feminism can accommodate all the activities of women named by socialist feminists as forms of labor only if the activity can somehow be sexualized. Reproduction had different tones of meanings for the two tendencies, one rooted in labor, one in sex, both calling the consequences of domination and ignorance of social and personal reality "false consciousness."

Beyond either the difficulties or the contributions in the argument of any one author, neither Marxist nor radical feminist points of view have tended to embrace the status of a partial explanation; both were regularly constituted as totalities. Western explanation has demanded as much; how else could the "Western" author incorporate its others? Each tried to annex other forms of domination by expanding its basic categories through analogy, simple listing, or addition. Embarrassed silence about race among white radical and socialist feminists was one major, devastating political consequence. History and polyvocality disappear into political taxonomies that try to establish genealogies. There was no structural room for race (or for much else) in theory claiming to reveal the construction of the category woman and social group women as a unified or totalizable whole.

The Informatics of Domination

In this attempt at an epistemological and political position, I would like to sketch a picture of possible unity, a picture indebted to socialist and feminist principles of design. The frame for my sketch is set by the extent and importance of rearrangements in worldwide social relations tied to science and technology. I argue for a politics rooted in claims about fundamental changes in the nature of class, race, and gender in an emerging system of world order analogous in its novelty and scope to that created by industrial capitalism; we are living through a movement from an organic, industrial society to a polymorphous, information system – from all work to all play, a deadly game.

We cannot go back ideologically or materially. It's not just that "god" is dead; so is the "goddess." In relation to objects like biotic components, one must think not in terms of essential properties, but in terms of strategies of design, boundary constraints, rates of flows, systems logics, costs of lowering constraints. Sexual reproduction is one kind of reproductive strategy among many, with costs and benefits as a function of the system environment. Ideologies of sexual reproduction can no longer reasonably call on the notions of sex and sex role as organic aspects in natural objects like organisms and families. Such reasoning will be unmasked as irrational, and ironically corporate executives reading *Playboy* and antiporn radical feminists will make strange bedfellows in jointly unmasking the irrationalism.

Likewise for race, ideologies about human diversity have to be formulated in terms of frequencies of parameters, like blood groups or intelligence scores. It is "irrational" to invoke concepts like primitive and civilized. For liberals and radicals, the search for integrated social systems gives way to a new practice called "experimental ethnography" in which an organic object dissipates in attention to the play of writing. At the level of ideology, we see translations of racism and colonialism into languages of development and underdevelopment, rates and constraints of modernization. Any objects or persons can be reasonably thought of in terms of disassembly and reassembly; no "natural" architectures constrain system design. The financial districts in all of the world's cities, as well as the export-processing and free trade zones, proclaim this elementary fact of "late capitalism." The entire universe of objects that can be known scientifically must be formulated as problems in communications

264

engineering (for the managers) or theories of the text (for those who would resist). Both are cyborg semiologies.

The dichotomies between mind and body, animal and human, organism and machine, public and private, nature and culture, men and women, primitive and civilized are all in question ideologically. The actual situation of women is their integration/exploitation into a world system of production/reproduction and communication called the informatics of domination. The home, workplace, market, public arena, the body itself — all can be dispersed and interfaced in nearly infinite, polymorphous ways, with large consequences for women and others — consequences that themselves are very different for different people and which make potent oppositional international movements difficult to imagine and essential for survival. One important route for reconstructing socialist-feminist politics is through theory and practice addressed to the social relations of science and technology, including crucially the systems of myth and meanings structuring our imaginations. The cyborg is a kind of disassembled and reassembled, postmodern collective and personal self. This is the self feminists must code.

Communications sciences and modern biologies are constructed by a common move — *the translation of the world into a problem of coding,* a search for a common language in which all resistance to instrumental control disappears and all heterogeneity can be submitted to disassembly, reassembly, investment, and exchange. In communications sciences, the translation of the world into a problem in coding can be illustrated by looking at cybernetic (feedback-controlled) systems theories applied to telephone technology, computer design, weapons deployment, or data base construction and maintenance. In each case, solution to the key questions rests on a theory of language and control; the key operation is determining the rates, directions, and probabilities of flow of a quantity called information. The world is subdivided by boundaries differentially permeable to information. Information is just that kind of quantifiable element (unit, basis of unity) which allows universal translation, and so unhindered instrumental power (called effective communication). The biggest threat to such power is interruption of communication. Any system breakdown is a function of stress. The fundamentals of this technology can be condensed into the metaphor C^3I, command-control-communication-intelligence, the military's symbol for its operations theory.

In modern biologies, the translation of the world into a problem in coding can be illustrated by molecular genetics, ecology, sociobiological evolutionary theory, and immunobiology. The organism has been translated into problems of genetic coding and readout. Biotechnology, a writing technology, informs research broadly. In a sense, organisms have ceased to exist as objects of knowledge, giving way to biotic components, i.e., special kinds of information-processing devices. The analogous moves in ecology could be examined by probing the history and utility of the concept of the ecosystem. Immunobiology and associated medical practices are rich exemplars of the privilege of coding and recognition systems as objects of knowledge, as constructions of bodily reality for us.

But these excursions into communications sciences and biology have been at a rarefied level; there is a mundane, largely economic reality to support my claim that these sciences and technologies indicate fundamental transformations in the structure of the world for us. Communications technologies depend on electronics. Modern states, multinational corporations, military power, welfare-state apparatuses, satellite systems, political processes, fabrication of our imaginations, labor-control systems, medical constructions of our bodies, commercial pornography, the international division of labor, and religious evangelism depend intimately upon electronics.

Microelectronics mediates the translations of labor into robotics and word processing; sex into genetic engineering and reproductive technologies; and mind into artificial intelligence and decision procedures. The new biotechnologies concern more than human reproduction. Biology as a powerful engineering science for redesigning materials and processes has revolutionary implications for industry, perhaps most obvious today in areas of fermentation, agriculture, and energy. Communications sciences and biology are constructions of natural-technical objects of knowledge in which the difference between machine and organism is thoroughly blurred; mind, body, and tool are on very intimate terms. The "multinational" material organization of the production and reproduction of daily life and the symbolic organization of the production and reproduction of culture and imagination seem equally implicated. The boundary-maintaining images of base and superstructure, public and private, or material and ideal never seemed more feeble.

The Homework Economy

The "new industrial revolution" is producing a new worldwide working class. The extreme mobility of capital and the emerging international division of labor are intertwined with the emergence of new collectivities, and the weakening of familiar groupings. These developments are neither gender- nor race-neutral. White men in advanced industrial societies have become newly vulnerable to permanent job loss, and women are not disappearing from the job rolls at the same rates as men. It is not simply that women in Third World countries are the preferred labor force for the science-based multinationals in the export-processing sectors, particularly in electronics. The picture is more systematic and involves reproduction, sexuality, culture, consumption, and production. In the prototypical Silicon Valley, many women's lives have been structured around employment in electronics-dependent jobs, and their intimate realities include serial heterosexual monogamy, negotiating childcare, distance from extended kin or most other forms of traditional community, a high likelihood of loneliness and extreme economic vulnerability as they age. The ethnic and racial diversity of women in Silicon Valley structures a microcosm of conflicting differences in culture, family, religion, education, and language.

Work is being feminized, whether performed by men or women. To be feminized means to be made extremely vulnerable; able to be disassembled, reassembled, exploited as a reserve labor force; seen less as workers than as servers; subjected to time arrangements on and off the paid job that make a mockery of a limited work day; leading an existence that always borders on being obscene, out of place, and reducible to sex. Deskilling is an old strategy newly applicable to formerly privileged workers. However, the homework economy does not refer only to large-scale deskilling, nor does it deny that new areas of high skill are emerging, even for women and men previously excluded from skilled employment. Rather, the concept indicates that factory, home, and market are integrated on a new scale and that the places of women are crucial – and need to be analyzed for differences among women and for meanings for relations between men and women in various situations.

The homework economy as a world capitalist organizational structure is made possible by (not caused by) the new technologies. The successs of the attack on relatively privileged, mostly white, men's unionized jobs is tied to the power of the new communications technologies to integrate and control labor despite extensive dispersion and decentralization. The consequences of the new technologies are felt by women both in the loss of the family (male) wage (if they ever had access to this white privilege) and in the character of their own jobs, which are becoming capital-intensive, e.g., office work and nursing.

The new economic and technological arrangements are also related to the collapsing welfare state and the ensuing intensification of demands on women to sustain daily life for themselves as well as for men, children, and old people. The feminization of poverty – generated by dismantling the welfare state, by the homework economy where stable jobs become the exception, and sustained by the expectation that women's wage will not be matched by a male income for the support of children – has become an urgent focus. The causes of various women-headed households are a function of race, class, and sexuality; but their increasing generality is a ground for coalitions of women on many issues. That women regularly sustain daily life partly as a function of their enforced status as mothers is hardly new; the kind of integration with the overall capitalist and progressively war-based economy is new. The particular pressure, for example, on US black women, who have achieved an escape

267

from (barely) paid domestic service and who now hold clerical and similar jobs in large numbers, has large implications for continued enforced black poverty *with* employment. Teenage women in industrializing areas of the Third World increasingly find themselves the sole or major source of a cash wage for their families, while access to land is ever more problematic. These developments must have major consequences in the psychodynamics and politics of gender and race.

Within the framework of three major stages of capitalism (commercial/early industrial, monopoly, multinational) – tied to nationalism, imperialism, and multinationalism, and related to Frederick Jameson's three dominant aesthetic periods of realism, modernism, and postmodernism – I would argue that specific forms of families dialectically relate to forms of capital and to its political and cultural concomitants. Although lived problematically and unequally, ideal forms of these families might be schematized as 1) the patriarchal nuclear family, structured by the dichotomy between public and private and accompanied by the white bourgeois ideology of separate spheres and nineteenth-century Anglo-American bourgeois feminism; 2) the modern family mediated (or enforced) by the welfare state and institutions like the family wage, with a flowering of feminist heterosexual ideologies, including their radical versions represented in Greenwich Village around World War I; and 3) the "family" of the homework economy with its oxymoronic structure of women-headed households and its explosion of feminisms and the paradoxical intensification and erosion of gender itself.

This is the context in which the projections for worldwide structural unemployment stemming from the new technologies are part of the picture of the homework economy. As robotics and related technologies put men out of work in "developed" countries and exacerbate failure to generate male jobs in Third World "development," and as the automated office becomes the rule even in labor-surplus countries, the feminization of work intensifies. Black women in the United States have long known what it looks like to face the structural underemployment ("feminization") of black men, as well as their own highly vulnerable position in the wage economy. It is no longer a secret that sexuality, reproduction, family, and community life are interwoven with this economic structure in myriad ways which have also differentiated the situations of white and black women. Many more women and men will contend with similar situations, which will make cross-gender and race alliances on issues of basic life support (with or without jobs) necessary, not just nice.

The new communications technologies are fundamental to the eradication of "public life" for everyone. This facilitates the mushrooming of a permanent high-tech military establishment at the cultural and economic expense of most people, but especially of women. Technologies like video games and highly miniaturized television seem crucial to production of modern forms of "private life." The culture of video games is heavily oriented to individual competition and extraterrestrial warfare. High-tech, gendered imaginations are produced here, imaginations that can contemplate destruction of the planet and a sci-fi escape from its consequences. More than our imaginations is militarized; and the other realities of electronic and nuclear warfare are inescapable.

The new technologies affect the social relations of both sexuality and of reproduction, and not always in the same ways. The close ties of sexuality and instrumentality, of views of the body as a kind of private satisfaction- and utility-maximizing machine, are described nicely in sociobiological origin stories that stress a genetic calculus and explain the inevitable dialectic of domination of male and female gender roles. These sociobiological stories depend on a high-tech view of the body as a biotic component or cybernetic communications system. Among the many transformations of reproductive situations is the medical one, where women's bodies have boundaries newly permeable to both "visualization" and "intervention." Of course, who controls the interpretation of bodily boundaries in medical hermeneutics is a major feminist issue. The speculum served as an icon of women's claiming their bodies in the 1970s; that handcraft tool is inadequate to express our needed body politics in the negotiation of reality in the practices of cyborg reproduction. Self-help is not enough. The technologies of visualization recall the important cultural practice of hunting with the camera and the deeply predatory nature of a photographic consciousness. Sex, sexuality, and reproduction are central actors in high-tech myth systems structuring our imaginations of personal and social possibility.

Another critical aspect of the social relations of the new technologies is the reformulation of expectations, culture, work, and reproduction for the large scientific and technical work force. A major social and political danger is the formation of a strongly bimodal social structure, with the masses of women and men of all ethnic groups, but especially people of color, confined to a homework economy, illiteracy of several varieties, and general redundancy and impotence, controlled by high-tech repressive apparatuses ranging from entertainment to surveillance and disappearance. An adequate socialist-feminist politics should address women in privileged occupational categories, and particularly in the production of science and technology that constructs scientific-technical discourses, processes, and objects.

This issue is only one aspect of inquiry into the possibility of a feminist science, but it is important. What kind of constitutive role in the production of knowledge, imagination, and practice can new groups doing science have? How can these groups be allied with progressive social and political movements? What kind of political accountability can be constructed to tie women together across the scientific-technical hierarchies separating us? Might there be ways of developing feminist science/technology politics in alliance with antimilitary science facility conversion action groups? Many scientific and technical workers in Silicon Valley, the high-tech cowboys included, do not want to work on military science. Can these personal preferences and cultural tendencies be welded into progressive politics among this professional middle class in which women, including women of color, are coming to be fairly numerous?

Women in the Integrated Circuit

Let me summarize the picture of women's historical locations in advanced industrial societies, as these positions have been restructured partly through the social relations of science and technology. If it was ever possible ideologically to characterize women's lives by the distinction of public and private domains – suggested by images of the division of working-class life into factory and home, of bourgeois life into market and home, and of gender existence into personal and political realms – it is now a totally misleading ideology, even to show how both terms of these dichotomies construct each other in practice and in theory. I prefer a network ideological image, suggesting the profusion of spaces and identities and the permeability of boundaries in the personal body and in the body politic. "Networking" is both a feminist practice and a multinational corporate strategy – weaving is for oppositional cyborgs.

The only way to characterize the informatics of domination is as a massive intensification of insecurity and cultural impoverishment, with common failure of subsistence networks for the most vulnerable. Since much of this picture interweaves with the social relations of science and technology, the urgency of a socialist-feminist politics addressed to science and technology is plain. There is much now being done, and the grounds for political work are rich. For example, the efforts to develop forms of collective struggle for women in paid work, like SEIU's District 925, should be a high priority for all of us. These efforts are profoundly tied to technical restructuring of labor processes and reformations of working classes. These efforts are also providing understanding of a more comprehensive kind of labor organization, involving community, sexuality, and family issues never privileged in the largely white male industrial unions.

The structural rearrangements related to the social relations of science and technology evoke strong ambivalence. But it is not necessary to be ultimately depressed by the implications of late-twentieth-century women's relation to all aspects of work, culture, production of knowledge, sexuality, and reproduction. For excellent reasons, most Marxisms see domination best and have

270

trouble understanding what can only look like false consciousness and people's complicity in their own domination in late capitalism. It is crucial to remember that what is lost, perhaps especially from women's points of view, is often virulent forms of oppression, nostalgically naturalized in the face of current violation. Ambivalence toward the disrupted unities mediated by high-tech culture requires not sorting consciousness into categories of "clearsighted critique grounding a solid political epistemology" versus "manipulated false consciousness," but subtle understanding of emerging pleasures, experiences, and powers with serious potential for changing the rules of the game.

There are grounds for hope in the emerging bases for new kinds of unity across race, gender, and class, as these elementary units of socialist-feminist analysis themselves suffer protean transformations. Intensifications of hardship experienced worldwide in connection with the social relations of science and technology are severe. But what people are experiencing is not transparently clear, and we lack sufficiently subtle connections for collectively building effective theories of experience. Present efforts – Marxist, psychoanalytic, feminist, anthropological – to clarify even "our" experience are rudimentary.

I am conscious of the odd perspective provided by my historical position – a PhD in biology for an Irish Catholic girl was made possible by Sputnik's impact on US national science education policy. I have a body and mind as much constructed by the post–World War II arms race and Cold War as by the women's movements. There are more grounds for hope by focusing on the contradictory effects of politics designed to produce loyal American technocrats, which as well produced large numbers of dissidents, rather than by focusing on the present defeats.

The permanent partiality of feminist points of view has consequences for our expectations of forms of political organization and participation. We do not need a totality in order to work well. The feminist dream of a common language, like all dreams for a perfectly true language, of perfectly faithful naming of experience, is a totalizing and imperialist one. In that sense, dialectics too is a dream language, longing to resolve contradiction. Perhaps, ironically, we can learn from our fusions with animals and machines how not to be Man, the embodiment of Western logos. From the point of view of pleasure in these potent and taboo fusions, made inevitable by the social relations of science and technology, there might indeed be a feminist science.

Cyborgs: A Myth of Political Identity

Earlier I suggested that "women of color" might be understood as a cyborg identity, a potent subjectivity synthesized from fusions of outsider identities. There are material and cultural grids mapping this potential. Audre Lorde

271

captures the tone in the title of her *Sister Outsider*. In my political myth, Sister Outsider is the offshore woman, whom US workers, female and feminized, are supposed to regard as the enemy preventing their solidarity, threatening their security. Onshore, inside the boundary of the United States, Sister Outsider is a potential amidst the races and ethnic identities of women manipulated for division, competition, and exploitation in the same industries. "Women of color" are the preferred labor force for the science-based industries, the real women for whom the worldwide sexual market, labor market, and politics of reproduction kaleidoscope into daily life. Young Korean women hired in the sex industry and in electronics assembly are recruited from high schools, educated for the integrated circuit. Literacy, especially in English, distinguishes the "cheap" female labor so attractive to the multinationals.

Contrary to orientalist stereotypes of the "oral primitive," literacy is a special mark of women of color, acquired by US black women as well as men through a history of risking death to learn and to teach reading and writing. Writing has a special significance for all colonized groups. Writing has been crucial to the Western myth of the distinction of oral and written cultures, primitive and civilized mentalities, and more recently to the erosion of that distinction in "postmodernist" theories attacking the phallogocentrism of the West with its worship of the monotheistic, phallic, authoritative, and singular word, the unique and perfect name. Contests for the meanings of writing are a major form of contemporary political struggle. Releasing the play of writing is deadly serious. The poetry and stories of US women of color are repeatedly about writing, about access to the power to signify; but this time that power must be neither phallic nor innocent. Cyborg writing must not be about the Fall, the imagination of a once-upon-a-time wholeness before language, before writing, before Man. Cyborg writing is about the power to survive, not on the basis of original innocence, but on the basis of seizing the tools to mark the world that marked them as other.

The tools are often stories, retold stories, versions that reverse and displace the hierarchical dualisms of naturalized identities. In retelling origin stories, cyborg authors subvert the central myths of origin of Western culture. We have all been colonized by those origin myths, with their longing for fulfillment in apocalypse. The phallogocentric origin stories most crucial for feminist cyborgs are built into the literal technologies – technologies that write the world, biotechnology and microelectronics – that have recently textualized our bodies as code problems on the grid of C^{3}I. Feminist cyborg stories have the task of recoding communication and intelligence to subvert command and control.

Figuratively and literally, language politics pervade the struggles of women of color; and stories about language have a special power in the rich contemporary writing by US women of color. For example, retellings of the story of the indigenous woman Malinche, mother of the mestizo "bastard" race of the new world, master of languages, and mistress of Cortes, carry special meaning for Chicana constructions of identity. Cherríe Moraga, in *Loving in the War Years,* explores the themes of identity when one never possessed the original language, never told the original story, never resided in the harmony of legitimate heterosexuality in the garden of culture, and so cannot base identity on a myth or a fall from innocence and right to natural names, mother's or father's. Moraga's writing, her superb literacy, is presented in her poetry as the same kind of violation as Malinche's mastery of the conqueror's language – a violation, an illegitimate production, that allows survival. Moraga's language is not "whole"; it is self-consciously spliced, a chimera of English and Spanish, both conqueror's languages. But it is this chimeric monster, without claim to an original language before violation, that crafts the erotic, competent, potent identities of women of color. Sister Outsider hints at the possibility of world survival not because of her innocence, but because of her ability to live on the boundaries, to write without the founding myth of original wholeness, with its inescapable apocalypse of final return to a deathly oneness that Man has imagined to be the innocent and all-powerful Mother, freed at the End from another spiral of appropriation by her son. Writing marks Moraga's body, affirms it as the body of a woman of color, against the possibility of passing into the unmarked category of the Anglo father or into the orientalist myth of "original illiteracy" of a mother that never was. Malinche was mother here, not Eve before eating the forbidden fruit. Writing affirms Sister Outsider, not the Woman-before-the-Fall-into-Writing needed by the phallogocentric Family of Man.

Writing is pre-eminently the technology of cyborgs, etched surfaces of the late twentieth century. Cyborg politics is the struggle for language and the struggle against perfect communication, against the one code that translates all meaning perfectly, the central dogma of phallogocentrism. That is why cyborg politics insist on noise and advocate pollution, rejoicing in the illegitimate fusions of animal and machine. These are the couplings which make Man and Woman so problematic, subverting the structure of desire, the force imagined to generate language and gender and so subverting the structure and modes of reproduction of "Western" identity, of nature and culture, of mirror and eye, slave and master, body and mind. "We" did not originally choose to be cyborgs, but choice grounds a liberal politics and epistemology that imagines the reproduction of individuals before the wider replications of "texts."

From the perspective of cyborgs, freed of the need to ground politics in "our" privileged position of the oppression that incorporates all other dominations, the innocence of the merely violated, the ground of those closer to nature, we can see powerful possibilities. Feminisms and Marxisms have run

273

aground on Western epistemological imperatives to construct a revolutionary subject from the perspective of a hierarchy of oppressions and/or a latent position of moral superiority, innocence, and greater closeness to nature. With no available original dream of a common language or original symbiosis promising protection from hostile "masculine" separation, but written into the play of a text that has no finally privileged reading or salvation history, to recognize "oneself" as fully implicated in the world, frees us of the need to root politics in identification, vanguard parties, purity, and mothering. Stripped of identity, the bastard race teaches about the power of the margins and the importance of a mother like Malinche. Women of color have transformed her from the evil mother of masculinist fear into the originally literate mother who teaches survival.

To recapitulate, certain dualisms have been persistent in Western traditions; they have all been systemic to the logics and practices of domination of women, people of color, nature, workers, animals – in short, domination of all constituted as *others*, whose task is to mirror the self. Chief among these troubling dualisms are self/other, mind/body, culture/nature, male/female, civilized/primitive, reality/appearance, whole/part, agent/resource, maker/ made, active/passive, right/wrong, truth/illusion, total/partial, God/man. The self is the One who is not dominated, who knows that by the service of the other; the other is the one who holds the future, who knows that by the experience of domination, which gives the lie to the autonomy of the self. To be One is to be autonomous, to be powerful, to be God; but to be One is to be an illusion, and so to be involved in a dialectic of apocalypse with the other. Yet to be other is to be multiple, without clear boundary, frayed, insubstantial. One is too few, but two are too many.

High-tech culture challenges these dualisms in intriguing ways. It is not clear who makes and who is made in the relation between human and machine. It is not clear what is mind and what body in machines that resolve into coding practices. Insofar as we know ourselves in both formal discourse (e.g., biology) and in daily practice (e.g., the homework economy in the integrated circuit), we find ourselves to be cyborgs, hybrids, mosaics, chimeras. Biological organisms have become biotic systems, communications devices like others. There is no fundamental, ontological separation in our formal knowledge of machine and organism, of technical and organic.

One consequence is that our sense of connection to our tools is heightened. The trance state experienced by many computer users has become a staple of science fiction film and cultural jokes. Perhaps paraplegics and other severely handicapped people can (and sometimes do) have the most intense experiences of complex hybridization with other communications devices. Why should our bodies end at the skin, or include at best other beings encapsulated by skin? From the seventeenth century till now, machines could be animated –

given ghostly souls to make them speak or move or to account for their orderly development and mental capacities. Or organisms could be mechanized – reduced to body understood as resource of mind. These machine/organism relationships are obsolete, unnecessary. For us, in imagination and in other practice, machines can be prosthetic devices, intimate components, friendly selves. We don't need organic holism to give impermeable wholeness, the total woman and her feminist variants (mutants?).

There are several consequences to taking seriously the imagery of cyborgs as other than our enemies. Our bodies, ourselves; bodies are maps of power and identity. Cyborgs are no exceptions. A cyborg body is not innocent; it was not born in a garden; it does not seek unitary identity and so generate antagonistic dualisms without end (or until the world ends); it takes irony for granted. One is too few, and two is only one possibility. Intense pleasure in skill, machine skill, ceases to be a sin, but an aspect of embodiment. The machine is not an *it* to be animated, worshiped and dominated. The machine is us, our processes, an aspect of our embodiment. We can be responsible for machines; *they* do not dominate or threaten us. We are responsible for boundaries, we are they. Up till now (once upon a time), female embodiment seemed to be given, organic, necessary; and female embodiment seemed to mean skill in mothering and its metaphoric extensions. Only by being out of place could we take intense pleasure in machines, and then with excuses that this was organic activity after all, appropriate to females. Cyborgs might consider more seriously the partial, fluid, sometimes aspect of sex and sexual embodiment. Gender might not be global identity after all.

Cyborg gender is a local possibility taking a global vengeance. Race, gender, and capital require a cyborg theory of wholes and parts. There is no drive in cyborgs to produce total theory, but there is an intimate experience of boundaries, their construction and deconstruction. There is a myth system waiting to become a political language to ground one way of looking at science and technology and challenging the informatics of domination.

Cyborg imagery can help express two crucial arguments in this essay: 1) the production of universal, totalizing theory is a major mistake that misses most of reality, probably always, but certainly now; 2) taking responsibility for the social relations of science and technology means refusing an anti-science metaphysics, a demonology of technology, and so means embracing the skillful task of reconstructing the boundaries of daily life, in partial connection with others, in communication with all of our parts. It is not just that science and technology are possible means of great human satisfaction, as well as a matrix of complex dominations. Cyborg imagery can suggest a way out of the maze of dualisms in which we have explained our bodies and our tools to ourselves. This is a dream not of a common language, but of a powerful infidel heteroglossia. It is an imagination of a feminist speaking in tongues to strike fear into

275

the circuits of the super-savers of the new right. It means both building and destroying machines, identities, categories, relationships, spaces, stories. Though both are bound in the spiral dance, I would rather be a cyborg than a goddess.

Notes

Socialist Review regrets that all the references that originally appeared in this article had to be cut due to space restraints. Many of the ideas in the piece emerged in relations to others, including several graduate students at the History of Consciousness program at the University of California, Santa Cruz.

PART IV

Unfinished Business

17

Production and Power in a Classless Society

A Critical Analysis of the Utopian Dimensions of Marxist Theory

(1981)

Carmen Sirianni

This essay develops a critique of existing Marxist approaches to the concept of a classless society. Its aim is to analyze some of the crucial questions, and critically to reformulate the problems of class and the division of labor, state power and bureaucratic organization, democracy and equality. The practical political import of these theoretical questions should be clear, especially in a world so pressured by egalitarian and democratic demands, and at a time when technological change promises to transform divisions of labor dramatically.

Utopia and Critique

A critical theory of society requires reference to utopian possibilities. The link between utopia and critique in Marx's work was part of the logic of explanation. Insofar as critical social science attempts systematically to uncover the empirical conditions that sustain domination, it must simultaneously formulate the conditions for overcoming that domination. The practical intent is inscribed in the core of critical analysis, if not always explicitly or coherently. A purely "negative critique" is ultimately groundless; a critical theory must justify its normative basis and attempt to elaborate the social possibilities of the human species if it is to have either explanatory or emancipatory power.

This critical logic operates in Marx's analysis of capitalist society. *Capital*'s critique of political economy bases itself on certain normative conceptions. In the first chapter of the first volume, Marx lays the basis for a critique of the commodity form of economic interaction (in which a "definite social relation between men . . . assumes, in their eyes, the fantastic form of a relation between things") by uncovering the particular social relations underlying what appears as simply natural. He historicizes and "denatures" the capitalist mode of production by comparing it to feudalism and a hypothetical Robinson Crusoe. His critique derives its force not simply from this historicization, but from a normative conception of non-alienated social production. In the same chapter of *Capital,* Marx refers to this as "a community of free individuals, carrying on their work with the means of production in common, in which the labour-power of all the different individuals is consciously applied as the combined labour-power of the community." This normative conception anticipates the good society in which the "practical relations of everyday life offer to man none but intelligible and reasonable relations with regard to his fellowmen and Nature," and in which there is no class domination. As an ideal, this retains the concepts that grounded his earlier critique of alienation and the state, namely, "free human production," "species being," "commonwealth" (*Gemeinwesen*), and "communist essence" (*das kommunistische Wesen*). The ideal of a free association of producers runs throughout his monumental critique.

Unfortunately, Marx did not remain consistently conscious of his own method, nor did he elaborate its implications for a critical theory of class. Part of the reason derives from his political battle with the utopian socialists, whom he saw as attempting to institute utopian experiments without understanding the developmental tendencies of capitalism. As a result of the polemics of Marx and Engels, "utopian" became a term of opprobrium for most Marxists. But the main reason seems to have been his own "latent positivism," reflected in his willingness to compare his "science" to the natural sciences, and his inclination towards a productivist interpretation of the forces of social change.

Freedom and equality: these ideals permeate Marx's work, and stamp the goal of a classless society. But their meaning for social theory – as distinct from philosophical speculation – is hardly clear. Where are their concrete possible meanings for social interaction and organization? While Jürgen Habermas has provided an important grounding for them, a general theory of communicative competence and ideal speech cannot *directly* provide the principles for political, economic, administrative, or cultural organization in a free and equal society, even if it must serve as an indispensable guide. Any attempt to theorize the possible institutional contours of a classless society must open itself to the entire range of relevant empirical studies and analytical concepts available in the social sciences, and must systematically formulate the empirical conditions and structural features that might limit the realization of the ideal. The status of such theorizations must, of course, remain tentative, as the truth of such theoretical analysis ultimately depends upon humanity's ability to transform the world in a utopian direction. The utopian theoretical project recognizes the necessity for revisions and variations, as well as the shifting boundaries between the possible and the inconceivable. It must even recognize that a completely classless society may ultimately be impossible, while simultaneously proceeding under a logic of justified hope and critical action and experimentation. Finally, utopian theorizing relevant for social-scientific analysis and political practice does not project the end of history, the elimination of conflict, or the perfect harmonization of individual and society, as does much traditional utopian thought. Inquiring about a free and equal society is not the same as dreaming of heaven on earth.

Class and the Division of Labor

The ideal of classlessness that motivates Marxist theory raises the question: What were the essential determinants of class for Marx? Marx never defined class in a formal and comprehensive manner, nor was his use of the term consistent. One thing it clearly was not, however, was an income category, in the sense either of amount or of source of income. Marx was concerned with a more elegant and structured classification than would result from the infinite fragmentation based on income determinations. Ownership of the means of production has been the most often used criterion among Marxists, and no doubt the one most frequently mentioned by Marx. The two major wings of political Marxism – social democracy and Leninism – have generally seen ownership as the basic criterion of class, and nationalization of the means of production as the decisive step towards socialism. Sociologists have generally agreed that property criteria were the most important for Marx, even when they have rejected those criteria themselves. Council communists, industrial democrats, and various other democratic socialists (including some within the social democratic and Leninist traditions) have claimed that ownership is the basic determinant only when linked to effective control, and thus that socialism implies the democratic control of the major means of production. Marx rarely, and never systematically, spoke about control as a fundamental criterion of class, but the idea is implicit in virtually everything he wrote. Marx's conception of class and his critique of class, however, were not confined to ownership and control. Both in his early and his later writings, the problem of class and its abolition was related to the division of labor itself.

Yet the relationship between class and the division of labor remains unclear. In *The German Ideology*, Marx characterized specialization in any activity as a sign of class organization, and postulated as an essential feature of a classless society the complete elimination of such specialization. In his *Critique of the Gotha Programme* some thirty years later, Marx again characterized communist society in terms of its elimination of the "enslaving subordination of individuals under the division of labor," and explicitly added the division between mental and manual labor. In the *Grundrisse,* the human being in communist society is one removed from the production process per se, who becomes a watchman and regulator, and whose necessary labor time is reduced to a minimum so as to provide time for the free development of the social individual. Such a vision implies the overcoming of the mental/manual division, the elimination of detail labor and, it would seem, the abolition of specialization itself, as in the more rustic imagery of *The German Ideology.*

In *Capital,* Marx developed his most extensive analysis of the connection between capitalist relations of production and the division of labor in the workplace. Capitalist class relations determine the fragmentation of factory work, the concentration of knowledge and control in the hands of the directors of the labor process, the separation of science and labor, and the conversion of the worker into a "crippled monstrosity." The worker, *formally* subsumed under the control of capital through capitalist property relations, becomes increasingly subsumed in a *real* sense as the result of the transformation of the labor process itself. Capitalist class relations express themselves in the very organization of the production process.

Marxists have recently developed this line of analysis, partly as a result of the publication in the West of the previously little-known section of *Capital* entitled "Results of the Immediate Process of Production." The work of Harry Braverman has been crucial in analyzing scientific management in terms of capitalist control of the labor process. The concentration of productive knowledge in management, the dissociation of the labor process from the skills of the workers, and the separation of conception and execution were all part of a capitalist strategy to ensure greater control of the labor process in the interests of profit. The very structure of productive organization, especially since the onset of scientific management, bore the imprint of class control. Since its publication in 1974, Braverman's *Labor and Monopoly Capital* has been criticized and supplemented in various ways. Changes in the organization of the production process, others have argued, cannot be analyzed apart from working-class struggle and organization, internal divisions and international constraints, state actions, and relatively autonomous input by managerial strata. Technical control has not been the final or even the predominant form of capitalist control, nor has there been a unidirectional tendency towards deskilling. The capitalist class has been neither an omniscient nor an omnipotent agent in the transformation of the labor process. Braverman remains ambivalent, however, on the crucial question on which many recent Marxist scholars seem clearly resolved: modern techniques and organizational forms such as the assembly line are primarily, or even solely, the result of the imperatives of class control. These productive forms are thus inherently class forms, and must be completely abolished in the process of creating a classless society.

Productive Integrity versus Global Pluralism

If the contention that modern forms of highly rationalized and fragmented production are *inherently* class forms is to be more than the trivial assertion that they developed in class society (first in capitalist, then, through imitation, in state capitalist or post-capitalist societies), then it must be shown that such productive forms are incompatible with any conception of a classless society, and that other forms of production are so compatible. In other words, the logic of explanation for this level of analysis of class and production under capitalism requires a conception of classlessness. One cannot demonstrate that class "imperatives" are built into particular forms of productive organization simply by showing that capitalists or engineers see them as part of a strategy of control, or even by showing that, under specific conditions of capitalist society, they do in fact enhance managerial control or increase the rate of surplus value. An argument about intention or effect in one mode of production cannot directly serve as an argument about structure or effect in another possible mode. And comparison to other forms of class society, such as feudalism, does not in itself provide the conceptual basis for saying anything about the *general* class character of the labor process. Only a conception of classlessness can permit assertions at this level.

An ideal model of productive organization has begun to emerge among Marxist scholars. I will call this model the "productive integrity" model, since its predominant imagery is that of holism in the production process. Proceeding on the basis of arguments in Marx, Mao, and Braverman, proponents of this model argue that productive organization in a classless society necessarily entails the reunification of socially divided labor, overcoming the split between mental and manual labor, and the reintegration of conception and execution, to permit all workers to understand and hence control the "entire production process." The image is that of a scientifically, technically, and culturally updated craft worker able to control the production process from beginning to end. Some seem to hold that all "fragmented" work is inherently exploitative, a sign of class division and domination. Braverman, in a lecture delivered after the publication of *Labor and Monopoly Capital*, suggested that this is perhaps not so, as long as all workers on the line also participate in engineering, repair, and the full range of more conceptual functions in production. Some, like Michael Burawoy and Stanley Aronowitz, suggest that the reunification of conception

283

and execution is absolutely necessary, but not sufficient. All proponents of the productive integrity model argue, however, that a classless society requires that all workers in each workplace possess the knowledge and skill to enable them to understand and control "the productive process as a whole. Braverman, for instance, outlines the socialization of labor in these terms:

> An automatic system of machinery opens up the possibility of the true control over a highly productive factory by a relatively small corps of workers, providing these workers attain the level of mastery over the machinery offered by engineering knowledge, and providing they then share out among themselves the routines of the operation, from the most technically advanced to the most routine.

In his sketch of a genuinely communist alternative in Eastern Europe, Rudolf Bahro presents a similar picture where "those who construct the machines also worked at them for prolonged periods." And, he continues,

> We can just as well imagine the everyday situation in a hospital, to take an example from a different sphere, one still more strongly burdened with the prejudices of the traditional division of labor, in which the entire staff consisted of people with full medical training, or other pertinent qualifications, who also took part in all nursing and ancillary work, and in social and economic functions as well.

This ideal conception of holism, where all workers share the full range of functions relevant to their particular sphere of work, has become the point of reference for virtually all critical accounts of the development of technology and productive organization under capitalism.

Yet this productive integrity model fails fundamentally as a conception of classlessness. It misconceives the problems and offers spurious and unnecessarily restrictive solutions, in regard to two basic dimensions of the question of class: 1) knowledge and control of societal processes, and 2) access to socially available life and work opportunities.

An adequate conception of class must include more than simple ownership of the means of production. Otherwise, Soviet-type societies which for decades have had nationalized ownership in the major means of production would not be analyzable as class societies, which they clearly are. Ownership is an overly formal criterion for class unless it is linked to control. Control, as productive integrity theorists insist, can be equally formal unless adequate knowledge is available. Knowledge and control together constitute basic determinants of class. Yet, if class is first of all a concept of society-wide dimensions, then knowledge and control must refer in the first instance to knowledge and control over the broadest options of social production and reproduction as a whole. Social class is primarily a global concept, and the knowledge and control that are constituent of it must likewise be of global dimensions.

This does not mean that every socially dominant class literally possesses global knowledge or control, though its decisions on the use of the major means of production do broadly determine the options for social and economic development. Class theory has to take into account class struggle, intra- and inter-national forms of organization, the relative autonomy of various institutions (most notably states), and other factors. The Marxian concept of a classless society, however, does imply the democratization of the control and knowledge relevant for determining the broadest forms of social production and reproduction. But knowledge and control at this level do not dictate particular forms of organization at other levels, including individual productive units. The question of social classlessness does not unambiguously indicate specific forms for the organization of knowledge and control in particular subunits of the social system. Democratization of knowledge and control at the global and local community levels might be consistent with various forms of organization in productive units, with various forms of social and technical relation in production, to use Burawoy's helpful terminology. Likewise, knowledge and control over the "production process as a whole," in the sense usually implied in the productive integrity model (i.e., over the "whole" of particular production processes), in no way directly implies knowledge and control at the societal level. Neither craft knowledge of a particular production process, nor even highly advanced scientific knowledge of an entire branch of production, in themselves provide understanding of global options. The relation between the whole and the parts in a classless society would be highly complex; the productive integrity model misleads when it tends to conflate the two. This conflation results from a peculiar form of productivism (still!) of this anti-productivist Marxism, so that the class division of labor tends to be reduced to the level of particular production processes and units, and the problem of the societal organization of control of productive options tends to get lost. Knowledge and control of "the production process as a whole" has become the naive wisdom of contemporary Marxist students of the labor process, as if the terms were clear, the boundaries defined.

If the knowledge and control implicit in the concept of classlessness refer first of all to the democratization of global options, then the question arises. what conditions might facilitate such general knowledge and control? The productive integrity model sees itself as rather unambiguously answering this question, when it directly links knowledge and control in each productive unit to knowledge and control at the societal level. The direct linkage seems to follow from Braverman's strict distinction between the social division of labor and the detailed division of labor. The former, of course, is inevitably present in all societies. But, while "the social division of labor subdivides *society,* the

285

detailed division of labor subdivides *humans* . . . [and] renders the workers inadequate to carry through any complete production process." The conclusion that tends to be drawn from this is that the worker is thereby also rendered incapable of understanding and intelligently participating in the decisions affecting social production and reproduction at the global level. The detailed division of labor must therefore be eliminated, or those engaging in it must also participate in the full range of more conceptual functions. Conception and execution must be reunited in each worker.

It is questionable whether such total incapacitation in production or in general social participation results even from the experience of highly fragmented work in capitalist society. Nor does it follow that all forms of rationalized and fragmented work would necessarily incapacitate people from general knowledge or control of societal decisions under socialism. First of all, the general conditions affecting knowledge and participation in public affairs are of a broad range, and include family and school socialization, level of education, participation in local politics, general sense of personal and political efficacy, and, clearly, experience at work. In a class society, some of these correlate in specific ways. Family and school socialization, for instance, correlate significantly with class position and parental work roles, though there is hardly strict determination here or between one's own work experience and political participation. Under conditions of formal democratic control of global production options, we would expect work experience to be a significant determinant of feelings of personal and political efficacy. However, we would expect other conditions to be important as well: organization of information, media, type of education, amount of free time, and more.

Second, a classless society can provide individuals a variety of concurrent options for productive activity, thus loosening the connection that exists between the experience of a worker in one particular productive unit and his or her general sense of personal and political efficacy. Clearly, one of the central aims of Marxism from the beginning has been the expansion of individual life and work opportunities, the development of what Bahro has recently called the "rich individuality" of all people. This implies a structure of work options conducive to relatively flexible and fluid individual life courses. Therefore, if the concept of class pertains not only to knowledge and control but also to the distribution of access to socially available life opportunities, and if the idea of going beyond class implies the relative equalization of both of these, it would seem unnecessarily restrictive to link the achievement of such equality to particular work roles. If a great variety of alternative opportunities exists for creative and fulfilling activity within and outside of socially necessary labor, then relative social equality and effective general knowledge and participation as a citizen need not directly depend on advanced or expert knowledge in every productive activity one performs. In other words, not all people who work in the production of transportation vehicles have to be electrical engineers, mechanics, or design technicians in order to be free, equal, active, and effective citizens. Some people who spend some of their time in such production don't have to be any of these and, indeed, may even work at relatively simple and repetitive tasks.

The "holistic" organization of productive units where all workers in each workplace share in the full range of tasks is neither theoretically necessary, practically possible, nor compellingly desirable as a premise for a classless division of labor. We can expect, on the contrary, that people might legitimately wish to have a good deal of flexibility in where and how they fulfill their work responsibilities. This is particularly true regarding tasks without a great deal of inherent interest, which lend themselves to flexibility because they are relatively easy to learn and do not require a high degree of continuity for their effective accomplishment. Among such reasons for flexibility are: 1) shifting patterns of friendship, love, and workmate relations over time; 2) conflicts between family needs and the spatio–temporal requirements of certain jobs; 3) the need for opportunities to test a range of occupational choices by engaging in less than high-level or long-term commitment; 4) health hazards that might be associated with the prolonged performance of certain tasks; 5) particular side-benefits of certain tasks that might warrant wide access and thus require rotation. The latter two raise the question not only of personal flexibility, but of equity and justice – a problem that will be discussed in more detail in the next section. But how could a strict application of holistic principles within particular work units ever establish the basis for relative equality in the societal distribution of work? Both the amount and the type of routine work *and* creative work would hardly be commensurate between different productive units. For instance, holistic production in coal mines and retail stores would hardly be relatively commensurate with holistic production in universities and research laboratories. Nor could we always be able (or want) to redefine and reorganize the units involved to eliminate such imbalances and inequalities without introducing structural inflexibility of other sorts. Just as the problem of distributive equality in material resources cannot be solved simply by participatory democracy within the workplace, so the problem of relative equality of work opportunities and contributions in the social division of labor cannot be solved by the principle of holism within individual work units. Indeed, holism within units could conceivably serve to legitimate significant and unacceptable inequalities between units, and hence among occupational groups and individuals. Broader principles are required to establish the basis for significant personal flexibility and relative social equality.

The key word here is "alternative." Any model of a free and equal classless society consistent with Marx's intention to expand individual life opportunities must encourage a great variety of personal and social alternatives for the use of productive resources. We cannot dogmatically rule out the possibility that people might choose to organize certain production processes in a relatively rationalized or fragmented manner, if it allows them more free time or options for creative work in other areas. Nor can we rule out less than "holistic" work commitments if this permits desired flexibility and relative equalization of other work opportunities. This is particularly important in view of the fact that alternatives must be created in the context of inherited technologies and divisions of labor in a world of extremely uneven development. The latter will inevitably leave their imprint on the creation of utopian forms, since the relative costs and benefits of various egalitarian strategies will vary considerably. Research in alternative forms of work organization has pointed to the relative autonomy of different levels of participation, and the significant impact on motivation and satisfaction of even relatively limited forms of job enrichment. Nothing in the empirical literature on political or industrial participation indicates that high-level holistic participation by each worker in each unit is *necessary* for an active and motivated laboring citizenry.

This by no means rules out the possibility of relative holism in some or many forms of work, nor does it ignore the problems of certain forms of flexible work arrangements. But a classless society must be fundamentally pluralist in the variety of options available for the satisfaction of individual and social needs, while securing relative equality and effective democratic control through global mechanisms (though not necessarily only global ones). To link either equality or global control to particular forms of productive activity seems unnecessarily restrictive, if not potentially repressive, and inevitably self-defeating. The relationship between micro- and macro-levels has never been simple and direct, and in a global pluralist model of a classless society it will be quite complex. Although it is understandable how Braverman, in the face of the dominant industrial sociology, could insist on a strict distinction between the division of labor in the workshop and in society, it is fundamentally misleading to premise the resolution of class divisions on the total reintegration of productive functions at the level of the individual productive unit. A theory of participation with emancipatory and egalitarian intentions must theorize the great array of conditions facilitating and impeding global knowledge and control of social production and reproduction, and not proceed from theoretically restrictive assumptions about the organization and experience of particular workplace units under capitalism or Soviet-style socialism.

Historical Materialism and the Exchange of Labor

My argument has been that the productive integrity model does not adequately conceptualize two central problems for any theory of a classless society: 1) the conditions for general knowledge and control over the global options of social reproduction; and 2) the conditions for relatively equal access to a pluralistic array of work and life opportunities. The alternative I have proposed asserts that there are many possibilities for organizing people's social contributions (i.e., necessary labor) in a way consistent both with adequate general knowledge and equal power to influence global decisions, and with securing relatively equal life opportunities. If this is correct, then Marxists face the challenge of articulating the principles according to which labor might be organized and exchanged in a classless society to ensure both relative equality and pluralism of options.

Paradoxically, little direct assistance for this task will be found in Marx. While the question of the organization and exchange of labor is central to Marxism, its problems vanish when Marx theorizes about the classless society. The problems disappear because, in his reflections on the higher stage of communism, Marx does not remain a consistent materialist. When Marx writes about the classless society, he crosses the boundary from a materialistically grounded critical-utopian social theory to traditional utopian thought rooted in the myth of total reconciliation and harmony.

"Economy of time, to this all economy ultimately reduces itself." Here Marx articulated what should be a fundamental tenet of a materialist social theory. *Capital* is itself a treatise on time, on the organization and forms of appearance of socially committed time under capitalism. Labor is a basic category of Marxism only insofar as it has temporal dimensions. And this is true even in a possible communist society. As Marx notes, the economy of labor time "remains the first economic law on the basis of communal production. It becomes law, there, to an even higher degree." Time, however, is *always relatively scarce,* and this fact impresses itself on every conceivable society faced with the task of organizing labor for the needs of its present and future members. No doubt the contours of our experience of time can change. Yet while revolutionaries may shoot the clocks, as they did in 1848, even a successful revolution under propitious conditions would have to reset them. The temporal tyranny of a civilization that commodifies our time hardly seems necessary in a rationally organized socialist society. But time, nonetheless, continues to "pass," with a very definite material relentlessness. And it always will.

The *relative* scarcity of time is a universal feature of individual and social life. Every commitment of socially necessary labor has costs, in the sense of possible alternative uses of relatively scarce labor time. It could never be a matter of general indifference either to society as a whole or to individual members how their time is organized. Every economy, then, including a possible classless economy, must organize relative scarcity. Marx, however, despite his brilliant analysis of the forms of labor time in *Capital,* loses sight of this in his discussions of communism. His vision of the future relies on an objectivistically conceived notion of the abolition of scarcity, as if there were some absolute point of general social affluence and productivity beyond which it would no longer be necessary to organize an economy of scarce time. Thus, he argues in *The German Ideology* that in a communist society each individual can "do one thing today and another tomorrow, to hunt in the morning, fish in the afternoon, rear cattle in the evening, criticize after dinner," *just as each has a mind to,* without any necessary special commitment to any of these activities. The possibility of a divergence between individual desire and social requirement has disappeared. The social regulation of productive commitments is no longer necessary. The continuity of commitments to specific tasks is no longer a problem.

In his *Critique of the Gotha Programme* thirty years later, Marx expresses the same perspective. As the division of labor breaks down and cooperative wealth flows abundantly, society can be organized according to the principle "from each according to his ability, to each according to his needs." Social and individual development are so great as to preclude any divergence between needs and contributions among people. No standards for the exchange of labor are therefore necessary. Even egalitarian standards reflect the "narrow horizon of bourgeois right," and will be "fully left behind." In these conceptions, the basic problems for any social division of labor have fallen out, and along with them the foundations of materialism itself. The invisible hand of a fully developed communism beyond scarcity now becomes the automatic regulator, ensuring the harmonization of individual needs and contributions. This is utopia as reconciliation myth, not utopia as the critical dimension of social theory.

Since time is always relatively scarce, and since, therefore, it could never be a matter of general indifference how it is utilized, even a classless society must develop social standards for the exchange of labor. The complexity of such standards increases with the complexity and specificity of the goals which the standards are designed to achieve. The global pluralist model attempts to secure: 1) a basic pluralism of options for the social and technical organization of various areas of production, depending on democratically mediated decisions as to the relative costs and benefits of these; 2) a basic pluralism of options for the individual fulfillment of one's share of socially necessary labor; and 3) the systematic distribution of life opportunities (creative work, free time, etc.) in a relatively egalitarian manner. Given the various types of work to be done and their different social and technical organization, we must also allow for the possibility that differential weight may be assigned to various jobs in the calculation of contributions to socially necessary labor (e.g., jobs that are particularly unpleasant, inconvenient, or hazardous, or that can't be widely rotated). In any case, these goals necessitate the development of standards for the exchange of necessary labor, standards through which contributions of

290

social labor can be made commensurate. Only through such standards could the relative equality of rights (and, implicitly, responsibilities) in the sphere of social production be determined at all. Indeed, the very meaning of "equality" in a classless society is linked to the articulation of such standards.

Standards for the equivalent exchange of labor in a system where production is socially regulated do not have to be based on abstract labor time, as they tend to be under capitalism (though various factors significantly modify this). Such standards can take into account various qualitative differences in concrete labor. They can express qualitative evaluations of different types of work, and they can be determined democratically. Hence, the meaning of particular types of standards can be debated. Indeed, public debate is absolutely crucial, if the system of social labor is not to be governed by "fetishized" relations, be they commodity relations or opaque administrative rules. Thus, even if it is conceivable to move beyond the law of value of capitalist society, some type of law of value will be essential to the regulation of production in a classless society. (Marx understood this in his economic writings, even though the principles he articulated in his utopian speculations on communism remove the basis for any determination of value standards.) Value standards will be necessary, if the distribution of social labor is to function in a *systematically* egalitarian manner, and yet permit a great array of options for social labor, and hence labor mobility. These standards provide the "discipline" in the system, analogous to the capitalist market.

Planning, councilist, and market socialist theories have not systematically raised the full range of questions relevant for a social system that might provide simultaneously for the elimination of a class division of labor, a pluralism of options for social labor, and the democratic determination of the criteria and mechanisms for its organization and exchange. Yet the very meaning of equality depends on the articulation of such models and criteria.

Class, Power, and Authority: Whither the State?

These reflections on class, the division of labor, and scarcity raise the issue of power and authority in social and political life. Marxism has typically linked these concepts by reducing the question of power to the question of class. This class reductionism has blocked the development of a general political and legal theory. (And under the conditions of revolutionary development in Russia, this reductionism encouraged the transformation of the Marxist theory of the state into a legitimating ideology for authoritarian statism.)

In a fully developed communist society, the Marxian wisdom goes, political power will disappear. With the elimination of classes, the abolition of the division between mental and manual labor, and the development of the productive forces by the associated producers, no special coercive apparatus will be necessary because there will be no class to be kept in subordination. "People will *grow accustomed* to observing the elementary conditions of social existence *without force and without subjection.*" Observance of the everyday rules of social life will become a habit. The responsibilities of work and the rewards of distribution will be allocated spontaneously and harmoniously, so that no calculation according to standards of justice and equality will be necessary. "From each according to his ability, to each according to his needs," will be the sole criterion for social contribution and individual reward. The social division of labor will thus be completely voluntary and no individual commitment to any necessary social task need be mandated. As the species' control over nature is perfected, the government of persons will be replaced by the "administration of things" and the "watching over of the true interests of society." The latter are unambiguous and served voluntarily, because they completely converge with every individual interest. The rules of social interaction become simply those of everyday civility. Democracy, which is nothing but the last and highest form of the state for the subjugation of the minority by the working majority, will itself become unnecessary and wither away.

This conception of the "withering of the state" is based on Marx's notion of the abolition of scarcity. Yet even a classless society must organize an economy of (scarce) time, and every decision to allocate resources implies a specific use of that time. The elimination of scarcity is inconceivable and so, therefore, is the dissolution of social power which is premised on it. Every ranking of needs implies that the priorities of some may not be satisfied. Conflict, therefore, will remain a basic feature of social life. Every allocation of social resources expresses social power. The "administration of things" can never be an apolitical or conflict-free process of resource adjustment, since "things" are ultimately reducible to human time and labor. The problem of social and political power, and hence of conflict, is not reducible to the problem of class.

Given relative scarcity and varied individual life possibilities, we can never assume the automatic harmonization of individuals' priorities for the use of their time. It is thus necessary to articulate the principles that organize socially necessary labor and socially available rewards. (The question of power in social life, of legal rights and responsibilities, is not one that can be theorized simply in relation to social labor. I make my argument here, since this is where Marx states his case most strongly.) There must be a system of norms governing access to work options – even in a society where the means of production are collectively owned and democratically managed, and where the class division of labor has been overcome. Standards reflecting equal rights must also denote equal responsibilities. Since the relations of value in the exchange of labor are based on such standards, the political economy of a classless society is fundamentally "political," and hence ultimately backed up by the possibility of coercion.

The *systematic application* of egalitarian *norms* for the organization of social labor and its fruits will thus be indispensable in the most highly developed classless society imaginable. This will be true *even if* the various levels of decentralized decision-making (networks of family, friends, workmates, local community) permit considerable flexibility in the application of such norms. And it will be true *even if* the "subsidization" of individuals and groups by others (e.g., through the assumption of extra work responsibilities) is so available, and the struggle for existence so pacified, that no meticulous calculation of fulfillment of responsibilities is necessary. Such possibilities for institutionalized and informal flexibility are crucial to a society that devotes itself to the development of each person's individuality. Indeed, here is the truth of Marx's dicta, "from each according to his ability, to each according to his needs," and "the free development of each is the condition for the free development of all." But the converse of this latter principle is just as important: equal opportunities for the free development of all are the condition for the free development of each. Thus, options for individual flexibility in social labor must proceed from the recognition of the prior right of every individual to relatively equal access to the social resources which are the condition for such individual development. This prior right entails the prior responsibility to fulfill the tasks allocated according to democratic and egalitarian norms (areas of both "autonomous decisions" and "mutual guarantees" beyond the reach of simple majorities can and should be collectively designated). Legitimate deviation must still be seen as deviation from an egalitarian norm and must occur according to rules consistent with such norms. Other forms of deviation, or the completely haphazard application of such norms, would implicitly deprive others of their equal rights to socially available "goods." And, perhaps equally important, it would deprive others of the rightful security of knowing where their social responsibility ended and their freely disposable personal time began.

The determination and systematic application of social norms to collectively made decisions on the use of social resources imply the delegation of legitimate *authority* for *monitoring* and *enforcing* such norms, and regulating possible conflict. Even a classless communist society, therefore, will require political and legal institutions through which such social decisions are made, alternative norms debated, and decisions enforced. As individuals in a classless society internalize the norms for the fulfillment of their responsibilities – and one would expect this to increase as existing social arrangements are seen as legitimate, equitable, and responsible – political and legal institutions would be able to operate less oppressively and obtrusively. Nor does the existence of such institutions presume any particular form of enforcement or sanction, or completely preclude informal moral pressure and communication/education as the more desirable forms for the expression of such sanctions. But such institutions – institutions that are focal points for the exercise of social power and not merely the neutral, nonpolitical administration of things – must exist if social interaction under conditions of relative scarcity is to be regulated at all. The complete "withering of the state" is inconceivable, even in a highly developed classless society. The need for a general Marxist political and legal theory with relevance to a "good society" must no longer be displaced by appeals to the abolition of classes and scarcity, to the "casting off of all natural limitations," to a unitary species subject or "the general interest," to the "new man" for whom work has become a vital need and the harmonization of all interests and needs occurs spontaneously. We cannot afford to take the idea of "free association" as self-explanatory, as Marx tended to do.

Paradoxes of Democracy

Although "democracy" would be central to a possible classless society, its meaning is far from unambiguous. Clearly, democracy implies some notion of universal and equal rights of participation in the polity, along with majority rule, procedural guarantees, and minority rights. In a complex society, however, the polity is highly differentiated into decision-making units of various competencies and constituencies, the relations among which can be quite multiform. In this section, I would like to raise some general questions about criteria for decision-making in a possible classless society, conceived in terms of global pluralism, in the hope that such reflection will contribute to more consistent theorizing.

At the global level of decision-making the criterion of universal and equal suffrage seems unproblematic as a measure of fair and democratic representation. The ideal of all citizens as equal members of the polity requires no justification in the democratic socialist tradition. But in any conceivable complex socialist society, as well as in all sizable subunits, it would be impossible for each citizen to participate and communicate *directly* with every other citizen in an effective two-way process – even given the most sophisticated communications media. Representation, therefore, would be indispensable. Communication must be asymmetrically structured, and information asymmetrically processed, since not everyone can effectively communicate on each decision, and not all relevant information can be effectively made available to everyone. Methods of direct democracy, while possible in small groups and organizations, are of restricted applicability in larger ones, and beyond a certain point have high costs that may undermine both democracy and efficiency.

The asymmetry of representative forms of democracy, however, need not contradict the symmetrical assumptions embodied in universal and equal political rights, if two conditions are met: effective mechanisms exist for public scrutiny and possible recall of elected officials by their electors; and political discussion and competition are organized so that the practical ramifications of alternative policies are clarified in a manner that is comprehensible to the ordinary citizen. Both these vertical and horizontal aspects – control and competition – are essential to our normative conception of democracy and the possibility of effective individual choice.

There is also no a priori reason to assume that democratic control over global options could maintain a relatively equal distribution of life opportunities *only* if politics were completely deprofessionalized. The elimination of the class division of labor does not necessarily imply the abolition of a division of labor in the sphere of political representation. Indeed, a certain degree of professionalization of politics would seem necessary if technical experts are not to assume control of the political agenda. As Weber noted long ago, in large organizations, or ones whose functions require technical training or continuity in policy, permanently appointed technical experts would tend to win the upper hand over government councils who were amateurs. A tendency toward technocratic solutions is permanent in any society dependent on a high level of technical expertise, including one that had abolished strict divisions between manual and mental labor. These technocratic tendencies may be controlled by institutionalizing various forms of competition so that a range of alternative technical arguments for any given problem will be publicly represented. Technocratic tendencies might also be checked by providing a continuity of political representatives responsible for the general articulation of overall options and their practical consequences. The latter cannot be left to technical experts as such. Yet political accountability requires a certain degree of continuity of service to be effective. Without professionalizing political tasks, technical rationales will tend to determine the political agenda. Such continuity places restrictions on office-holding by lot and rotation, and probably implies as well the aggregation of demands and proposals through competing political parties. Since there is never an unambiguous "general interest," it is unlikely that there could ever be a genuinely democratic government "above differences," and hence probably not one "above parties." To avoid institutionalizing such competition is to invite authoritarianism of one form or another. People who are professional "politicians" need not accumulate uncontrollable power or disproportionate material privileges. Such a tendency may be powerful. But so, indeed, may be the contradictions from which it arises, namely, the difficulties of achieving effective democratic control over highly complex issues without professionalizing responsibility and accountability. The range of possibilities for institutionalizing both relative social equality and effective political democracy in a complex society have yet to be seriously theorized in the Marxist tradi-

295

tion. Appeals to the myth of the Paris Commune are hardly an adequate substitute for social analysis.

Nor are the tasks of theorizing democracy as obvious as many proponents of workers' control would have us believe. If democracy is normatively unproblematic at the global level of a classless society (even if extremely complex and difficult to achieve), it can hardly be unproblematic in the multifarious units and networks that constitute the substructure. The criteria for decision-making most relevant at one institutional level are not necessarily most relevant in another. And workplace units present a set of very special problems.

Productive work can be organized in a great variety of ways, depending on the perceived balance of relative costs and benefits. Rationalized, relatively fragmented, and routine work is conceivable as a choice that people might wish to make for some work units, if the benefits in output, free time, or other work opportunities were seen to outweigh the costs. Significant levels of rotation or mobility of jobs not only within but among workplaces is also a likely, and probably very desirable, option. If either or both of these options were chosen to any significant degree, then 1) levels of workers' knowledge directly relevant to particular productive units would be uneven, and in many cases highly so; 2) the amount of time spent by workers in particular units would also be uneven; and 3) individual workers would be able to fulfill their responsibilities for social labor in a great variety of ways, and hence the overall number of units in which they worked would vary considerably.

Given the complex constellation of possibilities implied by even a limited application of pluralist principles for social labor, it becomes clear that the criteria for democracy in the polity as a whole are not necessarily directly relevant in each productive unit. Indeed, an across-the-board formula of one person, one vote in *all* matters pertaining to the operation of a particular unit could undermine overall principles of a classless society designed to secure equality and plurality of life chances on the basis of general democratic principles. Since such equality and plurality cannot be secured in any one productive unit, decision-making processes in particular units must operate within constraints decided at a more general level. This holds true even if there is significant decentralization, and lower-level units participate in establishing the guidelines of the higher levels. Democratic decisions taken by more general level units operating more uniformly according to principles of equal representation must take precedence over those units with very particular functions. The latter have intricate connections to, dependencies on, and definite effects upon other units, and hence affect the work and life options of people not in their immediate workplace constituency. The "system capacity" to provide egalitarian and pluralist options on a broad scale will place limits on the "citizen effectiveness" that tends to be more available in smaller units. Both equality and plurality of work and life options imply a prior status for global democratic forms. The inevitable competition among units operating in an environment of relatively scarce factors makes this global democratic priority even more necessary.

Nor do equality and plurality require total democratization within each productive unit. Where levels of relevant knowledge were highly unequal, such total democracy would inevitably remain formal in regard to technical questions. Even equal formal decision-making power for all workers in a productive unit (regardless of the amount of time they spend there, the continuity of their commitment, or the level of relevant knowledge they possess) offers neither an obviously fair way to distribute internal power nor a flexible approach to productive choices that bear directly on the life and work options of people outside of that unit.

"Workers' control" is a crucial aspect of any pluralist conception of a classless society. Clearly, for those people performing primarily routine tasks in certain work units (while performing more creative/conceptual ones in others), a voice in general working conditions and health and safety aspects is a minimal requirement, as would be definite procedures for grievances and technical recommendations as well. Beyond this there are many possibilities for participation and control, depending on the nature of the productive unit and the composition of the work force. My intention is not to restrict that range unnecessarily. Rather, I want to point to some ways in which full and equal suffrage in each productive unit might be inconsistent with more general forms of democracy, and the relative equality and plurality of life and work options that such general forms are intended to secure. Forms of authority in particular units should be analyzed in relation to broader decision processes and goals, as well as relevant local factors. We cannot proceed from the assumption that all forms of democracy are consistent with one another, or have no costs that might be questioned by rational, democratically minded people. *Equality of control over one's life, which is the aim of a global pluralist model, does not necessarily imply equality of control over each particular institutional sphere in which one is involved.*

The scarcity of time is fundamental to all social organization, as noted above. All participation in decision-making processes costs time, whether in meetings or in acquiring the knowledge and information relevant to such decisions. And time spent in such ways is time not spent on other things that might be of equal or more value to particular individuals or groups of people. As Robert Dahl has argued, the value of participating in decisions depends on a range of factors: the enjoyment derived from such participation, the importance of the matters being decided, and the differences at stake in the alternatives; the likelihood that one's participation will affect the outcome, and the competency of the participant. While participation would certainly be a very salient value in a democratic and egalitarian society, no philosophical or political justification permits considering it an absolute value, regardless of the costs, as many councilist and anarchist proponents imply.

Thus a genuinely democratic and pluralist society must recognize the right to limit participation in certain areas of decision-making according to agreed-upon criteria. It must recognize the right of individuals *not* to participate directly in certain decisions of institutions of which they are members. It must also recognize, as derivative of this, the right of majorities to circumscribe certain types of participation rights of all but specially delegated representatives. Without the possibility of such restrictions, majorities that might not view direct participation as a priority would be forced to participate or be subject to decisions made by unrepresentative minorities. And the necessity for calculating the relative importance of participation time increases with the expansion of the number of units of which one is a "member." Hence the more pluralist the work and life options available to people, the more likely that democracy will imply restricted participation rights of various sorts, though the latter by no means rules out recourse to general participatory controls when appropriate. Not to recognize the necessity for restrictions, however, contradicts the principles of democracy and pluralism that are essential to the idea of a classless society.

These theoretical problems in the theory of democracy are inevitable. They could be avoided only by making very questionable assumptions about the possible uniformity of people's preferred needs and uses of their time, or by postulating an easy harmonization of needs among individuals and among the various units of decision-making. Both the productive integrity model, and a community integrity model akin to it, tend to make such assumptions. Thus the former never even poses the question of multiple possibilities for organizing work and for fulfilling responsibilities for social labor. It simply assumes that all would want to spend the better part of their socially committed time in one particular unit, acquire advanced knowledge and skill relevant to the functioning of that unit, and spend a great deal of time participating in its decisions. André Gorz goes so far as to prescribe the costs of large-scale technologies that *must* be renounced, if the autonomy and conviviality of "real communities" is to be preserved. Not only are options unilaterally preempted, but a further assumption is made: that people will agree on the relative importance to them of such "real" productive communities. The presumption is that all members of a particular productive or territorial unit would seek "holistic" satisfactions from it, or be easily capable and desirous of transplanting themselves to find such. A genuinely pluralist conception of a classless society cannot theoretically predefine the range of alternatives through which people will seek productive or personal and interpersonal fulfillments. To prescribe the ideal and encompassing Gemeinschaft at this stage of urban civilization seems both fruitless and uninspiring. Our task is to expand the range of options consistent with overall equality and democracy, and to analyze the possible costs and benefits of various social rules, organizational models, and community forms. It is not to construct libertarian cages for our ideally communal and convivial comrades to inhabit.

Equal power in every sphere or over every decision in a workplace has not been shown to be a precondition for equal respect, solidarity, or personal growth – all of which can be nourished through multiple sources. And yet relatively equal power must exist widely, if a democratic ethos is to flourish. Transitory orientations to work units may undermine solidaristic social relations and even organizational maintenance. And yet arrangements flexible enough to facilitate other work and learning experiences, to mitigate emotional intensity and burnout, and to permit a broader range of interpersonal relations may in fact provide other conditions for mutual support, respect, and stable commitment. Such arrangements may relieve individuals of the all-or-nothing choice of full membership, and lessen the strong tendency for participatory institutions to dissolve after relatively short periods of time – leading in many cases to cynicism about some of the very values that motivated participation and commitment in the first place. Institutions must be designed such that their *overall impact* fosters mutuality, equality, personal self-confidence and initiative, even where full equality of power or knowledge in every sphere does not exist. And relations among family and friends, in school and at play, can and should nourish such values, so that people can move between work roles requiring various levels of knowledge and participation without undermining the general bases of equality. The tensions are permanent, and different individuals will inevitably seek different institutional supports. But holistic work arrangements hardly appear as the only (or always the best) way of nurturing egalitarian, democratic, and solidaristic values.

Expertise and Bureaucracy

The problem of expertise in the division of labor was noted above in connection with global democracy and the division of political tasks. It will exist at many levels of a possible classless society, since people with specialized knowledge on whom other people depend will be indispensable. Relative scarcity necessitates economization and hence an unavoidably uneven distribution of knowledge. Even if such an uneven distribution were avoidable within particular work units, it would be inescapable in society at large. The relative scarcity of time limits the extent of training and retraining opportunities, the tolerable degree of discontinuity in the discharge of technical functions, the thematization of technically based discussion, and the communication of technically relevant information. The absorption of technical knowledge by individuals no doubt also has definite limits. And even if these were vastly broader than they seem today, a pluralist conception of a classless society cannot make overly grand assumptions about how much technical knowledge people would want to attain. In addition, since neither the distribution of people with specialized knowledge nor their competence could ever become a matter of general indifference under conditions of relative scarcity, definite rules of access and performance would be required. Breaking down the class division of labor does not, therefore, imply complete deprofessionalization.

But the existence of professionals and experts inevitably poses problems. At a basic level, there is the question of preventing and correcting local abuses and limiting the mystifications of specialized knowledge and professional practices. More directly relevant for a theory of class, however, is the problem of preventing the power that invariably accompanies unevenly distributed expertise from accumulating so that particular corporate groups can generalize their power to the societal level. Such a possibility would probably be greatest among those who were professional politicians, technical experts, or both. Making experts "red" does not solve the problem. A "red" perspective can quite easily transform itself into an inclination to impose on others a very particular shade of red. The possibility that all might be expert in some area, as well as share in the more routine work of the society, would also be likely to lessen the sense of exclusiveness among corporate professional groups. But the problem of controls over such groups remains. The question of organization remains foremost, whether such controls take the form of workers' control, consumer and client control in formulating policies and monitoring performance, parliamentary or administrative control, internal professional control, or a combination of these. It is impossible to conceive of breaking down class divisions in this area apart from specific forms of organizational control.

Similar conclusions can be drawn about the related problem of bureaucracy. From Marx's early writings, through his analysis of the Paris Commune, to Lenin's analyses during and after the Russian Revolution, Marxism has seen itself as anti-bureaucratic, going so far at times as to postulate the abolition of bureaucracy in a classless society. The later critiques of the "bureaucratic degeneration" of existing socialist societies have rendered the idea of bureaucracy odious among virtually all Marxists not concerned to legitimate existing power relations in such societies. Yet Marxists have not adequately analyzed the problem of bureaucracy at a level general enough to be of relevance to the theory of a possible classless society. It is simply assumed that bureaucracy implies domination, and that a classless society will be able to do without it.

Nonsense. We do not have to agree with Weber's view of an inevitable iron cage of bureaucratic rationality to recognize that routine administration according to formalized rules will be indispensable to any conceivable complex classless society. The problem of administrative power, like the problem of power in general, will never go away. To recognize this is not to succumb to the "metaphysical pathos" of organizational pessimism and fatalism that had so long been dominant in American sociology. If I emphasize constraints here it is not to bury democratic hopes, but to counter that peculiarly Marxian naiveté whose disappointment perennially regenerates the pathos of pessimism. The hope of democracy and equality rests on both recognizing *and* testing limits through analysis of specific organizational types, formalized rules, and bureaucratic procedures, not on simply reducing bureaucracy to domination.

Given the limits on time and on the possible holistic organization of productive units analyzed above, the achievement of general fairness and democratic control seems linked as much to the formulation and regular application of formalized rules as to permanent or unrestricted participation. Small units whose work forces are relatively homogeneous in relevant skills and/or commitment to the organization may function according to more radically participatory methods, but even then not without considerable costs. But a search for alternatives cannot be guided by a commitment to an ideal type of participatory collective that presents itself as the sole or primary bearer of value-rationality in social organization. Rather, we must analyze in an open-ended fashion the spheres where formalized rules might be relevant or desirable, what kind of rules these might be, and what mechanisms might be available for applying, amending, or suspending them. Among the constraints that might make rule-formalization relevant are size, heterogeneity of participation (in knowledge, skill, and commitment to the collective), types of technologies and production-flows, and health and safety hazards. Among the goals of such formalization might be economy of time, interpersonal tension-reduction, predictability and continuity, and general protection against arbitrariness and favoritism (from which participatory collectives and elected representatives are certainly not immune). Even modified application of meritocratic standards in employment and advancement, which would be indispensable in a complex and just society, requires rule formalization. And the ability to determine one's personal time rhythms is highly dependent on the kind of predictability in one's environment that likewise derives from formalization. Marxist analyses that trace all bureaucracy in the workplace to the needs of capitalist domination and control misunderstand the significance of workers' struggles for such rule-formalization and for procedures protecting *individual* rights – struggles that would undoubtedly continue under socialism.

The most suitable forms of organization in particular productive units, therefore, cannot be decided a priori, but only in the context of the *totality* of relevant constraints and goals both within and across particular units. There can be no *general* theory of self-management at the level of the economic unit. Not all types of rule-formalization and bureaucracy are the same. If we are to escape from the polarity of unregenerate fatalism and unreflective optimism that often accompanies broad generic uses of the term "bureaucracy," we must specify alternative types in much greater detail.

When we direct our attention to global problems in a possible classless society, the inevitability of certain forms of bureaucracy seems even more obvious. The institutionalization of a genuine plurality of life and work options, such as to secure equality, represents a problem of enormous complexity. And the complexity grows, the greater the options available and the more relatively equal the outcomes desired. Not all life and work options, and all equalization, require formal administration. But the latter is necessary if these goals are to be achieved on a *societal* level in a *systematic* manner. Given the multiform interrelations among units and individuals, the complexity of the tasks, and the relative scarcity of the environment in which they are to be achieved, economization and formalization of administration become indispensable. Neither an unregulated market nor an essentially informal or haphazard application of rules could conceivably achieve systematic equality. Indeed, long-established, stable routines may best reveal the consequences over time of various alternative policies. Hence, the possibility of thematizing such alternatives (e.g., standards of labor exchange) fundamentally depends on formalization and routinization. Historically such formal-legal rationalization has been a bulwark against arbitrary power; democracy in a complex classless society *requires* bureaucracy.

But does it require bureaucrats? Several considerations suggest that, even where everyone in the society shared the more boring and less desirable tasks, and even where administration was simple enough to be performed by the ordinary citizen, a certain degree of professionalization of administrative work might be necessary, or at least preferable. Indeed, bureaucratic work might be considered *both* less desirable (because routine) *and* necessarily "professional," requiring a definite degree of continuity in the performance of such tasks. First of all, continuity is economical, at least up to a certain point. Even if administrative tasks are intellectually undemanding (which would not always be the case), learning them can be time-consuming. The routines and formal rules of an office can be extremely complex. The costs of rotation beyond a certain point might outweigh the benefits – a calculation that would depend on a range of other factors, such as the amount of time doing such work, and other work and life options available. In addition, rotation may have definite limits if a bureau is to function at all, since everyday operations depend on interpersonal factors achieved through stable interaction. Perhaps more important, however, accountability requires continuity.

If the existence of "bureaucrats" is not to undermine the premises of a classless society, then the organization of accountability becomes the crucial question. Bureaucrats do not inevitably represent domination – class or otherwise – if their privileges can be contained and their actions held accountable. The possible elimination of a class division of labor does not imply the abolition of an administrative division of labor or the total deprofessionalization of such. There may be a permanent tendency towards unchecked power or disengagement in bureaucracies – even if bureaucrats themselves have no sinister motives. But nothing dooms that tendency to go unrestrained. Various mechanisms are available, and indeed many have already been used to some effect: supervision and investigation by elected political bodies (such as parliamentary commissions), removal and sanctions against those violating legally established norms, public access to information, mechanisms for appeal and rectification of decisions, and specifically appointed or elected popular commissions. It should not be assumed, however, that the latter, and other possible forms of "radical democratic" controls, would be the most effective. Indeed, in penetrating the operations of bureaucracies, more regular checks by those with special knowledge may be more effective.

All of these mechanisms of control, however, can work in a consistently democratic fashion only if a more general condition is met: effective public discussion and debate of formal rules of administration. Such a discussion must attempt to clarify the possible outcomes of the application of alternative rules, so that costs and benefits can be calculated, and the tendency for decisions to be made according to bureaucratic rationality alone can be checked. This implies a regular process of monitoring systematic outcomes and unanticipated consequences. If such a public discussion is effectively institutionalized, and mechanisms to check and remove abuses exist, the routine application of formalized rules by regularly tenured staff can become an extremely effective "neutral" instrument of democracy. Under conditions of relative scarcity that necessitate *some* transmission of social requirements to individual citizens, no other conceivable instrument might simultaneously provide flexibility of choice among an array of life and work options *and* relative equality of outcomes in a *systematic* fashion.

Beyond Class

I have tried to clarify some of the problems of theorizing about a society beyond class. A critical theory of class necessarily implies the tentative articulation of a concept of classlessness. The idea of a classless society is laden with normative elements. If the truth value of such a concept ultimately depends on its actual realization, the latter itself would depend on the normative judgment of its citizens. A value-free validation either here or beyond is inconceivable. The values I have emphasized – equality, democracy, plurality of choice – have not received extensive philosophical justification here. A rejection of these values obviously makes the entire discussion beside the point. Acceptance of them at least allows the issues to be engaged at the level of social-scientific discourse, and debated within the framework of pluralist and democratic theory.

Classlessness cannot be conceived as an "objective state" that is "reached," or a set of "objective positions" that are "filled." Rather, it is a totality of relationships in a permanent process of *struggle*. A society without conflict and struggle is inconceivable. Not every set of standards and institutional mechanisms for achieving one desired objective coincides with every other objective. Democracy, equality, and plurality may represent a totality, but their institutional embodiment would inevitably be contradictory in some ways. All rules define a set of options, and restrict others. All sets of rules generate problems. *Struggle* – because in an environment of relative scarcity, organizational and role conflicts are inevitable; because communication can never be instantaneous, "complete," or undistorted. There can be no "general interest" or "radical needs" completely apart from the particular interests and needs that people have as a result of their positions in the division of labor, and the peculiar perceptions and interpretations that result from the intersection of their individual life histories with societal processes. *Struggle* – because power cannot wither away. *Class struggle* – not in the sense of polarized groups with dichotomous positions of power and privilege, but struggle *over* class, struggle over the meaning of class and the tolerable and intolerable forms of inequality. The various inequalities that will inevitably accompany complex social differentiation provide a permanent ground for class (re)formation. There is not reason to believe that, beyond the capitalist and party-dominated collectivist societies existing today, there could not be various forms of class society, i.e., societies that systematically reproduce inequalities that are judged significant, unacceptable, and not correctable through the regular redistributive mechanisms available.

Struggle – because permanent tensions run throughout the social totality, tensions determined by the materiality of our existence itself. Time is scarce. This first principle of political economy is also a first principle of moral economy. The two are inextricably woven. We produce ourselves and construct our meanings in the face of the limits of existential time, of loss and death, and the permanent fragility of life itself. All culture must ultimately confront these material realities that pierce through the human project – even culture produced under utopian conditions. Power must be organized because the stakes are so high: the conditions under which we can weave the fabric of life's meaning in the face of its very definite boundaries and scarcity.

18

Reaganism and Neoliberalism

(1986)

David Plotke

Facing the overall state of national political forces today, what should "the left" do? And what is "the left"? The term has at least three referents. One is everything to the left of center in contemporary politics. Given Reagan's successes, this left covers a vast territory, such that it has little substantive political content. Sometimes "the left" means the socialist and radical left, including socialist organizations and institutions as well as the radical sections of the feminist, black, and other movements. This left is electorally insignificant, but ideologically influential in some milieus.

The third "left" is hardest to define. It includes the second left, but its main forces are neither socialist nor radical – they are left-liberal, populist, and sometimes social-democratic. This left includes sections of the unions, and of the organized feminist and black movements. It includes parts of the gay movements and the environmental movement, as well as the organized opposition to United States policy in South Africa and Central America. Electorally, it is roughly demarcated by the combined vote for Jesse Jackson and George McGovern in the 1984 Democratic primaries, plus perhaps 20 percent of the primary vote of Hart and Mondale.

Thus while the socialist and radical left is politically marginal, the other two lefts are not well organized, ideologically clear, or programmatically coherent. Nor are they enthusiastic about the proposals of socialists! What should one do in this situation, if one is a socialist interested in having a significant effect on the course of national politics?

The political record of the various lefts over the last decade is bad enough to encourage all sorts of wishful thinking, and to nourish insular tendencies within the shrinking political space these lefts can call their own. One proposal that has surfaced regularly over the last decade amounts to a call to assemble the many sections of the left-liberal, populist, and social-democratic lefts into a more coherent force. This prospective left would assemble a range of interest groups and movements and advance a broad program for social and economic democracy. It would be democratic, and probably Democratic; it would be well to the left of center, but not socialist.

Yet while this proposal has been made often, such a left hasn't appeared. Nor are there strong signs that it is about to. This proposal falls short because it is much more a statement of desire than a strategy linked to the overall configuration of national political forces. Advocates of this course too often hesitate before asking themselves practical strategic questions about influencing national politics.

A first question: Would this proposed mass left be an immediate candidate for national power, or part of a broader array of governing forces? The clear answer is that only the latter is a feasible conception in the medium term. Even assembling this mass left is a five- to ten-year task, and it will not immediately gain the strength, diversity, and resources to win national power. Given this reality, those who propose to consolidate a "new American left" are advocating a good thing, but they are only beginning a discussion. When they claim that this course is a full strategy, they fail to engage the real choices we face.

Today there is a central question that offers a point of strategic reference for all the "lefts." As Reagan's administration ends, will Reaganism be consolidated as a durable regime? Despite the scale of Reagan's two victories, and the great changes in policy and political debates that have occurred, this consolidation has not yet been achieved. Reagan's popularity is extraordinary. But it is both cause and result of a political process. "Reaganism" combines several major themes: energetic and nationalistic patriotism; enthusiasm for entrepreneurial activity and the market in general; cultural conservatism; and hostility to expanding state social spending past the programs of the New Deal. These themes are advanced by distinct but overlapping forces in a broad coalition.

Several Reaganite coalitions are conceivable, all of them multi-class and popular, but with varying social and regional bases, and different ideological emphases. One such coalition might be able to shape a long period in which Reaganite Republicans and conservative Democrats dominate the field of national politics. This coalition would not win every presidential election, or always control Congress, but would set a policy framework and structure political discourse. The obvious analogy is to the long New Deal period of Democratic domination.

Many of the possible prerequisites are in place. Reagan enjoys great political support (though it is weaker than his personal support), and major shifts to the right have occurred in the last decade. His administration has delivered on its promises in two crucial respects. First, while economic growth has been uneven, and its future is uncertain, the 1980s look very good compared to the stagnation and unraveling of the 1970s, which is a crucial point of political reference now. Second, while Reagan has spent a fortune on the military, his administration has mainly avoided direct American military engagement. He still scares people – but insofar as relative peace is a collective good (and can easily be confused with security), it has been delivered.

The fate of all the lefts in a durable Reaganite regime would be bleak enough that trying to prevent this outcome should be our priority. Thus a "progressive majority" – there are several possible variants – is now virtually any majority that effectively blocks the consolidation of Reaganism.

The gap between a new mass "left" and an imagined "progressive majority" – the awkward character of both terms suggests our distance from what they point to! – stems from the weakness of popular forces, and the relative strength of variants of neoliberalism. Imagining that a mass left and a new "progressive" majority are identical is wishful, and leads us away from thinking about the overall field of strategic political action in the United States, towards a narrow focus on how to unify (at most) the left 15 to 20 percent of the electorate.

Here I will discuss the *most likely* progressive majority, one vastly more likely than a social-democratic or left-populist majority. This possible majority also has some substantive virtues compared with other conceivable progressive majorities beyond its greater practical chances to block Reaganism.

The most likely progressive majority to emerge would be mainly "neoliberal." To stop the consolidation of Reaganism, we – both the socialist "we" and the populist and left-liberal "we" – have to make very broad alliances, including a crucial alliance with neoliberalism. Rather than attacking neoliberals (whose positions will need criticizing), we should recognize that largely by default, neoliberalism is the most promising candidate for a leading role in a credible and even moderately progressive alternative to Reaganism. Such an alliance at best might even recall the main moments of democratic reform in this century, which conjoined progressive and popular-democratic impulses.

I will argue for this view in discussing: 1) economic programs and their problems; 2) the electoral-demographic logic of neoliberalism; and 3) the special-interest problem. If I sometimes use the names of 1984's Democratic candidates in referring to political tendencies within and around the Democratic Party – conservative, traditional liberal, neoliberal, and left-liberal – these names are metaphors for broad projects, including presidential and local electoral and constituency politics.

307

Political Economy of a Progressive Majority

A progressive majority requires a credible and workable political-economic project. Yet, at the moment, the left's alternatives are not credible in popular political conflict. There have been many efforts to propose an alternative economic program to Reaganism. On the left, these have usually involved a combination of proposals for an active industrial policy, social and economic protectionism (both in international trade and domestic policy), expanded social welfare expenditures, and Keynesian approaches to government spending and wages.

The political problem is that on the whole the left's policies are not taken seriously as an alternative to Reaganism – and this is due in part to their actual deficiencies. Reading most works of left economic analysis or program, one hears about an economic crisis. Is the "crisis" because

(a) there is no growth occurring, or not enough growth?
(b) growth is too erratic and uncertain?
(c) growth is unbalanced across regions and sectors?
(d) growth is unfair, marginalizing some groups and making
     others miserable in their inclusion?

Our complaints combine these themes. The problem is that socialists, other leftists, and Democrats have not demonstrated much recent competence. Socialists and other radicals have the (slightly whiny if true) excuse of not having been given a "real" chance. Left-liberal and other Democrats have not done much with their actual chances, most recently under Carter. Partly as a result, they have no public credibility on (a) and (b). That is, no one believes that leftists or Democrats know how to produce more growth than the Reagan administration has. Nor do many people believe that we could produce steadier growth.

We do have some credibility on (c) and (d). It is believed – and it's true – that we know how to redistribute the results of growth and compensate the most disadvantaged. But there is a problem. It is also believed that our policies are at least self-defeating, if not actively hostile to growth: our redistributive and protective social and economic policies would produce short-run benefits, but their unintended consequences would limit economic growth in ways that undermined even those benefits.

While many valuable proposals have been made, even the most sympathetic reading of left and Democratic programs can't miss a basic problem. These programs often seem to amount to a list of good things, without much attention to the interaction among either the aims or the measures taken to achieve them. Nor are the arguments that predict a spell of terrible economic trouble persuasive. There is always the possibility of a catastrophe, but the main arguments don't come close to showing its likelihood. We're likely to see continued severe economic problems, including another substantial recession, along with major episodes and areas of economic growth. As the last decade made clear, there is no reason to think that severe economic problems will send people off to the left.

Neoliberal Advantages

Given the popular resistance to Democratic and left economic approaches, the tendency with the unhappy name of neoliberalism tends to win politically – if mainly by default, rather than by virtue. Yet its advantages are not purely political. Of the main contenders on the scene, only neoliberalism now makes a sustained case for a positive view of the possibilities of contemporary economic and social development. While most liberal and left-liberal stances seem on balance antagonistic to socioeconomic change, neoliberalism has at least tried to offer elements of a policy approach aimed both at encouraging growth and shaping it in better rather than worse ways.

1. Neoliberal arguments and policies encourage development, which they properly recognize as postindustrial – meaning both a sectoral shift from manufacturing to other activities, and an expansion of labor-saving and knowledge-intensive forms across sectors.

2. Neoliberal approaches raise issues about how to shape growth patterns, not only regarding the balance among industries and sectors, but also concerning productivity and work relations.

3. Neoliberals have recognized a positive role for government in human capital efforts, such as social expenditures in education and training, which are correctly viewed as productive.

4. Both because of its emphasis on human capital, and because it is connected to the liberal Democratic tradition, neoliberalism facilitates social expenditures aimed at people whose economic and social prospects have been damaged by growth, or who have been excluded.

Taken together, these themes make neoliberal perspectives at least as analytically persuasive as those competing with them in the Democratic Party and on the left. Given that they are also strategically better with respect to electoral conflict, they have a considerable overall advantage. These themes offer a starting point for a way out of the current left/Democratic isolation, in which Democrats are seen as incompetent to produce real socioeconomic development, or opportunistically opposed to it for the sake of protecting traditional votes.

If neoliberal themes are only the best of an uninspired lot of political-economic projects, the irony is that neoliberalism is occupying some of the space "we" – the various "we's" on the left – should have occupied. Neoliberalism partially fills the empty space in which a positive, progressive conception of postindustrial socioeconomic development might appear. We are now paying the political costs of having spent too much of our time denouncing socioeconomic modernization without proposing feasible alternative growth models. Without such models, we are treated either as opposed to growth, or as vaguely in favor of all economic good things such that their sum signifies our program. Thus a political alliance with neoliberalism is required both by the latter's programmatic emphases, and the left's failures to address the same issues in a more convincing way.

We need to be able to make and defend the claim that we have reasonable criteria by which to choose among the bundle of possible socioeconomic changes linked to new technologies – that we can help choose the changes to be supported, and those to be reshaped or even prevented. And we need to be able to show that we have ways of making such choices that do not themselves destroy growth mechanisms.

We need to be able to say how we would address the pain and hardship of those for whom postindustrial development will be at least a serious temporary loss (and sometimes a permanent disaster) – rather than appearing mainly interested in stopping the changes, which renders us even less able to deal with their consequences when we fail.

To protect those who are dislocated and those who are marginalized, we need to encourage sufficient growth so that demands can be made and won both for compensation and for paying the large "costs of entry" for marginalized groups. Without growth, the cost of economic hardship will be greater than with it, for most groups. And in the practical politics of the present and near future, the main payment for such costs comes from the middle and working classes, with negative political results that are by now familiar.

Despite these economic and political realities, we of the various lefts often now seem to be saying that growth is not happening, that it is not really possible, and that it is mostly a bad thing. The truth is that growth and development are occurring, although unevenly. In this area, some neoliberal themes are not only electorally appealing, but defensible on other grounds – we should have made them ours, but with our own quite different formulations, some time ago.

The Electoral and Demographic Framework

There is more to a "progressive" majority than an economic approach. Other factors also make a neoliberal project the most likely center of such a majority. A neoliberal-dominated coalition is demographically more feasible than the alternatives. The Republican Party is now competitive in every region in the country in presidential politics. That is not true for the Democrats. Traditional liberal politics are uncompetitive in the West and South. Left-liberal politics are uncompetitive in both these regions, and in much of the Midwest. And neoliberalism (though perhaps not in its more conservative variants) is uncompetitive in much of the South. Given the choices, a neoliberal effort has the virtue of being the *least uncompetitive* Democratic possibility. It has the best chance of winning parts of the West, which is essential given the Democratic decline in the South.

A neoliberal coalition would not necessarily produce major defections by existing Democratic supporters. What matters is how an overall coalition is constructed. Can bridges be built between neoliberalism and labor; can other popular-democratic groupings be engaged in a serious mobilization effort?

For many groups, the major reason for participating in a neoliberal-led coalition will be the usual uninspiring but powerful motive – it is the least bad alternative. This will likely be the case for labor. For the black and feminist movements, the danger of antagonism may be even greater. This is partly because some neoliberals indulge in abrasive critiques of these movements. More important, the neoliberal style of politics, firmly in the Progressive tradition, offers a relatively narrow role for a politics of mass mobilization and local organizing (especially given the current campaign technologies). In this area the various lefts could play a critical role, by helping to build a coalition to which mass forces can devote energy with the assurance that their efforts will make a difference not only for electoral outcomes but for program and policy.

Neoliberalism also has a chance of winning back middle-class and upper-working-class constituencies who are in danger of becoming durably Republican, or at least anti-Democratic. Many voters are pro-growth in one sense or another, and also relatively liberal on "social" issues, especially concerning women's rights. In this area, neoliberalism can help split part of the Reagan electoral coalition off from future Republican candidates, given the likely ties of the latter to the new/far right.

In all these respects, a neoliberal coalition/majority is not ideal, but has better electoral prospects than the alternatives. Thus to block the construction of a durable Reaganism, we need to reach an accommodation with neoliberalism, to help create a coalition between neoliberal and other forces, realizing that such a coalition will be mainly neoliberal. This overall direction does not dictate a single organizational strategy or set of political tactics, and

311

involves both conflict and compromise. It might be unnecessary had the left(s) somehow managed successfully to occupy the terrain that neoliberalism now occupies as the main heir to traditional liberalism. We did not succeed in doing this, and have to make strategic calculations on a terrain not to our liking.

Despite our weakness, what we do in the next several years matters, especially in determining the extent to which neoliberalism is influenced significantly by left-liberal and popular-democratic ideas and political forces. Such influences are a good thing, and not only because neoliberalism needs them to have a chance at the political mobilization required for electoral success against a popular adversary.

The Neoliberals' Special-Interest Problem, and Ours

The lefts' critique of neoliberalism has generally boiled down to the claim that under the guise of a critique of special-interest politics, neoliberalism expresses the political impulses of mildly reformist, modernizing sections of the middle classes. That claim is partly true. Yet if we stop there we risk ignoring the historical precedents for the shaping of American progressive majorities. And we avoid facing the deep problems of relations among popular movements and constituencies.

"Progressive" is now a word leftists use to identify themselves, without being clear about where the progress is headed. In the early twentieth century, "progressive" meant modernizing, efficient, honest reform. Many such efforts were middle class in inspiration. Yet the main periods of democratic social reform in this century – aspects of the Progressive period, in the 1930s, and in the 1960s – were marked by a widening of this term, so that "progressive" meant both modernizing and democratic impulses.

Another such period, if we were so lucky, would probably have the same character. The only way it might be avoided would be if popular movements were large and politically mature enough to dominate a coalition with modernizing progressives, to focus the coalition on democratic aims. If this did not happen in the 1960s, does the state of popular movements make it likely today?

In this context, to denounce neoliberalism is simply to wish away a crucial precondition for an effective reform effort, especially in a period of economic and social transformation. If part of our job on the left is to build the popular and democratic side of a reform coalition, that is not likely to be done by concentrating our energies on abusing our possible partners for their failure to be radical democrats.

The weakness of popular movements is only part of the reason that a nationally successful left-liberal coalition is very unlikely (i.e., a winning coalition in which progressive liberalism takes a back seat). For the left(s) to be the leading force in a new progressive majority, we would have to accomplish something we have so far failed to do.

There is now no credible political form of popular unity among democratic movements. There are lists of groups and demands with little unity, or political projects that express the immediate interests of one group in forms that can't be acceptable to the others. Republican charges of special-interest politics – and neoliberal charges – are sometimes mean-spirited, but they signal the fragmentation of the popular left. This fragmentation appears as a profound lack of trust. It also expresses a legitimate refusal to accept that any group has an intrinsic right, due to its experience, previous political behavior, or structural position, to lead a popular coalition. No group has such a right today. When some try to claim it, any (temporary) gain in power usually comes at the expense of prospects for durable alliances.

Neoliberalism's political prospects are enhanced inasmuch as it offers a (pseudo)solution to this fragmentation: all popular movements will be kept at arm's length, where they can be supervised and mediated by a farseeing political leadership. This approach does derive partly from neoliberal elitism and nervousness about popular movements. Yet it speaks to a real problem, and its appeal has a logic beyond its origins, even among the groups neoliberals call "special interests."

Each such group might most strongly prefer that a coalition be led by a candidate and identified with a program stamped mainly with its own identity and aspirations. Failing to achieve that – or failing to do so in an electorally viable form – the groups face a choice. They can either support a project clearly identified with another group, in which case their subordinate position will be apparent. Or they can support an allegedly neutral arbiter, friendly to all the groups, but independent.

The logic of this situation will lead many groups to support the second option. They may judge that their specific interests are less likely to be taken into account in an alliance dominated by another group with its own interest-linked agenda. So, for example, feminist political elites might just as soon deal with a neoliberal arbiter as with Jesse Jackson; black political elites might as soon deal with such an arbiter as with a new Mondale. Many groups will deal with a neoliberal who seems to be no one's captive rather than a more "progressive" candidate whose agenda includes their own program only at the end of a long and clearly ordered list.

The arbiter role is partly illusory – due to the weight of "middle class" interests and also due to the willingness of neoliberals to engage in interest-group politics when it suits their immediate needs. It is also partly real, enough so to be attractive among troubling options.

313

Neoliberalism here fills another empty space, albeit inadequately: the space for new forms of mediation among popular movements and organizations. These forms are crucial to the emergence of a positive substantive vision of a "progressive" public interest. Simply by recognizing the need to fill this space, neoliberalism has gained a crucial advantage over its competitors to the left of center. Neoliberalism has recognized that a compelling vision has to go beyond summing up a range of demands for good things, and give some account of how those goods are interconnected. A credible vision has to acknowledge tensions, and suggest how they might be addressed.

If workable new forms of mediation were built, beyond those neoliberalism envisages, it would be reasonable to ask a question that sections of the popular left see as almost a provocation: How are the demands of your group related to an overall conception of the public good? This question seems to challenge hard-won rights to autonomy and the expression of difference.

In practice, a stance focused on criticizing neoliberalism might at best lead to the day-to-day politics of defending the immediate interests of various popular movements. Some successes might result, perhaps moving parts of the movements slightly to the left. But amidst the ongoing fragmentation, such successes would not contribute much to creating a new, positive dynamic among the movements and groups.

Individual and local successes wouldn't add up any more than they have in the last decade. Aside from all the differences of style, interest, and perspective, there is a built-in reason why it is so hard to sum up the activities of disparate movements and groups in a "left" form. In a sentence, it is almost impossible to unite the "left" 15 to 20 percent of the electorate on its own, without a strategic perspective in which such unity is seen as part of an even broader coalition-building perspective, aimed at governing.

Why? The elements of a proposed left political force are spread across a range of interest groups and movements. Every element is subject to dual loyalties – on the one hand, to the labor movement, the women's movement, and so on; on the other hand, to a vision of an intergroup left alternative. If strategy is reduced to drawing together the most "left" sections of these groups and movements, the "unifying" project will fail because it seems to be sectarian and narrowly ideological. Its practical result would be to jeopardize each left element's relations with the mass forces in its movement. Unless a "left" unity is conceived as part of a process of forming and influencing a governing coalition, each prospective component of the imagined "left" will reasonably seek its own accommodation with whatever governing coalition does take shape.

314

Prospects and Choices

In the near future, a phase of democratic reform would be both progressive and popular-democratic. A progressive majority dominated by neoliberalism would have many defects. Is there any reason to be excited about it? As I argued before, aiming at such a coalition is a response to the overall shape of national politics. Framed by a negative aim, it is limited. Yet it would be hard to overestimate the bleakness of all the lefts' medium-term futures were Reaganism consolidated into a durable popular majority, a right-center coalition lasting for decades.

There are also some positive prospects. First, there's the hope of retaking the high ground in debates on political-economic program. Second, there's the possibility of being able to fight to include the excluded and marginalized, to exit from the downward spiral of defending hard-to-defend welfarist policies. Third, it would be exciting to enter a situation where we can try to broaden and extend democratic forms, rather than devoting ourselves to defending hard-won gains from bitter attacks.

The argument I've made doesn't dictate a single immediate strategic choice. There are many ways to develop such an approach, depending on the features of various states and cities. Two sorts of activity seem especially appropriate. One is direct involvement in neoliberal projects, aimed partly at building bridges to the organizations and movements of the popular democratic left. Such efforts would be important in posing an alternative to the alliance with Southern conservative Democrats which appeals to at least some neoliberals.

A second effort would aim to build bridges from the other direction. It would focus on mobilizing popular-democratic movements against Reaganism in ways that open up the possibility of a coalition with neoliberal forces (and enhance the left's role within it). Such efforts will certainly embroil those involved in sharp conflicts. They may find themselves opposing groups who want to start from the 1984 Jackson campaign with the aim of building a quasi-autonomous political faction within and around the Democratic Party. Such an effort is mainly concerned with securing its own political and organizational identity, and is willing, even eager, to define a mainly antagonistic relation with neoliberalism and the remains of traditional liberalism.

Yet it would be wrong to end on too conciliatory a note. I have been trying to criticize the strategic approaches that dominate much of the left. One course means wishful waiting for an economic situation so bad that our long lists of virtuous economic outcomes will be mistaken for a workable program. Another is the militant insistence that by attaching ourselves to the interest-group politics of one or another social force we will make others accept a coalition on our terms – and that coalition will somehow become majoritarian. A third, more sophisticated, recommends a broad coalition of

315

popular forces, but in a vacuum, without linking this coalition to an overall political strategy. All these approaches turn aside from the real world of national politics and confine their attention to building various forms of a marginalized "left."

Engaging national politics is hard now, given how far to the right things have slipped. It is difficult even to enter the main public debates, let alone to show that what we want immediately and later is workable and responsible to a popular, general interest. Yet the risks and problems of these efforts can be avoided only by giving up on influencing national political life in the remainder of this decade.

Postscript – 1990

Written well before the 1988 election, when there appeared to be a significant prospect of electoral success for an alternative to the Republican course, this article took that prospect as the point of reference for the many lefts, and argued that attempting to realize it required building a center-left coalition.

This position was regarded, within parts of the left, as a conservative turn that neglected the importance of autonomous political and cultural development for various forces well to the left of center. As it turned out, my analysis was in certain respects wishful and too optimistic. What I proposed was wishful regarding the capacity of anti-Republican forces, especially on the left, to undertake the sort of strategic action required to influence national presidential politics. And despite the cautious tone of the article, I may have been too optimistic about the prospects of a neoliberal candidacy.

It would require a full article to make a precise assessment of the relative weight of the more and less contingent elements in the 1988 election, for example, Dukakis's rigid and charmless persona against economic prosperity. Despite the scale of the eventual defeat, it was not wholly determined, and at least Democratic respectability was a serious possibility.

Nonetheless, the Democratic defeat and the ensuing high levels of public support for Bush indicate the scope and depth of the conservative turn in contemporary American politics. From the late 1970s through Bush's victory and beyond, considerable effort has gone into debating whether any real move to the right has occurred in American politics, with many analysts on the left searching eagerly for evidence to the contrary. These debates should now be considered closed by the dramatic string of presidential successes for conservative Republicans who campaigned energetically against Democratic liberalism, though we can still debate how this conservative shift occurred, and argue about the respective roles of its mass and elite components.

Republican success does not guarantee permanence, as though that party's presidential domination has now become a political second nature. Nonetheless, we confront a political reality very different from that expected by those who began *Socialist Review* twenty years ago. While the first few issues of *Socialist Revolution* were generally free of the apocalyptic imagery that plagued the late New Left, radical political and social change were believed to be on the medium-term agenda. Given this view, the sharpening of a strong critique of advanced liberalism was regarded as a central political and theoretical task.

For much of *Socialist Review*'s history, its main targets were mainstream Democratic liberalism in politics and more-or-less orthodox Marxism in theory. Yet in these twenty years only one Democrat has been elected president. The strength and vitality of anti-liberal currents, from Wallace to Reagan and beyond, has regularly exceeded the expectations of *SR* and the broader circles of academics and activists of which it is a part. A thorough diagnosis of these misjudgments would help illuminate the long series of unsuccessful efforts to undermine Republican domination. And understanding those efforts opens onto all the daunting problems that face attempts to redefine a democratic, modern left in the US, amid domestic and international circumstances dramatically different from those of two decades ago.

19

Socialism as Ethics
(1986)
Jeffrey Escoffier

The classical vision of socialism is moribund. No "actually existing" socialist society offers the democracy, justice, and freedom that socialism promises. Nor has any social democratic society yet embarked on a transition to socialism. Defeated by powerful political and cultural forces, the left has not achieved a place in political life after years of growth during the sixties and early seventies. We are now in a period of decline and discouragement. We have no objective guarantee that the working class recognizes capitalism as the cause of the injustice and inequalities of American life. The recent history of the American working class clearly shows that it lacks the organizational and political capacity to struggle effectively for the fundamental transformation of society.

Profound disappointments and doubts have shattered our faith in the objective and strategic possibilities implied by Marxist interpretations of history. Many of us are now adrift. Is socialism a meaningful political stance? If so, how is it? How can we maintain our commitment and seek to realize our hopes politically? Our political crisis is experienced as deeply personal and demoralizing. As socialists we may still believe in equality, justice, and democracy, but whether we like it or not, all of us are riddled with doubt and are searching for new foundations for our political commitments.

The Flawed Vision

The classical socialist vision was predicated on the inevitable achievement of a socialist society – according to some interpretations, sometimes helped along by a vanguard party. The historical inevitability of socialism emerged from the dynamics of the capitalist system as it generated a large population of disenfranchised laborers. The doctrine of historical inevitability both framed the left's strategic choices and sustained the individual militant's commitment to the cause of socialist revolution. In periods of defeat and discouragement, the promise of inevitability kept hope and commitment alive. Perhaps most importantly, political defeats were mitigated by a sense of cumulative achievement on the road to socialism. Socialists could also count on the inevitable development of productive forces to undermine the stability of the capitalist system, since classical socialism was unalterably grounded in the belief in progress. Since Marx it has been almost impossible to expunge the progressive interpretation of history from the left's psychological frame of reference – hence the contemporary euphemism, "progressive."

Today, however, we have grown skeptical about Marxism's objective laws of historical change, in part because socialism remains blocked in the advanced industrial countries; state socialism in the Soviet Union has been a disaster; the imposed revolution in Eastern Europe has failed; and yet forms of socialism have emerged in unlikely places such as China, Tanzania, and Cuba. All too often history has seemed to "require" sacrificing human lives or civil liberties.

We are forced to wonder whether there are real political movements that "naturally" lead the left and strive to achieve radical social transformation. Classical socialism offered sophisticated theoretical and empirical arguments that only the working class could achieve a socialist society. Nevertheless, when the American labor movement failed to act as a "left" in the post–World War II period, New Left intellectuals went in search of "revolutionary subjects." The New Left generation repeatedly took up emerging social movements as the agents of revolution – blacks, students, the poor, the Third World, and various social movements of the early seventies. Some members of the New Left generation also attempted to return to the working class. But our chronic mythologizing of a succession of social movements produced a chronic disillusionment.

Our overinvestment in the revolutionary potential of many social movements has fostered dependence on the welfare state. Almost all the political strategies that social movements took up in the sixties and seventies (and that the left supported) relied upon expanding the welfare state. Virtually all of these movements – black civil rights, the environmental movement, the women's movement, gay rights – demanded new or expanded social services, more rigorously protected civil rights, and tougher regulation of big business. These strategies were based on the recognition of the social character of political rights, economic well-being, and a healthy and viable natural environment. The expansion of the welfare state genuinely improved the well-being of many of the poor and disadvantaged, but it also produced dependency in its wake. These demands on the welfare state were said (by conservatives and business leaders) to have created a fiscal crisis because they conflicted with the state's role in capital accumulation. Some of us hoped that the fiscal crisis would "heighten the contradictions." This hope was only one more example of the left's naive faith in the "progressive" resolution of political contradictions.

The recurring discovery of each new social movement's revolutionary potential solved our emotional needs for moral legitimacy. We tried to fashion a morally perfect culture. Cultural forms, artistic expressions, and social values had to be purified of all traces of the morally corrupt, dominant culture. Consequently the ethically serious but fervently moral perfectionism on the left and in various social movements during the seventies often turned into intolerance and sectarianism. The political culture of the left did not always provide exemplary models for radically democratic dialogue among those who held different but equally passionate convictions.

None of this means that we should abandon social movements – only our exalted dreams that they will necessarily produce radical social change. The search for privileged agents of social change is an illusion that has led us to feel betrayed when activists in these social movements achieve integration in the American mainstream or proclaim themselves "populists." There are no historically guaranteed revolutionary subjects. Political subjects seeking radical social change create themselves in the process of their struggles for emancipation. Our political strategies must take into account the historical conditions of a political subject's emergence, both those that they create and those that constrain them. Our egalitarianism and our sense of justice are the legitimate reasons for participating in these social movements.

Socialist Politics and Ethics

The failure of the traditional working class and labor movements to achieve political dominance and to reform capitalism has set us adrift both strategically and morally. The failure of the actually existing socialist societies to achieve real democracy and genuine self-management has betrayed the promise of historical materialism. The belief in either historical inevitability (classical socialism) or privileged revolutionary subjects (Western Marxism) guaranteed both a movement and a strategy. The Marxist interpretations of history offered strategic guidance to our political actions. They allowed us to measure our political "progress." Without either canonized political subjects or strategic inevitability, all our political choices are risky and uncertain.

Therefore we must root our politics in an ethics of social transformation grounded in a solidarity that is not metaphysical, essentialist, nostalgic, or

321

transhistorical. Our ethics of transformation must be grounded in historical realities, it must recognize the contingency of social life. Though a theory of history remains a requirement of any strategy, we cannot continue to rely on a theory of history that resolves all contradictions with reference to a mythical totality. We must face up to the need for a utopian socialist vision and socialist principles of political action.

Socialism remains a theory of justice based on the critique of capitalism developed through the Marxist tradition. But socialism is also an ethics of solidarity that requires both structural change (rooted in an empirical knowledge of history) and individual commitment. Socialist principles call for the transformation of social structures that exploit and maim workers, oppress racial and ethnic minorities, restrict the autonomy of women, proscribe forms of sexuality, and destroy the natural environment. Socialist politics are grounded on the critical edge between *what is* and *what should be;* these cannot be identified without free discussion, public debate, tolerance of difference, and voluntary association. Socialist politics must be a synthesis of ethics and strategy. Any political strategy without an ethics can only lead to opportunism, while an ethics that refuses to commit itself to a strategy can only create a new moralism. We must continue to build on the empirical understanding of history that the socialist tradition has encouraged, but we must also recognize ourselves as an ethical movement. Only then can we address the problem of our commitment to the socialist project in an era of disillusion and decline.

20

Socialism and Beyond
Remaking the American Left
(1983)
Stanley Aronowitz

The cleavages in the United States between socialism and the social movements for sexual freedom, ecology, and race and national autonomy are by no
means as wide as they presently are in Western Europe. Nevertheless,
American socialism shares with its international counterparts a pervasive sense
of crisis. The crisis in socialism grows out of the problems associated with
"actually existing socialism."[1] For much of the contemporary world the Soviet
Union and its allies are what is meant by socialism. The socialist movement
must take responsibility for the totalitarian character of these societies by engaging in a process of self-examination. What tendencies within the socialist
tradition generated the conflict between "democracy" and "nationalization"?
How have some socialists been able to accept the systematic repression of
political and cultural freedom in much of Eastern Europe, China, Cuba, and
other actually existing socialist states?

The tradition of what I shall call *authoritarian* socialism identified the abolition of private ownership of the means of production with the first stage of the
transition from capitalism to socialism. The "temporary" suspension of political
and social liberty is regarded as a tragic but necessary price for making the first
revolutionary steps. Of course, there is an alternate socialist tradition that has
rejected Stalinism as a model, that insisted in the post-Bolshevik era on the
irreducibility of democracy, of parliamentary pluralism, and of cultural liberty.
Democratic socialism renounces the revolutionary model of the transition even
though it adopts the viewpoint that socialism necessarily implies economic
planning and a strong welfare state. Its economic program seeks to create a
"mixed economy" where the most decisive, large-scale industries are national-

ized; this applies particularly to financial institutions that can control investment. In recent decades Western socialism has confined its appeal to economic welfare; the Marxist insistence on the ineluctable tie between economic, political, and ideological spheres is denied, not so much on theoretical grounds, but on the view that socialism need not concern itself with knotty and divisive issues such as the family, art, and sexuality.

Socialism remains an essential moment in the movement towards human emancipation, but is no longer identical with it. The crisis of socialism is the crisis in the emancipatory vision, shattered by the perceived disparity between cultural radicalism and economic equality. Socialists may still hold to a relatively uncritical perspective on the domination of nature, nuclear power, and the ideal of industrialization. The American left has only recently begun to confront these problems. By its historical experience, socialism no longer evokes subversive images in society. Thus democratic socialists have confined their political interventions to "real" politics, and their strategy for building the socialist movement tends to merge socialism with progressivism. Democratic socialists are good precinct walkers for liberal legislators, but produce scarcely a tremble in the executive suite. True to the presuppositions of Bernstein, the "movement" is everything for most of the democratic socialists, and the goal has tended, in effect, to become nothing.

Therefore, all tendencies on the American left undervalue the importance of creating a socialist public sphere. In theory, the labor and socialist movements operate in three spheres: the trade unions, which are responsible for conducting the struggle at the point of production; the political party that fights for workers' interests against and within the state; and the alternative institutions – cultural, social, educational. In the left's traditional conception, the public sphere is constituted by these alternative institutions (the socialist schools, publications, social clubs, singing societies, and on a more informal level, bars, cabarets, and dance halls).[2] In the early socialist movement of the nineteenth century, none of these forms of organization held any particular privilege. Nevertheless, European socialism came to be centered on the parliamentary party because the state increasingly became a major site of capitalist hegemony. In the United States, without a labor party, the labor movement became identical with the trade unions.

In the history of American socialism, the only flourishing public sphere was created by the nationality federations affiliated with the Socialist Party at the turn of the century. They eventually became the mass base of American communism after the Bolshevik victory. These federations, organized among nearly every major group of foreign-born workers, were veritable "states within a state." They formed burial societies, social organizations, and with the collaboration of socialist-led trade unions, taught hundreds of thousands of workers how to read and write along with elements of politics, economics, and socialist ideology.

Since the Second World War, the alternate institutions of American socialism and the labor movement have shriveled. No major union operates a workers' school that compares with the great Brookwood Labor College or the Highlander Folk School of the CIO organizing drives of the 1930s.[3] DSA and some independent Marxists have formed socialist schools in New York, Los Angeles, Chicago, and the San Francisco Bay Area. However, the concept that the socialist movement is, in part, a sphere for broad discussions of politics and culture, has fallen into disrepair. The left is not a place where an individual becomes genuinely educated; at best, left organizations are places for mobilizing around specific issues. The "party" is more than a place for reform struggles, but less than an emancipated territory.

The left public sphere in America is now constituted by journals (the cultural radical papers, the socialist periodicals, the left academic journals). Here one may encounter the vocabularies of Marxism, gay and lesbian liberation, feminism, black nationalism, etc. These journals create a discourse among various constituencies. Yet institutions of face-to-face discourse – where people create common languages, argue, learn, and share a broad emancipatory vision – are scarce. The breakup of the old working-class culture is matched by the fragmentation of the traditional intellectual centers. Thus the left is reduced not only by its own antipathy to social and critical theory, but by the circumstances of its daily existence.

Consequently, left organizations tend to build microspheres, arranging themselves along a spectrum of possible mainstream interventions, ranging from single-issue struggles to activities in trade unions and the political parties. Or, in the most wizened instances, the left colonizes itself – the smaller organizations constituting a pimple on the ass of the larger. In practice the left public sphere becomes an endless contest of competing ideologies rather than a site of genuine discussion and debate.

Under these circumstances, left organizations push and shove each other, creating only a microsphere of political discourse in which the world appears bounded by the panoply of left ideologies. Their frequent ventures into the world of mainstream politics do not endanger their respective ideological stances, because, with the exception of the democratic socialists for whom the mainstream is identical with the movement, they have generated powerful devices aimed at preserving the distance between themselves and the "others" – competing left sects and progressive movements. For the Communists, support for the Soviet Union performs the function of isolating them but also protecting the apparatus. For this reason, the mass American public still regards the CP as the genuine revolutionary article despite its predominant strategy of creating a series of popular-front coalitions. The orthodox Trotskyists distinguish themselves ideologically by their critique of the Soviet Union "from within" and distance themselves from the CP and socialists' penchant for Democratic Party tailing. Since most of the Trotskyist groups have little or no public intellectual presence, they are not capable of attracting a sizable group of intellectuals, as their equally small European counterparts have done. Without the romance of the Chinese revolution to buttress their fortunes, the erstwhile Maoist groups have fallen apart. The democratic socialists, cultural radicals, and non-socialist local insurgents are, therefore, the only possible cores for the creation of a serious left wing in the United States.

Since the left has no immediate prospects for broad influence, much less creating a large socialist movement, its independent role is primarily to create a left "public sphere," that is, to find the basis for enlarging the left political culture in ways that address existing conditions, but also to find ways of going beyond them. This task has several practical specifications: 1) a major effort to study the formation of intellectuals in the American context, both those who were destined to serve the prevailing order and those who attempted to define themselves as the opposition; 2) recognition that mass communications is the mainstream public sphere in which political and social ideas are disseminated and sometimes debated – mostly among the organic intellectuals of capital; 3) investigation into the relations between economic, political, and ideological spheres in the United States as a specifically "late" capitalist society; and 4) a concrete and unsentimental analysis of the evolution and devolution of the American working class – particularly its ideological formation and changing composition – and the trade unions. This would deepen our understanding of the centrality of race, sex, and ecological politics in both the discourses of domination and the political culture of the left.

Of course, the main barrier to the realization of this program within the organized left is its profound contempt for and fear of theoretical work and the intellectuals who are, in the current division of labor, condemned to perform it. The roots of left anti-intellectualism are overdetermined. American ideology has been marked by its break from the traditional intellectual cultures of Europe. Since the effective disappearance of the European immigration, the left has been formed by the ideological precepts of pragmatism.

The American reception of pragmatism in ideological state apparatuses such as schools and political parties and its acceptance as a semi-official American ideology has affected the left as much as other tendencies on the political spectrum. Americans of nearly all ideological hues glorify "practice" as both the criterion of truth and a world-transforming activity. But American radicals have consistently confused the *dialectical* theory of practice, which has a reflexive theoretical moment, with the *pragmatic* view in which theoretical activity is dismissed as metaphysics. The criterion of utility has always dominated the choice of political priorities in left organizations of every variety. Sometimes "theory" is identified with "utopian" thought and is curtly

326

dismissed. Or the concept is taken to mean a semi-religious study of the sacred Leninist texts, which are taken as a "guide to action." The truth of these texts is assumed prior to their being tested in American circumstances, and they are applied to American conditions only rhetorically.

The history of the organized left's relation to intellectuals is analogous to the "instrumental" view of the relation of ideas and critical thinking to the revolutionary process. When writers, artists, scholars, and social and political theorists are not used as legitimating notables in popular-front efforts to achieve visibility and acceptability with middle-class constituencies, they are relegated to the role of a "technical" intelligentsia within progressive movements. Trade-union leaders and party officials view intellectuals with profound suspicion because they fear the critical function of thought when directed to the movement and to its policies. Intellectuals are employed as journalists, research analysts, and publicists for left and trade-union groups. And, of course, the leadership of socialist and progressive organizations contains a large number of intellectuals-turned-administrators, organizers, and political leaders. But these leadership bodies recognize few, if any, intellectuals whose work is primarily devoted to theoretical and political/cultural critique rather than engaged in generating positive knowledge according to a priori categories that fit into the strategy of left and progressive movements.

Analogously, the American left is philistine on questions of art and its relation to politics. Virtually no left organization allows art to have a special place in its internal life or in its political perspective. When it recognizes art, the left instrumentalizes it in the manner of socialist realism in the world communist movement or, more typically, it adopts a "populist" theory of art that is merely a native version of socialist-realist concepts. In this respect, the continuity between the contemporary American left and its progenitors is remarkable, despite the widespread ignorance of cultural history shared by most radicals.

Of course, intellectuals do become politically committed. When they choose to commit themselves to radical politics, however, their decision often entails the desire to escape the narrow confines of their academic life. Yet rarely, if ever, do American radical groups offer outlets for an alternative intellectual life. The left parties and movements are places where a committed activist may use the "technical" skills of economic analysis, writing, and other skills that are usually subordinated in American universities to dubious ends. In effect, intellectuals of the left are only marginally different from their liberal or conservative colleagues. In most cases they are obliged to observe the positivist procedures demanded by various disciplines in order to legitimate their academic status. For the most part, their politics are subjective; that is, their work entails no radical break from bourgeois science. Nor is the left concerned with the problem of the ideological hegemony enjoyed by instrumentalist and positivist paradigms in American intellectual life, since it is earnestly opposed to theoretical discourse, which it claims is mainly concerned with issues that have no place in socialist practice.

Thus, socialist organizations, as distinct from caucuses within the academic professions, engage in intellectual activity that is typically issue-oriented. The questions raised by feminism, for example, are seen exclusively within their practical political context. The left is interested in fighting alongside blacks, feminists, or ecologists in order to enhance its own influence or build coalitions around "progressive" issues. This form of instrumentalization effectively excludes the theoretical questions involved in changing relations between men and women, humans and nature – concerns that are further from the everyday interests of the left than they are from those of millions of Americans. To the extent that the left remains epistemologically isolated from political and cultural reality, its approach to social issues tends to be construed within the framework of its organizational interests. Independent leftists know this about the socialist organizations and maintain their distance as much as possible, except in specific coalitions or struggles.

Creating a socialist public sphere where the rapidly changing character of the world system as well as late capitalist societies is debated as a concomitant to evolving a new strategy of historical transformation exceeds the capacity of the existing left. The task would be difficult if the left *wanted* to create institutions that could occasion the forms of interactions, dialogue, and debate necessary to constitute such a sphere. The chief obstacles are well known: given the power of mass media and large corporations in conjunction with the executive to set the agenda of public debate, left political and social thought is drawn to engaging within this agenda rather than setting a new agenda. Under these circumstances, transformation of all intellectuals into a technical intelligentsia makes critical thought itself problematic. In an era when thought is reduced to so many instruments of socially acceptable practice, the discomfiture intellectuals might have experienced within a corporate-dominated public sphere tends to dissipate as alternative ways of thinking are increasingly unavailable despite the proliferation of Marxist texts. All that is left is a vague feeling of discontent, or opposition to particular items on the corporate agenda.

The trouble is that few individuals and groups want to explore the preconditions for the emergence of a left public sphere. In America most socialist journals are sequestered on the left wing of particular academic disciplines; the few general political and theoretical journals are obliged to distance themselves from the organized socialists. In the United States, the failure of the socialist left has been so monumental that most political intellectuals for whom theoretical activity retains its practical force cannot conceive merging this work with any existing group, even if they affiliate personally.

There are nevertheless compelling reasons for breaking this isolation, generating a left public sphere, and expanding its debate on key theoretical and strategic questions. Apart from the practicality of such an enterprise, given the paucity of available options, the most important reason is the crisis in Marxism, which has several specifications: widespread disillusionment both with the Soviet Union and China and the patent reformism of Western European socialism, which has eroded a clear image of the socialist alternative; the profound conservatism of the American working class, as well as its decline and recomposition, which has raised serious questions about its future (of course, the situation in the working class is an expression of the transformation of the productive forces – in particular, the rise of knowledge as the major productive force); the widespread deindustrialization of major regions; the sharp increase in women, black, and Hispanic workers in the labor force and the trade unions; the escalation of ecological concerns to the proportions of a major social movement.

The second reason is that the organized left's political legitimacy, even among radicals, has suffered severe erosion since the end of the Vietnam War. Americans have little contact with socialists, as a result of sectarian trends and the decline of the left's public activity. This is in contrast to the 1966–1973 period when the left, although by no means a mass phenomenon, was visible and socialists were able to recruit. Only if the left opens up a public debate on its long-cherished political and theoretical positions can it hope to recover the shreds of legitimacy it once enjoyed.

Beyond the New Deal: Economic Strategy and Social Domination

In the United States, the "popular left" has lost ideological hegemony and therefore has no chance to recover political hegemony or to reconstitute itself as a power bloc until it redefines the composition of the bloc on the one hand, and establishes a new common sense on the other. One of its major errors since the rise of neoconservative hegemony has been its penchant to fight for the reestablishment of the old bloc based upon the old "New Deal" common sense. The principal argument for this strategy is the degree to which the fundamental assumptions of the welfare state are being challenged by the new hegemonic forces. The "old faith" held that the struggle for economic justice was the political condition for social struggles concerned with gender, sexuality, race, and other issues.

This proposition is troublesome not because of its emphasis on the importance of the gains made since 1936 by workers and by blacks and other minorities, but because the question here is one of strategy.

The fundamental weakness of the left is as an educational movement. It is not a movement articulating a new critical view of the current political and social conjuncture; indeed, its intellectuals are stuck in the moral-political awareness appropriate to the industrializing period of capitalist development, infatuated with the ideologies of national liberation movements which are not suitable to our situation, or locked into the assumptions of the interventionist state.

Three key social movements that emerged in the United States in the late 1960s have generated organic intellectuals who have begun to articulate elements of a new critical culture. Feminism, ecology, and gay and lesbian movements have raised, in an ambiguous and halting but increasingly sharp manner, a series of questions about the domination of nature and the character of social and sexual relations that contest the old class-based common sense of both socialism and progressivism. In the past decade the opposition to the new conservative hegemony has been defined, to a great degree, by these movements and their intellectuals. They have been obliged to defend, on the terrain of conventional civil liberties, the gains already won by mobilizing millions of people to establish a new regime in our relations of gender and sexuality.

The successful resistance of the feminist and ecology movements during the Reagan era attests to the power of social radicalism. Pressed by its neoconservative wing, the Reagan Administration repeatedly tried to impose legislative restrictions on abortion rights to circumvent the 1973 Wade decision by the Supreme Court. It has also made a concerted attack on the environmental protections enacted by previous administrations, and has tried to relax the Civil Rights Act protecting black and minority voting rights. Despite a massive and expensive ideological campaign against these gains, the right has been able to achieve little more than it can accomplish by administrative fiat. In fact, the right-wing juggernaut helped solidify the social movements which (with the partial exception of the extension of some environmental protections) had been stalled throughout the 1970s during a conservative Democratic administration.

During the 1981–82 fights to save abortion rights and the basic ecological restraints on the exploitation of nature, leaders from the old New Deal bloc: (most liberal politicians, some trade-union leaders, leaders of black organizations) gave only lip service to "social" issues, while privately insisting that a determined battle around them would be an obstacle to effective resistance on the main front, i.e., economic policy. Most progressives failed to recognize the link between economic and social conservatism – that the campaigns against social gains were effectively splitting the progressive opponents of reactionary economic policies. The attack on the welfare system was not only a racist assault on the black and Latino poor, it was also an attack on women. Similarly, the sweeping rollbacks initiated by Interior Secretary Watt were directed as much against the progressive coalition as they were against the mainstream environmentalism of the Audubon Society and the Sierra Club.

The unity of the conservative program consisted precisely in its explicit soldering of the discourses of capitalist expansion, social austerity, and puritanism. The contradictory ideological appeal was no more anomalous than the Protestant ethic itself: humankind could only redeem its original sin by means of sexual repression and the domination of nature; the domination of nature is the site of sublimated eros.

Despite the failure of Reagan's economic policies, neoconservatism retains its political force because of its onslaught on social gains, particularly those won by women and gay people. While it may not have achieved much at a legislative level, it has succeeded in setting the agenda on social issues. It has imposed questions of moral conduct that have provoked cultural radicals to defend their positions by invoking basic rights of privacy rather than boldly defending the morality of sexual freedom. In fact, even within the feminist and gay movements, frank discussions of sexuality are regarded as disruptive to the main strategy, which poses many of these cultural issues as civil liberties questions.

The success of conservatism in simultaneously attacking the material conditions of the working class and leading the resistance to the gains made by the civil rights movement and the so-called new social movements of women and gay people, has made the task of organizing a left response especially difficult. Many on the left waffle in their defense of the gains of women and gays and persist in the advocacy of essentially defensive economic struggle. But on tactical grounds alone, a strategy of defending the gains of workers along the old lines is simply not feasible. Rather, a more appropriate strategy would involve both a broadening of the economic struggle and an effort to link economic and class-based approaches to more creative efforts to advance the goals of the new social movements.

More specifically, the left must be prepared to acknowledge that the current situation cannot be reversed without a fundamental transfer of control over investment from the transnational corporations to the state. Short of this eventuality, which is highly improbable under current political conditions, a left program should focus on making links to "progressive" unions, ecologists, blacks, the aged, and the displaced workers in the heartland of large-scale industry.

The heart of a new economic discourse should focus on justice and control rather than on job creation by private-sector growth. All of these arguments have been heard before. The new feature is an ideological one: ecologists have already argued against further industrial growth because they believe that it overloads the biosphere and endangers the species. But such a rhetoric isolates them from other progressive forces. Since modern liberals have recoiled from openly renouncing growth, because to do so would open the door to a discourse about class and class struggle, they have chosen a corporatist strategy.

Productivity increases and growth policies make possible greater opportunities for those historically excluded from social mobility. Thus, despite the long decline in the American economy, despite the failure of state intervention, they have remained faithful to the old-time religion. A radical economic program would not dispute the necessity of state intervention or growth, but it would be frankly redistributive in content. It would openly declare political war on those whom Franklin Roosevelt called the "economic royalists."

If the popular left adopted such an ideology and program it would surely remain a minority factor in American politics for some time to come. But it would finally stake out a definite position in the political spectrum and thus become a force in future political struggles. The social and cultural left, at the most general level, is challenging the capitalist domination of nature. Earlier radical movements regarded scientific and technical "progress" as a social goal. They mounted a critique of the profit system, in part, on the basis of the failure of capital to develop the beneficent effects of scientific discovery. In contrast, over the past two decades "new" movements have challenged the underlying rationale of modern technology and scientific theory – the domination of nature. For Herbert Marcuse, Murray Bookchin, and other critics of technological society, science and technology are not neutral: the domination of nature leads to the domination of humanity.[4] Progressive reason, that unchallenged ideology of the Enlightenment, held out the hope that humanity could transcend the realm of necessity by unleashing the Promethean powers of science. Scientifically based technology would eliminate most backbreaking labor, provide more leisure for ordinary people, and reduce world hunger. Thus, humanism was not only linked to the arts but was based on science as well in eighteenth- and nineteenth-century thought.

Although Marx offered a critique of the degradation of labor that resulted from technological development, he ascribed the worst effects of technological change to capitalist social relations. In the history of Marxist thought, the question of the nature of the labor process was "forgotten" until recently. The political-economic focus on labor power as the source of surplus value narrowed the analysis of labor in orthodox Marxism and contributed to the benign attitude (of the Soviets and Western social democrats) toward the regimen of the assembly line, Taylorism, and finally the mechanization and chemicalization of agricultural production. The 1960s were marked by new interest in the intrinsic issues raised by both technological applications of science in production and the problem of science as an ideology. Harry Braverman, André Gorz, Sergio Bologna, and others argued that we can no longer place our faith in progressive reason.[5] The most dramatic challenge to the exploitation of science in capitalist society's drive to subordinate the external world was provided by the environmental and ecological movements, which in the late 1960s began to transform both law and social consciousness in the United States. The most basic ecological critiques of industrial (not necessarily capitalist) societies argued that rather than constituting the source of human salvation, technology, constrained by hierarchical social relations, was destroying civilization. The most advanced thinkers (notably Dubos, Bookchin, and the Frankfurt School) advocated the "re-enchantment" of nature as the first step towards saving it. This implied rejecting the scientific method's reduction of nature to its quantitative dimensions, which is the basis of its ability to predict and control the external world. The critiques of Ernst Bloch and the Frankfurt School, and, more recently, Murray Bookchin's social ecology, are frankly utopian perspectives on the social effects of science and technology. However, the idea of nature's enchantment is little more than a return to religious mysticism. Yet the absence of utopian thought in the twentieth century, with its critiques of technology, has produced near-disaster for our biosphere. Consequently, it is not only the forces of capital that have promoted nuclear energy, untrammeled industrial development, and the litany of productivism, but the countries undergoing development, many of which call themselves socialist. Nuclear plant development is the hallmark of the French Socialist government's energy program, and the Soviet Union boasts of its extensive nuclear energy system.

The ideology of racism seeks to legitimate oppressive practices by posing "blackness" as alien from "whiteness." "Black" is defined as the absence of humanity, a category like nature. The sexual myths link blacks to the exotic and the primitive. Consequently, just as our society exploits a mute nature, Western societies have constituted blacks as mute and invisible.

The movements that focus on the deleterious effects of the domination of nature challenge the Marxist conception of the advance of the forces of production as the heart of progress. The ecological and feminist movements and the movement for cultural and political autonomy for African and Afro-American peoples experience the domination of nature as the heart of darkness. In the last two decades these emerging movements have shaken the critical elements of the old strategy – the primacy of economic contradictions in the struggle for liberation – and thereby the centrality of the old configurations for achieving a new society.

These movements speak to the human condition in ways never dreamed of by the older working class. Marx and Gramsci observe that every class seeking power in society must present itself as a universal class, and these movements, which speak to the effects of nature-domination and offer us a vision of the future society, correspond more to their notion of the universal class than does the working class in late capitalist societies. Feminism and social ecology propose a new way of shaping social relations that builds upon the promise of social emancipation. If the most radical feminist, ecological, and self-management programs were to be implemented, the type of social investment, work

333

relations, and the construction of everyday life would change radically.

First, much of the chemical, plastics, and other industries that produce non-degradable raw materials for packaging would be reduced; society might ban automobiles in the cities and expand public transportation; the huge investment in nuclear weapons and nuclear energy would be diverted to other needs.

Second, a feminist approach to work would value housework and traditional wage labor equally. Men and women would equally share raising children and the other work of society. Thus, although the eight-hour day might not be eliminated in the short run, wage labor might be reduced to four hours.

Third, the commitment to eliminate racism would generate a new concept of the relation between society's productive labor and income. An economics of income sharing would have to be instituted, together with a different concept of the value of labor power. Reverse work hierarchies might be required to make more equal the social distribution of income after investment. That is, rather than rewarding intellectual labor with higher income, heavy labor such as sanitation, building maintenance, and foundry work, and unstimulating labor, such as clerical and service labor, would receive relatively higher remuneration.

Fourth, political and social relations would change. A new program would have to take into account the fact that demands for social and political autonomy have become central to the feminist, black and Hispanic, and gay and lesbian movements. It is not a question of fighting for the hegemony of Marxism or socialist ideology over these movements, but of offering a counterhegemonic program of *no* hegemony. That is, Gramsci's projection to our era of class hegemonies of earlier historical periods may be outmoded in the wake of the new circumstances. In the earlier periods, contending classes presented themselves as the best leaders in the universal struggle for the domination of nature. The bourgeoisie won over the scientific intellectuals and placed them in the marketplace against the old religious intellectuals who opposed the Enlightenment. By the end of the eighteenth century the battle was essentially over. The value of the domination of nature, the identification of freedom with individual liberty, and the definition of private property were unquestioned. Knowledge became power, but also a productive force of capital. This arrangement has remained in force for more than two centuries.

The working class and its parties entered the historical stage as the "representative" of the new scientific productive forces in the period of imperialism when the bourgeoisie transformed these knowledges into a force of destruction. Marxism lays claim to the scientific-technological revolution because the world crisis of capitalism (manifested as wars and depressions) distorts the fruits of the progress made possible by science. At the same time, Marxism presented itself as a new "science," a counterhegemony to bourgeois politics and social theory. As with many other events, history has played a cruel trick on Marxism: capital proved itself capable of developing the productive forces engendered by scientific knowledge and carried the scientific-technological revolution to an undreamed-of frontier. In the process, it has tended to eliminate the old proletariat in the advanced countries and to transfer the site of industrial production to the Third World. At the same time, capital has generated a new world economic order, a new international division of labor that no longer divides along the older East/West ideological lines. Now the whole industrialized world stands in opposition to the underdeveloped regions, particularly Asia, Africa, and Latin America. And, within this division of labor, the working classes are themselves divided. Now a new international subproletariat is formed whose sites are global, no longer confined to the underdeveloped societies. Labor becomes as migratory as in the industrializing era for the Western countries. Now as before, agricultural areas are the recruiting ground for new sources of wage labor. Of course, consonant with earlier practices, many of these Asians, Africans, and Latin Americans find their way to factories and mines, as often as not brought to industrial regions by contractors and state terror as well as by hunger.

Unlike the earlier immigration to the United States, the new subproletariat is not integrated into the mainstream of the economy – its most technologically advanced sectors. Instead, the new underclass becomes permanently marginal in the sense that it occupies economic and political niches of the least developed sectors, constituting in the process the labor force of a new sector – the underground or illegal economy. While Europe consigned this labor force to temporary status by regarding its members as guest laborers, the United States has kept millions undocumented and made them vulnerable to deportation.

Today, in all advanced capitalist countries, the working classes are divided against themselves. The traditional base of socialist power, the industrial working class, has been decimated by the new economic order. Two new strata have been called into being by new productive forces and capitalist relations of production – one variously termed new and middle strata, professional-managerial class, technical intelligentsia, etc.; the other a mass underclass arising from the expansion of services and the revival of manufacturing in competitive, low-technology industries that employ labor under substandard conditions.

The new social movements are recruited from a fraction of the middle strata in the most technologically advanced sectors, particularly those engaged in education, health, and information and communications industries, and public employees. In the main, they are educated intellectual workers. But unlike earlier periods when these strata were linked politically and ideologically to capital, their proletarianization, which has resulted from the shift in the

335

technical composition of capital, has generated a new politics. Their access to knowledge of the issues generated by the domination of nature has turned them against the prevailing ethos that subordinates health, work satisfaction, and even human survival to accumulation of capital. A politically significant minority of the middle strata have renounced consumption as ideology, as well as economic growth as the condition of human happiness. On the other hand, the profound dissatisfaction among these groups concerning their position within occupational and social hierarchies has not, with the notable exception of professional women, translated into struggles for new work relations. Only among public employees, especially teachers, clerical workers, and blue-collar workers, has any appreciable increase in trade-union organization occurred. Otherwise, the issues of social rights – i.e., of nuclear power, environmental protection, women's equality, and the right to sexual preference, rather than questions of workplace democracy – have dominated the political awakening of these strata.

Unfortunately, the new immigration, which has reached nearly 1 million a year since 1970, has received scant attention from the left. In contrast to the earlier immigration when workers brought socialist and anarchist traditions into the factories and mines, the new immigrants have been segregated not only in marginal economic sectors but in inner cities, where they have formed enclaves. There, they are able to preserve their culture and language and protect themselves against deportation. Chinese and immigrants from Central America and the Caribbean have become the major groups in the garment industry. Chicanos are the workforce of agriculture and light industry in the West. Koreans, Vietnamese, and other Asians have occupied the niches formerly held by Jews and Italians in the small retail food shops. Many of the new immigrants constitute the new proletariat. Their relations with the traditional industrial working class in heavy industries and skilled trades are not even mediated by trade unions, which (except for the needle trades and the farm workers' unions) have not attempted to organize them or to fight for their right to work and live here.

Lacking an alternative economic discourse, American workers and their unions are condemned to fight to preserve jobs in two ways: on the right, they have adopted an unfortunate protectionist stance exemplified by buy-American campaigns; on the left, they have tried to restrict the power of capital to contract out work to non-union areas at home and abroad (outsourcing). If seen as a temporary program to ameliorate immediate conditions, these are inadequate but could be effective responses. The most serious problem facing traditional industrial workers is that neither their unions nor other forces on the left of American politics have succeeded in offering a new approach to the effects of the economic crisis that could constitute the basis for a mass campaign. Although legislation to control the flight of capital and a shorter work week without pay losses are no panaceas, they are better solutions, combined with stronger language within the contract against outsourcing.

The Machinists Union has proposed a program to deal with technological change that is, perhaps, the most advanced in the trade-union movement. The Machinists Bill of Rights would require bilateral negotiations between the union and management before a new technology is introduced. Management's violation of this provision would be a strikable issue. Further, the union declares that no technological change could result in job losses. Instead, the rights bill proposes to retrain displaced workers, at company expense, to perform the new jobs generated by technological transformation. Combined with a strong legislative program against capital flight, these measures to limit the power of capital investment by protecting jobs and work relations constitute a valuable advance over proposals that would merely deal with the effects of unilateral management initiatives.[6]

The complexity of the American situation defies an easy or clear strategic course. Since our economic, social, and ideological relations are marked by unevenness, the perspectives for the formation of a new historic bloc able to contest political power are extremely frail. But the ideological left could begin to offer a perspective for the formation of alliances that embrace those for whom the domination of nature has become problematic and those concerned with inventing a new economic discourse that links with new social arrangements. Necessarily, such an ideology takes on some of the utopian dimension which the popular and the ideological left have condemned in the past. Yet at a time when the old politics is in disarray in both the popular and ideological left camps, efforts to reproduce the old alignments will certainly fail unless a bold new approach is taken.

This approach cannot rest on the traditional Marxist formulae. It must question the assumptions of historical materialism concerning the primacy of economic relations. It is obliged to reconsider the progressive rationality of science and technology and to challenge Marxism's complicity in perpetuating the illusion of the algebra of revolution that holds to the following formula: economic crisis plus working-class organization plus a strong hegemonic socialist party equals revolution. The crisis is, more broadly, a social crisis, which various classes and sectors resist differently. In the older terminology, capital suffers from a legitimation crisis arising from its crisis of moral and intellectual leadership as much as from its accumulation problems. Certainly there are no "organic" intellectuals of the working class to challenge that leadership, leaving a large vacuum. The counterhegemony in virtually every advanced capitalist country is provided by the social movements concerned with nature, sexuality, and race. A fraction of intellectuals have emerged to link with these movements and, today, constitute the most consistent opposi-

UNFINISHED BUSINESS: TWENTY YEARS OF SOCIALIST REVIEW

tion to the historical assumptions of the bourgeois enlightenment and its aftermath. The major weakness of their discourses consists in the failure to acknowledge the unevenness of social and economic development. The claim of what I call social ecology to universality is hampered by this blindness. This is precisely the place where a socialist left could create a public sphere linking the discourses of economic and social justice. It will have to theorize the link between the *class* and the *social* opposition to capital, which now defines the terrains upon which wars of position must be fought – cities, social institutions, the workplace, and the erogenous zones.

Notes

1. Rudolph Bahro, *The Alternative in Eastern Europe*, London: Verso 1978.

2. My discussion of the political party is based on a talk at the New York Socialist School by Bogdan Denitch in the fall of 1982. The best English-language source for an early formulation of the theory of the public sphere is Jürgen Habermas, "The Public Sphere," *New German Critique*, no. 3 (Fall 1974), pp. 49–55.

3. Jonathan P. Blum, "Brookwood Labor College, 1923–1931: Training Ground for Union Organizers," PhD dissertation, Rutgers University, 1978; Chris Ridzig, "Brookwood Labor College," senior thesis, Hampshire College; Frank Adams, *Unearthing Seeds of Fire: The Idea of Highlander*, Winston-Salem, N.C.: John F. Blair 1975.

4. Herbert Marcuse, *Eros and Civilization*, Boston: Beacon Press 1955, and *One-Dimensional Man*, Boston: Beacon Press 1964; Murray Bookchin, *The Ecology of Freedom*, Palo Alto, Calif.: Cheshire Books 1982; Carolyn Merchant, *The Death of Nature: Women, Ecology, and the Scientific Revolution*, San Francisco: Harper & Row 1980.

5. Harry Braverman, *Labor and Monopoly Capital: The Degradation of Work in the Twentieth Century*, New York: Monthly Review Press 1974; André Gorz, "Technology, Technicians, and Class Struggle," in André Gorz, ed., *The Division of Labour*, Atlantic Highlands, N.J.: Humanities Press 1976; Sergio Bologna, "Class Composition and the Theory of the Party at the Origin of the Workers' Council Movement," in *The Labour Process and Class Strategies*, London: Conference of Socialist Economists 1976.

6. International Association of Machinists, *The Technology Bill of Rights*; see also the report of the 1982 Engineers and Technicians Conference.

Notes on Contributors

STANLEY ARONOWITZ teaches sociology at the Graduate Center of the City University of New York. He is the author of *False Promises: The Shaping of American Working Class Consciousness* (1974); *Science as Power: Discourse and Ideology in Modern Society* (1988); and, with Henry Giroux, of *Education under Siege: The Conservative, Liberal and Radical Debate over Education* (1985).

FRED BLOCK currently teaches sociology at the University of California, Davis. His most recent books are *Postindustrial Possibilities: A Critique of Economic Discourse* (1990) and *Revising State Theory: Essays in Politics and Postindustrialism* (1987).

GARY DELGADO is the founder and general director of the Center for Third World Organizing in Oakland, California, which develops organizers in Asian, Latino, African-American, and Native American communities in the United States. Delgado currently teaches young people of color ways of challenging elected officials and corporate decision-makers. He is author of *Organizing the Movement: The Roots and Growth of ACORN* (1986).

BARBARA EHRENREICH is a writer, lecturer, feminist, and activist living in New York. Her most recent work is the award-winning *Fear of Falling: The Inner Life of the Middle Class* (1989). She is a co-chair of the Democratic Socialists of America.

STEVEN EPSTEIN is a member of the Bay Area collective of *Socialist Review* and a graduate student in sociology at the University of California, Berkeley. He is a coauthor of *Learning by Heart: AIDS and Schoolchildren in America's Communities* (1989).

JEFFREY ESCOFFIER is the former Executive Editor of *Socialist Review*. He is currently a literary agent and publisher of *Out/Look: National Lesbian and Gay Quarterly*. He is working on a book about intellectuals and social movements.

DONNA HARAWAY received her PhD in biology. She is the author of *Crystals, Fabrics, and Fields* (1976), and *Primate Visions: Gender, Race and Nature in the World of Modern Science* (1989). She teaches in the History of Consciousness Program at the University of California, Santa Cruz.

JACK KLOPPENBURG, JR. continues work on the political economy of genetic resources. DANIEL LEE KLEINMAN is completing a dissertation on the creation of the National Science Foundation and the prospects for democratic control of science. Both are associated with the sociology program, University of Wisconsin-Madison.

ERNESTO LACLAU and CHANTAL MOUFFE are the authors of *Hegemony and Socialist Strategy: Towards a Radical Democratic Politics* (1989).

JACK METZGAR is director of the Labor Education Program at Roosevelt University in Chicago and is editor of *Labor Research Review,* the semi-annual journal of the Midwest Center for Labor Research.

MICHAEL OMI teaches in the Asian-American Studies and Ethnic Studies programs at the University of California, Berkeley. HOWARD WINANT teaches sociology at Temple University in Philadelphia. They are coauthors of *Racial Formation in the United States: From the 1960s to the 1980s* (1986).

DAVID PLOTKE teaches political science at Yale. He is the author of a forthcoming book on the Democratic Party from the New Deal to the 1970s, and is working on a study of contemporary social movements and interest groups. He has been associated with *Socialist Review* since 1972.

RAYNA RAPP teaches anthropology at The New School for Social Research in New York. She helps to edit *Feminist Studies* and has been active in the women's studies movement and the reproductive rights movement for twenty years.

CARMEN SIRIANNI teaches sociology at Brandeis University. He is the author of *Workers Control and Socialist Democracy: The Soviet Experience* (1982) and articles on the sociology of time.

JUDITH STACEY teaches sociology and women's studies at the University of California, Davis. She is author of *Patriarchy and Socialist Revolution in China* (1983) and *Brave New Families: Stories of Domestic Upheaval in Late Twentieth-Century America* (1990).

THOMAS WEISSKOPF teaches Economics and Social Science at the University of Michigan. He helped found the Union for Radical Political Economics (URPE) in 1968 and has been an active member ever since. He is coauthor of *The Capitalist State* (1972), *Beyond the Wasteland* (1983) and *After the Wasteland* (1991) and is a member of Democratic Socialists of America.

ROBERT E. WOOD teaches sociology at Rutgers University, Camden, New Jersey, and is the author of *From Marshall Plan to Debt Crisis* (1986). He was part of the *SR* Boston collective for five years.

THE HAYMARKET SERIES

Already Published

Forthcoming

THE ARCHITECTURE OF COMPANY TOWNS *by Margaret Cameron*

ENCOUNTERS WITH THE SPHINX: Journeys of a Radical in Changing Times
by Alexander Cockburn

WAR AND TELEVISION *by Bruce Cumings*

SHADES OF NOIR *Edited by Mike Davis and Joan Copjec*

THE MERCURY THEATER: Orson Welles and the Popular Front *by Michael Denning*

NO CRYSTAL STAIR: African Americans and the City of Angels *by Lynell George*

THE POLITICS OF SOLIDARITY: Central America and the US Left *by Van Gosse*

JAMAICA 1945–1984 *by Winston James*

BLACK RADICAL TRADITIONS *by Cynthia Hamilton*

THE OTHER SIDE: Los Angeles from Both Sides of the Border *by Rubén Martínez*